First World War
and Army of Occupation
War Diary
France, Belgium and Germany

21 DIVISION
Headquarters, Branches and Services
General Staff
1 September 1918 - 31 March 1919

WO95/2134

The Naval & Military Press Ltd
www.nmarchive.com
Published in association with The National Archives

Published by

The Naval & Military Press Ltd

Unit 10 Ridgewood Industrial Park,

Uckfield, East Sussex,

TN22 5QE England

Tel: +44 (0) 1825 749494

www.naval-military-press.com

www.nmarchive.com

This diary has been reprinted in facsimile from the original. Any imperfections are inevitably reproduced and the quality may fall short of modern type and cartographic standards.

Contents

Document type	Place/Title	Date From	Date To
Heading	21 Div Hon. & Awards Removed Belong In His Box C F 16/8/2012		
Heading	21 Division Gen Staff 1918 September		
Heading	21st Div. G.S. Sept, 1918		
Miscellaneous			
War Diary	Le Sars	01/09/1918	04/09/1918
War Diary	T.3.d.4.4	05/09/1918	07/09/1918
War Diary	Le Mesnil En Arrouaise.	07/09/1918	30/09/1918
Map	Enemy Organisation, 17-7-18		
Map			
Miscellaneous	51 Copies 57D SE Old		
Miscellaneous	Report On Operation August 21st to September 3rd, 1918.	03/09/1918	03/09/1918
Miscellaneous	Copy of Telegrams to accompany Summary of Operations for period 20th Aug. to 3rd Sept.	03/09/1918	03/09/1918
Miscellaneous	21st Division. Summary of Casualties August 21st-Sept 14th (inc.)	21/09/1918	21/09/1918
Miscellaneous	Copy of Telegrams to accompany Summary of Operations for Period 20th Aug. to 3rd Sept.	20/08/1918	20/08/1918
Miscellaneous	21st Division. Summary of Casualties-August 21st Sept 14th	21/08/1918	21/08/1918
Miscellaneous	21 Div. G. 37.	18/10/1918	18/10/1918
Miscellaneous	Report on Operations From 4th Sept. to 16th Sept. 1918.	16/09/1918	16/09/1918
Miscellaneous	Report On Operations August 21st to September 3rd, 1918.	21/08/1918	21/08/1918
Miscellaneous	Telegrams to accompany Report On Operations from 4th to 16th September, 1918.	04/09/1918	04/09/1918
Miscellaneous	Report On Operations From 4th Sept. to 16th Sept. 1918.	04/09/1918	04/09/1918
Miscellaneous	21st Division. Summary of Casualties from Sept. 4th-16th (inclusive) 1918.	04/09/1918	04/09/1918
Miscellaneous	Report On Operations From 17th to 20th September 1918.	17/09/1918	17/09/1918
Miscellaneous	Telegrams to accompany Report On Operations from 17th to 20th September 1918.	17/09/1918	17/09/1918
Miscellaneous	21st Division. Summary of Casualties Sept 17th-20th 1918 (inclusive).	17/09/1918	17/09/1918
Miscellaneous	Summary Of Operations for period Sept. 26th to Oct. 10th. 1918.	26/10/1918	26/10/1918
Miscellaneous	Copy of Telegrams to accompany 21st Division Summary of Operations for period 26.9.18 to 10.10.18.	26/09/1918	26/09/1918
Miscellaneous	Telegram. App I		
Miscellaneous	Telegram App II		
Miscellaneous	Telegram.		
Miscellaneous	Telegram		
Miscellaneous	Telegram.		
Miscellaneous	Telegram. App 8		
Miscellaneous	Telegram App 9		
Miscellaneous	Telegram App 10		

Miscellaneous	Telegram App II		
Miscellaneous	Telegram App 12		
Miscellaneous	Telegram. App 13		
Miscellaneous	Telegram. App 14		
Operation(al) Order(s)	21st Division Order No. 233. App 15	16/09/1918	16/09/1918
Miscellaneous	Appendix A. Assembly Arrangements.		
Miscellaneous	Appendix "B" to 21st Division Order No. 233. Artillery Arrangements.		
Miscellaneous	Appendix "C" to 21st Division Order No. 233. Consolidations of Objectives And Work Of R.E. & Pioneers.		
Operation(al) Order(s)	Appendix "D" to 21st Division Order No. 233. Intelligence.		
Map	Enemy Organisation.		
Operation(al) Order(s)	21st Division Order No. 237.	26/09/1918	26/09/1918
Operation(al) Order(s)	All Recipients of Divl. Order No. 237.	26/09/1918	26/09/1918
Map	To accompany 21st. Div. Order No 237		
Miscellaneous	Message Form.		
Miscellaneous	Appendix A Assembly And Preliminary Arrangements.		
Miscellaneous	Appendix 'B'. Artillery Arrangements.		
Miscellaneous	Intelligence. Appendix 'C'.		
Diagram etc	21 Div. Communications.		
Miscellaneous	Tanks. Appendix 'G'.		
Miscellaneous	Miscellaneous. Appendix 'H'.		
Miscellaneous	Telegram. App 20		
Miscellaneous	Telegram. App 21		
Miscellaneous	Telegram. App 22		
Miscellaneous	Telegram. App 23		
Miscellaneous	Telegram. App 24		
Miscellaneous	Report on examination of Prisoners of 44th Reserve Division captured at Beaulencourt on morning of 1st September, 1918. App 26	01/09/1918	01/09/1918
Miscellaneous	Telegram. App 27		
Miscellaneous	Report on examination of Prisoners of War captured 2nd September 1918. App 28	02/09/1918	02/09/1918
Miscellaneous	Policy For Immediate Future. App 29	10/09/1918	10/09/1918
Miscellaneous	C Form. Messages And Signals.		
Miscellaneous	Report On The Examination Of Prisoners Of War Of 2nd Coy and 9th Coy. 403rd I.R. Captured In W.24.a and o. on 11th September 1918. App 30	11/09/1918	11/09/1918
Miscellaneous	Report On Examination Of Prisoners Of the 401st and 402nd I.Rs, 201st Division Captured on the Morning of the 13th September 1918. app31	13/09/1918	13/09/1918
Miscellaneous	Proceeding Of Conference Held At Divisional Headquarters, 23rd Sept. 1918. App 32	23/09/1918	23/09/1918
Miscellaneous	Forecast Of Future Policy. App 33	29/09/1918	29/09/1918
Miscellaneous	Telegram. App 3		
Miscellaneous	Telegram. App II		
Miscellaneous	Telegram.		
Miscellaneous	Telegram App. 5		
Miscellaneous	Telegram App 6		
Miscellaneous	Telegram App 7		
Miscellaneous	Telegram		
Miscellaneous	Telegram.		
Heading	War Diary. General Staff. 21st Division. October 1918. (Report On operations attached).		

Heading	War Diary of "G" Branch, Headquarters 21st Division. From:- 1st Oct. 1918. To:- 31st Oct. 1918.		
War Diary	Equancourt.	01/10/1918	07/10/1918
War Diary	Bantouzeele. M.32.b.7.1.	08/10/1918	09/10/1918
War Diary	Walincourt.	10/10/1918	22/10/1918
War Diary	Inchy	23/10/1918	23/10/1918
War Diary	Neuvilly.	24/10/1918	26/10/1918
War Diary	Neuvilly	27/10/1918	30/10/1918
War Diary	Ovillers.	30/10/1918	31/10/1918
Operation(al) Order(s)	21st Division Order No. 242. App I	02/10/1918	02/10/1918
Miscellaneous	Telegram. App 2		
Miscellaneous	C Form Messages And Signals.		
Miscellaneous	Telegram. App 3		
Miscellaneous	C Form. Messages And Signals.		
Miscellaneous	Telegram. App 4		
Miscellaneous	C Form. Messages And Signals.		
Miscellaneous	Report On Prisoners of War examined on 6th instant.	07/10/1918	07/10/1918
Operation(al) Order(s)	21st Division Order No. 246. App 5	07/10/1918	07/10/1918
Miscellaneous	Assembly Arrangements. Appendix 'A'.		
Operation(al) Order(s)	With reference to 21st Divisional Order No. 246. Appendix "B".		
Diagram etc	Divisional Communications After 8.O. AM		
Map	France		
Miscellaneous	Telegram. App		
Miscellaneous	21st Division Instructions for forthcoming Operations-Series G.F. No. 1. App 7	18/10/1918	18/10/1918
Miscellaneous	21st Division Instructions For Forthcoming Operations. Series G.F. No. 2	19/10/1918	19/10/1918
Miscellaneous	21st Division Instructions For Forthcoming Operation	21/10/1918	21/10/1918
Miscellaneous	21st Division Instructions For Forthcoming Operations. Series G.F. No. 4.	21/10/1918	21/10/1918
Miscellaneous	21st Division Instruction For Forthcoming Operations. Series G.F. No. 5.	19/10/1918	19/10/1918
Miscellaneous	21st Division Instructions For Forthcoming Operations. Series G.F. No. 6.	21/10/1918	21/10/1918
Miscellaneous	21st Division Instructions For Forthcoming Operations. Series G.F. No. 7. Miscellaneous.	21/10/1918	21/10/1918
Map			
Miscellaneous	C Form. Messages And Signals.		
Miscellaneous	21st Division Order No. 247.	21/10/1918	21/10/1918
Operation(al) Order(s)	All recipients of Div. Order No. 247.		
Miscellaneous	Telegram.		
Map	W X		
Miscellaneous	C Form. Messages And Signals.		
Miscellaneous			
Miscellaneous	Telegram App 9		
Miscellaneous	Telegram. App 10		
Miscellaneous	A Form. Messages And Signals.		
Miscellaneous	Telegram App 12		
Miscellaneous	Telegram App 13		
Miscellaneous	Telegram. App 14		
Miscellaneous	C Form. Messages And Signals.	25/10/1918	25/10/1918
Miscellaneous	C Form. Messages And Signals.		
Miscellaneous	App 15		
Operation(al) Order(s)	21st Division Order No. 253. App 16	26/10/1918	26/10/1918
Miscellaneous	Table To Accompany 21st Division Order No. 253.		

Miscellaneous	A Form Messages And Signals. App 17		
Operation(al) Order(s)	21st Division Order No. 254. App 18	28/10/1918	28/10/1918
Miscellaneous	Table to accompany Divisional Order No. 254.		
Miscellaneous	Telegram. App 19		
Operation(al) Order(s)	21st Division Order No. 255. App 20.	31/10/1918	31/10/1918
Miscellaneous	21 Div. G. 329.	28/10/1918	28/10/1918
Miscellaneous	21st Division.	02/10/1918	02/10/1918
Miscellaneous	21st Division. Summary of Information from 0600 3rd to 0600 4th Octr. 1918.	04/10/1918	04/10/1918
Miscellaneous	21st Division. Summary Of General Information 6th October 1918.	06/10/1918	06/10/1918
Miscellaneous	Defensive Arrangements Left Division, V Corps. App 22	25/10/1918	25/10/1918
Miscellaneous	Proceedings of Conference held at Divisional Headquarters, 28th Oct. 1918. App 23	28/10/1918	28/10/1918
Miscellaneous	Mentions Of The 21st Division In The Commander-In-Chief's Dispatches From January To October. 1918. App 24	30/10/1918	30/10/1918
Miscellaneous	Telegram.		
Miscellaneous	Report On Operations August 21st to September 3rd, 1918. App 25	03/09/1918	03/09/1918
Miscellaneous	Copy of Telegrams to accompany Summary of Operations for period 20th Aug. to 3rd Sept.	20/08/1918	20/08/1918
Miscellaneous	Report On Operations From 4th Sept. to 16th Sept. 1918. App 26	04/09/1918	04/09/1918
Miscellaneous	Telegrams to accompany Report On Operations from 4th to 16th September 1918	04/09/1918	04/09/1918
Miscellaneous	Report On Operations From 17th to 20th September 1918.	17/09/1918	17/09/1918
Miscellaneous	Telegrams to accompany Report On Operations from 17th to 20th September 1918.	17/09/1918	17/09/1918
Miscellaneous	Summary Of Operations for period Sept. 26th to Oct. 10th. 1918. App 28	26/09/1918	26/09/1918
Miscellaneous	Copy of Telegrams to accompany 21st Division Summary of Operations for Period 26.9.18 to 10.10.18.	26/09/1918	26/09/1918
Operation(al) Order(s)	All recipients of Div. Order No. 237.	27/09/1918	27/09/1918
War Diary	Telegram.		
Miscellaneous	Telegram.		
Map	W X		
Map	V W		
Miscellaneous	21st Div Map		
Miscellaneous	Account Of Operation From 22nd October to 26th October, 1918.	22/10/1918	22/10/1918
Miscellaneous	Proceedings of Conference held at Divisional Headquarters, 28th Oct. 1918.	28/10/1918	28/10/1918
Miscellaneous	Copy of Telegrams to accompany 21st Division Summary of Operations for period 26.9.18 to 10.10.18.	26/09/1918	26/09/1918
Miscellaneous	Summary Of Operations From August 1st To 31st 1918. App 25	01/08/1918	01/08/1918
Miscellaneous	G.X. 151.	23/10/1918	23/10/1918
Miscellaneous	Telegram		
Heading	21st Div G.S., November 1918		
Heading	D.A.G. G.H.Q. 3rd Echelon AFC 2118		
Heading	War Diary "G" Branch, Headquarters, 21st Division. November 1st-30th 1918.		
War Diary	Ovillers.	01/11/1918	01/11/1918

War Diary	Neuvilly	02/11/1918	03/11/1918
War Diary	Poix. Du Nord.	04/11/1918	05/11/1918
War Diary	Foresters Institute. Near Locquignol.	05/11/1918	07/11/1918
War Diary	Berlaimont.	07/11/1918	12/11/1918
War Diary	Aulnoye	12/11/1918	30/11/1918
Miscellaneous			
Miscellaneous	Telegram. App III		
Miscellaneous	A Form Messages And Signals. App II		
Miscellaneous	Telegram.		
Miscellaneous	Telegram. App VI		
Miscellaneous	A Form Messages And Signals.		
Miscellaneous	21 Div. G. 617. App XIV	11/11/1918	11/11/1918
Miscellaneous	Proceedings Of Conference Held At Divisional Headquarters November 11th. 1918.	11/11/1918	11/11/1918
Map	4th Army		
Miscellaneous	21 Division Gen Staff 1918 Dec-1919 Mar		
Heading	21st Div. G.S. December 1918		
Miscellaneous	J. Lyons & Co Lin.		
Heading	War Diary Of "G" Branch, Headquarters, 21st Division. From:- 1st December 1918. To:- 31st December 1918. Vol 40		
War Diary	Aulnoye.	01/12/1918	31/12/1918
Miscellaneous	Table To Accompany Warning Order G. 840.		
Miscellaneous	21st Division Warning Order. App I	04/12/1918	04/12/1918
Miscellaneous	21 Div G. 829	03/12/1918	03/12/1918
Operation(al) Order(s)	21st Division Order No. 266.	06/12/1918	06/12/1918
Miscellaneous	Table To Accompany 21st Division Order No. 266.		
Miscellaneous	Recipients Of Div. Order No.266.	15/12/1918	15/12/1918
Miscellaneous	Proceedings Of Conference Held At Divisional Headquarters On 21st December 1918. App IV	21/12/1918	21/12/1918
Miscellaneous	Proceedings Of Conference Held At Divisional Headquarters, 30th December 1918. App V	30/12/1918	30/12/1918
War Diary	War Diary of "G" Branch., Headquarters, 21st Division. From:- 1st January 1919. To:- 31st January 1919. Vol 41		
War Diary		01/01/1919	31/01/1919
War Diary	War Diary Of "G" Branch, Headquarters, 21st Division. From:- 1st February 1919. To:- 28th February. 1919. Vol 42		
War Diary		01/02/1919	28/02/1919
War Diary	Molliens Vidame.	01/03/1919	31/03/1919
Map	To Accompany 21st Div Order No. 233		
Miscellaneous	21 Div. G. 419.	24/09/1918	24/09/1918
Map	21st Div		
Map	France		
Miscellaneous			
Map	France		
Map	References Of Enemy Organisation.		
Miscellaneous	H.Q. Logon O.D		
Map	Enemy Organisation.		
Miscellaneous	Reference 21st Division Operation Order No. 257. Appendix D.		

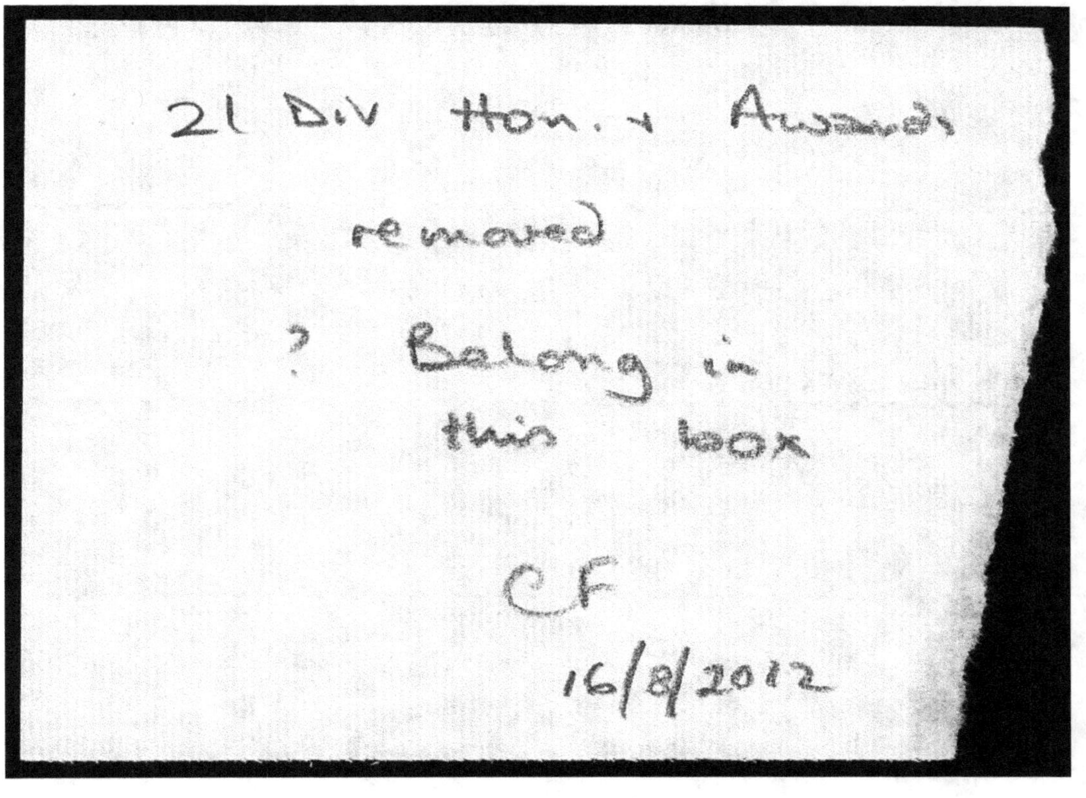

21 Div Hon. + Awards
removed
? Belong in
this box

CF
16/8/2012

21 DIVISION

GEN. STAFF

1918 SEPTEMBER

21ST. DIV.

G. S.

SEPT, 1918

On His Majesty's Service.

ECRET

The Officer i/c
DAG's Office
at the Base

GENERAL STAFF,
VI CORPS.

C 412

Instructions regarding War Diaries and Intelligence Summaries are contained in F. S. Regs., Part II. and the Staff Manual respectively. Title pages will be prepared in manuscript.

WAR DIARY
or
INTELLIGENCE SUMMARY.
(Erase heading not required.)

Army Form C. 2118.

Place	Date	Hour	Summary of Events and Information	Remarks and references to Appendices
LE SARS.				
	Sept.	1st.	8.10 a.m. BEAULENCOURT captured by 110 Inf. Bde. Enemy counter-attack beaten off. Attack on SUGAR FACTORY held up by M.G. fire from LE TRANSLOY.	
			8.5 p.m. 21st Division G.X.734 issued detailing 62nd Inf. Bde. to have Battalion in YELLOW CUT, one Bn. WARLENCOURT, one Bn. LE SARS.	
			8.15 p.m. 21st Division Order No.221 issued detailing attack on SUGAR FACTORY and LABDA COPSE by 110 and 64th Inf. Bdes. respectively. See App.	App I.
			Prisoners during day 100 other ranks - 2 - 77 mm. guns and 30 M.Gs.	
	:	2nd	6.10 a.m. SUGAR FACTORY captured but pocket of enemy still between the Factory and BEAULENCOURT.	
			7.20 a.m. LABDA COPSE captured and situation in vicinity of SUGAR FACTORY cleared up. Prisoners during day 16 Officers 123 other ranks.	App II
			6.15 p.m. 21st Div. withdrawn to Corps Reserve less 110 Inf. Bde. which took over front held by 64th Inf. Bde.	
			11.45 p.m. V Corps G.180 received ordering Div. to withdraw 110 Inf. Bde. to Valley West of BEAULENCOURT, which was done accordingly.	
	:	3rd	Division resting and to be disposed as follows :- Div.H.Q. ... LE SARS. 62nd Inf. Bde. ... LES BOEUFS. 64th : : ... BLUE CUT - LE BARQUE. 110th : : BEAULENCOURT.	
			12.10 p.m. Vth Corps G.197 issued detailing 21st Division less Artillery to be prepared to move forward on Sept. 4th to neighbourhood of EQUANCOURT.	

Instructions regarding War Diaries and Intelligence Summaries are contained in F. S. Regs., Part II, and the Staff Manual respectively. Title pages will be prepared in manuscript.

WAR DIARY
or
INTELLIGENCE SUMMARY.
(Erase heading not required.)

Army Form C. 2118.

Place	Date	Hour	Summary of Events and Information	Remarks and references to Appendices
			8 p.m. 21st Div. Order No. 223 issued ordering 62nd Inf. Bde. to march on 4th inst to ROCQUIGNY - BARASTRE area and placing 64th and 110th Inf. Bdes. under one hour's notice to move.	App III
	Sept.	4th.	11.30 a.m. Warning order received from Corps for relief of 38th Division by 21st Division on September 5th and 21st Div. Order No. 224 issued in consequence. Division still in Corps Reserve.	App IV
T.3.d.4.4.	Sept.	5th.	3.30 p.m. Divisional Headquarters opened T.3.d.4.4.	
			6.50 p.m. 21st Division Order No.225. issued detailing policy to be followed by 62nd Inf. Bde. on taking over line. During the afternoon 64th Inf. Bde. relieved the 113th and 115th Inf. Bdes, 38th Division in Support in Trench System U.5, 11, 17 and 10. Relief complete 11.20 p.m. Heavy mustard gas shelling of ETRICOURT - MANANCOURT Valley.	App V
	:	6th.	During the night 62nd Inf. Bde. relieved 114th Inf. Bde. 38th Division, in the front line. Relief complete 6.40 a.m.	
			10 a.m. 21st Div. G.X. 851 issued giving the line of 62nd Inf. Bde. V.3.d.3.2. - V.9.a.5.0. to V.15.a.3.1.	
			1 p.m. 62nd Inf. Bde. report their troops in trenches V.22. b and d. and EQUANCOURT WOOD and Village.	
			3.45 p.m. 21st Div. G.X.864 issued giving situation and ordering 64th Inf. Bde. to move one Battalion to high ground W. of ETRICOURT and 64th Inf. Bde. to occupy ground E. of Canal as soon as 62nd Inf. Bde. had cleared trench system V.10 to 22.	
			8 p.m. 21st Division Order No.226. issued.	App VI
			10.15 p.m. 62nd Inf. Bde. line runs spur W.19.a & c. - SOREL LE GRAND - FINS.	

D. D. & L., London, E.C.
(A7883) Wt. W809/M1672 350,000 4/17 Sch. 52a Forms/C/2118/14

Army Form C. 2118.

Instructions regarding War Diaries and Intelligence Summaries are contained in F. S. Regs., Part II. and the Staff Manual respectively. Title pages will be prepared in manuscript.

WAR DIARY
or
INTELLIGENCE SUMMARY.
(Erase heading not required.)

Place	Date	Hour	Summary of Events and Information	Remarks and references to Appendices
	Sept. 7th.	8.45 a.m.	62nd Inf. Bde. report left Battalion advancing W.9.a. without opposition Right Battalion have reached high ground W.20.c. but held up by Machine Gun fire from ridge S. of HEUDECOURT.	
LE MESNIL EN ARROUAISE.		12. noon.	Divisional Headquarters opened at U.5.c.3.2. (LE MESNIL EN ARROUAISE)	
		9.45 a.m.	21st Division G.X. 694 issued detailing advances of Brigades consequent upon advance of 62nd Inf. Bde.	App VII
		4 p.m.	21st Div. G.X.899 issued detailing movement of 110th Inf. Bde. to area between area CANAL DU NORD and a line due N. and S. through MESNIL before dark.	
		4.5 p.m.	21st Div. G.X.901. issued detailing 64th Inf. Bde. to move one Battalion to neighbourhood of SORAL LE GRAND.	
		8 p.m.	21st Div. Order No.227. issued giving situation and detaling 62nd Inf. Bde. to send forward advanced guards at 6 a.m. 8th inst, but no large attack to be undertaken without reference to Div. H.Q. 64th Inf. Bde. to carry our reconnaissances with ~~xx~~ a view to relieving 62nd Inf. Bde.	App VIII
	Sept. 8th	1.10 p.m.	REVELON FARM captured and patrol pushed forward into GENIN WELL COPSE. Heavy Machine Gun fire encountered.	
		2.30 p.m.	Our troops in W.24.d. driven back to W.24.c. by counter-attack.	
		10.10 p.m.	21st Div. Order No.228. issued detailing attack on CHAPEL HILL and W.11.d. by 64th Inf. Bde. on 9th inst.	App IX

D. D. & L., London, E.C.
(A7883) Wt. W809/M1672 350,000 4/17 Sch. 52a Forms/C/2118/14

Instructions regarding War Diaries and Intelligence Summaries are contained in F. S. Regs., Part II. and the Staff Manual respectively. Title pages will be prepared in manuscript.

WAR DIARY
or
INTELLIGENCE SUMMARY.
(Erase heading not required.)

Army Form C. 2118.

Place	Date	Hour	Summary of Events and Information	Remarks and references to Appendices
	Sept. 9th.	12.40 p.m.	Little progress made by 64th Inf. Bde. Objectives not reached owing to M.G. fire from flanks. Captures, 50 prisoners, 20 Machine Guns.	
		8 p.m.	21st Division Order No.229. issued detailing attack on CHAPEL HILL on 10th inst.	App X
	Sept. 10th.	10.40 a.m.	Attack on CHAPEL HILL did not succeed.	
		1.56 p.m.	Policy of harassing the enemy ordered by Vth Corps.	App XI
	Sept. 11th.		110th Inf. Bde. relieves 64th Inf. Bde. 110th Inf. Bde. H.Q. V.18.c.1.9. 110th Inf. Bde. attacked and captured Trench System in W.23.d.85.30 to W.18.c.9.9. at 3 a.m. - line now runs W.23.d.8.0. along line of trenches to W.18.c.8.9. - W.18.a.8.4. - LOWLAND SUPPORT - N. Div. Boundary. Prisoners taken in operation 50 O.R. Artillery gas shoots on selected areas were carried out during the night. At 1.30 a.m. and 2.5 a.m. 99 drums of gas were fired on CHAPEL CROSSING and VAUCELLETTE FARM.	
	Sept. 12th.	6 a.m.	Enemy attempted to bomb down trench leading to our line at W.11.c.8.6. but was repulsed. Heavy shelling of back areas.	
		2 p.m.	Enemy attempted to raid Post at W.17.b.6.9 but was repulsed.	
	Sept. 13th	9.55 a.m.	Enemy opened heavy bombardment on Left Battn. front from N. Div. boundary - LOWLAND SUPPORT to W.18.Cent. followed up by an Infantry attack which was accompanied by Flammenwerfer. Enemy completely repulsed. At W.11.c.8.6. where the enemy entered our lines, he was promptly ejected by counter-attack. None of our men are missing - 11 prisoners taken.	

D. D. & L., London, E.C.
(A7883) Wt. W809/M1672 350,000 4/17 Sch. 52a Forms/C/2118/14

Instructions regarding War Diaries and Intelligence Summaries are contained in F. S. Regs., Part II. and the Staff Manual respectively. Title pages will be prepared in manuscript.

WAR DIARY
or
INTELLIGENCE SUMMARY.
(Erase heading not required.)

Army Form C. 2118.

Place	Date	Hour	Summary of Events and Information	Remarks and references to Appendices
	Sept. 14th.		3 a.m. 60 gas drums discharged against W.30.b.95.75 at 2 a.m. and 2.30 a.m. Retaliation slight.	
			7.30 a.m. 21st Division Order No.232 issued detailing the relief of 110th Inf. by 64th Inf. Bde. Order subsequently cancelled (G.X.84).	App XII
			11.30 a.m. Corps Commander's Conference at Div. H.Q. One E.A. night flying bombing machine brought down in our lines and Officer pilot taken prisoner. Enemy attempted to raid our trenches at W.18.b.7.4. at 7 a.m. but was repulsed by rifle and M.G. fire before entering our lines.	
	Sept. 15th.		Hostile artillery active. 110th Inf. Bde. were relieved by the 19th Inf. Bde. 33rd Division during night 15/16th and Command of the Sector passed to G.O.C. 33rd Division. On relief the 110th Inf. Bde. withdrew to Camps just E. of the CANAL DU NORD. 110th Inf. Bde. H.Q. established at U.12.d.5.7.	App XIII
	Sept. 16th.		9.30 a.m. G.O.C. held a Conference at 62nd Inf. Bde. H.Q. at 9.30 a.m. The day spent resting and reorganizing. 62nd Inf. Bde. relieved the part of 19th Inf. Bde. 33rd Div. in the line on the night 16/17th. Relief complete 5.35 a.m. Divl. Order No.233 issued.	App XIV
			5.15 p.m. Enemy gas shelled area V.9.c. and d., V.15 and 16.c & d. with Blue Cross.	
	Sept. 17th.		Desultory shelling of forward area. Occasional H.V. shelling of MANANCOURT and ETRICOURT.	App XV
	Sept. 18th.		7 a.m. Verbal report that 62nd Inf. Bde. in BROWN LINE and advance progressing well.	
			7.45 a.m. GREEN LINE captured by 62nd Inf. Bde. and 64th and 110th Inf. Bdes advancing on RED line.	

D. D. & L., London, E.C.
(A7883) Wt W809/M1672 350,000 4/17 Sch. 52a Forms/C/2118/14

Instructions regarding War Diaries and Intelligence Summaries are contained in F. S. Regs., Part II, and the Staff Manual respectively. Title pages will be prepared in manuscript.

WAR DIARY
or
INTELLIGENCE SUMMARY.
(Erase heading not required.)

Army Form C. 2118.

Place	Date	Hour	Summary of Events and Information	Remarks and references to Appendices
			10.30 a.m. Left Battn, 64th Inf. Bde. report 10.40 a.m. MEUNIER SUPPORT Trench occupied. One battery 4.2" guns captured complete with horses and personnel. Right Brigade troops seen nearing MEATH POST. Heavy M.G. fire from LIMERICK POST. Left Battn. during advance met counter-attack coming down LINNET VALLEY, which it repulsed.	
			12.55 p.m. 21st Div. G.X.252 issued placing one Coy. of left Battn. 62nd Inf. Bde. at the disposal of 64th Inf. Bde. to relieve a Coy. of 64th Inf. Bde, if necessary. 12th Division on right unable to make progress. Situation in EPEHY and PEIZIERE still obscure.	
			2.30 p.m. Troops at GAUCHE WOOD fell back slightly but situation quickly restored. Touch with 17th Division retained.	
			3 p.m. 64th Inf. Bde. hold whole of final objective from left Boundary to LEITH WALK in X.15.d. 110th Inf. Bde. continues line S.W. to X.21.a.9.7. in MEATH LANE - thence to junction of POPLAR TRENCH and Road in X.26.a.	
			5.35 p.m. 21st Div. G.X.262 issued detailing one Coy. 1st Lincolns at present holding RACKET TRENCH to be at disposal of 64th Inf. Bde. to replace one Coy. 15th Durham Light Infantry used to reinforce left flank.	App XVI
			7.30 p.m. Left Brigade unchanged, with defensive flank from X.15.d.8.9. to X.15.c.central approx. Right Brigade X.15.c.Central - X.21.a.5.6. - MEATH LANE - Road in X.20.b. and d. Division on right reports enemy in POPLAR TRENCH - CHESTNUT AVENUE - CULLEN POST.	
			8.30 p.m. Harassing fire to be active during night. Counter preparation carried out by all artillery 4.45 a.m. to 5.10 a.m.	
			11.30 p.m. The Army Commander and Corps Commander sent their congratulations and thanks to the Division.	

D. D. & L., London, E.C.
(A7883) Wt W809/M1672 350,000 4/17 Sch. 52a Forms/C/2118/14

Army Form C. 2118.

Instructions regarding War Diaries and Intelligence Summaries are contained in F. S. Regs., Part II, and the Staff Manual respectively. Title pages will be prepared in manuscript.

WAR DIARY
or
INTELLIGENCE SUMMARY.
(Erase heading not required.)

Place	Date	Hour	Summary of Events and Information	Remarks and references to Appendices
	Sept. 19th.	4.15 a.m.	Enemy counter-attacked in X.21.a. (S. of VILLERS GUISLAIN) and was repulsed, - situation unchanged.	
		6.45 p.m.	Enemy bombed up MEUNIER TRENCH (S. of VILLERS GUISLAIN) and drove our troops back slightly, attempts made to drive him back to original positions. Divisions on our right had not reached their final objectives and our troops in MEUNIER TRENCH were very exposed on their right flank.	
	Sept. 20th.	4.15 a.m.	33rd Division took over from 21st Division, less Artillery. 21st Division now in Corps Reserve. 62nd Inf. Bde. located in LE MESNIL EN ARROUAISE, 110th Inf. Bde. at ETRICOURT and MANANCOURT and 64th Inf. Bde. at LES BOEUFS (staged at ETRICOURT, arrived LES BOUEFUS 21st Sept).	App XVII
	Sept 21st.		Cleaning up and reorganization of Brigades.	
	Sept 22nd		Training.	
	Sept 23rd		Training.	
	Sept 24th		62nd Inf. Bde. marched from LES BOEUFS to vicinity of ETRICOURT.	
	Sept 25/26th.	3 a.m.	21st Division relieved 17th Division in left Sector of Vth Corps front. 62nd and 110th Inf. Bde. in front line, 62nd Inf. Bde, on left. 64th Inf. Bde. in reserve in the ETRICOURT area.	App XVIII
	Sept 26th.		Enemy very quiet.	
	Sept 27th	7.52 a.m.	62nd Inf. Bde. attacked AFRICAN TRENCH within Divisional Boundaries in conjunction with an attack by the Third Army on CAMBRAI FRONT. Attack succeeded, but casualties fairly	App XIX

D. D. & L., London, E.C.
(A7883) Wt. W809/M1672 350,000 4/17 Sch. 52a Forms/C/2118/14

Instructions regarding War Diaries and Intelligence Summaries are contained in F. S. Regs., Part II. and the Staff Manual respectively. Title pages will be prepared in manuscript.

WAR DIARY
or
INTELLIGENCE SUMMARY.
(*Erase heading not required.*)

Army Form C. 2118.

Place	Date	Hour	Summary of Events and Information	Remarks and references to Appendices
			heavy. 5th Division on our left did not take their part of the trench; accordingly bombing block was established on the Div. Boundary. 8 prisoners of 80th R.I.R. captured.	
			8.2 a.m. 150 drums of oil fired on GOUZEAUCOURT.	
			7 p.m. Enemy put down a very heavy barrage on African trench and retook it. No strong efforts made to retain it owing to pending more extensive operations. Enemy artillery inactive that night.	
	Sept 28th		10.40 a.m. Enemy evacuated the portion of AFRICAN TRENCH taken by us on 27th.	
			11 a.m. Patrols reached West edge of GOUZEAUCOURT without being fired on.	
			1 p.m. Group of Snipers reported in QUENTIN QUARRY (R.31.c.).	
			1.58 p.m. Patrols reached line of Railway E. of GOUZEAUCOURT.	
			3 p.m. Patrols reached GOUZEAUCOURT - VILLERS PLUICH Road N. of the Village and located the enemy in FLAG RAVINE (R.25.b.). VILLERS TRENCH and GREEN LANE occupied. 15 prisoners and one M.G. captured.	App XX
			6.30 p.m. 110th Inf. Bde. established Headquarters at CHAPEL HILL.	
			9.10 p.m. Line runs VILLERS TRENCH along GREEN LANE and GREEN SWITCH to R.26.c.4.0. Enemy holding Reserve Line in front of GONNILIEU as main line of resistance.	
	Sept. 29th		3.2 a.m. 62nd and 110th Inf. Bdes. attacked GONNILIEU which was found to be very strongly held with many M.Gs. 62nd Inf. Bde. on left held up by M.G. fire from GONNELIEU. 110th Inf. Bde. on right held up by M.G. fire from VILLERS GUISLAIN. 4 tanks were co-operating in the attack. As a result of the attack we hold VILLERS GUISLAIN, Cemetery X.2.d. and the VILLERS-GUISLAIN - GOUZEAUCOURT Road. Prisoners captured, 60.	App XXI

Instructions regarding War Diaries and Intelligence Summaries are contained in F. S. Regs., Part II. and the Staff Manual respectively. Title pages will be prepared in manuscript.

WAR DIARY
or
INTELLIGENCE SUMMARY.
(Erase heading not required.)

Army Form C. 2118.

Place	Date	Hour	Summary of Events and Information	Remarks and references to Appendices
			<u>10.50 a.m.</u> Troops of Division on our left (5th) had reached LA VACQUERIE ROAD R.21. 21st Division was ordered to send three Battalions round into the left Divisional area to occupy the BANTEUX spur E. of GONNELIEU (R.28.Central.) One Battn. attached from 110th to 62nd Inf. Bde. to assist them.	
			<u>4.35 p.m.</u> Situation on 5th Div. front very obscure and Battalion unable to proceed as ordered.	
			<u>5.15 p.m.</u> Ordered by Vth Corps to reorganize, leading Brigades prepara-tory to renewing attack tonight. 3 Battns. ordered back to their Brigades. This was not complete until 3 a.m. as one Battalion had to be relieved by the 5th Division in FERN TRENCH.	App XXII
			<u>9 p.m.</u> Order for attack cancelled. Troops to be reorganized and rested as much as possible.	
	Sept.30th.		<u>2.30 a.m.</u> Reserve line and GONNELIEU found by patrols to be strongly held by the enemy.	
			<u>5 a.m.</u> Patrols report reserve line still held but enemy very quiet.	
			<u>9.25 a.m.</u> Patrols of 5th Division have entered GONNELIEU from its N. and report also having entered BANTEUX.	
			<u>10.15 a.m.</u> One Battalion 62nd Inf. Bde. has gone through GONNELIEU.	
			<u>12.10 p.m.</u> 64th Inf. Bde. ordered to QUENTIN Ridge and to be prepared to cross the canal and occupy the HINDENBURG LINE.	App XXIII
			<u>12.45 p.m.</u> Patrols of 62nd and 110th Inf. Bdes. E. of GONNELIEU and are advancing to BANTEUX Spur.	
			<u>4.45 p.m.</u> 62nd Inf. Bde. patrols heavily fired on by M.Gs. from E. bank of canal. Patrols now working down BANTEUX - GONNILIEU Road.	

D. D. & L., London, E.C.
(A7883) Wt. W809/M1672 350,000 4/17 Sch. 52a Forms/C/2118/14

Instructions regarding War Diaries and Intelligence Summaries are contained in F. S. Regs., Part II, and the Staff Manual respectively. Title pages will be prepared in manuscript.

WAR DIARY
or
INTELLIGENCE SUMMARY.
(Erase heading not required.)

Army Form C. 2118.

Place	Date	Hour	Summary of Events and Information	Remarks and references to Appendices
			7.30 p.m. Policy of Division to hold line of RIBBLE - ROSE and FIVES Trenches in R.35 and X.5. and patrol ground down to the Canal. Crossings over the Canal to be repaired if possible.	App XXIV
			10 p.m. All crossings over Canal found to be broken. Post established on BANTEUX - HONNECOURT Road. Enemy holding trench 300 yards E. of Canal.	
			Captures during day 4 - 77 mm guns, one 4.2" how. 4 heavy M.Gs. 16 Light M.Gs. 4 Minnenwerfer and 2 anti-tank rifles.	
			15th Oct. 1918.	
			[signature] Lieut-Col. GS for Major-General, Commanding 21st Division.	

D. D. & L., London, E.C.
(A7883) Wt W809/M1672 350,000 4/17 Sch. 52a Forms/C/2118/14

Army Form C. 2118.

Instructions regarding War Diaries and Intelligence Summaries are contained in F. S. Regs., Part II. and the Staff Manual respectively. Title pages will be prepared in manuscript.

WAR DIARY
or
INTELLIGENCE SUMMARY.
(Erase heading not required.)

Place	Date	Hour	Summary of Events and Information	Remarks and references to Appendices
			Summary of Operations from 1st to 31st August, 1918.	App.25.
			Report on examination of prisoners of 44th Reserve Division.	App.26.
			Message of congratulation from the Corps Commander.	App.27.
			Report on examination of prisoners captured 2nd Sept. 1918.	App.28.
			Policy of Division for immediate future.	App.29.
			Report on examination of Prisoners of 403rd I.R.	App.30.
			Report on examination of Prisoners of 401st, 201st Division.	App.31.
			Proceedings of Conference held at Div. H.Q. 23rd Sept. 1918.	App.32.
			Forecast of future policy of Division.	App.33.

D. D. & L., London, E.C.
(A7883) Wt W809/M1672 350,000 4/17 **Sch. 52a** Forms/C/2118/14

SCALE 1:20,000
BRITISH TRENCHES IN RED.
Trenches revised from information received to 17-7-18
FRANCE
GERMAN TRENCHES IN BLUE.
Trenches revised from information received to 17-7-18
EDITION 5.e (Local)
SHEET 57D S.E.
ENEMY ORGANISATION, 17-7-18
Varennes
Hedauville
ALBERT
Contalmaison
Field Survey Bn. (10693) 22-7-18.
Scale 1:20,000

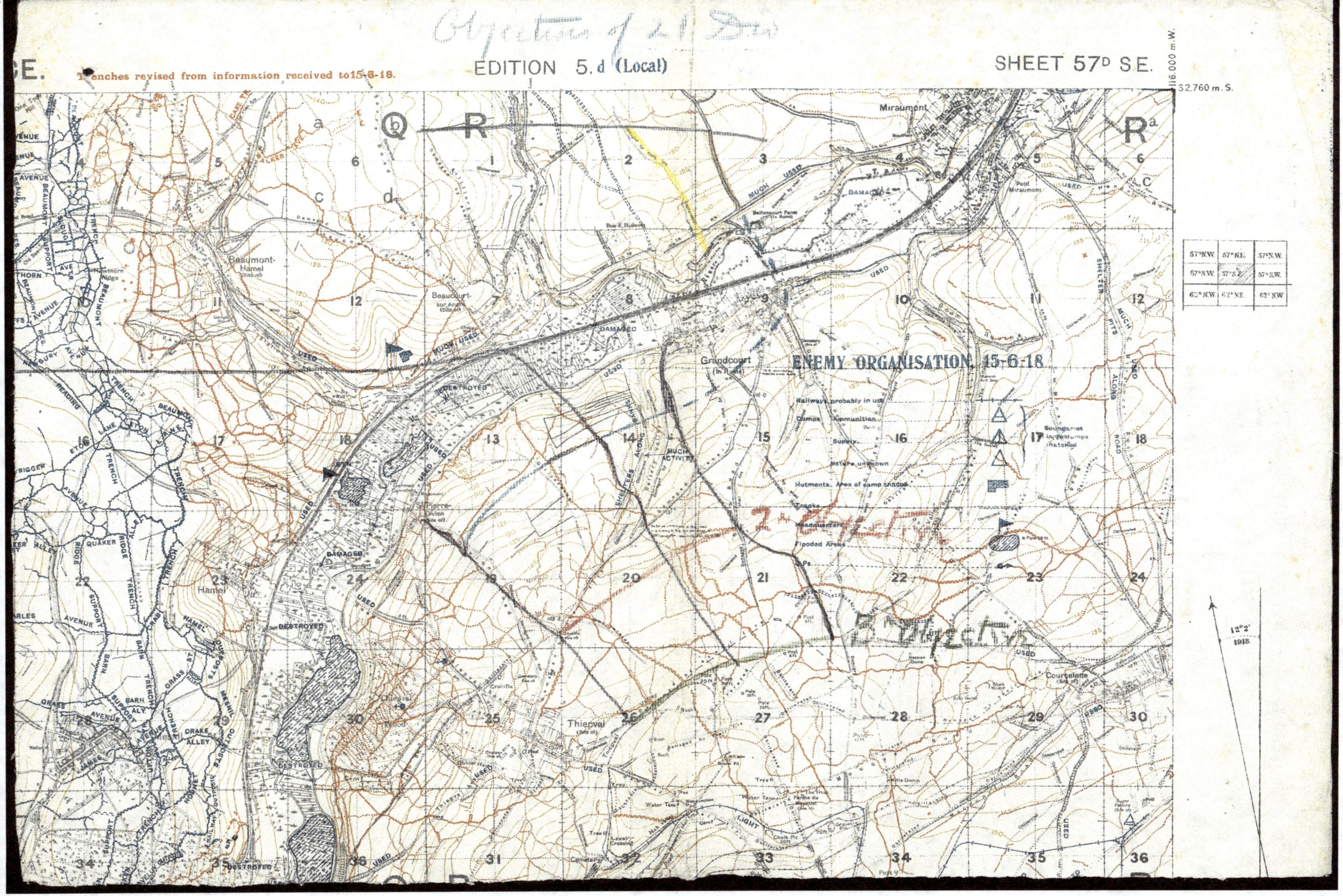

Objective of 21 Div
Trenches revised from information received to 15-6-18.
EDITION 5.d (Local)
SHEET 57D S.E.
ENEMY ORGANISATION 15-6-18
Railways probably in use
Dumps Ammunition
Supply
Nature unknown
Hutments. Area of camp shaded
Headquarters
Flooded Areas
Boundaries of large dumps hatched
2nd Objective
3rd Objective
Miraumont
Petit Miraumont
Beaumont-Hamel
Beaucourt-sur-Ancre
Grandcourt
Thiepval
Hamel
Courcelette
MUCH ACTIVITY
DAMAGED
DESTROYED
USED
57D N.W.
57D N.E.
57C N.W.
57D S.W.
57D S.E.
57C S.W.
62D N.W.
62D N.E.
62C N.W.
12°2' 1918.
32.760 m. S.
116.000 m. W.

5 Copies 57P9E
OLD

With August diary

21 Div.
G. 748.

REPORT ON OPERATIONS AUGUST 21st to SEPTEMBER 3rd, 1918.

Reference Maps Sheets
57.B. D. and C. 1/40,000.

On August 19th orders were received from V Corps that the Division would take part in an attack on the enemy's lines in conjunction with the Corps on either flank, the Division being ordered to carry out an attack on BEAUCOURT and the Sunken Road R.3.a.3.2 (Div. Order No.205).

On August 20th, Divisional Headquarters closed at RAINCHEVAL and opened at ACHEUX.

August 21st, 1918.

12 Midnight. The enemy commenced a heavy area bombardment with gas shell on Q.6.c. and Q.11.b. This bombardment lasted about three quarters of an hour.

5.45 a.m. The 62nd Infantry Brigade advanced to the attack on BEAUCOURT and Sunken Road R.3.a.

7.45 a.m. The 62nd Infantry Brigade reported that they had captured BEAUCOURT and had reached the railway embankment East of the Village. About 90 prisoners had been captured, our casualties being reported as very slight. Our troops were also well on the way to the Sunken Road in R.3.a.

8.25 a.m. 1 N.C.O. and 12 men of the V Corps Cyclist Regiment were ordered to report to the 64th Infantry Brigade Headquarters to assist in exploitation. (G.X.449).

9.30 a.m. The 2nd Linc. Regiment held the line of the railway embankment from R.9.d.0.3 to R.8.c.0.5 with patrols working down the MIRAUMONT ROAD. A post had been established at R.7.d.4.8. Patrols of the 12/13 North'd Fus. had passed through BEAUCOURT on their way to the Blue Line South of the River ANCRE. About 120 prisoners so far counted.

10.20 a.m. The 62nd Infantry Brigade were ordered as soon as the Brown Line (R.3.a.) was captured, to move two Companies to the line of the River ANCRE from R.4.c.6.7 to R.4.a.0.5. Piquets were to be placed on all bridges over the ANCRE. Patrols were also to be pushed forward into the S.W. outskirts of MIRAUMONT. The 64th Infantry Brigade were to place two Companies at the disposal of the 62nd Infantry Brigade to act as Brigade Reserve. (G.X.452).

10.30 a.m. Orders received from Corps to hold the 64th Infantry Brigade in readiness to move along the BEAUCOURT - MIRAUMONT ROAD, cross the River ANCRE in R.3. & 4 and to move via BATTERY VALLEY so as to threaten THIEPVAL from the rear. (V Corps G.396).

11.50 a.m....

11.00 a.m. Situation. Our troops were reported by the Royal Air Force to be on the line R.3.c.7.3 - R.3.c.4.8 - R.3.a.2.0 - R.2.b.9.6. Touch gained with troops on left. The 110th Infantry Brigade were unable to cross the ANCRE owing to very strong opposition, the enemy holding the West bank with Machine Guns.

12.20 p.m. The 62nd Infantry Brigade were ordered to attack and capture the remainder of the Brown Line. The 64th Infantry Brigade, less portion already South of the ANCRE, were ordered to assemble about R.1 and R.2. If the 62nd Infantry Brigade should fail to capture the Brown Line, the 64th Infantry Brigade were then to carry out this operation. On the Brown Line being captured, the 64th Infantry Brigade were to cross the ANCRE and move up SIXTEEN ROAD through R.16.a. & c. on to the Green Line with left flank guard along BOOM RAVINE. (Div. Order No.206).

(Owing to events detailed below, this turning movement could never be put into operation).

1.20 p.m. One Battalion 110 Infantry Brigade was placed at the disposal of the 64 Infantry Brigade. (G.X.455).

3.25 p.m. Owing to IRLES having not yet been captured, and, in consequence of this, the 42nd Division on the left having not yet entered MIRAUMONT, the 64th Infantry Brigade were ordered to take special precautions regarding their Eastern flank after crossing the ANCRE. The 62nd Infantry Brigade were to make every endeavour to throw bridges across the ANCRE between BEAUCOURT and GRANDCOURT, in order to give the 64th Infantry Brigade an alternative line for withdrawal in case of necessity. The 64th Infantry Brigade were to send patrols towards GRANDCOURT after crossing the ANCRE to connect with 62nd Infantry Brigade and also to cover bridge-heads. (G.X.460).

3.40 p.m. 110 Infantry Brigade reported that the 6th Leic. Regt. had two patrols just across the ANCRE Q.18.d.4.6 and Q.13.c.7.9. Both patrols were unable to make further advance owing to enemy fire.

3.50 p.m. 110 Infantry Brigade were ordered to hold another Battalion in readiness to join 64th Infantry Brigade. (G.X.641).

The 64 Infantry Brigade were ordered to relieve two Companies 62 Infantry Brigade in R.14.a. & b. during the night, these Companies to come under orders of 62 Infantry Brigade. 1st Wilts Regt. were to remain with 64th Infantry Brigade but were not to be used except in case of emergency. Brigades were to improve and if possible increase the present crossings over the ANCRE with the aid of attached R.E. Sections. (Div. Order No.209).

5.5 p.m. 110 Infantry Brigade reported that the 6th Leic. Regt. were heavily fired at as soon as the ANCRE at R.13.a.3.7 was crossed. LOGGING TRENCH and LOGGING LANE were reported as being strongly held by the enemy.

6 p.m. Under orders from Corps, the Division was ordered to consolidate the final objective from the ANCRE at BAILLESCOURT FARM to R.3.a.0.8 with one Brigade, touch to be maintained with 42nd Division on left. One Brigade was to be in position to support the front Brigade or to re-new the offensive across the ANCRE at short notice. The 3rd Brigade was to be in position South and West of BEAUMONT HAMEL. (V Corps G.241).

/7.20 p.m....

7.20 p.m. Situation at 7 p.m. 62nd Infantry Brigade attacked at 2 p.m. with objective R.4.c.5.6. to R.4.a.0.5. The attack was held up by Machine Gun and Artillery fire. The attack was renewed with 6 Companies about 4 p.m. and was successful. Two Companies 62nd Infantry Brigade crossed the ANCRE at 4 p.m. and gained the Blue Line from LITTLE TRENCH to R.14.b.8.3. The dispositions of 62nd Infantry Brigade were as follows :-

Two Companies from R.4.c.4.8. along road to R.3.a.9.9. where touch had not been gained with 42nd Division. Two Companies between Brown and Yellow Lines and Two Companies on Blue Line. Four Companies about R.2.c. and Two Companies in BEAUCOURT.

8.30 p.m. Orders issued for 62nd Infantry Brigade to maintain their present dispositions and to gain touch with 42nd Division. The two Companies in BEAUCOURT were to be relieved by one Company at present at R.4.c. and were then to be withdrawn into Reserve. 64th Infantry Brigade were to establish Bridgeheads over the ANCRE at selected points between R.4.d.3.4. and R.1.a.1.9. connecting with 62nd Infantry Brigade at R.4.a.5.1. 62nd Infantry Brigade to form Bridgeheads from R.9.a.1.9. to BEAUCOURT inclusive. 110th Infantry Brigade to form Bridgeheads from BEAUCOURT (exclusive) to MILL BRIDGE in area Q.6, Q.12, R.1 and R.7. One Battalion 110th Infantry Brigade to remain attached to 64th Infantry Brigade (Div. Order No.208).

10.40 p.m. Situation unchanged. Heavy hostile Machine Gun fire coming from MIRAUMONT. Prisoners so far counted 3 Officer, 156 Other Ranks.

10.50 p.m. Orders issued to the 64th Infantry Brigade that the two rear Battalions of that Brigade and One Battalion 110th Infantry Brigade attached, were not to move forward without reference to Divisional Headquarters (G.X.476).

11.58 p.m. All Brigades and Divisional Artillery were warned that owing to the trend of hostile movement during the evening having been towards MIRAUMONT and ACHIET LE GRAND, hostile counterattack was possible either tonight or tomorrow morning. The action of the two rear Battalions of the 64th Infantry Brigade and the attached Battalion 110th Infantry Brigade, would, therefore, be defensive until further orders. At dawn tomorrow 110th Infantry Brigade were to endeavour to push patrols across the ANCRE and gain the Blue Line. As soon as the Blue Line was consolidated patrols were to be pushed forward to the Red Line. (GX.477).

22nd August 1918.

3.52 a.m. Report received from 64th Infantry Brigade that the bridges at R.9.b.6.7. and R.3.D.9.2. were in good condition. The 97th Field Company R.E. had constructed a footbridge at R.9.a.9.7. over which a Platoon of the 1st East Yorkshire Regt. had crossed about 2.15 a.m. and had met with heavy Machine Gun fire from about R.9.b.2.2.

/4 a.m......

4 a.m. Enemy heavily gas shelled the area between ARTILLERY LANE and LUMINOUS AVENUE.

7.35 a.m. 62nd Infantry Brigade reported that enemy had put down a barrage on the Brown Line, which, however, only lasted about 10 minutes. No Infantry action followed.

8.45 a.m. 110th Infantry Brigade report timed 8.20 a.m. gave the situation East of the ANCRE as follows :- At 5 a.m. two Platoons were established in LOGGING TRENCH and a third Platoon was moving along CANDY LANE with objective LOGGING SUPPORT. During the night crossings over the ANCRE at Q.18.d.4.7. and Q.18.b.9.3. were made passable for Infantry.

9.40 a.m. Situation unchanged since last report. Up to about 8 a.m. there was continuous hostile shelling of forward area, but after this hour shelling became much less and very scattered. Enemy reported to be holding Railway Embankment in R.10. in strength.

9.40 a.m. 62nd Infantry Brigade were ordered to push forward Patrols from Blue Line to portion of Red Line in their area and also to GRANDCOURT. If Red Line occupied by our patrols, 64th Infantry Brigade were to be prepared to send two Companies to garrison it (G.X.486).

10 a.m. 62nd Infantry Brigade reported that a Patrol of the 12/13th Northumberland Fusiliers was observed to be pushing South from Blue Line. No Machine Gun fire had been encountered from THIEPVAL RIDGE for the last hour. 64th Infantry Brigade reported that the Platoon of the 1st East Yorks Regt. South of the River in N.9.b. had been driven to the North of the River where they had taken up a position covering the crossing.

12.15 p.m. 110th Infantry Brigade report, timed 11 a.m. gave the situation as follows :- Bombing Party had succeeded in reaching point in LOGGING TRENCH North of the enemy Post R.13.c.1.4. This party was working in conjunction with bombing party from the South to capture this Post. A Patrol had proceeded up CANDY AVENUE to about R.19.b.35.60. and had located enemy Machine Gun at Q.13.c.9.2. which would be dealt with by Platoon which was working down LITTLE TRENCH and LUFF AVENUE. (R?)

1.30 p.m. 62nd Infantry Brigade reported that the Valley in R.1.b. and forward area was being continuously shelled by guns of all calibre. The 2nd Lincolnshire Regt. reported that their left flank was being turned in R.3.b.

4.10 p.m. Situation. 62nd Infantry Brigade unchanged. Lewis Gun Section of North Irish Horse (Corps Cyclists) sent to reinforce the left flank in R.3.b. Situation on that flank was not satisfactory owing to the 42nd Division having their right at R.2.b.5.0. 110th Infantry Brigade held the Blue Line from LUFF AVENUE inclusive to junction of LOGGING SUPPORT and CANDY AVENUE. A Platoon was being sent along CANDY AVENUE to clear COMMON LANE. Enemy Post at R.13.c.2.6. had been rushed and garrison killed. Patrols advancing to Red Line were held up by heavy Machine Gun fire in R.14.c.Central. At 3 p.m. enemy opened a very heavy barrage on Valley in R.1.b. but shelling had now died down.

/5 p.m.....

5 p.m. 110th Infantry Brigade report that LUFF AVENUE and LOGGING SUPPORT to junction of CANDY AVENUE had been captured. Touch had been obtained with the 62nd Infantry Brigade in the Blue line. Considerable Machine Gun fire was being met with from COMMON LANE. Further Platoons were being Moved up to consolidate the Blue Line and capture COMMON LANE.

6.30 p.m. Orders received from Vth Corps that one Brigade 17th Division would relieve and take over one Brigade front at present held by 110th Infantry Brigade on night of 22nd/23rd. The boundary between the 21st and 17th Divisions would be a line running from R.21.d.0.0., R.14.c.0.0., Q.12.c.6.0., thence West along grid line between Q.11. and Q.17. 17th Divisional Artillery at present under orders of C.R.A. 21st Division would revert to C.R.A. 17th Division at 4 a.m. 23rd inst. (Vth Corps G.466., R.A. 1163 and G.X.496.).

9.55 p.m. 62nd Infantry Brigade reported that at 8.15 p.m. enemy put down a barrage including smoke on the Brown Line and in the ANCRE Valley near GRANDCOURT. The enemy were reported to have attacked and to have driven back part of the garrison of the Brown line. No news received about situation in the Yellow Line, but this line believed to be intact. One Battalion 64th Infantry Brigade was holding intermediate system along ARTILLERY LANE and another Battalion was being ordered up to PUISIEUX Road to restore situation if required.

10.5 p.m. Orders sent to the 62nd Infantry Brigade that if any portion of the Brown Line had been lost it was to be restored by a counter-attack in conformity with an attack of 42nd Division at 2.30 a.m. August 23rd. (G.X.503).

11.15 p.m. Situation. Enemy attacked Brown Line about 8 p.m. Attack was repeated twice afterwards. Each attack was beaten off with heavy casualties to the enemy. A few enemy reached the Brown line but were immediately ejected. Our casualties were fairly heavy. Situation was now quiet.

23rd August 1918.

1.20 a.m. 110th Infantry Brigade reported that Platoon Posts had been established at R.19.a.4.0. R.19.a.6.5., R.13.a.6.3., R.13.d.5.6., R.14.c.3.9., R.13.c.1.4., R.13.a.6.0., and one over the ST. PIERRE DIVION Caves at Q.24.b.6.1. COMMON LANE South of R.19.a.4.0. was destroyed by shell fire and not occupied by the enemy.

5.a.m. 62nd Infantry Brigade reported that the situation in the BROWN Line had been entirely restored and that touch had been gained with the 42nd Division on the left.

6.15 a.m. The relief of the 110th Infantry Brigade by one Brigade 17th Division was reported complete.

9.55 a.m. Situation unchanged. Enemy was shelling PUISIEUX Road in R.7.c. with heavy guns. Snipers and Machine Guns were active from R.15.a.

/1.30 p.m.

1.30 p.m. Situation 12 Noon. Enemy put down a heavy barrage on our front line in response to attack carried out by troops on our left. Enemy in small parties were seen going East and S.E. from R.16.c.2.3. 12/13 North'd Fus. reported that some of their men had reached BATTERY VALLEY but had to withdraw owing to hostile M.G. fire from Eastern edge of Valley.

2.50 p.m. All Lewis Gunners of North Irish Horse (Corps Cyclists) except those belonging to 'A' Squadron were ordered to rejoin their own Unit. (G.X.521 and V Corps G.511).

3.15 p.m. Orders issued for the continuation of the attack. 64 Inf. Bde. to attack at 1 a.m. with first objective Brown Line from R.20.a.9.3 to R.8.b.7.2 and second objective Red Line from R.21.d.0.0 through R.15.Central to railway at R.9.b.3.3. The 110 Inf. Bde. to attack at 5 a.m. with objective the Blue Line R.27.b.2.8 along SIXTEEN ROAD to R.4.c.5.7 with bridge-head at R.2.d.8.4. After capture of this line, exploitation to be carried out towards LE SARS and PYS. (D.O.210).

5.55 p.m. Situation. North of river unchanged. South of River our patrols were working towards the Red Line. About 100 enemy dead had been counted in front of the Brown Line as the result of the counter-attack the day before.

7 p.m. Divisional Headquarters closed at ACHEUX and opened at MAILLY MAILLET.

8.50 p.m. Divisional Order No.210 was amended as follows :- The advance to the Green Dotted Line was to be carried out as soon as possible. 64 Inf. Bde. were to advance with its left on the River ANCRE with objective Green Dotted Line in R.11.b. & d. 110 Inf. Bde. to advance in rear of 64 Inf. Bde. and connect right of 64 Inf. Bde. with 17th Division on Green Dotted Line. (G.X.529).

11 p.m. 62 Inf. Bde. were ordered to concentrate all troops less garrison of Brown Line at once, and as soon as reliable information received that MIRAUMONT had been captured, the garrison in the Brown Line was to concentrate with its own Unit. 62 Inf. Bde. was to be prepared to cross River ANCRE either by the railway bridge or the Bridge in GRANDCOURT. (G.X.535).

24th August, 1918.

12.30 a.m. Report received from 64 Inf. Bde. that the Red Line had been captured. The right flank of this Brigade appeared to be in the air and was being continually harassed by the enemy.

12.40 a.m. 62 Inf. Bde. were ordered to be prepared to concentrate in BATTERY VALLEY or valley in R.9.d. and R.15.b. (G.X.541).

1.35 a.m. 64 Inf. Bde. reported that they were firmly established on the Red Line, but owing to fighting and broken state of ground Units were somewhat dis-organised. The Brigade was being re-organised and advance would be continued to the high ground in R.11 and R.12 at about 3.30 a.m. The right flank of the Brigade was very exposed and no touch could be obtained with any other troops.

/7.10 a.m.....

7.10 a.m. 62 Infantry Brigade were ordered to concentrate their whole Brigade less the two Companies in the Brown Line, on South bank of ANCRE, in BATTERY VALLEY and R.14.a. (G.X.545).

7.40 a.m. 110 Infantry Brigade ordered to push on by easiest route possible irrespective of left of 17th Division and to get touch with right of 64th Infantry Brigade (D.O.211).

In R.11.b. No touch had been gained

8.45 a.m. Report received from 64th Infantry Brigade that their troops had reached final objective/on either flank and the enemy were reported as working round flanks. Line very weakly held and reinforcements were urgently required.

9.20 a.m. Pigeon message was received from 64th Infantry Brigade timed 7.28 a.m. reporting that they were holding high ground in R.11.b. but that the enemy had completely surrounded them and were very active with Machine Guns, Snipers and Trench Mortars. Casualties appeared to be heavy. The enemy had counter-attacked both flanks but had been completely repulsed.

9.30 a.m. Situation. 64 Infantry Brigade still held high ground R.11.b. but were entirely surrounded. 110 Infantry Brigade moving forward to support the right of the 64th Infantry Brigade on Green Dotted Line. In course of the advance they successfully attacked enemy post at R.14.d.0.0 capturing three Trench Mortars and killing between 30 and 40 of the enemy.

11 a.m. Owing to the B.G.C. 64 Infantry Brigade having been wounded, B.G.C. 110 Infantry Brigade was ordered to take command of both 64th and 110th Infantry Brigades. He was ordered to take the high ground in R.11.b. & d. and when this ground had been captured the 62nd Infantry Brigade was to pass through and advance in the direction of PYS. (D.O.1).

12 Noon. R.A.F. observer reported 11.30 a.m. that our troops were still holding out in R.11.b.Central with enemy at R.10.d.8.7 and in BOOM RAVINE.

12.16 p.m. 110 Infantry Brigade were ordered to expedite their attack as much as possible in order to relieve the 64th Infantry Brigade who were still holding out on high ground R.11.b. (D.O.3).

1.25 p.m. Situation of 64th Infantry Brigade unchanged. 110 Infantry Brigade were advancing in R.16 but exact position not definitely known.

2.30 p.m. Report received from 110 Infantry Brigade timed 1.15 p.m. that they had definitely gained touch with 64th Infantry Brigade on high ground R.11.b. & d. Small parties of the enemy were still holding out in BOOM RAVINE but were being mopped up. Touch not yet gained with 17th Division on right but the 7th Leicestershire Regiment had been ordered to occupy the remainder of the Green Dotted Line from R.17.d.0.0. to Southern Divisional Boundary and to gain touch with 17th Division.

4 p.m. The high ground R.11.b and d and R.17.b and d. now occupied. The right of the Division was at R.17.d.2.2. where it was reported to be in touch with 17th Division. 62nd Infantry Brigade were moving forward to gain touch with 42nd Division at PYS.

/under.....

~~Under instructions received from Corps one Cavalry Troop was~~ being allotted to this Division as Divisional Cavalry. (Corps G.567).

4.50 p.m. R.A.F. report our men seen in M.1.b and d. and R.23 about 4 p.m.

4.55 p.m. Orders issued that the Division would advance on LE SARS. 110th Infantry Brigade were to advance forthwith and capture the line M.20.b.0.3., M.15.Central. M.10.Central, patrols being sent forward to LE SARS and DESTREMONT FARM. The 62nd Infantry Brigade to concentrate on Road R.12, R.18. ready to move through 110th Infantry Brigade and take up the advance. 64th Infantry Brigade to reorganize in BOOM RAVINE (Div. Order No.212).

5 p.m. 62nd Infantry Brigade report that 12/13th Northumberland Fusiliers had moved up into position as ordered in G.C.1. The remainder of the Brigade were moving to BOOM RAVINE.

5.45 p.m. Orders issued that if LE SARS was found empty, it was to be occupied and patrols sent on to the BUTTE DE WARLENCOURT (G.X.570).

10.40 p.m. Orders issued for the continuation of the advance on the 25th with BEAULENCOURT as objective. The advance would be carried out by 62nd Infantry Brigade who, moving through 110th Infantry Brigade, were to capture the line M.24.a.3.0., N.7.a.0.0. When this line captured, 110th Infantry Brigade would move through 62nd Infantry Brigade to line of Road N.21.d.4.0., N.9.b.6.0. Advance would then be continued by 62nd Infantry Brigade to the BAPAUME - SAILLY SAILLISEL Road, touch being obtained with the IV Corps at RIENCOURT. 64th Infantry Brigade would remain in present position as Divisional Reserve (D.O.213.).

11.25 p.m. 110th Infantry Brigade moved from GREEN DOTTED Line towards LE SARS. Otherwise situation unchanged.

25th August 1918.

8 a.m. Divisional Headquarters closed MAILLY MAILLET and opened GRANDCOURT.

9 a.m. 64th Infantry Brigade were ordered to move at once to line of Road in R.12 and R.18. Units were to remain concentrated and obtain as much rest as possible, but to be prepared to hold the line of this road in case of necessity. (G.A.1.).

9.15 a.m. Patrol from Divisional Cav. Troop reported that the enemy were holding the Wood in N.12.b. and N.7.a. with Infantry and Machine Guns.

9.30 a.m. Pigeon message received from 62nd Infantry Brigade timed 8.55 a.m. stated that the Brigade moved without difficulty to the WARLENCOURT - COURCELETTE Road, where the 1st Wiltshire Regt. were found to be 300 yards South of it in M.14.d. with two Coys. of the 6th Leicestershire Regt. on their left. The position of the remainder of the 110th Infantry Brigade had not yet been ascertained. 62nd Infantry Brigade continued the advance but were unable to reach the summit of the ridge through M.10.Central, M.15. Central, owing to heavy Machine Gun fire from LE SARS.

9.45 a.m. 62nd Infantry Brigade reported that Artillery barrage ~~had been~~ arranged on LE SARS and that advance would be continued under this fire.

/the......

The enemy were showing signs of retiring. Touch had been gained with the 17th Division on the right near COURCELLETTE, and troops of the 42nd Division on the left had been seen near LITTLE WOOD. The high ground in M.15.c. had been gained and troops were working along high ground in M.9.d. and M.10.c.

<u>1 p.m.</u> 62nd Infantry Brigade were instructed to carry out the task allotted to the 110th Infantry Brigade in order No.213 if latter Brigade were not ready to carry it out (B.C.5.).

<u>1.10 p.m.</u> Information was received from the Corps on right that the enemy were massing for counter-attack in N.9.c. and d. and N.16.a. Instructions were sent to the 60 pdrs. attached to this Division to engage this target.

<u>1.25 p.m.</u> Situation at 1 p.m. 62nd Infantry Brigade attacked LE SARS and captured it. The QUARRY in M.15.a. was attacked under cover of Stokes Mortars and captured, 17 Germans being killed. The BUTTE DE WARLENCOURT was also captured, 1 Officer and 30 men being taken prisoner. Touch had been gained with 63rd Division on left, but not with 17th Division on right.

<u>2.50 p.m.</u> 64th Infantry Brigade were ordered to be ready to move at once in view of the possibility of the enemy counter-attacking from the direction of EAUCOURT L'ABBAYE (C.A.7.).

The 21st Battalion Machine Gun Corps was ordered to send its reserve Company to take up position on the road R.18, R.12. covering the Divisional front. (G.A.8.).

<u>3.20 p.m.</u> Situation as follows :- 62nd Infantry Brigade on line of Road M.24.a. and M.18.b. and d. touch being established with the 63rd Division on the left. At 2.15 p.m. the enemy delivered a heavy counter-attack against the right of the 62nd Infantry Brigade from the South and South East. 110th Infantry Brigade, who were on the move to pass through the 62nd Infantry Brigade were diverted to prolong the right of the former Brigade in order to gain touch with the 17th Division. The counter-attack was repulsed at 2.45 p.m. some prisoners being taken.

<u>4 p.m.</u> The 64th Infantry Brigade were ordered to sit easy but to be ready to move at 6 p.m. (G.A.10.).

<u>4.30 p.m.</u> Orders were issued to the 62nd Infantry Brigade and 110th Infantry Brigade that the Division would probably remain in its present position for the remainder of the day. The 62nd Infantry Brigade were to be prepared, however, to advance its left to keep touch with troops on its left, should they go forward. Should the 17th Division advance, and take EAUCOURT L'ABBAYE the 110th Infantry Brigade were to be prepared to carry on the advance (G.A.11.).

<u>7.30 p.m.</u> Orders were issued for the 62nd and 110th Infantry Brigades to hold their present positions during the night. The 64th Infantry Brigade were to move forthwith to the high ground M.15 and M.20 and to be prepared to hold this line. The reserve Machine Gun Company was to be prepared to occupy positions on the ridge R.12 R.18. At 5.30 a.m. August 26th, 64th Infantry Brigade were to take up the advance and move through the 62nd Infantry Brigade and capture the line of the Road N.21.b.6.0. - N.9.b.7.0. When the 64th Infantry Brigade had made good this objective, the 62nd Infantry Brigade were to advance to the

/SAILLY......

SAILLY SAILLISEL - BAPAUME ROAD. The 110 Infantry Brigade as soon the 62nd Infantry Brigade advanced, were to concentrate in M.17 and would be in Divisional Reserve. One Squadron, Corps Cyclists were placed under the orders of the 64th Infantry Brigade for the first operation and the 62nd Infantry Brigade for the second. Div. Cav. Troop were ordered to work in front of the Infantry and report the situation to leading Brigade. The 95th Bde. R.F.A. were placed under the orders of the leading Brigade. (D.O.214).

10.15 p.m. In continuation of Order No.214, 62nd Infantry Brigade were to first make good, as intermediate objective, the line of the road N.19.b. & N.17.b., the advance to the further objective not being carried out without orders from Divisional Headquarters. As soon as the 17th Division on the right commenced their advance, 110 Infantry Brigade were to concentrate in M.17. (G.X.587).

10.45 p.m. Div. Cav. Troop were ordered to withdraw to MIRAUMONT if they had not been relieved by 7.30 p.m. on the 26th instant. (G.X.589).

10.55 p.m. Message was sent to the 63rd Division stating that it was improbable that troops of that Division who were in this Divisional area would be relieved tonight. Orders had been given to the leading Brigade to extend their left on the 26th instant to the North. (G.X.588).

26th August, 1918.

5.30 a.m. Situation unchanged during the night. Some desultory shelling over forward area about 4.50 a.m.

9.25 a.m. Situation. 64th Infantry Brigade passed through 62nd Infantry Brigade but met with heavy Machine Gun fire coming from the direction of LUISENHOF FARM. No signs of troops advancing on the right flank.

10.45 a.m. Situation. 64 Infantry Brigade reported at 9.20 a.m. that their right Battalion appeared to be approaching the objective. The left Battalion had reached the line N.7.b.5.9 to N.13.a.7.1. where they were held up by heavy Machine Gun fire. Artillery barrage was being arranged and the advance would then be continued. Hostile resistance on the Divisional front had distinctly stiffened since yesterday. The right of the 63rd Division was in rear of our left and no touch had been gained with the 17th Division on the right.

12.35 p.m. Situation. Right Battalion, 64th Infantry Brigade, gained objectives South of LUISENHOF FARM. Left Battalion was held up on the line N.13.a.5.0 - N.7.a.5.0. 64th Infantry Brigade had two Battalions in front and one in reserve with one Cyclist Squadron and one Brigade R.F.A. attached.
62 Infantry Brigade disposed in depth with leading troops in YELLOW CUT with their left on South edge of LE BARQUE.
110 Infantry Brigade in Divisional Reserve with one Battalion at EAUCOURT L'ABBAYE, one Battalion in M.17.a. and one Battalion M.14.d. and M.15.a.

/4.15 p.m....

4.15 p.m. Situation. 64 Infantry Brigade report timed 3.15 p.m. stated that the right Battalion had been forced to withdraw and now held line of Sunken Road in N.19.a. and N.19.c. Left Battalion continued this line to N.7.b.2.0. Touch had not been gained on either flank. Cyclist Squadron were in touch with enemy at M.24.c.4.4.

7.30 p.m. Situation. Enemy counter-attacked 64th Infantry Brigade at 4 p.m. but were repulsed by rifle and Lewis Gun Fire. Heavy hostile Machine Gun fire from LIGNY and LIGNY THILLOY prevented our troops from approaching LUISENHOF FARM Road. Much enemy movement had been seen in trenches N.2.b. and N.2.c.

8.30 p.m. 64th Infantry Brigade ordered to find outposts on the general line now held. 62nd Infantry Brigade were .. to hold YELLOW CUT as main line of resistance. 110th Infantry Brigade were to concentrate each Unit and allow the men to rest, but were also to be prepared to hold the line DESTREMONT FARM - Road Junction M.16.b.3.3. - WARLENCOURT in case of necessity. 64th Infantry Brigade were to continue the advance on the 27th inst on BEAULENCOURT and occupy as first objective, line of the road N.19.b. - N.7.b. The 110th Infantry Brigade would then advance through the 64th Infantry Brigade with objective high ground N.20.central - N.14.b.5.0. - N.8.Central. Cyclists and Div. Cavalry Troop with Mobile Newton Mortar would work with leading Brigade. 94th Brigade R.F.A. were placed under the orders of 64th Infantry Brigade and 95th Brigade R.F.A. under the orders of 110th Infantry Brigade (Div. Order No. 215.).

27th August 1918.

5.45 a.m. Situation unchanged during the night. Patrols of 64th Infantry Brigade reported the enemy occupying LIGNY THILLOY and LUISENHOF FARM at 3 a.m.

11.50 a.m. Orders were issued cancelling Order No.215 and ordering the 64th Infantry Brigade to make good LUISENHOF FARM and the line of Road for 400 yards on each side of it, throwing refused flanks back to join with flank Divisions. This operation to be carried out by patrols, garrisons being sent forward to hold ground gained. 62nd Infantry Brigade would relieve the 64th Infantry Brigade during the night 27th/28th inst, and would also continue to hold the YELLOW CUT. On relief, the 64th Infantry Brigade would withdraw to Valley M.9. 18 and 14. (GX.622).

12.30 p.m. Situation. 64th Infantry Brigade reported that leading troops had reached line of road North of LUISENHOF FARM but were being badly enfiladed by Machine Guns from THILLOY. Very little hostile shelling.

2.45 p.m. 64th Infantry Brigade were holding line as previously reported with patrols on the road in N.13.b. and d. LUISENHOF FARM was reported unoccupied. Cyclist Sqdn. had established a Post at FACTORY CORNER (N.19.d.). Enemy Machine Guns were active from about N.7.d.9.9. Owing to reports being received that the enemy were retiring South of the SOMME, Brigades were instructed to keep close touch with the enemy, especially during the night.

/6 p.m.......

6 p.m. Situation remained unchanged. Small parties of the enemy were seen during the afternoon to come down the Valley in N.5.c. towards THILLOY.

6.30 p.m. Owing to the possibilty of the enemy evacuating BAPAUME during the night of 27th/28th, harassing fire by artillery was ordered to be carried out actively during the night.

10.10 p.m. 62nd Infantry Brigade were ordered to continue the advance on the 28th inst. under an Artillery barrage commencing at 5.30 a.m. with the objective high ground N.14. N.15. (D.O.216).

28th August 1918.

7.30 a.m. 62nd Infantry Brigade reported that LUISENHOF FARM and the road in N.7.d. and N.13.b. were strongly held by the enemy. Machine Gun fire was opened on both flanks of our patrol and owing to the very heavy fire from the direction of LIGNY THILLOY it had been found impossible to advance. Large numbers of the enemy were reported to be moving into THILLOY.

9.10 a.m. 62nd Infantry Brigade reported that THILLOY and Sunken Road from LIGNY THILLOY to LUISENHOF FARM still strongly held by the enemy, as was also the trench in N.9.a, c and d. The right Battalion reported no enemy could be seen on the above road from N.13.d.6.9. to N.19.a.1.3.

4.15 p.m. 110th Infantry Brigade were ordered to relieve the 62nd Infantry Brigade in the line during the night 28th/29th inst. On relief, 62nd Infantry Brigade were to take over the present dispositions and defence arrangements of 110th Infantry Brigade. The Cyclist Squadron would come under the orders of 110th Infantry Brigade on completion of relief (D.O.217.).

7.15 p.m. Orders were issued to the effect that as the 38th Division were attacking the high ground East of GINCHY on the 29th Machine Gun and Artillery barrages were to be put down on the Divisional front in order to assist this advance. 110th Infantry Brigade were to be ready to push forward advanced guards on any slackening of the enemy's resistance being noticed, but the main body of this Brigade was not to advance without orders from Divisional Headquarters (D.O.218.).

The situation on the Divisional front remained unchanged for the remainder of the day.

29th August.1918.

The situation remained unchanged during the night. No enemy Machine Gun or Artillery activity.

8 a.m. Divisional Cavalry Troop were ordered to send a patrol under a N.C.O. to report to B.G.C., 110th Infantry Brigade. The remainder of the troop was to be ready to move at short notice but not saddled up.(G.X.653.)

9.20 a.m. Owing to the 38th Division meeting no opposition in their attack this morning, 110th Infantry Brigade were ordered to push forward advanced guards followed by the remainder of the

/Brigade......

Brigade if feasable, and make good the following successive lines:- LUISENHOF FARM ROAD - Road N.21 - N.9.a. Spur N.22.a.0.0. - Cross Roads N.9.d.7.2. along road to N.9.b.8.0. - Cross Roads N.24.a.5.1. - BEAULENCOURT and Road from N.11.d.5.0. to N.11.b.7.0. 62nd Infantry Brigade will be in Support to 110th Infantry Brigade and would move to LUISENHOF FARM Road when 110th Infantry Brigade had made good the road in N.21.a. N.9.a. moving on to the Spur in N.22.a. when 110th Infantry Brigade had reached BEAULENCOURT. Further orders would be issued for the move of 64th Infantry Brigade and Reserve Machine Gun Coy. (G.X.654).

10.40 a.m. 95th Brigade R.F.A. were placed under the orders of 110th Infantry Brigade and 94th Brigade R.F.A. under the orders of 64th Infantry Brigade. 94th Brigade R.F.A. were to assist however, in covering the advance of the 110th Infantry Brigade (G.X.659.)

11 a.m. Situation. Advanced Guards of the Right Battalion, 110th Infantry Brigade had reached the Ridge N.14.Central and reported it clear of the enemy. Divisional Cavalry Troop had gained touch with the 42nd Division and reported THILLOY to have been evacuated by the enemy.

12.10 p.m. Orders issued in continuation of G.X.654 for the 64th Infantry Brigade to become Support Brigade in place of the 62nd Infantry Brigade and to be prepared to move to YELLOW CUT on receipt of orders from Divisional Headquarters. 94th Brigade R.F.A. would now come under the orders of the 64th Infantry Brigade (G.X.661.).

12.15 p.m. Main Guards had occupied LUISENHOF FARM ROAD with vanguards advancing over high ground N.14 and 15. Some hostile Machine Gun fire encountered from N.3.c. otherwise no touch with the enemy yet obtained.

2 p.m. 64th Infantry Brigade ordered to move forthwith to YELLOW CUT (G.X.665).
Situation. Infantry Patrols had reached line in N.16.c. and were encountering Machine Gun fire from Sunken Road N.16 a and b. Infantry advanced guards were on Ridge N.15.a and c. and main body was crossing the LUISENHOF FARM ROAD.

4.30 p.m. 110th Infantry Brigade report timed 2 p.m. stated that advanced guards had reached the line of trenches in N.16, N.9. and were in touch with the 17th Division on the Right and 42nd Division on the left. Main body had reached line of the road N.21.a, N.9.a at 3.25 p.m.

6 p.m. Situation at 5.30 p.m. Main body had reached line of trenches N.16.d. to N.9.d. and were in touch on both flanks. Advanced guards were endeavouring to make progress towards BEAULENCOURT, but were encountering very heavy Machine Gun and rifle fire from the Western edge of the Village.

9.20 p.m. Message sent to Vth Corps asking for as much artillery fire as possible to be brought to bear on BEAULENCOURT during the night. All fire on the village to cease at 2 a.m. 30th inst, when patrols would enter the village (G.X.673.).

/10.20 p.m.....

10.20 p.m. Orders issued for the 110th Infantry Brigade to send forward fighting patrols to ascertain the situation as regards BEAULENCOURT and to occupy the village if found empty. 110th Infantry Brigade were also to endeavour to resume the advance to the fourth objective early tomorrow, August 30th. When this objective had been taken, one Coy and one Section of Machine Guns were to be sent to LUBDA COPSE to form defensive flank facing North. As soon as the PERONNE - BAPAUME Road had been crossed, the Division would come into Corps reserve about LE TRANSLOY. Until further orders the 64th and 62nd Infantry Brigades would remain in their present positions, the 64th Infantry Brigade being ready to occupy YELLOW CUT at short notice. The Cyclist Squadron and Divisional Cavalry Troop would remain under the orders of 110th Infantry Brigade (D.O.219).

30th August 1918.

The situation during the night remained unchanged with very little enemy activity.

12 noon. Divisional Hdqrs. closed at GUEUDECOURT and opened N.9.c.70.05.

12.5 p.m. Situation. Patrols report BEAULENCOURT still occupied. Machine Guns and snipers very active from the Western outskirts of the Village.

7.15 p.m. Situation throughout the day remained unchanged. Enemy artillery fire was negligible. Our Artillery shelled BEAULENCOURT and engaged Machine Guns which had been located in the Western outskirts of the village. Large explosions occurred at N.11.d.5.8. and N.5.c.3.6. between 5.30 and 6.5 p.m.

7.30 p.m. Orders were issued to the Divisional Cavalry Troop to rejoin their Squadron near COURCELETTE by 8.30 a.m. 31st August (G.A.684).

31st August 1918.

5.20 a.m. The situation remained unchanged during the night. Patrols had endeavoured to enter BEAULENCOURT but were stopped by Machine Gun fire. Much enemy movement was heard in BEAULENCOURT during the night. At South end of the village wiring was believed to be in progress. There was considerable random shelling of our back areas during the night.

8.50 a.m. Under instructions received from Corps one Troop of Carabineers was placed under the orders of the Division as Divisional Cavalry. The Troop was ordered to bivouac near the BUTTE DE WARLENCOURT and was placed under the orders of 110th Infantry Brigade (G.A.688).

10.25 a.m. Instructions were received from Corps for intense harassing fire by artillery not only on enemy known communications but also on all known positions held by him (Vth Corps A.A.30/44).

/9 p.m......

9 p.m. Orders were issued for 110th Infantry Brigade to capture and occupy BEAULENCOURT during the night, Zero hour being 2.30 a.m. The infantry were to form up on the line N.10.Cent. N.11.b.2.9. and attack Southwards. When the village had been captured, 110th Infantry Brigade were to carry out a second operation at 5.40 a.m. (in conjunction with 17th Division who were to take LE TRANSLOY) with objective the SUGAR FACTORY N.24.Central. 64th Infantry Brigade were to take over the present positions of 110th Infantry Brigade when vacated by latter Brigade (D.O.220.). The situation throughout the night remained unaltered, all attempts by patrols to enter BEAULENCOURT being frustrated by Machine Gun fire.

1st September 1918.

7.45 a.m. 110th Infantry Brigade report that all objectives in the first attack had been gained and an enemy counter-attack easily beaten off. Our casualties were believed to be slight. About 100 prisoners were captured and two 77 mm guns. Touch had not yet been gained with 42nd Division but patrols were being sent out to do so.

9.50 a.m. Situation. 110th Infantry Brigade report timed 9.30 a.m. states that troops detailed to take the SUGAR FACTORY were unable to enter it owing to Machine Gun fire from LE TRANSLOY. They have occupied trench in N.24.a. just North of Factory. An Officer who had just returned from BEAULENCOURT reports many German dead in the Village. Touch had been gained with 42nd Division about N.11.d.3.9. 30 enemy Machine Guns had already been counted in the Village.

6.40 p.m. Situation remained unchanged throughout the day. Enemy shelled BEAULENCOURT and trenches in N.16. Shelling ceased about 6 p.m.

8.5 p.m. 62nd Infantry Brigade were ordered to take up the following dispositions by 5 a.m. 2nd September. One Battalion in YELLOW CUT, one Battalion WARLENCOURT, and one Battalion in bivouacs near LE SARS. (G.A.734).

8.15 p.m. Orders issued that in conjunction with the attack by IV Corps on September 2nd, the 110th Infantry Brigade were to capture the SUGAR FACTORY N.24.Central. After capture of SUGAR FACTORY, 110th Infantry Brigade were to push out a force not exceeding one Coy. to about O.19.d.central with object of preventing withdrawal of garrison of LE TRANSLOY.

This attack to take place at 2 a.m.

In conjunction with main attack of IV and Vth Corps which was to take place later in the morning the 64th Infantry Brigade were to capture LABDA COPSE, at 5.15 a.m. at which hour the 42nd Division on the left would be attacking VILLERS AU FLOS. After capture of LABDA COPSE, 64th Infantry Brigade were to effect a junction with 42nd Division at Cross Roads O.13.a.2.4. and were also to establish a line from LABDA COPSE to SUGAR FACTORY and get in touch with 110th Infantry Brigade. (D.O. 221).

2nd September 1918.

5.45 a.m. Report received from 110th Infantry Brigade that the SUGAR FACTORY had been captured but that the attacking Coys. of 7th Leicestershire Regt had been unable to gain touch with their

/supporting....

Company. The runner who brought back the message states that enemy with Machine Guns were still in position between SUGAR FACTORY and BEAULENCOURT. The 1st Wiltshire Regt. were sending one Coy. forward to clear up the situation and to gain touch with troops of the 7th Leicester Regt. in the SUGAR FACTORY.

__7.20 a.m.__ 64th Infantry Brigade reported LABDA COPSE to have been captured with about 30 prisoners and 6 - 77 mm guns. A pocket of Germans in N.18.b. was being dealt with by Stokes Mortars. Situation at SUGAR FACTORY now reported as being satisfactory.

__10.40 a.m.__ Report received from 64th Infantry Brigade that owing to Machine Gun fire from the Southern outskirts of VILLERS AU FLOS and N.E. Corner of LE TRANSLOY, the 1st East Yorkshire Regt. had been withdrawn from LABDA COPSE. This Battalion was now holding trench from N.18.Central to about O.13.a.6.0. The road from LE TRANSLOY to BEAULENCOURT was being swept by Machine Gun fire from LE TRANSLOY. Touch with 110th Infantry Brigade in the SUGAR FACTORY had not been gained owing to fire from small enemy pockets about O.19.a.

__11.15 a.m.__ 64th Infantry Brigade reported that LABDA COPSE had been reoccupied. The line now ran O.13.b.3.1. where in touch with 42nd Division through O.13.d.3.0. to O.19.b.0.8. 110th Infantry Brigade report that counter-attack from LE TRANSLOY drove their troops out of all except N.W. portion of the SUGAR FACTORY. A fresh attack was being organized to retake the FACTORY.

__12.30 p.m.__ 110th Infantry Brigade reported that 7th Leicester Regt. have retaken SUGAR FACTORY and are pushing up the Spur towards LABDA COPSE. Troops of the 17th Division had just passed through and could be seen on high ground in O.19.a.

__6.15 p.m.__ Orders issued for 110th Infantry Brigade to relieve forward Battalion of 64th Infantry Brigade during night 2nd/3rd September. The 110th Infantry Brigade would then hold SUGAR FACTORY and LABDA COPSE, maintaining touch with 42nd Division at O.13.b.3.1. 110th Infantry Brigade were also to garrison the defences of BEAULENCOURT, maintaining at least one Battalion in Brigade reserve in Valley West of the main PERONNE - BAPAUME Road. The 64th Infantry Brigade, after relief of the 1st East Yorkshire Regt. by 110th Infantry Brigade, were to be prepared to hold general line N.22.Central - N.10.Central. 62nd Infantry Brigade were to move to area near LESBOEUFS forthwith (D.O.222.).

The situation during the day remained unchanged. Very little hostile fire of any kind.

__3rd September 1918.__

__12.30 a.m.__ Instructions received from Corps to withdraw the 110th Infantry Brigade to Valley West of BEAULENCOURT as soon as possible to rest. Time of withdrawal to be arranged mutually between 21st and 17th Divisions (Vth Corps G.180.).

/5.45 a.m......

5.45 a.m. All moves ordered by Divisional Order No.222. were complete.

3.30 p.m. Orders issued to all Brigades to give instructions to Cyclists to concentrate at N.13.d.3.3. where they were to be ready to move at 1 hours notice. (G.X.780 and G.X.781).

10.25 p.m. Orders issued to the effect that 21st Division would remain in Corps Reserve on September 4th. The 62nd Infantry Brigade group would move to area about O.20 and O.21. on the 4th instant, so as to clear LE TRANSLOY by 10 a.m. Observation posts were to be established in the trench system East of ROCQUIGNY, as soon as this system was vacated by 17th Division. 110th Infantry Brigade and 64th Infantry Brigade Groups would probably not move but 64th Infantry Brigade group would be ready to move at one hour's notice. (D.O.223.).

During the above operations the following prisoners and guns were captured by the Division :-

	Officers.	Other Ranks.
Prisoners	45	1,242.
Guns.	12. (including two 8" hows.)	

Copy of Telegrams to accompany Summary of Operations
for period 20th Aug. to 3rd Sept.

G.X.449.

Send one N.C.O. and 12 men to report to 64th Inf. Bde. at Q.10.b.8.4 at once AAA Addsd Corps Cyclists reptd V Corps and 64th Inf. Bde.

G.X.452.

Our troops have entered ACHIET LE PETIT and are moving on IRLES AAA As soon as Brown Line captured 62nd Inf. Bde. will move two Reserve Companies preceded by patrols to line River ANCRE at R.4.c.6.7 Road junc. R.4.a.5.1 to R.4.a.0.5. AAA Picquets will be placed on all bridges over ANCRE between above line and Brown Line AAA 62 Inf. Bde. will push patrols from new line into S.W. outskirts of MIRAUMONT AAA 64th Inf. Bde. will place two Coys. at disposal of 62nd Inf. Bde. to act as Brigade Reserve AAA Ack

G.396 from Corps.

In event of IV Corps taking IRLES and the fire from THIEPVAL RIDGE not being heavy be prepared move your 3rd Bde. rapidly along BEAUCOURT - MIRAUMONT Road and cross ANCRE in R.3 and 4 moving thence on THIEPVAL holding BOOM RAVINE to cover movement AAA

G.X.455.

One Battalion 110 Inf. Bde. is placed at disposal of 64th Inf. Bde. AAA Battalion will reach BEAUMONT RESERVE Area about 2 p.m. AAA 64th Inf. Bde. will send orders to 110th Inf. Bde. H.Q. as to further move of Battalion AAA

G.X.460.

IRLES has not yet been captured by us AAA In consequence 42nd Div. have not yet entered MIRAUMONT AAA 64th Inf. Bde. will therefore take special precautions regarding his Eastern flank after crossing ANCRE AAA 62 Inf. Bde. will make every endeavour to throw bridges across the ANCRE between BEAUCOURT and GRANDCOURT so as to give 64th Inf. Bde. alternative line for withdrawal in case of necessity AAA 64th Inf. Bde. will send patrols towards GRANDCOURT after crossing ANCRE to connect with 62nd Inf. Bde. and to ensure connection between these bridge-heads AAA

G.X.461.

Reference G.X.455 AAA 110th Inf. Bde. will hold another Battalion in readiness to join 64th Inf. Bde, if ordered to do so from Div. H.Q. AAA Ack

G.421 from Corps.

21st Div. will consolidate final objective from River by BAILLESCOURT FARM Sunken Road to R.3.a.0.8 with one Bde. connecting with 42nd Div. on left AAA One Brigade in position to support front Bde. or to renew the offensive across the ANCRE at short notice AAA Rear Bde. S. and W. of BEAUMONT HAMEL in positions to be selected and reported AAA Ack

G.X.476.

Two rear Battalions 64th Inf. Bde. and 1 Battalion 110th Inf. Bde. attached 64th Inf. Bde. will NOT be ~~forward~~ moved forward without reference to Div. H.Q.

G.X.477.

Trend of hostile movement this evening has been towards MIRAUMONT and ACHIET LE GRAND AAA Hostile counter-attack is

therefore possible tonight or tomorrow morning AAA All Commanders will be warned accordingly AAA Action of two Rear Battalions of 64th Inf. Bde. and attached Battalion from 110 Inf. Bde. will be defensive until further orders AAA They will be prepared to support 62nd Inf. Bde. to meet a counter-attack from the East AAA At Dawn tomorrow Aug. 22nd 110 Inf. Bde. will endeavour to push patrols across the ANCRE to the Blue Line also a patrol in conjunction with 38th Div. AAA When Blue Line has been made good and consolidated 110th Inf. Bde. will push patrols to Red Line AAA 62 Inf. Bde. will push patrols to Blue Dotted Line AAA Leading Battalion of 64th Inf. Bde. will push patrols acress ANCRE to try and get touch with enemy. AAA Ack

22.9.18. G.X.486.

62 Inf. Bde. will push patrols forward from Blue Line to portion of Red Line in their area as well as to GRANDCOURT AAA If Red Line occupied by our patrols 64th Inf. Bde. will be prepared to send two Coys. to garrison it AAA Ack

G.466 from Corps.

A Brigade 17th Division will relieve and take over a one Brigade front at present held by 110th Inf. Bde. 21st Division tonight (22nd/23rd) AAA Relief to be complete by 5 a.m. 23rd AAA Boundary between 21st and 17th Divs. will be line from R.21.d.0.0 - R.14.c.0.0 to Q.12.c.6.0 thence West along grid line between Q.11 and Q.17 AAA S. Boundary 17th Div. will be THIEPVAL Road (exclusive) to Q.24.a.6.0 thence West along grid line Q.23.Central - Q.22.Central AAA Ack

R.A.1163 from Corps.

Reference V Corps G.466 AAA 17th Divl. Arty. will come under orders of C.R.A. 17th Div. at 4 a.m. on 23rd AAA The two 60 - pdr. Batteries will remain under C.R.A. 21st Div. AAA Ack

G.X.503.

If Brown Line or any portion of it has been lost it must be restored by a counter-attack in conformity with attack of Div. on your left at 2.30 a.m. Aug. 23rd AAA Arrange Arty. support with affiliated Brigade R.F.A. AAA Gain touch with 42nd Div. after counter-attack AAA Ack

23rd ~~September~~ AUGUST, 1918.

G.511 from Corps.

A Company, Cyclists Battalion, is allotted to each Div. AAA Coy. has already been detailed to 21st and 38th Divs AAA Remaining Coy. now allotted to 17th Div. under arrangements to be made direct between Headquarters 17th Division and O.C. Cyclist Bn. AAA Lewis Gun Detachments now attached 21st Division will revert to their CompaniesAAA O.C. Cyclist Bn. and Adjutant will act as liaison Officers between Divisions ~~xxx~~ and will be attached 17th Division under arrangements to be made direct AAA Ack

G.X.521.

Order all Lewis Gunners N.I.H. except those belonging to "A" Squadron to rejoin their own Units AAA Ack

G.X.535.

Confirmation of telephone conversation AAA 62 Inf. Bde. will concentrate all troops less garrison of Brown Line at once AAA As soon as reliable information is received that MIRAUMONT has been captured the garrison of the Brown Line will concentrate with its own Units AAA You will then be prepared to cross the ANCRE either by the railway bridge or the bridge in GRANDCOURT AAA

24th ~~September~~ August, 1918.

G.X.541.

In continuation of G.X.535 62nd Inf. Bde. will on receipt of orders from 21 Div. H.Q. be prepared to concentrate either in BATTERY VALLEY or Valley in R.9.d. and R.15.b.

G.X.545.

Concentrate your Brigade less two Coys. left in the Brown Line on the South bank of the ANCRE in BATTERY VALLEY and R.14.a.

D.C.1 to G.O.C. 110 Inf. Bde.

1. You will take Command of 64th and 110 Inf. Bdes.

2. 42nd Division are attacking North of MIRAUMONT through IRLES on to PYS. You will attack high ground in R.11.b. & d. 17th Div. have been ordered to move to R.17 to protect your flanks.

3. When attack has succeeded 62nd Inf. Bde. will pass through moving along ridge running in N.E. direction to PYS and will join hands with 42nd Division.

4. The attack will be pushed with the greatest vigour.

D.C.3 to G.O.C. 110 Inf. Bde.

Reference my D.C.2 parties of our men have been definitely located holding out in R.11.a. AAA Please expedite attack as much as possible to relieve these men AAA Barrage will be arranged to miss them AAA

G.567 from Corps.

One Regiment 1st Cavalry Division allotted to V Corps AAA will march this afternoon from SARTON to LINES in vicinity of CONTAY AAA H.Q. accommodation in CONTAY on application to 18th Div. AAA Regt. will be used as Corps Cavalry one troop will be attached each Div. as Divl. Cavalry.

G.X.570.

Reference Order No.212 AAA If LE SARS found empty it will be occupied and patrols sent on to BUTTE DE WARLENCOURT AAA If 110th Inf. Bde. moves H.Q. it will be along the general line R.17.Central - M.15.Central AAA Ack.

G.A.1.

64th Inf. Bde. will move at once to line of road in R.12 and R.18. AAA Units will remain concentrated and obtain as much rest as possible but be prepared to hold line of road in case of need AAA

D.C.5 to G.O.C. 62 Inf. Bde.

Reference SPICERS message approve of you carrying out roll allotted 110 Inf. Bde. if latter are not ready to do it. Inform G.O.C. 110 Inf. Bde. who must then carry out your original role

G.A.7.

Get ready to move at once but don't fall in until you receive further orders AAA Have look-out post to watch country in direction of LE SARS as enemy are counter-attacking from EAUCOURT L'ABBAYE.

G.A.8.

Send Reserve Coy. to take up position on road R.12 R.18 covering Divl. front AAA Enemy are counter-attacking from direction of EAUCOURT L'ABBAYE.

25th ~~September~~ August, 1918.

G.A.10.

Sit easy AAA Be prepared to move at 6 p.m.

G.A.11.

In confirmation of telephone message AAA 21st Division will probably remain in present position for today AAA However 62nd Inf. Bde. will be prepared to advance its left to keep touch with troops on its left should they go forward AAA Should 17th Div. advance and take EAUCOURT L'ABBAYE 110 Inf. Bde. will be prepared to carry on the general advance AAA

Order No.214.

17th Division are holding East of MARTINPUICH with their left in M.22.c. 63rd Division hold LE BARQUE and YELLOW CUT AAA 62 Inf. Bde. will hold present line in M.18 and 24. AAA 110th Inf. Bde. will protect the right of 62nd Inf. Bde. until 17th Div. left reaches M.24.c. when 110th Inf. Bde. will concentrate West of BLUE CUT and ready to hold that line AAA 64th Inf. Bde. will move to high ground M.15 and 20 and be prepared to hold this line AAA Reserve M.Gs will prepare to occupy positions on ridge R.12 and R.18 AAA 64th Inf. Bde. will advance at 5.30 a.m. Aug. 26th and move through 62nd Inf. Bde. with objective line of road N.21.b.6.0 - N.9.b.7.0. AAA When 64th Inf. Bde. has passed road N.19.b. N.7.b. 62nd Inf. Bde. will advance to it AAA When 64th Inf. Bde. ~~made~~ objective made good 62nd Inf. Bde. will advance to SAILLY SAILLISEL - BAPAUME Road AAA 110th Inf. Bde. if not already concentrated in M.17 will do so when 62nd Inf. Bde. advances and be in Divisional Reserve AAA One Coy. Cyclists works under 64th Inf. Bde. for first operation and 62nd Inf. Bde. for second AAA One Troop Div. Cav. under special instructions issued to O.C. will work in front of Infantry reporting situation to leading Brigade AAA 94th Bde. R.F.A. under orders 64th Inf. Bde. for first operation AAA 95th Bde. R.F.A. under 62nd Inf. Bde. for second AAA Mobile Newton Mortar works with leading Brigade reporting 62nd Inf. Bde. H.Q. early tomorrow AAA Infantry will not move extended across country unless under aimed small arm fire AAA Div. H.Q. remain GRANDCOURT AAA ACK

G.X.587.

Ref. Order No. 214 AAA 64th Inf. Bde. will first make good intermediate objective line of road N.19.b. N.17.b. reporting capture to Div. H.Q. AAA 64th Inf. Bde. will not advance to further objective without orders from Div. H.Q. AAA 62nd Inf. Bde. will not advance to their objective without reference to Div. H.Q. AAA As soon as 17th Division start advancing on right of 110 Inf. Bde., 110 Inf. Bde. will concentrate in M.17 AAA

G.X.589.

Reference instructions issued you today if Infantry have not relieved you by 7 p.m. you will withdraw to MIRAUMONT AAA If state of ground tomorrow does not permit of you moving faster than the Infantry you will return to MIRAUMONT and report to Div. H.Q. for further orders AAA

G.X.588.

If as is probable relief of your troops in our area not carried out tonight AAA Brigade which moves through our leading Bde. at 7.30 a.m. have particular orders to get their left on Northern Div. Boundary. AAA

29th ~~September~~ August, 1918.

G.X.653.

Send a patrol under a N.C.O. to report to B.G.C. 110th Inf. Bde. as soon as possible AAA Remainder of Troop to be ready to move at short notice but not saddled up AAA

G.X.654.

38th Division report that they met no opposition this morning AAA There are other indications that enemy are retiring AAA 110th Inf. Bde. will push forward Advanced Guards followed if feasible by remainder of Brigade and make good following successive bounds AAA LUISENHOF FARM ROAD AAA Road N.21.a. N.9.a. AAA Spur N.22.a.00 to Cross Rds N.9.d.7.2 along road to N.9.b.8.0 AAA Cross Rds N.24.a.5.1 BEAULENCOURT and road from N.11.d.5.0 to N.11.b.7.0 AAA 62nd Inf. Bde. will support 110 Inf. Bde. moving to LUISENHOF FARM Rd. when 110 Inf. Bde. has made good road N.21.a. N.9.a. AAA N.2 Spur N.22.a.0.0 Cross Rds. N.9.d. when 110 Inf. Bde. has reached BEAULENCOURT AAA Moves of 64th Inf. Bde. and Reserve M.Gs will be ordered direct from Div. H.Q. AAA Successive Report Centres at BUTTE DE WARLENCOURT LUISENHOF FARM and Sunken Road N.15.d.4.7 AAA

G.X.659.

95th Bde. R.F.A. will act under orders of leading Brigade AAA 94th Bde. R.F.A. under orders of supporting Brigade but will assist in covering advance of leading Brigade AAA

G.X.661.

Ref. G.X.654 of today AAA 64 Inf. Bde. will become supporting Brigade instead of 62nd Inf. Bde. AAA 64 Inf. Bde. will be prepared to move to YELLOW CUT on receipt of orders from Divisional H.Q. AAA 94th Bde. R.F.A. now come under orders 64th Inf. Bde. AAA

G.X.665.

64 Inf. Bde. will move forthwith to YELLOW CUT AAA Completion of move to be reported to 21st Div. H.Q. AAA

G.X.673.

In confirmation of telephone conversation AAA As much Arty. fire as possible is required on BEAULENCOURT tonight AAA All fire on Village to cease at 2 a.m. 30th instant when patrols will enter the village AAA Could 4th Corps be asked to shell the village as well AAA

30th ~~September~~ August, 1918.

G.X.684.

Under orders from Corps you are to rejoin your Squadron at Cross Roads COURCELLETTE at 8.30 a.m. tomorrow August 31st AAA

31st August, 1918.

G.X.688.

You will bivouac near the BUTTE DE WARLENCOURT AAA Until further orders you will be under the 110 Inf. Bde. who will issue the necessary orders for your employment AAA Please report to these Brigade H.Q. at N.13.d.6.4 as soon as possible leaving the troop in bivouacs.

31st August, 1918.

R.A.30/44 from Corps.

It is essential that enemy should be prevented from improving his present positions by making secure M.G.posts improving his trenches and putting up wire AAA All Artillery will be active not only on communications but on the positions now held by enemy

1st September, 1918.

G.X.734.

62 Inf. Bde. will have one Battalion holding YELLOW CUT by 5 a.m. Sept. 2nd AAA Another Battalion of 62nd Inf. Bde. will be at WARLENCOURT and the third in bivouacs near LE SARS by same hour AAA 62nd Inf. Bde. will establish Brigade Headquarters at BUTTE DE WARLENCOURT ~~xxx~~ by 11 a.m. AAA

2nd September, 1918.

G.180 from Corps.

21st Division will withdraw Brigade now holding LABDA COPSE SUGAR FACTORY BEAULENCOURT as soon as possible to rest AAA Time of withdrawal to be arranged mutually between 21st and 17th Divs.

3rd September, 1918.

G.X.780.

110 Inf. Bde. will issue instructions to Cyclists to concentrate at the BUTTE forthwith AAA 62nd and 64th Inf. Bdes. will send all cyclists at present ~~to~~ with them to rejoin their Unit at the BUTTE AAA Cyclist Squadron will keep orderlies at the BUTTE Telephone Exchange AAA After concentration Cyclists will be ready to move at one hours' notice AAA

G.X.781.

Ref. G.X.780 AAA Cyclists will now concentrate at N.13.d.3.3 and NOT at the BUTTE AAA Cyclists will keep orderlies at 110th Inf. Bde. H.Q.

21st D I V I S I O N.

Summary of Casualties - August 21st - Sept 14th (inc.)

U N I T.	Killed.		Wounded.		Missing.		TOTAL.	
	Off.	O.R.	Off.	O.R.	Off.	O.R.	Off.	O.R.
62nd Inf. Brigade.								
12/13th North Fus.	2	44	15	278	-	21	17	343
1st Lincoln Regt.	3	39	10	208	-	17	13	264
2nd Lincoln Regt.	1	31	5	133	-	7	6	171
62nd T.M.Battery.	-	1	-	17	-	-	-	18
Total.	6	115	30	636	-	45	36	796
64th Inf. Brigade.HQ	-	-	1	-	-	-	1	-
1st E.Yorks Regt.	7	54	12	193	4	205	23	452
9th K.O.Y.L.I.	6	42	18	270	-	39	24	351
15th Durham L.I.	9	74	15	344	1	112	25	530
64th T.M.Battery.	-	-	1	2	-	-	1	2
Total.	22	170	47	809	5	356	74	1335
110th Inf. Brigade.								
6th Leicester Regt.	2	21	5	170	1	9	8	200
7th Leicester Regt.	2	16	12	218	1	32	15	266
1st Wilts Regt.	2	17	10	154	-	6	12	177
110th T.M.Battery.	2	3	-	11	-	-	2	14
Total.	8	57	27	553	2	47	37	657
14th North Fus (P).	-	2	2	26	-	-	2	28
21st Bn M.G.Corps.	1	7	8	51	-	2	9	60
Divl. Artillery.								
94th Brigade RFA.	-	-	2	8	-	-	2	8
95th Brigade RFA.	-	1	3	15	-	-	3	16
21st D.A.C.	-	-	-	2	-	-	-	2
21st T.M.Brigade.	-	-	-	-	-	-	-	-
Total.	-	1	5	25	-	-	5	26
Divl. Engineers.								
97th Field Coy RE.	-	-	-	9	-	-	-	9
98th Field Coy RE.	-	-	2	37	-	-	2	37
126th Field Coy RE.	-	-	-	9	-	-	-	9
Total.	-	-	2	55	-	-	2	55
R. A. M. C.								
Regtl. M.O's.	1	-	-	-	-	-	1	-
63rd Field Amb.	-	-	-	7	-	-	-	7
64th Field Amb.	-	1	-	6	-	-	-	7
65th Field Amb.	-	2	-	16	-	-	-	18
Total.	1	3	-	29	-	-	1	32
21st Div.Train. ASC.	-	-	-	2	-	-	-	2
33rd Mob.Vet.Sec. AVC.	-	-	-	1	-	-	-	1
Army Chaplains Dept.	-	-	1	-	-	-	1	-
T O T A L.	38	355	122	2187	7	450	167	2992

------0------

Copy of Telegrams to accompany Summary of Operations
for period 20th Aug. to 3rd Sept.

21

G.X.449.

Send one N.C.O. and 12 men to report to 64th Inf. Bde. at Q.10.b.8.4 at once AAA Addsd Corps Cyclists reptd V Corps and 64th Inf. Bde.

G.X.452.

Our troops have entered ACHIET LE PETIT and are moving on IRLES AAA As soon as Brown Line captured 62nd Inf. Bde. will move two Reserve Companies preceded by patrols to line River ANCRE at R.4.c.6.7 Road junc. R.4.a.5.1 to R.4.a.0.5. AAA Picquets will be placed on all bridges over ANCRE between above line and Brown Line AAA 62 Inf. Bde. will push patrols from new line into S.W. outskirts of MIRAUMONT AAA 64th Inf. Bde. will place two Coys. at disposal of 62nd Inf. Bde. to act as Brigade Reserve AAA Ack

G.396 from Corps.

In event of IV Corps taking IRLES and the fire from THIEPVAL RIDGE not being heavy be prepared move your 3rd Bde. rapidly along BEAUCOURT - MIRAUMONT Road and cross ANCRE in R.3 and 4 moving thence on THIEPVAL holding BOOM RAVINE to cover movement AAA

G.X.455.

One Battalion 110 Inf. Bde. is placed at disposal of 64th Inf. Bde. AAA Battalion will reach BEAUMONT RESERVE Area about 2 p.m. AAA 64th Inf. Bde. will send orderly to 110th Inf. Bde. H.Q. as to further move of Battalion AAA

G.X.460.

IRLES has not yet been captured by us AAA In consequence 42nd Div. have not yet entered MIRAUMONT AAA 64th Inf. Bde. will therefore take special precautions regarding his Eastern flank after crossing ANCRE AAA 62 Inf. Bde. will make every endeavour to throw bridges across the ANCRE between BEAUCOURT and GRANDCOURT so as to give 64th Inf. Bde. alternative line for withdrawal in case of necessity AAA 64th Inf. Bde. will send patrols towards GRANDCOURT after crossing ANCRE to connect with 62nd Inf. Bde. and to ensure connection between these bridge-heads AAA

G.X.461.

Reference G.X.455 AAA 110th Inf. Bde. will hold another Battalion in readiness to join 64th Inf. Bde, if ordered to do so from Div. H.Q. AAA Ack

G.421 from Corps.

21st Div. will consolidate final objective from River by BAILLESCOURT FARM Sunken Road to R.3.a.0.8 with one Bde. connecting with 42nd Div. on left AAA One Brigade in position to support front Bde. or to renew the offensive across the ANCRE at short notice AAA Rear Bde. S. and W. of BEAUMONT HAMEL in positions to be selected and reported AAA Ack

G.X.476.

Two rear Battalions 64th Inf. Bde. and 1 Battalion 110th Inf. Bde. attached 64th Inf. Bde. will NOT be ~~formerx~~ moved forward without reference to Div. H.Q.

G.X.477.

Trend of hostile movement this evening has been towards MIRAUMONT and ACHIET LE GRAND AAA Hostile counter-attack is

therefore possible tonight or tomorrow morning AAA All Commanders will be warned accordingly AAA Action of two Rear Battalions of 64th Inf. Bde. and attached Battalion from 110 Inf. Bde. will be defensive until further orders AAA They will be prepared to support 62nd Inf. Bde. to meet a counter-attack from the East AAA At Dawn tomorrow Aug. 22nd 110 Inf. Bde. will endeavour to push patrols across the ANCRE to the Blue Line also a patrol in conjunction with 38th Div. AAA When Blue Line has been made good and consolidated 110th Inf. Bde. will push patrols to Red Line AAA 62 Inf. Bde. will push patrols to Blue Dotted Line AAA Leading Battalion of 64th Inf. Bde. will push patrols across ANCRE to try and get touch with enemy. AAA Ack

22.9.18. G.X.486.

62 Inf. Bde. will push patrols forward from Blue Line to portion of Red Line in their area as well as to GRANDCOURT AAA If Red Line occupied by our patrols 64th Inf. Bde. will be prepared to send two Coys. to garrison it AAA Ack

G.466 from Corps.

A Brigade 17th Division will relieve and take over a one Brigade front at present held by 110th Inf. Bde. 21st Division tonight (22nd/23rd) AAA Relief to be complete by 5 a.m. 23rd AAA Boundary between 21st and 17th Divs. will be line from R.21.d.0.0 - R.14.c.0.0 to Q.12.c.6.0 thence West along grid line between Q.11 and Q.17 AAA S. Boundary 17th Div. will be THIEPVAL Road (exclusive) to Q.24.a.6.0 thence West along grid line Q.23.Central - Q.22.Central AAA Ack

R.A.1163 from Corps.

Reference V Corps G.466 AAA 17th Divl. Arty. will come under orders of C.R.A. 17th Div. at 4 a.m. on 23rd AAA The two 60 - pdr. Batteries will remain under C.R.A. 21st Div. AAA Ack

G.X.503.

If Brown Line or any portion of it has been lost it must be restored by a counter-attack in conformity with attack of Div. on your left at 2.30 a.m. Aug. 23rd AAA Arrange Arty. support with affiliated Brigade R.F.A. AAA Gain touch with 42nd Div. after counter-attack AAA Ack

23rd ~~September~~ August, 1918.

G.511 from Corps.

A Company, Cyclists Battalion, is allotted to each Div. AAA Coy. has already been detailed to 21st and 38th Divs AAA Remaining Coy. now allotted to 17th Div. under arrangements to be made direct between Headquarters 17th Division and O.C. Cyclist Bn. AAA Lewis Gun Detachments now attached 21st Division will revert to their CompaniesAAA O.C. Cyclist Bn. and Adjutant will act as liaison Officers between Divisions ~~xxx~~ and will be attached to 17th Division under arrangements to be made direct AAA Ack

G.X.521.

Order all Lewis Gunners N.I.H. except those belonging to "A" Squadron to rejoin their own Units AAA Ack

G.X.535.

Confirmation of telephone conversation AAA 62 Inf. Bde. will concentrate all troops less garrison of Brown Line at once AAA As soon as reliable information is received that MIRAUMONT has been captured the garrison of the Brown Line will concentrate with its own Units AAA You will then be prepared to cross the ANCRE either by the railway bridge or the bridge in GRANDCOURT AAA

August

24th [redacted]r, 1918.

G.X.541.
In continuation of G.X.535 62nd Inf. Bde. will on receipt of orders from 21 Div. H.Q. be prepared to concentrate either in BATTERY VALLEY or Valley in R.9.d. and R.15.b.

G.X.545.
Concentrate your Brigade less two Coys. left in the Brown Line on the South bank of the ANCRE in BATTERY VALLEY and R.14.a.

D.C.1 to G.O.C. 110 Inf. Bde.
1. You will take Command of 64th and 110 Inf. Bdes.

2. 42nd Division are attacking North of MIRAUMONT through IRLES on to PYS. You will attack high ground in R.11.b. & d. 17th Div. have been ordered to move to R.17 to protect your flanks.

3. When attack has succeeded 62nd Inf. Bde. will pass through moving along ridge running in N.E. direction to PYS and will join hands with 42nd Division.

4. The attack will be pushed with the greatest vigour.

D.C.3 to G.O.C. 110 Inf. Bde.
Reference my D.C.2 parties of our men have been definitely located holding out in R.11.a. AAA Please expedite attack as much as possible to relieve these men AAA Barrage will be arranged to miss them AAA

G.567 from Corps.
One Regiment 1st Cavalry Division allotted to V Corps AAA will march this afternoon from SARTON to LINES in vicinity of CONTAY AAA H.Q. accommodation in CONTAY on application to 18th Div. AAA Regt. will be used as Corps Cavalry one troop will be attached each Div. as Divl. Cavalry.

G.X.570.
Reference Order No.212 AAA If LE SARS found empty it will be occupied and patrols sent on to BUTTE DE WARLENCOURT AAA If 110th Inf. Bde. moves H.Q. it will be along the general line R.17.Central - M.15.Central AAA Ack.

G.A.1.
64th Inf. Bde. will move at once to line of road in R.12 and R.18. AAA Units will remain concentrated and obtain as much rest as possible but be prepared to hold line of road in case of need AAA

D.C.5 to G.O.C. ~~XXX~~ 62 Inf. Bde.
Reference SPICERS message approve of you carrying out role allotted 110 Inf. Bde. if latter are not ready to do it. Inform G.O.C. 110 Inf. Bde. who must then carry out your original role

G.A.7.
Get ready to move at once but don't fall in until you receive further orders AAA Have look-out post to watch country in direction of LE SARS as enemy are counter-attacking from EAUCOURT L'ABBAYE.

G.A.8.
Send Reserve Coy. to take up position on road R.12 R.18 covering Divl. front AAA Enemy are counter-attacking from direction of EAUCOURT L'ABBAYE.

25th August, 1918.

G.A.10.

Sit easy AAA Be prepared to move at 6 p.m.

G.A.11.

In confirmation of telephone message AAA 21st Division will probably remain in present position for today AAA However 62nd Inf. Bde. will be prepared to advance its left to keep touch with troops on its left should they go forward AAA Should 17th Div. advance and take EAUCOURT L'ABBAYE 110 Inf. Bde. will be prepared to carry on the general advance AAA

Order No.214.

17th Division are holding East of MARTINPUICH with their left in M.22.c. 63rd Division hold LE BARQUE and YELLOW CUT AAA 62 Inf. Bde. will hold present line in M.18 and 24. AAA 110th Inf. Bde. will protect the right of 62nd Inf. Bde. until 17th Div. left reaches M.24.c. when 110th Inf. Bde. will concentrate West of BLUE CUT and ready to hold that line AAA 64th Inf. Bde. will move to high ground M.15 and 20 and be prepared to hold this line AAA Reserve M.Gs will prepare to occupy positions on ridge R.12 and R.18 AAA 64th Inf. Bde. will advance at 5.30 a.m. Aug. 26th and move through 62nd Inf. Bde. with objective line of road N.21.b.6.0 - N.9.b.7.0. AAA When 64th Inf. Bde. has passed road N.19.b. N.7.b. 62nd Inf. Bde. will advance to it AAA When 64th Inf. Bde. objective made good 62nd Inf. Bde. will advance to SAILLY SAILLISEL - BAPAUME Road AAA 110th Inf. Bde. if not already concentrated in M.17 will do so when 62nd Inf. Bde. advances and be in Divisional Reserve AAA One Coy. Cyclists works under 64th Inf. Bde. for first operation and 62nd Inf. Bde. for second AAA One Troop Div. Cav. under special instructions issued to O.C. will work in front of Infantry reporting situation to leading Brigade AAA 94th Bde. R.F.A. under orders 64th Inf. Bde. for first operation AAA 95th Bde. R.F.A. under 62nd Inf. Bde. for second AAA Mobile Newton Mortar works with leading Brigade reporting 62nd Inf. Bde. H.Q. early tomorrow AAA Infantry will not move extended across country unless under aimed small arm fire AAA Div. H.Q. remain GRANDCOURT AAA ACK

G.X.587.

Ref. OrderNo. 214 AAA 64th Inf. Bde. will first make good intermediate objective line of road N.19.b. N.17.b. reporting capture to Div. H.Q. AAA 64th Inf. Bde. will not advance to further objective without orders from Div. H.Q. AAA 62nd Inf. Bde. will not advance to their objective without reference to Div. H.Q. AAA As soon as 17th Division start advancing on right of 110 Inf. Bde., 110 Inf. Bde. will concentrate in M.17 AAA

G.X.589.

Reference instructions issued you today if Infantry have not relieved you by 7 p.m. you will withdraw to MIRAUMONT AAA If state of ground tomorrow does not permit of you moving faster than the Infantry you will return to MIRAUMONT and report to Div. H.Q. for further orders AAA

G.X.588.

If as is probable relief of your troops in our area not carried out tonight AAA Brigade which moves through our leading Bde. at 7.30 a.m. have particular orders to get their left on Northern Div. Boundary. AAA

29th ~~September~~ August, 1918.

G.X.653.

Send a patrol under a N.C.O. to report to B.G.C. 110th Inf. Bde. as soon as possible AAA Remainder of Troop to be ready to move at short notice but not saddled up AAA

G.X.654.

38th Division report that they met no opposition this morning AAA There are other indications that enemy are retiring AAA 110th Inf. Bde. will push forward Advanced Guards followed if feasible by remainder of Brigade and make good following successive bounds AAA LUISENHOF FARM ROAD AAA Road N.21.a. N.9.a. AAA Spur N.22.a.00 to Cross Rds N.9.d.7.2 along road to N.9.b.8.0 AAA Cross Rds N.24.a.5.1 BEAULENCOURT and road from N.11.d.5.0 to N.11.b.7.0 AAA 62nd Inf. Bde. will support 110 Inf. Bde. moving to LUISENHOF FARM Rd. when 110 Inf. Bde. has made good road N.21.a. N.9.a. AAA N.2 Spur N.22.a.0.0 Cross Rds. N.9.d. when 110 Inf. Bde. has reached BEAULENCOURT AAA Moves of 64th Inf. Bde. and Reserve M.Gs will be ordered direct from Div. H.Q. AAA Successive Report Centres at BUTTE DE WARLENCOURT LUISENHOF FARM and Sunken Road N.15.d.4.7 AAA

G.X.659.

95th Bde. R.F.A. will act under orders of leading Brigade AAA 94th Bde. R.F.A.under orders of supporting Brigade but will assist in covering advance of leading Brigade AAA

G.X.661.

Ref. G.X.654 of today AAA 64 Inf. Bde. will become supporting Brigade instead of 62nd Inf. Bde. AAA 64 Inf. Bde. will be prepared to move to YELLOW CUT on receipt of orders from Divisional H.Q. AAA 94th Bde. R.F.A. now come under orders 64th Inf. Bde. AAA

G.X.665.

64 Inf. Bde. will move forthwith to YELLOW CUT AAA Completion of move to be reported to 21st Div. H.Q. AAA

G.X.673.

In confirmation of telephone conversation AAA As much Arty. fire as possible is required on BEAULENCOURT tonight AAA All fire on Village to cease at 2 a.m. 30th instant when patrols will enter the village AAA Could 4th Corps be asked to shell the village as well AAA

30th ~~September~~ August, 1918.

G.X.684.

Under orders from Corps you are to rejoin your squadron at Cross Roads COURCELLETTE at 8.30 a.m. tomorrow August 31st AAA

31st August, 1918.

G.X.688.

You will bivouac near the BUTTE DE WARLENCOURT AAA Until further orders you will be under the 110 Inf. Bde. who will issue the necessary orders for your employment AAA Please report to these Brigade H.Q. at N.13.d.6.4 as soon as possible leaving the troop in bivouacs.

21st August, 1918.

R.A.30/44 from Corps.

It is essential that enemy should be prevented from improving his present positions by making secure M.G.posts improving his trenches and putting up wire AAA All Artillery will be active not only on communications but on the positions now held by enemy

1st September, 1918.

G.X.734.

62 Inf. Bde. will have one Battalion holding YELLOW CUT by 5 a.m. Sept. 2nd AAA Another Battalion of 62nd Inf. Bde. will be at WARLENCOURT and the third in bivouacs near LE SARS by same hour AAA 62nd Inf. Bde. will establish Brigade Headquarters at BUTTE DE WARLENCOURT xxx by 11 a.m. AAA

2nd September, 1918.

G.180 from Corps.

21st Division will withdraw Brigade now holding LABDA COPSE SUGAR FACTORY BEAULENCOURT as soon as possible to rest AAA Time of withdrawal to be arranged mutually between 21st and 17th Divs.

3rd September, 1918.

G.X.780.

110 Inf. Bde. will issue instructions to Cyclists to concentrate at the BUTTE forthwith AAA 62nd and 64th Inf. Bdes. will send all cyclists at present with them to rejoin their Unit at the BUTTE AAA Cyclist Squadron will keep orderlies at the BUTTE Telephone Exchange AAA After concentration Cyclists will be ready to move at one hours' notice AAA

G.X.781.

Ref. G.X.780 AAA Cyclists will now concentrate at N.13.d.3.3 and NOT at the BUTTE AAA Cyclists will keep orderlies at 110th Inf. Bde. H.Q.

21st DIVISION.

Summary of Casualties - August 21st - Sept 14th (inc.)

UNIT.	Killed. Off.	Killed. O.R.	Wounded. Off.	Wounded. O.R.	Missing. Off.	Missing. O.R.	TOTAL. Off.	TOTAL. O.R.
62nd Inf. Brigade.								
12/13th North Fus.	2	44	15	278	-	21	17	343
1st Lincoln Regt.	3	39	10	208	-	17	13	264
2nd Lincoln Regt.	1	31	5	133	-	7	6	171
62nd T.M.Battery.	-	1	-	17	-	-	-	18
Total.	6	115	30	636	-	45	36	796
64th Inf. Brigade.HQ	-	-	1	-	-	-	1	-
1st E.Yorks Regt.	7	54	12	193	4	205	23	452
9th K.O.Y.L.I.	6	42	18	270	-	39	24	351
15th Durham L.I.	9	74	15	344	1	112	25	530
64th T.M.Battery.	-	-	1	2	-	-	1	2
Total.	22	170	47	809	5	356	74	1335
110th Inf. Brigade.								
6th Leicester Regt.	2	21	5	170	1	9	8	200
7th Leicester Regt.	2	16	12	218	1	32	15	266
1st Wilts Regt.	2	17	10	154	-	6	12	177
110th T.M.Battery.	2	3	-	11	-	-	2	14
Total.	8	57	27	553	2	47	37	657
14th North Fus (P).	-	2	2	26	-	-	2	28
21st Bn M.G.Corps.	1	7	8	51	-	2	9	60
Divl. Artillery.								
94th Brigade RFA.	-	-	2	8	-	-	2	8
95th Brigade RFA.	-	1	3	15	-	-	3	16
21st D.A.C.	-	-	-	2	-	-	-	2
21st T.M.Brigade.	-	-	-	-	-	-	-	-
Total.	-	1	5	25	-	-	5	26
Divl. Engineers.								
97th Field Coy RE.	-	-	-	9	-	-	-	9
98th Field Coy RE.	-	-	2	37	-	-	2	37
126th Field Coy RE.	-	-	-	9	-	-	-	9
Total.	-	-	2	55	-	-	2	55
R. A. M. C.								
Regtl. M.O's.	1	-	-	-	-	-	1	-
63rd Field Amb.	-	-	-	7	-	-	-	7
64th Field Amb.	-	1	-	6	-	-	-	7
65th Field Amb.	-	2	-	16	-	-	-	18
Total.	1	3	-	29	-	-	1	32
21st Div.Train. ASC.	-	-	-	2	-	-	-	2
33rd Mob.Vet.Sec. AVC.	-	-	-	1	-	-	-	1
Army Chaplains Dept.	-	-	1	-	-	-	1	-
TOTAL.	38	355	122	2187	7	450	167	2992

------0------

SECRET.

21 Div.
G.37.

GENERAL STAFF.
V CORPS.
No. G.X. 4513
Date 18.10.18.

Vth Corps.

Herewith Reports on Operations of the 21st Division from 4th to 16th September and from 17th to 20th September, 1918, all dates inclusive.

R.H. Macdougall Major
G.S. for
Major General
Commanding 21st Division.

18th October 1918.

21 Div.
G. 989.

REPORT ON OPERATIONS FROM 4th SEPT. to 16th SEPT. 1918.

4th September, 1918.

Orders were issued for the Division to relieve the 38th Division in the line, the 62nd Inf. Bde. being the leading Brigade, with 64th Inf. Bde. in support and 110 Inf. Bde. in Reserve. (Order No.224 and G.X.806 and G.X.808).

Instructions received from Corps that operations on a large scale would not be undertaken for the present. The enemy rear-guards, however, were to be engaged and pressed by our advanced guards and every opportunity taken of gaining ground.(Corps G.247).

5th September, 1918.

12.40 p.m. Orders issued for the 64 Inf. Bde. to relieve the 113th and 115th Inf. Bdes., 38th Division, in the trench system U.5. U.11 U.17.a. and U.10. 110 Inf. Bde. were to move to the area West of SAILLY SAILLISEL. (Order No.224a).

3.30 p.m. Divisional Headquarters closed at M.9.c.70.05 and opened at LES BOEUFS. (T.3.d.4.4).

6.50 p.m. Orders issued for active patrolling to be carried out during the night and the following day. If enemy resistance showed signs of slackening, the 62 Inf. Bde. were to push forward advanced guards and be prepared to follow with remainder of the Brigade. The advance would be continued until the objective W.22.c.0.4 - REVELON - W.10.Central was reached, when orders for a fresh advance would be issued from Divisional Headquarters. The 62 Inf. Bde. were not to engage in a serious attack unless instructions were issued from Divisional Headquarters to that effect. The 64 Inf. Bde. were to be prepared to hold the line ST. MARTINS WOOD to LE MESNIL - en - ARROUAISE, but efforts were to be concentrated on keeping troops fresh. 110 Inf. Bde. were to remain in their present position. (Order No.225).

/6th Sept.......

6th September, 1918.

6.15 a.m. The relief of the 38th Division was complete and G.O.C. 21st Division assumed command of the sector. The line taken over ran V.9.a.7.2 - V.15.a.3.1 - V.14.c.2.5 - V.20.a.0.0. The enemy was inactive, but there was slight gas shelling of valley near MANANCOURT and ETRICOURT.

8.5 a.m. Left Battalion 62 Inf. Bde. reported that the enemy still held EQUANCOURT TRENCH. Touch had been obtained with troops on the left.

10.30 a.m. The line now ran V.3.d.3.2 - V.9.a.5.0 - V.15.a.3.1 - V.14.c.2.6 - V.20.a.0.0. Owing to troops of the 12th Division having withdrawn from FAUCON TRENCH this trench had been occupied by the Right Battalion, 62 Inf. Bde. and an unconfirmed report stated that touch had been gained with 12th Division about V.22.b.7.1.

1 p.m. Situation. 62 Inf. Bde. reported that their right Battn. was established in trenches V.22.b. & d. and were believed to be in trenches in V.16.d. Patrols of the Left Battalion were in EQUANCOURT WOOD.

1.15 p.m. Report received that EQUANCOURT Village and Wood were now occupied by our troops.

2 p.m. Two Mobile Newton Mortars were ordered to proceed to 62 Inf. Bde. under whose orders they would act. (G.X.856).

3.10 p.m. Situation. Right Battalion, 62 Inf. Bde., were holding trenches in V.23.b. & d. and V.17.d. Left Battalion was in trenches V.17.a.0.5 and along trench system V.11.a. & c. Touch had been gained with 12th Division on right. No definite opposition had been encountered.

3.45 p.m. Orders were issued to the 64 Inf. Bde. to move one Battalion to the high ground East of ETRICOURT. As soon as the 62 Inf. Bde. had cleared the trench system running through V.10. to V.22 the 64 Inf. Bde. were to move two Battalions up to this line, ready to occupy it in depth, one Battalion remaining West of the Canal. (G.X.864).

/4.35 p.m....

4.35 p.m. Situation. Right Battalion, 62 Inf. Bde. had reached the line of the road V.23.b.3.1 to V.18.c.1.9 with advanced guard pushing on to SOREL LE GRAND. The left Battalion had encountered opposition from the trenches V.11.b. and a. but this opposition was being dealt with.

5.15 p.m. Report received from the Corps Cavalry Troop, timed 4.5 p.m., that the 2nd Linc. Regt. had a patrol in SOREL LE GRAND, and that the 1st Linc. Regt. was pushing round the North of FINS.

8 p.m. Orders issued to the 62 Inf. Bde. to continue the advance on the following day, the main guard moving forward at 6 a.m.
Objectives :-
(1) Brown Line W.22.c. - W.16.Central - W.10.a.0.0 - W.9.a.8.9.
(2) Northern end of PEIZIERE - VAUCELLETTE FARM - CHAPEL CROSSING.
64 Inf. Bde. to move forward by stages until the EQUANCOURT TRENCH SYSTEM was occupied, when further orders would be issued. The 110 Inf. Bde. to remain in present position. (D.O.226).

10.15 p.m. Situation. Line ran, Spur in W.19.a. & c. SOREL LE GRAND inclusive. Touch had been gained with 17th Division in V.6.d. Situation in FINS was uncertain.

....

7th September, 1918.

12.45 a.m. FINS had been definitely captured and was being heavily gas shelled by the enemy.

5.15 a.m. With the exception of the gas shelling of FINS, the enemy were inactive during the night.

8.40 a.m. Report from 62 Inf. Bde. timed 8.30 a.m. stated that the left Battalion was advancing through W.8 and W.9, apparently without opposition. Right Battalion was echeloned in rear owing to troops on right not commencing the advance until 8 a.m. No news of progress of this Battalion had yet been received, but hostile M.G. fire had been heard.

9.45 a.m. Orders were issued to the effect that when the 62 Inf. Bde. had occupied the whole of the first objective, the 64 Inf. Bde. were to move one Battalion to occupy SOREL LE GRAND. When the reserve Battalion 62 Inf. Bde. had moved forward from first objective, the 64 Inf. Bde. were to send one Battalion to W.8.Central and another to about W.20.a. & c. keeping one Battalion in SOREL LE GRAND. When 62 Inf. Bde. had gained the whole of the

/second....

second objective, the 64 Inf. Bde. were/to dispose their troops so as to be able to occupy the first objective in case of need, or to take up the advance on the following day. The 110 Inf. Bde. were warned that they would probably move to ground East of the Canal du Nord during the evening. (G.X.894).

10 a.m. Report received from the 62 Inf. Bde. timed 9.45 a.m. that the right Battalion held the ridge W.20.a. & c. but were held up by M.G. fire coming from about W.26.d. The left Battn. of the 12th Division held the ridge W.25. and were also held up by M.G. fire. The left Battalion 62 Inf. Bde. had reached W.9.Central and had been ordered to push on to REVELON RIDGE. Enemy had been seen retiring out of HEUDECOURT.

12 Noon. Divisional Headquarters closed at LES BOEUFS and opened at LE MESNIL EN ARROUAISE (U.5.c.3.2).

4 p.m. 110 Inf. Bde. were ordered to move to bivouacs in the area between Canal du Nord and a line running North and South through LE MESNIL en ARROUAISE before dark tonight. (G.X.899).

The reserve M.G. Coy. were ordered to reconnoitre positions in trench system V.22.b. - V.16.b. & d. - W.11.a. & c. These positions were to be occupied before dark. (G.X.900).

4.5 p.m. The 64 Inf. Bde. were ordered to move one Battalion to the neighbourhood of SOREL LE GRAND. (G.X.901).

4.25 p.m. 62 Inf. Bde. reported the situation at 1 p.m. as under :-

Right Battalion were in W.27.b. Left Battalion had been reported by the Corps Cavalry to be on the general line W.9.Cen. to railway North of HEUDECOURT. HEUDECOURT was reported to have been captured.

4.50 p.m. Situation. Right/Bn. 62 Inf. Bde. held trenches in W.23.a. & c. with advanced posts in W.22.d. Left Battalion held trenches in W.9.b. and W.10.c. and was advancing to the attack on REVELON RIDGE. The right Battalion was advancing to the spur W.23.Central in order to cover the left flank of the 12th Division.

8 p.m. Orders issued for the 62 Inf. Bde. to send forward advanced guards at 6 a.m. tomorrow to try and capture the second objective. If the enemy's resistance had slackened, advanced guards were to be supported, but no serious attack

/was.......

was to be undertaken without reference to Div. H.Q. 94th and 95th Bdes. R.F.A. were placed under the orders of 62 Inf. Bde. Artillery and Machine Guns were to be freely used for harassing fire. 64 and 110 Inf. Bdes. would remain in their present positions but the 64 Inf. Bde. were to carry out the necessary reconnaissances with a view to relief of 62 Inf. Bde. on the night 8th/9th. (D.O.227).

8th September, 1918.

5.40 a.m. Situation unchanged during the night. There was spasmodic shelling throughout the night of roads, tracks and villages in the forward area. Hostile night bombing squadrons were very active.

8.45 a.m. Situation. Enemy held RAILTON - REVELON - W.10.Central. 1st Linc. Regt. had an encounter with an enemy patrol near RAILTON, in which four prisoners were captured. Enemy attempted to raid one of our posts at 5.30 a.m. but was repulsed before entering our lines.

9.45 a.m. Owing to the enemy putting down a very heavy barrage on the Division on our left, the 62 Inf. Bde. called on the leading Battalion of the 64 Inf. Bde. to form a defensive flank facing North in case of necessity. (G.X.919).

10.50 a.m. Situation. The right Battalion 62 Inf. Bde. attacked at 7.30 a.m. in conjunction with 58th Division on right and captured the KNOLL at W.23.Central with little opposition. The Battalion was moving on the second objective, the trench line W.24.c. - W.23.d. which objective was also later reported as captured. Troops were pushed down railway through W.24.c. & d. to connect with left of 58th Division who were believed to have captured PEIZIERE. This village, however, was not captured.

12.20 p.m. Trenches in W.23.Central and W.21.a & c. were being consolidated. RAILTON was being mopped up and a few prisoners had been taken.

1.10 p.m. Situation. REVELON FARM was reported captured and Battalions had been pushed forward to GENIN WELL COPSE. Heavy M.G. fire was being encountered from LOWLAND SUPPORT.

/2.30 p.m.

2.30 p.m. Report received from 62 Inf. Bde. that their troops had worked along the railway at W.24.d. but had been driven back by a counter-attack. They also reported that PEIZIERE was strongly held by the enemy.

10.10 p.m. Orders issued to the 64 Inf. Bde. to attack tomorrow at 4 a.m. in conjunction with the 17th Division on their left. The objectives were CHAPEL HILL and high ground in W.11.d. After capture of these objectives, the 62 Inf. Bde. were to push patrols to VAUCELLETTE FARM, which was to be occupied in absence of resistance. The 110 Inf. Bde. were to have two Battalions in the vicinity of, and ready to occupy, EQUANCOURT TRENCH SYSTEM by 6 a.m. tomorrow morning. The third battalion was to move to the neighbourhood of SOREL LE GRAND. The 62 Inf. Bde. would be withdrawn gradually under orders of Div. H.Q. to MANANCOURT and ETRICOURT and to ground just East of Canal. (D.O.228).

9th September, 1918.

5.30 a.m. Situation. Very little activity during the night. Enemy harassed RAILTON Cross roads with Artillery. No news had yet been received from the attacking Battalions.

7 a.m. 64 Inf. Bde. reported that the first objective in W.11.d. had been captured, but this report had not been confirmed. The enemy were heavily shelling RAILTON and REVELON.

8.10 a.m. Situation. Owing to GENIN WELL COPSE No.2 not having been held by our troops during the night it had to be taken by the attacking troops this morning, and consequently these troops lost the barrage. The line now reported ran W.18.c.9.9 along rly. to W.17.b.4.8. thence along LOWLAND SUPPORT to Northern Divl. Boundary.

Three Machine Guns and some prisoners were captured.

4.30 p.m. Situation remained unchanged. There was some hostile shelling of back areas.

5 p.m. 64 Inf. Bde. reported that they were continuing the attack at 5.30 p.m. in order to gain the final objectives.

/8 p.m.....

8 p.m. 64 Inf. Bde. were ordered that unless attack delivered at 5 p.m. was successful, the attack would be continued in conjunction with 17th Division at 4 a.m. the following day. The objectives would be CHAPEL HILL thence along CAVALRY TRENCH and LOWLAND TRENCH to junction with 17th Division at W.12.a.0.0. At 5.15 a.m. the 58th Division on the right were attacking EPEHY and PEIZIERE at which hour the 64 and 110 Inf. Bdes. were to advance and occupy the YELLOW LINE under a creeping barrage. In view of this the 110 Inf. Bde. would be relieving the 62 Inf. Bde. in the Brown Line and at KNOLL W.23.Central during the night. 110 Inf. Bde. were also to be prepared to occupy REVELON FARM and GENIN WELL COPSE No.1 if vacated by forward move of troops of 64 Inf. Bde. On relief, 62 Inf. Bde. was to move to the EQUANCOURT - ETRICOURT Area. (D.O.229).

10th September, 1918.

6.35 a.m. Situation: Heavy shelling of trench system W.24.a. & c. during the night. No news had yet been received of the attack. There was heavy rain and wind during the night.

10.40 a.m. Report received from 64 Inf. Bde. that the attack on CHAPEL HILL and high ground in W.11.d. was not successful. No details had yet been received.

11.30 a.m. Warning order issued that the 110 Inf. Bde. would relieve the 64 Inf. Bde. during the night. The 110 Inf. Bde. was also to be prepared to advance under a barrage and occupy the Yellow Line from CHAPEL HILL to Southern Divisional Boundary. On relief, the 64 Inf. Bde. would move to the EQUANCOURT TRENCH SYSTEM with one Battalion about SOREL LE GRAND. (G.X.693).

7.30 p.m. Orders issued for the 110 Inf. Bde. to advance under a barrage and make good the whole of the Yellow Line within the Divisional Sector. 110 Inf. Bde. would also relieve the 64 Inf. Bde. in the line. (D.O.230).

11.25 p.m. 64 Inf. Bde. reported that a patrol of the 15th Durham L.I. had reached point W.18.c.4.7 where they encountered heavy M.G. fire from both sides. Patrol reported the Yellow Line to be occupied in W.18.c. and W.24.a.

/11th Sept. ......

11th September, 1918.

5.20 a.m. Situation. The attack by the 110 Inf. Bde. started at 3 a.m. and the objectives were now reported as captured, but this report not yet confirmed. Enemy retaliation was slight in the forward area, but heavy on back area, where all valleys were being gassed. The relief of the 64 Inf. Bde. by the 110 Inf. Bde. was complete at 2.45 a.m.

12.30 p.m. Report received from the 110 Inf. Bde. giving situation as follows. One Coy. in trench system from W.23.d.85.30 to W.24.c.45.95. One Platoon in trench system W.24.a.6.2, one Coy. W.18.c.9.3 to W.18.c.9.6. Hostile counter-attack from direction of CHAPEL HILL had been repulsed. This trench system was being heavily shelled by the enemy and the dispositions of the remaining troops could not be ascertained.

2.15 p.m. 110 Inf. Bde. were informed that gas would be projected on CHAPEL CROSSING and VAUCELLETTE FARM between 1.30 a.m. and 2.30 a.m. Sept. 12th. (G.X.5).

2.15 p.m. Brigades were ordered to send all Cavalry and Cyclists attached to them to concentrate in EHRICOURT where they would be under the orders of the 62 Inf. Bde. (G.X.6.).

4.30 p.m. Situation. Line ran W.23.d.8.0 along line of trenches W.18.c.8.9 where a small gap still existed. Line was continued from W.18.a.8.4 along LOWLAND SUPPORT to Northern Divl. Boundary. Touch had been gained on both flanks. Endeavours were being made to clear up the situation in the gap. Enemy trench mortars were active from LOWLAND TRENCH, but were being engaged by Stokes mortars.

12th September, 1918.

12.30 a.m. Report received from the 110 Inf. Bde. that the 1st Bn. Wilts. Regt. had been unable to gain touch with the 7th Leic. Regt. in the Yellow Line. The patrol had been attacked with M.G. fire and bombed by the enemy who were holding a strong post about W.18.a.8.4.

6 a.m. Situation during the night unchanged. Gas was successfully projected at 1.30 a.m. Practically no hostile retaliation.

/11.30 a.m.

11.30 a.m. Situation. No activity on the right Battalion front. Left Battalion front was heavily shelled from W.17.b.9.9 to W.11.c.8.6 between 5 a.m. and 7 a.m. At 6 a.m. the enemy attempted to bomb down trench leading to our line at W.11.c.8.6. but were repulsed. Touch had not yet been obtained between 7th Leic. Regt. and 1st Wilts. Regt.

6 p.m. Situation unchanged during the day. At 2 p.m. the enemy attempted to raid the post at W.17.b.6.9 but was repulsed before entering our line.

13th September, 1918.

5.25 a.m. The situation remained quiet and unchanged during the night. Touch had now been gained between the 7th Leic. Regt. and the 1st Wilts. Regt., the enemy pocket which had existed between these two Battalions being cleared up.

9 a.m. 110 Inf. Bde. caught a deserter who stated that the enemy would make an attack on our present line on CHAPEL HILL at 10 a.m. The attack would be accompanied by flammenwerfer. This attack was carried out.

1.5 p.m. 110 Inf. Bde. were informed that gas would be projected on to the railway cutting W.35.b.95.70 between 1.30 a.m. and 2.30 a.m. 14th instant. (G.X.23).

2 p.m. Report received from 110 Inf. Bde. timed 12.30 p.m. that the enemy attacked with flammenwerfer at 10 a.m. and obtained a temporary footing in our line at the trench junction W.11.c.8.6. He was immediately counter-attacked and driven out, 12 men and 1 M.G. being captured. The enemy's losses were reported as being very heavy. Our line was intact and in touch on both flanks. None of our men were missing. The enemy attack was accompanied by heavy Artillery and Trench Mortar bombardment.

The situation for the remainder of the day remained unchanged. There was no enemy activity.

14th September, 1918.

5.25 a.m. There was no change in the situation during the night which passed quietly. An enemy bombing aeroplane was brought down in our lines at 10.30 p.m., the Officer Pilot being captured.

/9.5 a.m......

9.5 a.m. Report received from the 110 Inf. Bde. that preceded by a Trench Mortar bombardment about 20 of the enemy attempted to enter our line at W.18.a.7.4 but were entirely repulsed by rifle and Lewis Gun fire.

4.30 p.m. Situation. Up to 1 p.m. the enemy artillery was fairly active on back areas, but after that hour there was practically no fire.

15th September, 1918.

5.15 a.m. Situation during the night remained unchanged. Enemy Artillery was comparatively quiet but increased slightly at 4 a.m. Some hostile trench mortar fire on the front line in the right sector.

4 p.m. Orders issued that the 110 Inf. Bde. would be relieved by the 19th Inf. Bde. in the line tonight 15th/16th instant. On relief, the 110 Inf. Bde. would move to ETRICOURT and MANANCOURT. The Coys. of the 21st Bn. M.G.C. in the line would not be relieved. (D.O.231).

5.36 p.m. Situation remained unchanged except for some shelling of HEUDECOURT. Our Artillery carried out the usual harassing fire.

16th September, 1918.

2.20 a.m. The relief of the 110 Inf. Bde. by the 19th Inf. Bde. was complete and command of the sector passed to the G.O.C. 33rd Division.

5.15 a.m. The enemy opened a bombardment of the area V.9.c. & d. V.15, V.16.c. & d. where the 62 and 64th Inf. Bdes. were bivouaced, with H.E. and gas. The bombardment ceased at 5.45 a.m. A few casualties were caused.

During the above operations, the following prisoners were captured by the Division.

Officers.	O.R.
5	246

21 Div.
G. 748.

REPORT ON OPERATIONS AUGUST 21st to SEPTEMBER 3rd, 1918.

Reference Maps Sheets
57.B. D. and C. 1/40,000.

On August 19th orders were received from V Corps that the Division would take part in an attack on the enemy's lines in conjunction with the Corps on either flank, the Division being ordered to carry out an attack on BEAUCOURT and the Sunken Road R.3.a.3.2 (Div. Order No.205).

On August 20th, Divisional Headquarters closed at RAINCHEVAL and opened at ACHEUX.

August 21st, 1918.

12 Midnight. The enemy commenced a heavy area bombardment with gas shell on Q.6.c. and Q.11.b. This bombardment lasted about three quarters of an hour.

5.45 a.m. The 62nd Infantry Brigade advanced to the attack on BEAUCOURT and Sunken Road R.3.a.

7.45 a.m. The 62nd Infantry Brigade reported that they had captured BEAUCOURT and had reached the railway embankment South of the Village. About 90 prisoners had been captured, our casualties being reported as very slight. Our troops were also well on the way to the Sunken Road in R.3.a.

8.25 a.m. 1 N.C.O. and 12 men of the V Corps Cyclist Regiment were ordered to report to the 64th Infantry Brigade Headquarters to assist in exploitation. (G.X.449).

9.30 a.m. The 2nd Linc. Regiment held the line of the railway embankment from R.9.d.0.3 to R.8.c.0.5 with patrols working down the MIRAUMONT ROAD. A post had been established at R.7.d.4.8. Patrols of the 12/13 North'd Fus. had passed through BEAUCOURT on their way to the Blue Line South of the River ANCRE. About 120 prisoners so far counted.

10.20 a.m. The 62nd Infantry Brigade were ordered as soon as the Brown Line (R.3.a.) was captured, to move two Companies to the line of the River ANCRE from R.4.c.6.7 to R.4.a.0.5. Picquets were to be placed on all bridges over the ANCRE. Patrols were also to be pushed forward into the S.W. outskirts of MIRAUMONT. The 64th Infantry Brigade were to place two Companies at the disposal of the 62nd Infantry Brigade to act as Brigade Reserve. (G.X.452).

10.30 a.m. Orders received from Corps to hold the 64th Infantry Brigade in readiness to move along the BEAUCOURT - MIRAUMONT ROAD, cross the River ANCRE in R.3. & 4 and to move via BATTERY VALLEY so as to threaten THIEPVAL from the rear. (V Corps G.396).

11.50 a.m....

11.30 a.m. Situation. Our troops were reported by the Royal Air Force to be on the line R.3.c.7.3 - R.3.c.4.8 - R.3.a.2.0 - R.2.b.9.6. Touch gained with troops on left. The 110th Infantry Brigade were unable to cross the ANCRE owing to very strong opposition, the enemy holding the West bank with Machine Guns.

12.20 p.m. The 62nd Infantry Brigade were ordered to attack and capture the remainder of the Brown Line. The 64th Infantry Brigade, less portion already South of the ANCRE, were ordered to assemble about R.1 and R.2. If the 62nd Infantry Brigade should fail to capture the Brown Line, the 64th Infantry Brigade were then to carry out this operation. On the Brown Line being captured, the 64th Infantry Brigade were to cross the ANCRE and move up SIXTEEN ROAD through R.16.a. & c. on to the Green Line with left flank guard along BOOM RAVINE. (Div. Order No.206).

(Owing to events detailed below, this turning movement could never be put into operation).

1.20 p.m. One Battalion 110 Infantry Brigade was placed at the disposal of the 64 Infantry Brigade. (G.X.455).

3.25 p.m. Owing to IRLES having not yet been captured, and, in consequence of this, the 42nd Division on the left having not yet entered MIRAUMONT, the 64th Infantry Brigade were ordered to take special precautions regarding their Eastern flank after crossing the ANCRE. The 62nd Infantry Brigade were to make every endeavour to throw bridges across the ANCRE between BEAUCOURT and GRANDCOURT, in order to give the 64th Infantry Brigade an alternative line for withdrawal in case of necessity. The 64th Infantry Brigade were to send patrols towards GRANDCOURT after crossing the ANCRE to connect with 62nd Infantry Brigade and also to cover bridge-heads. (G.X.460).

3.40 p.m. 110 Infantry Brigade reported that the 6th Leic. Regt. had two patrols just across the ANCRE Q.18.d.4.6 and Q.13.c.7.9. Both patrols were unable to make further advance owing to enemy fire.

3.50 p.m. 110 Infantry Brigade were ordered to hold another Battalion in readiness to join 64th Infantry Brigade. (G.X.641).

The 64 Infantry Brigade were ordered to relieve two Companies 62 Infantry Brigade in R.14.a. & b. during the night, these Companies to come under orders of 62 Infantry Brigade. 1st Wilts Regt. were to remain with 64th Infantry Brigade but were not to be used except in case of emergency. Brigades were to improve and if possible increase the present crossings over the ANCRE with the aid of attached R.E. Sections. (Div. Order No.209).

5.5 p.m. 110 Infantry Brigade reported that the 6th Leic. Regt. were heavily fired at as soon as the ANCRE at R.13.a.3.7 was crossed. LOGGING TRENCH and LOGGING LANE were reported as being strongly held by the enemy.

6 p.m. Under orders from Corps, the Division was ordered to consolidate the final objective from the ANCRE at BAILLESCOURT FARM to R.3.a.0.8 with one Brigade, touch to be maintained with 42nd Division on left. One Brigade was to be in position to support the front Brigade or to re-new the offensive across the ANCRE at short notice. The 3rd Brigade was to be in position South and West of BEAUMONT HAMEL. (V Corps G.241).

7.20 p.m. Situation at 7 p.m. 62nd Infantry Brigade attacked at 2 p.m. with objective R.4.c.5.6. to R.4.a.0.5. The attack was held up by Machine Gun and Artillery fire. The attack was renewed with 6 Companies about 4 p.m. and was successful. Two Companies 62nd Infantry Brigade crossed the ANCRE at 4 p.m. and gained the Blue Line from LITTLE TRENCH to R.14.b.8.3. The dispositions of 62nd Infantry Brigade were as follows :-

Two Companies from R.4.c.4.8. along road to R.3.a.9.9. where touch had not been gained with 42nd Division. Two Companies between Brown and Yellow Lines and Two Companies on Blue Line. Four Companies about R.2.c. and Two Companies in BEAUCOURT.

8.30 p.m. Orders issued for 62nd Infantry Brigade to maintain their present dispositions and to gain touch with 42nd Division. The two Companies in BEAUCOURT were to be relieved by one Company at present at R.4.c. and were then to be withdrawn into Reserve. 64th Infantry Brigade were to establish Bridgeheads over the ANCRE at selected points between R.4.d.3.4. and R.1.a.1.9. connecting with 62nd Infantry Brigade at R.4.a.5.1. 62nd Infantry Brigade to form Bridgeheads from R.9.a.1.9. to BEAUCOURT inclusive. 110th Infantry Brigade to form Bridgeheads from BEAUCOURT (exclusive) to MILL BRIDGE in area Q.6, Q.12, R.1 and R.7. One Battalion 110th Infantry Brigade to remain attached to 64th Infantry Brigade (Div. Order No.208).

10.40 p.m. Situation unchanged. Heavy hostile Machine Gun fire coming from MIRAUMONT. Prisoners so far counted 3 Officer, 156 Other Ranks.

10.50 p.m. Orders issued to the 64th Infantry Brigade that the two rear Battalions of that Brigade and One Battalion 110th Infantry Brigade attached, were not to move forward without reference to Divisional Headquarters (G.X.476).

11.58 p.m. All Brigades and Divisional Artillery were warned that owing to the trend of hostile movement during the evening having been towards MIRAUMONT and ACHIET LE GRAND, hostile counterattack was possible either tonight or tomorrow morning. The action of the two rear Battalions of the 64th Infantry Brigade and the attached Battalion 110th Infantry Brigade, would, therefore, be defensive until further orders. At dawn tomorrow 110th Infantry Brigade were to endeavour to push patrols across the ANCRE and gain the Blue Line. As soon as the Blue Line was consolidated patrols were to be pushed forward to the Red Line. (GX.477).

22nd August 1918.

3.52 a.m. Report received from 64th Infantry Brigade that the bridges at R.9.b.6.7. and R.3.D.9.2. were in good condition. The 97th Field Company R.E. had constructed a footbridge at R.9.a.9.7. over which a Platoon of the 1st East Yorkshire Regt. had crossed about 2.15 a.m. and had met with heavy Machine Gun fire from about R.9.b.2.2.

/4 a.m......

4 a.m. Enemy heavily gas shelled the area between ARTILLERY LANE and LUMINOUS AVENUE.

7.35 a.m. 62nd Infantry Brigade reported that enemy had put down a barrage on the Brown Line, which, however, only lasted about 10 minutes. No Infantry action followed.

8.45 a.m. 110th Infantry Brigade report timed 8.20 a.m. gave the situation East of the ANCRE as follows :- At 5 a.m. two Platoons were established in LOGGING TRENCH and a third Platoon was moving along CANDY LANE with objective LOGGING SUPPORT. During the night crossings over the ANCRE at Q.18.d.4.7. and Q.18.b.9.3. were made passable for Infantry.

9.40 a.m. Situation unchanged since last report. Up to about 8 a.m. there was continuous hostile shelling of forward area, but after this hour shelling became much less and very scattered. Enemy reported to be holding Railway Embankment in R.10. in strength.

9.40 a.m. 62nd Infantry Brigade were ordered to push forward Patrols from Blue Line to portion of Red Line in their area and also to GRANDCOURT. If Red Line occupied by our Patrols, 64th Infantry Brigade were to be prepared to send two Companies to garrison it (G.X.486).

10 a.m. 62nd Infantry Brigade reported that a Patrol of the 12/13th Northumberland Fusiliers was observed to be pushing South from Blue Line. No Machine Gun fire had been encountered from THIEPVAL RIDGE for the last hour. 64th Infantry Brigade reported that the Platoon of the 1st East Yorks Regt. South of the River in N.9.b. had been driven to the North of the River where they had taken up a position covering the crossing.

12.15 p.m. 110th Infantry Brigade report, timed 11 a.m. gave the situation as follows :- Bombing Party had succeeded in reaching point in LOGGING TRENCH North of the enemy Post R.13.c.1.4. This party was working in conjunction with bombing party from the South to capture this Post. A Patrol had proceeded up CANDY AVENUE to about R.19.b.35.60. and had located enemy Machine Gun at Q.13.c.9.2. which would be dealt with by Platoon which was working down LITTLE TRENCH and LUFF AVENUE.

1.30 p.m. 62nd Infantry Brigade reported that the Valley in R.1.b. and forward area was being continuously shelled by guns of all calibre. The 2nd Lincolnshire Regt. reported that their left flank was being turned in R.3.b.

4.10 p.m. Situation. 62nd Infantry Brigade unchanged. Lewis Gun Section of North Irish Horse (Corps Cyclists) sent to reinforce the left flank in R.3.b. Situation on that flank was not satisfactory owing to the 42nd Division having their right at R.2.b.5.0. 110th Infantry Brigade held the Blue Line from LUFF AVENUE inclusive to junction of LOGGING SUPPORT and CANDY AVENUE. A Platoon was being sent along CANDY AVENUE to clear COMMON LANE. Enemy Post at R.13.c. 2.6. had been rushed and garrison killed. Patrols advancing to Red Line were held up by heavy Machine Gun fire in R.14.c.Central. At 3 p.m. enemy opened a very heavy barrage on Valley in R.1.b. but shelling had now died down.

/5 p.m.....

5 p.m. 110th Infantry Brigade report that LUFF AVENUE and LOGGING SUPPORT to junction of CANDY AVENUE had been captured. Touch had been obtained with the 62nd Infantry Brigade in the Blue line. Considerable Machine Gun fire was being met with from COMMON LANE. Further Platoons were being Moved up to consolidate the Blue Line and capture COMMON LANE.

6.30 p.m. Orders received from Vth Corps that one Brigade 17th Division would relieve and take over one Brigade front at present held by 110th Infantry Brigade on night of 22nd/23rd. The boundary between the 21st and 17th Divisions would be a line running from R.21.d.0.0., R.14.c.0.0., Q.12.c.6.0., thence West along grid line between Q.11. and Q.17. 17th Divisional Artillery at present under orders of C.R.A. 21st Division would revert to C.R.A. 17th Division at 4 a.m. 23rd inst. (Vth Corps G.466., R.A. 1163 and G.X.496.).

9.55 p.m. 62nd Infantry Brigade reported that at 8.15 p.m. enemy put down a barrage including smoke on the Brown Line and in the ANCRE Valley near GRANDCOURT. The enemy were reported to have attacked and to have driven back part of the garrison of the Brown line. No news received about situation in the Yellow Line, but this line believed to be intact. One Battalion 64th Infantry Brigade was holding intermediate system along ARTILLERY LANE and another Battalion was being ordered up to PUISIEUX Road to restore situation if required.

10.5 p.m. . . Orders sent to the 62nd Infantry Brigade that if any portion of the Brown Line had been lost it was to be restored by a counter-attack in conformity with an attack of 42nd Division at 2.30 a.m. August 23rd. (G.X.503).

11.15 p.m. Situation. Enemy attacked Brown Line about 8 p.m. Attack was repeated twice afterwards. Each attack was beaten off with heavy casualties to the enemy. A few enemy reached the Brown line but were immdiately ejected. Our casualties were fairly heavy. Situation was now quiet.

23rd August 1918.

1.20 a.m. 110th Infantry Brigade report-ed that Platoon Posts had been established at R.19.a.4.0. R.19.a.6.5., R.13.a.6.3., R.13.d.5.6., R.14.c.3.9., R.13.c.1.4., R.13.a.6.0., and one over the ST. PIERRE DIVION Caves at Q.24.b.6.1. COMMON LANE South of R.19.a.4.0. was destroyed by shell fire and not occupied by the enemy.

5.a.m. 62nd Infantry Brigade reported that the situation in the BROWN Line had been entirely restored and that touch had been gained with the 42nd Division on the left.

6.15 a.m. The relief of the 110th Infantry Brigade by one Brigade 17th Division was reported complete.

9.55 a.m. Situation unchanged. Enemy was shelling PUISIEUX Road in R.?.c. with heavy guns. Snipers and Machine Guns were active from R.15.a.

/1.30 p.m.

1.30 p.m. Situation 12 Noon. Enemy put down a heavy barrage on our front line in response to attack carried out by troops on our left. Enemy in small parties were seen going East and S.E. from R.16.c.2.3. 12/13 North'd Fus. reported that some of their men had reached BATTERY VALLEY but had to withdraw owing to hostile M.G. fire from Eastern edge of Valley.

2.50 p.m. All Lewis Gunners of North Irish Horse (Corps Cyclists) except those belonging to 'A' Squadron were ordered to rejoin their own Unit. (G.X.521 and V Corps G.511).

3.15 p.m. Orders issued for the continuation of the attack. 64 Inf. Bde. to attack at 1 a.m. with first objective Brown Line from R.20.a.9.3 to R.8.b.7.2 and second objective Red Line from R.21.d.0.0 through R.15.Central to railway at R.9.b.3.3. The 110 Inf. Bde. to attack at 5 a.m. with objective the Blue Line R.27.b.2.8 along SIXTEEN ROAD to R.4.c.5.7 with bridge-head at R.2.d.8.4. After capture of this line, exploitation to be carried out towards LE SARS and PYS. (D.O.210).

5.55 p.m. Situation. North of river unchanged. South of River our patrols were working towards the Red Line. About 100 enemy dead had been counted in front of the Brown Line as the result of the counter-attack the day before.

7 p.m. Divisional Headquarters closed at ACHEUX and opened at MAILLY MAILLET.

8.50 p.m. Divisional Order No.210 was amended as follows :- The advance to the Green Dotted Line was to be carried out as soon as possible. 64 Inf. Bde. were to advance with its left on the River ANCRE with objective Green Dotted Line in R.11.b. & d. 110 Inf. Bde. to advance in rear of 64 Inf. Bde. and connect right of 64 Inf. Bde. with 17th Division on Green Dotted Line. (G.X.529).

11 p.m. 62 Inf. Bde. were ordered to concentrate all troops less garrison of Brown Line at once, and as soon as reliable information received that MIRAUMONT had been captured, the garrison in the Brown Line was to concentrate with its own Unit. 62 Inf. Bde. was to be prepared to cross River ANCRE either by the railway bridge or the Bridge in GRANDCOURT. (G.X.535).

24th August, 1918.

12.30 a.m. Report received from 64 Inf. Bde. that the Red Line had been captured. The right flank of this Brigade appeared to be in the air and was being continually harassed by the enemy.

12.40 a.m. 62 Inf. Bde. were ordered to be prepared to concentrate in BATTERY VALLEY or valley in R.9.d. and R.15.b. (G.X.541).

1.35 a.m. 64 Inf. Bde. reported that they were firmly established on the Red Line, but owing to fighting and broken state of ground Units were somewhat dis-organised. The Brigade was being re-organised and advance would be continued to the high ground in R.11 and R.12 at about 3.30 a.m. The right flank of the Brigade was very exposed and no touch could be obtained with any other troops.

/7.10 a.m.....

7.10 a.m. 62 Infantry Brigade were ordered to concentrate their whole Brigade less the two Companies in the Brown Line, on South bank of ANCRE, in BATTERY VALLEY and R.14.a. (G.X.545).

7.40 a.m. 110 Infantry Brigade ordered to push on by easiest route possible irrespective of left of 17th Division and to get touch with right of 64th Infantry Brigade (D.O.211).

In R.11.b. No touch had been gained

8.45 a.m. Report received from 64th Infantry Brigade that their troops had reached final objective/on either flank and the enemy were reported as working round flanks. Line very weakly held and reinforcements were urgently required.

9.20 a.m. Pigeon message was received from 64th Infantry Brigade timed 7.28 a.m. reporting that they were holding high ground in R.11.b. but that the enemy had completely surrounded them and were very active with Machine Guns, Snipers and Trench Mortars. Casualties appeared to be heavy. The enemy had counter-attacked both flanks but had been completely repulsed.

9.30 a.m. Situation. 64 Infantry Brigade still held high ground R.11.b. but were entirely surrounded. 110 Infantry Brigade moving forward to support the right of the 64th Infantry Brigade on Green Dotted Line. In course of the advance they successfully attacked enemy post at R.14.d.O.O capturing three Trench Mortars and killing between 30 and 40 of the enemy.

11 a.m. Owing to the B.G.C. 64 Infantry Brigade having been wounded, B.G.C. 110 Infantry Brigade was ordered to take command of both 64th and 110th Infantry Brigades. He was ordered to take the high ground in R.11.b. & d. and when this ground had been captured the 62nd Infantry Brigade was to pass through and advance in the direction of PYS. (D.C.1).

12 Noon. R.A.F. observer reported 11.30 a.m. that our troops were still holding out in R.11.b.Central with enemy at R.10.d.8.7 and in BOOM RAVINE.

12.16 p.m. 110 Infantry Brigade were ordered to expedite their attack as much as possible in order to relieve the 64th Infantry Brigade who were still holding out on high ground R.11.b. (D.C.3).

1.25 p.m. Situation of 64th Infantry Brigade unchanged. 110 Infantry Brigade were advancing in R.16 but exact position not definitely known.

2.30 p.m. Report received from 110 Infantry Brigade timed 1.15 p.m. that they had definitely gained touch with 64th Infantry Brigade on high ground R.11.b. & d. Small parties of the enemy were still holding out in BOOM RAVINE but were being mopped up. Touch not yet gained with 17th Division on right but the 7th Leicestershire Regiment had been ordered to occupy the remainder of the Green Dotted Line from R.17.d.O.O. to Southern Divisional Boundary and to gain touch with 17th Division.

4 p.m. The high ground R.11.b and d and R.17.b and d. now occupied. The right of the Division was at R.17.d.2.2. Where it was reported to be in touch with 17th Division. 62nd Infantry Brigade were moving forward to gain touch with 42nd Division at PYS.

/under......

Under instructions received from Corps one Cavalry Troop was being allotted to this Division as Divisional Cavalry. (Corps G.567).

4.50 p.m. R.A.F. report our men seen in M.1.b and d. and R.23 about 4 p.m.

4.55 p.m. Orders issued that the Division would advance on LE SARS. 110th Infantry Brigade were to advance forthwith and capture the line M.20.b.0.3., M.15.Central. M.10.Central, patrols being sent forward to LE SARS and DESTREMONT FARM. The 62nd Infantry Brigade to concentrate on Road R.12, R.18. ready to move through 110th Infantry Brigade and take up the advance. 64th Infantry Brigade to reorganize in BOOM RAVINE (Div. Order No.212).

5 p.m. 62nd Infantry Brigade reported that 12/13th Northumberland Fusiliers had moved up into position as ordered in G.C.1. The remainder of the Brigade were moving to BOOM RAVINE.

5.45 p.m. Orders issued that if LE SARS was found empty, it was to be occupied and patrols sent on to the BUTTE DE WARLENCOURT (G.X.570).

10.40 p.m. Orders issued for the continuation of the advance on the 25th with BEAULENCOURT as objective. The advance would be carried out by 62nd Infantry Brigade who, moving through 110th Infantry Brigade, were to capture the line M.24.a.3.0., N.7.a.0.0. When this line captured, 110th Infantry Brigade would move through 62nd Infantry Brigade to line of Road N.21.d.4.0., N.9.b.6.0. Advance would then be continued by 62nd Infantry Brigade to the BAPAUME - SAILLY SAILLISEL Road, touch being obtained with the IV Corps at RIENCOURT. 64th Infantry Brigade would remain in present position as Divisional Reserve (D.O.213.).

11.25 p.m. 110th Infantry Brigade moved from GREEN DOTTED Line towards LE SARS. Otherwise situation unchanged.

25th August 1918.

3 a.m. Divisional Headquarters closed MAILLY MAILLET and opened GRANDCOURT.

9 a.m. 64th Infantry Brigade were ordered to move at once to line or Road in R.12 and R.18. Units were to remain concentrated and obtain as much rest as possible, but to be prepared to hold the line of this road in case of necessity. (G.A.1.).

9.15 a.m. Patrol from Divisional Cav. Troop reported that the enemy were holding the Wood in N.12.b. and N.7.a. with Infantry and Machine Guns.

9.30 a.m. Pigeon message received from 62nd Infantry Brigade timed 8.55 a.m. stated that the Brigade moved without difficulty to the WARLENCOURT - COURCELETTE Road, where the 1st Wiltshire Regt. were found to be 300 yards South of it in M.14.d. with two Coys. of the 6th Leicestershire Regt. on their left. The position of the remainder of the 110th Infantry Brigade had not yet been ascertained. 62nd Infantry Brigade continued the advance but were unable to reach the summit of the ridge through M.10.Central, M.15. Central, owing to heavy Machine Gun fire from LE SARS.

9.45 a.m. 62nd Infantry Brigade reported that Artillery barrage had been arranged on LE SARS and that advance would be continued under this fire.

/the......

The enemy were showing signs of retiring. Touch had been gained with the 17th Division on the right near COURCELLETTE, and troops of the 42nd Division on the left had been seen near LITTLE WOOD. The high ground in M.15.c. had been gained and troops were working along high ground in M.9.d. and M.10.c.

1 p.m. 62nd Infantry Brigade were instructed to carry out the task allotted to the 110th Infantry Brigade in order No.213 if latter Brigade were not ready to carry it out (D.C.5.).

1.10 p.m. Information was received from the Corps on right that the enemy were massing for counter-attack in N.9.c. and d. and N.16.a. Instructions were sent to the 60 pdrs. attached to this Division to engage this target.

1.35 p.m. Situation at 1 p.m. 62nd Infantry Brigade attacked LE SARS and captured it. The QUARRY in M.15.a. was attacked under cover of Stokes Mortars and captured, 17 Germans being killed. The BUTTE DE WARLENCOURT was also captured, 1 Officer and 30 men being taken prisoner. Touch had been gained with 63rd Division on left, but not with 17th Division on right.

2.50 p.m. 64th Infantry Brigade were ordered to be ready to move at once in view of the possibility of the enemy counter-attacking from the direction of EAUCOURT L'ABBAYE (G.A.7.).

The 21st Battalion Machine Gun Corps was ordered to send its reserve Company to take up position on the road R.18, R.12. covering the Divisional front. (G.A.8.).

3.20 p.m. Situation as follows :- 62nd Infantry Brigade on line of Road M.24.a. and M.18.b. and d. touch being established with the 63rd Division on the left. At 2.15 p.m. the enemy delivered a heavy counter-attack against the right of the 62nd Infantry Brigade from the South and South East. 110th Infantry Brigade, who were on the move to pass through the 62nd Infantry Brigade were diverted to prolong the right of the former Brigade in order to gain touch with the 17th Division. The counter-attack was repulsed at 2.45 p.m. some prisoners being taken.

4 p.m. The 64th Infantry Brigade were ordered to sit easy but to be ready to move at 6 p.m. (G.A.10.).

4.30 p.m. Orders were issued to the 62nd Infantry Brigade and 110th Infantry Brigade that the Division would probably remain in its present position for the remainder of the day. The 62nd Infantry Brigade were to be prepared, however, to advance its left to keep touch with troops on its left, should they go forward. Should the 17th Division advance, and take EAUCOURT L'ABBAYE the 110th Infantry Brigade were to be prepared to carry on the advance (G.A.11.).

7.30 p.m. Orders were issued for the 62nd and 110th Infantry Brigades to hold their present positions during the night. The 64th Infantry Brigade were to move forthwith to the high ground M.15 and M.20 and to be prepared to hold this line. The reserve Machine Gun Company was to be prepared to occupy positions on the ridge R.12 R.18. At 5.30 a.m. August 26th, 64th Infantry Brigade were to take up the advance and move through the 62nd Infantry Brigade and capture the line of the Road N.21.b.6.0. - N.9.b.7.0. When the 64th Infantry Brigade had made good this objective, the 62nd Infantry Brigade were to advance to the

/SAILLY.....

SAILLY SAILLISEL - BAPAUME ROAD. The 110 Infantry Brigade as soon the 62nd Infantry Brigade advanced, were to concentrate in M.17 and would be in Divisional Reserve. One Squadron, Corps Cyclists were placed under the orders of the 64th Infantry Brigade for the first operation and the 62nd Infantry Brigade for the second. Div. Cav. Troop were ordered to work in front of the Infantry and report the situation to leading Brigade. The 95th Bde. R.F.A. were placed under the orders of the leading Brigade. (D.O.214).

10.15 p.m. In continuation of Order No.214, 62nd Infantry Brigade were to first make good, as intermediate objective, the line of the road N.19.b. & N.17.b., the advance to the further objective not being carried out without orders from Divisional Headquarters. As soon as the 17th Division on the right commenced their advance, 110 Infantry Brigade were to concentrate in M.17. (G.X.587).

10.45 p.m. Div. Cav. Troop were ordered to withdraw to MIRAUMONT if they had not been relieved by 7.30 p.m. on the 26th instant. (G.X.589).

10.55 p.m. Message was sent to the 63rd Division stating that it was improbable that troops of that Division who were in this Divisional area would be relieved tonight. Orders had been given to the leading Brigade to extend their left on the 26th instant to the North. (G.X.588).

26th August, 1918.

5.30 a.m. Situation unchanged during the night. Some desultory shelling over forward area about 4.50 a.m.

9.25 a.m. Situation. 64th Infantry Brigade passed through 62nd Infantry Brigade but met with heavy Machine Gun fire coming from the direction of LUISENHOF FARM. No signs of troops advancing on the right flank.

10.45 a.m. Situation. 64 Infantry Brigade reported at 9.20 a.m. that their right Battalion appeared to be approaching the objective. The left Battalion had reached the line N.7.b.5.9 to N.13.a.7.1. where they were held up by heavy Machine Gun fire. Artillery barrage was being arranged and the advance would then be continued. Hostile resistance on the Divisional front had distinctly stiffened since yesterday. The right of the 63rd Division was in rear of our left and no touch had been gained with the 17th Division on the right.

12.35 p.m. Situation. Right Battalion, 64th Infantry Brigade, gained objectives South of LUISENHOF FARM. Left Battalion was held up on the line N.13.a.5.0 - N.7.a.5.0. 64th Infantry Brigade had two Battalions in front and one in reserve with one Cyclist Squadron and one Brigade R.F.A. attached.
62 Infantry Brigade disposed in depth with leading troops in YELLOW CUT with their left on South edge of LE BARQUE.
110 Infantry Brigade in Divisional Reserve with one Battalion at EAUCOURT L'ABBAYE, one Battalion in M.17.a. and one Battalion M.14.d. and M.15.a.

/4.15 p.m....

4.15 p.m. Situation. 64 Infantry Brigade report timed 3.15 p.m. stated that the right Battalion had been forced to withdraw and now held line of Sunken Road in N.19.a. and N.19.c. Left Battalion continued this line to N.7.b.2.0. Touch had not been gained on either flank. Cyclist Squadron were in touch with enemy at M.24.c.4.4.

7.30 p.m. Situation. Enemy counter-attacked 64th Infantry Brigade at 4 p.m. but were repulsed by rifle and Lewis Gun Fire. Heavy hostile Machine Gun fire from LIGNY and LIGNY THILLOY prevented our troops from approaching LUISENHOF FARM Road. Much enemy movement had been seen in trenches N.2.b. and N.2.c.

8.30 p.m. 64th Infantry Brigade ordered to find outposts on the general line now held. 62nd Infantry Brigade were .. to hold YELLOW CUT as main line of resistance. 110th Infantry Brigade were to concentrate each Unit and allow the men to rest, but were also to be prepared to hold the line DESTREMONT FARM - Road Junction M.16.b.3.3. - WARLENCOURT in case of necessity. 64th Infantry Brigade were to continue the advance on the 27th inst on BEAULENCOURT and occupy as first objective, line of the road N.19.b. - N.7.b. The 110th Infantry Brigade would then advance through the 64th Infantry Brigade with objective high ground N.20.central - N.14.b.5.0. - N.8.Central. Cyclists and Div. Cavalry Troop with Mobile Newton Mortar would work with leading Brigade. 94th Brigade R.F.A. were placed under the orders of 64th Infantry Brigade and 95th Brigade R.F.A. under the orders of 110th Infantry Brigade (Div. Order No. 215.).

27th August 1918.

5.45 a.m. Situation unchanged during the night. Patrols of 64th Infantry Brigade reported the enemy occupying LIGNY THILLOY and LUISENHOF FARM at 3 a.m.

11.50 a.m. Orders were issued cancelling Order No.215 and ordering the 64th Infantry Brigade to make good LUISENHOF FARM and the line of Road for 400 yards on each side of it, throwing refused flanks back to join with flank Divisions. This operation to be carried out by patrols, garrisons being sent forward to hold ground gained. 62nd Infantry Brigade would relieve the 64th Infantry Brigade during the night 27th/28th inst. and would also continue to hold the YELLOW CUT. On relief, the 64th Infantry Brigade would withdraw to Valley M.9. 15 and 14. (GX.622).

12.30 p.m. Situation. 64th Infantry Brigade reported that leading troops had reached line of road North of LUISENHOF FARM but were being badly enfiladed by Machine Guns from THILLOY. Very little hostile shelling.

2.45 p.m. 64th Infantry Brigade were holding line as previously reported with patrols on the road in N.13.b. and d. LUISENHOF FARM was reported unoccupied. Cyclist Sqdn. had established a Post at FACTORY CORNER (N.19.d.). Enemy Machine Guns were active from about N.7.d.9.9. Owing to reports being received that the enemy were retiring South of the SOMME, Brigades were instructed to keep close touch with the enemy, especially during the night.

/6 p.m.......

6 p.m. Situation remained unchanged. Small parties of the enemy were seen during the afternoon to come down the Valley in N.5.c. towards THILLOY.

6.30 p.m. Owing to the possibility of the enemy evacuating BAPAUME during the night of 27th/28th, harassing fire by artillery was ordered to be carried out actively during the night.

10.10 p.m. 62nd Infantry Brigade were ordered to continue the advance on the 28th inst. under an Artillery barrage commencing at 5.30 a.m. with the objective high ground N.14. N.15. (D.O.216).

28th August 1918.

7.30 a.m. 62nd Infantry Brigade reported that LUISENHOF FARM and the road in N.7.d. and N.13.b. were strongly held by the enemy. Machine Gun fire was opened on both flanks of our patrol and owing to the very heavy fire from the direction of LIGNY THILLOY it had been found impossible to advance. Large numbers of the enemy were reported to be moving into THILLOY.

9.10 a.m. 62nd Infantry Brigade reported that THILLOY and Sunken Road from LIGNY THILLOY to LUISENHOF FARM still strongly held by the enemy, as was also the trench in N.9.a, c and d. The right Battalion reported no enemy could be seen on the above road from N.13.d.6.9. to N.19.a.1.3.

4.15 p.m. 110th Infantry Brigade were ordered to relieve the 62nd Infantry Brigade in the line during the night 28th/29th inst. On relief, 62nd Infantry Brigade were to take over the present dispositions and defence arrangements of 110th Infantry Brigade. The Cyclist Squadron would come under the orders of 110th Infantry Brigade on completion of relief (D.O.217.).

7.15 p.m. Orders were issued to the effect that as the 38th Division were attacking the high ground East of GINCHY on the 29th Machine Gun and Artillery barrages were to be put down on the Divisional front in order to assist this advance. 110th Infantry Brigade were to be ready to push forward advanced guards on any slackening of the enemy's resistance being noticed, but the main body of this Brigade was not to advance without orders from Divisional Headquarters (D.O.218.).

The situation on the Divisional front remained unchanged for the remainder of the day.

29th August.1918.

The situation remained unchanged during the night. No enemy Machine Gun or Artillery activity.

8 a.m. Divisional Cavalry Troop were ordered to send a patrol under a N.C.O. to report to B.G.C., 110th Infantry Brigade. The remainder of the troop was to be ready to move at short notice but not saddled up. (G.X.653.)

9.20 a.m. Owing to the 38th Division meeting no opposition in their attack this morning, 110th Infantry Brigade were ordered to push forward advanced guards followed by the remainder of the

/Brigade.....

Brigade if feasable, and make good the following successive lines:- LUISENHOF FARM ROAD - Road N.21 - N.9.a. Spur N.22.a.0.0. - Cross Roads N.9.d.7.2. along road to N.9.b.8.0. - Cross Roads N.24.a.5.1. - BEAULENCOURT and Road from N.11.d.5.0. to N.11.b.7.0. 62nd Infantry Brigade will be in Support to 110th Infantry Brigade and would move to LUISENHOF FARM Road when 110th Infantry Brigade had made good the road in N.21.a. N.9.a. moving on to the Spur in N.22.a. when 110th Infantry Brigade had reached BEAULENCOURT. Further orders would be issued for the move of 64th Infantry Brigade and Reserve Machine Gun Coy. (G.X.654).

10.40 a.m. 95th Brigade R.F.A. were placed under the orders of 110th Infantry Brigade and 94th Brigade R.F.A. under the orders of 64th Infantry Brigade. 94th Brigade R.F.A. were to assist however, in covering the advance of the 110th Infantry Brigade (G.X.659.)

11 a.m. Situation. Advanced Guards of the Right Battalion, 110th Infantry Brigade had reached the Ridge N.14.Central and reported it clear of the enemy. Divisional Cavalry Troop had gained touch with the 42nd Division and reported THILLOY to have been evacuated by the enemy.

12.10 p.m. Orders issued in continuation of G.X.654 for the 64th Infantry Brigade to become Support Brigade in place of the 62nd Infantry Brigade and to be prepared to move to YELLOW CUT on receipt of orders from Divisional Headquarters. 94th Brigade R.F.A. would now come under the orders of the 64th Infantry Brigade (G.X.661.).

12.15 p.m. Main Guards had occupied LUISENHOF FARM ROAD with vanguards advancing over high ground N.14 and 15. Some hostile Machine Gun fire encountered from N.3.c. otherwise no touch with the enemy yet obtained.

2 p.m. 64th Infantry Brigade ordered to move forthwith to YELLOW CUT (G.X.665).

Situation. Infantry Patrols had reached line in N.16.c. and were encountering Machine Gun fire from Sunken Road N.16 a and b. Infantry advanced guards were on Ridge N.15.a and c. and main body was crossing the LUISENHOF FARM ROAD.

4.30 p.m. 110th Infantry Brigade report timed 3 p.m. stated that advanced guards had reached the line of trenches in N.16, N.9. and were in touch with the 17th Division on the Right and 42nd Division on the left. Main body had reached line of the road N.21.a, N.9.a at 3.25 p.m.

6 p.m. Situation at 5.30 p.m. Main body had reached line of trenches N.16.d. to N.9.d. and were in touch on both flanks. Advanced guards were endeavouring to make progress towards BEAULENCOURT, but were encountering very heavy Machine Gun and rifle fire from the Western edge of the Village.

9.20 p.m. Message sent to Vth Corps asking for as much artillery fire as possible to be brought to bear on BEAULENCOURT during the night. All fire on the village to cease at 2 a.m. 30th inst, when patrols would enter the village (G.X.673.).

/10.20 p.m.....

10.20 p.m. Orders issued for the 110th Infantry Brigade to send forward fighting patrols to ascertain the situation as regards BEAULENCOURT and to occupy the village if found empty. 110th Infantry Brigade were also to endeavour to resume the advance to the fourth objective early tomorrow, August 30th. When this objective had been taken, one Coy and one Section of Machine Guns were to be sent to LESBOEUFS COPSE to form defensive flank facing North. As soon as the PERONNE - BAPAUME Road had been crossed, the Division would come into Corps reserve about LE TRANSLOY. Until further orders the 64th and 62nd Infantry Brigades would remain in their present positions, the 64th Infantry Brigade being ready to occupy YELLOW CUT at short notice. The Cyclist Squadron and Divisional Cavalry Troop would remain under the orders of 110th Infantry Brigade (D.O.219).

30th August 1918.

The situation during the night remained unchanged with very little enemy activity.

12 noon. Divisional Hdqrs. closed at GRANDCOURT and opened M.9.c.70.05.

12.5 p.m. Situation. Patrols report BEAULENCOURT still occupied. Machine Guns and snipers very active from the Western outskirts of the Village.

7.15 p.m. Situation throughout the day remained unchanged. Enemy artillery fire was negligible. Our Artillery shelled BEAULENCOURT and engaged Machine Guns which had been located in the Western outskirts of the village. Large explosions occurred at N.11.d.5.8. and N.5.c.3.6. between 5.30 and 6.5 p.m.

7.30 p.m. Orders were issued to the Divisional Cavalry Troop to rejoin their Squadron near COURCELETTE by 8.30 a.m. 31st August (G.A.684).

31st August 1918.

5.20 a.m. The situation remained unchanged during the night. Patrols had endeavoured to enter BEAULENCOURT but were stopped by Machine Gun fire. Much enemy movement was heard in BEAULENCOURT during the night. At South end of the village wiring was believed to be in progress. There was considerable random shelling of our back areas during the night.

8.50 a.m. Under instructions received from Corps one Troop of Carabineers was placed under the orders of the Division as Divisional Cavalry. The Troop was ordered to bivouac near the BUTTE DE WARLENCOURT and was placed under the orders of 110th Infantry Brigade (G.A.688).

10.25 a.m. Instructions were received from Corps for intense harassing fire by Artillery not only on enemy known communications but also on all known positions held by him (Vth Corps R.A.30/44).

/9 p.m......

9 p.m. Orders were issued for 110th Infantry Brigade to capture and occupy BEAULENCOURT during the night. Zero hour being 2.30 a.m. The infantry were to form up on the line N.10.Cent. N.11.b.2.9. and attack Southwards. When the village had been captured, 110th Infantry Brigade were to carry out a second operation at 5.40 a.m. (in conjunction with 17th Division who were to take LE TRANSLOY) with objective the SUGAR FACTORY N.24.Central. 64th Infantry Brigade were to take over the present positions of 110th Infantry Brigade when vacuted by latter Brigade (D.O.220.). The situation throughout the night remained unaltered, all attempts by patrols to enter BEAULENCOURT being frustrated by Machine Gun fire.

1st September 1918.

7.45 a.m. 110th Infantry Brigade report that all objectives in the first attack had been gained and an enemy counter-attack easily beaten off. Our casualties were believed to be slight. About 100 prisoners were captured and two 77 mm guns. Touch had not yet been gained with 42nd Division but patrols were being sent out to do so.

9.50 a.m. Situation. 110th Infantry Brigade report timed 9.30 a.m. states that troops detailed to take the SUGAR FACTORY were unable to enter it owing to Machine Gun fire from LE TRANSLOY. They have occupied trench in N.24.a. just North of Factory. An Officer who had just returned from BEAULENCOURT reports many German dead in the Village. Touch had been gained with 42nd Division about N.11.d.3.9. 30 enemy Machine Guns had already been counted in the Village.

6.40 p.m. Situation remained unchanged throughout the day. Enemy shelled BEAULENCOURT and trenches in N.16. Shelling ceased about 6 p.m.

8.5 p.m. 62nd Infantry Brigade were ordered to take up the following dispositions by 5 a.m. 2nd September. One Battalion in YELLOW CUT. one Battalion WARLENCOURT, and one Battalion in bivouacs near LE SARS. (G.A.734).

8.15 p.m. Orders issued that in conjunction with the attack by IV Corps on September 2nd, the 110th Infantry Brigade were to capture the SUGAR FACTORY N.24.Central. After capture of SUGAR FACTORY, 110th Infantry Brigade were to push out a force not exceeding one Coy. to about O.19.d.central with object of preventing withdrawal of garrison of LE TRANSLOY.

This attack to take place at 4 a.m.

in conjunction with main attack of IV and VI Corps which was to take place later in the morning the 64th Infantry Brigade were to capture LABDA COPSE, at 5.15 a.m.at which hour the 42nd Division on the left would be attacking VILLERS AU FLOS. After capture of LABDA COPSE, 64th Infantry Brigade were to effect a junction with 42nd Division at Cross Roads O.13.a.2.4. and were also to establish a line from LABDA COPSE to SUGAR FACTORY and get in touch with 110th Infantry Brigade. (D.O. 221).

2nd September 1918.

5.45 a.m. Report received from 110th Infantry Brigade that the SUGAR FACTORY had been captured but that the attacking Coys. of 7th Leicestershire Regt had been unable to gain touch with their

/supporting....

Company. The runner who brought back the message states that enemy with Machine Guns were still in position between SUGAR FACTORY and BEAULENCOURT. The 1st Wiltshire Regt. were sending one Coy. forward to clear up the situation and to gain touch with troops of the 7th Leicester Regt. in the SUGAR FACTORY.

7.20 a.m. 64th Infantry Brigade reported LABDA COPSE to have been captured with about 30 prisoners and 6 - 77 mm guns. A pocket of Germans in N.18.b. was being dealt with by Stokes Mortars. Situation at SUGAR FACTORY now reported as being satisfactory.

10.40 a.m. Report received from 64th Infantry Brigade that owing to Machine Gun fire from the Southern outskirts of VILLERS AU FLOS and N.E. Corner of LE TRANSLOY, the 1st East Yorkshire Regt. had been withdrawn from LABDA COPSE. This Battalion was now holding trench from N.18.Central to about O.13.a.6.0. The road from LE TRANSLOY to BEAULENCOURT was being swept by Machine Gun fire from LE TRANSLOY. Touch with 110th Infantry Brigade in the SUGAR FACTORY had not been gained owing to fire from small enemy pockets about O.19.a.

11.15 a.m. 64th Infantry Brigade reported that LABDA COPSE had been reoccupied. The line now ran O.13.b.3.1. where in touch with 42nd Division through O.13.d.3.0. to O.19.b.0.8. 110th Infantry Brigade report that counter-attack from LE TRANSLOY drove their troops out of all except N.W. portion of the SUGAR FACTORY. A fresh attack was being organised to retake the FACTORY.

12.30 p.m. 110th Infantry Brigade reported that 7th Leicester Regt. have retaken SUGAR FACTORY and are pushing up the Spur towards LABDA COPSE. Troops of the 17th Division had just passed through and could be seen on high ground in O.19.a.

6.15 p.m. Orders issued for 110th Infantry Brigade to relieve forward Battalion of 64th Infantry Brigade during night 2nd/3rd September. The 110th Infantry Brigade would then hold SUGAR FACTORY and LABDA COPSE, maintaining touch with 42nd Division at O.13.b.3.1. 110th Infantry Brigade were also to garrison the defences of BEAULENCOURT, maintaining at least one Battalion in Brigade reserve in Valley West of the main PERONNE - BAPAUME Road. The 64th Infantry Brigade, after relief of the 1st East Yorkshire Regt. by 110th Infantry Brigade, were to be prepared to hold general line N.22.Central - N.10.Central. 62nd Infantry Brigade were to move to area near LESBOEUFS forthwith (D.O.222.).

The situation during the day remained unchanged. Very little hostile fire of any kind.

3rd September 1918.

12.30 a.m. Instructions received from Corps to withdraw the 110th Infantry Brigade to Valley West of BEAULENCOURT as soon as possible to rest. Time of withdrawal to be arranged mutually between 21st and 17th Divisions (Vth Corps G.180.).

/5.45 a.m.......

5.45 a.m. All moves ordered by Divisional Order No.222. were complete.

3.30 p.m. Orders issued to all Brigades to give instructions to Cyclists to concentrate at N.13.d.3.3. where they were to be ready to move at 1 hours notice. (G.X.780 and G.X.781).

10.25 p.m. Orders issued to the effect that 21st Division would remain in Corps Reserve on September 4th. The 62nd Infantry Brigade group would move to area about O.20 and O.21. on the 4th instant, so as to clear LE TRANSLOY by 10 a.m. Observation posts were to be established in the trench system East of ROCQUIGNY, as soon as this system was vacated by 17th Division. 110th Infantry Brigade and 64th Infantry Brigade Groups would probably not move but 64th Infantry Brigade group would be ready to move at one hour's notice. (D.O.223.).

During the above operations the following prisoners and guns were captured by the Division :-

	Officers.	Other Ranks.
Prisoners	45	1,242.
Guns.	12. (including two 8" hows.)	

Telegrams to accompany REPORT ON OPERATIONS from
4th to 16th September, 1918.

4th ~~October~~ September 1918.

G.X.806. Ref. 21st Div. Order 224 AAA Field Coys R.E. Pioneer Bn and M.G. Bn. less 3 Coys will move between 2 p.m. and 8 p.m. tomorrow Sept.5th to Bivouaacs on COMBLES - SAILLY SAILLISEL Rd. AAA Route via LES BOEUFS and MORVAL AAA Exact Location of bivouaacs from 'Q'

G.X. 808. Cyclist Squadron will come under orders of 62nd Inf. Bde. tomorrow and will report to 62nd Inf. Bde. H.Q.O.31.b.33 before 12 noon AAA 62nd Inf. Bde. will issue necessary orders for future employment.

G.247. Operations on a large scale will not be undertaken for the present and our resouces must be husbanded and communications improvised with a view to the resumption of a vigorous offensive in the near future AAA Divisions will be in depth on a one Brigade front AAA Corps Cav. will be withdrawn to BAZETIN LE GRAND keeping in touch with the situation by patrols AAA Adv. Guards will continue to press the enemy driving in his rearguards AAA On Adv. Guards gaining any hostile position they will be reinforced sufficiently from main bodies to resist any local counter-attack AAA Valleys should be avoided on account of gas shelling AAA Reserve Bdes. of forward Divisions and the Reserve Division will rest and train AAA

September 6th. 1918.

G.X.856. Two Mobile Newton Mortars being sent at once to 60 pounder Bridge MANANCOURT V.13.d.5.2. AAA Arrange guide to meet them.

G.X.864. 62nd Inf. Bde. has occupied Equancourt and is advancing on FINS and SOREL AAA 64th Inf. Bde. will move one Bn. to the high ground West of ETRICOURT AAA As soon as 64th Inf. Bde. has cleared the trench system running through V.10. to V.22. 64th Inf. Bde. will occupy with two Battns. disposed in depth the ground East of Canal AAA One Battn. will remain West of the Canal AAA 64th Inf. Bde. will be prepared to occupy the above trench system in case of necessity AAA

7th September 1918.

G.X.899. 110th Inf. Bde. will move to bivouaacs in area between CANAL DU NORD and a line due North and South through MESNIL before dark tonight AAA 110th Inf. Bde. will report hour of moving and hour of arrival AAA

G.X.900. Instruct Reserve M.G. ~~Battn.~~Coy. to reconnoitre positions in Trench System V.22.b. - V.16.b and d - V.11 a and c. AAA These positions will be occupied before dark tonight AAA Coy. will report that positions have been taken up to Div. H.Q.

G.X.901. Confirming telephone conversation to 64th Inf. Bde AAA 64th Inf. Bde. will move one Battalion to neighbourhood of SOREL LE GRAND forthwith AAA 64th Inf. Bde. will report arrival and disposition of this Battalion.

8th September 1918.

G.X.919. Enemy are putting down a heavy barrage on Division on our left AAA 62nd Inf. Bde. have called on leading Battn. of 64th Inf. Bde to form defensive flank facing North in case of need AAA Battalion H.Q. 1st E.York Regt. at W.18.c.8.4 AAA

11th September, 1918.

G.X.5. Gas will be projected on CHAPEL CROSSING and VAUCELLETTE FARM between 1.30 and 2.30 a.m. September 12th AAA Further details will be sent to 110 Inf. Bde. AAA

G.X.6. Brigades will instruct all Cavalry and Cyclists attached to them to concentrate in ETRICOURT AAA Both Div. Cav. and Cyclists will come under orders of 62 Inf. Bde. until further orders AAA 62 Inf. Bde. will arrange billets and also baths AAA

13th September, 1918.

G.X.53. Gas will be projected on to railway cutting W.30.b.95.70 tonight AAA Position of projectors sunken road W.23.d. AAA Zero between 1.30 a.m. and 2.30 a.m. 14th instant AAA Further details to 110 Inf. Bde. later AAA

5th September 1918.

G.X.822./ Ref 21 Div Order No.224. AAA 64th Inf. Bde. group will relieve 113th and 115th Bdes. in Trench System U.5, U.11, U.17.a. and U.10. this afternoon AAA Both these Brigades are very weak AAA Exact positions occupied by 38 Div need not be taken up AAA Woods and valleys are full of gas and will be avoided AAA 64th Bde. H.Q. will be established at 113 Bde.H.Q. U.8.a.5.5. from 3 p.m. AAA Leading Troops 64th Bde. will cross main LE TRANSLOY - SAILLY SAILLISEL Road at 3.30 p.m. AAA Movement by Platoons AAA 64th Bde. will wire exact position of Battns. on completion of relief AAA Dispositions of 113 and 115 Bdes by wire for 64th Bde only. 110th Bde. will move to area W. of SAILLY SAILLISEL AAA Starting point LE TRANSLOY SUGAR FACTORY at 4.30 p.m. AAA 110th Bde. H.Q. will be established at 115th Bde.H.Q. U.14.a.0.4. from 5 p.m.

7th September 1918.

G.X.894. Ref. 21 Div. Order 226. When 62nd Inf. Bde. has occupied whole of 1st objective 64th Bde. will move one Battn. to occupy SOREL LE GRAND AAA When 62ND Bde. Reserve Bn. moves forward from 1st objective, 64th Bde. will move one Battn. to about W.8. Cent. and another to about W.20 a and c. maintaining one Battn. in SOREL AAA When 62nd Inf. Bde. reports whole of 2nd objective captured 64th Bde. will dispose Brigade so as to be able to occupy 1st objective in case of need or to take up advance tomorrow AAA 110th Bde. will probably move to ground E. of CANAL DU NORD this evening so all preparations should be made AAA Reserve M.G. Coy. will move via EQUANCOURT to about V.17.d. forthwith.AAA This Coy. will move in future when leading Bde.H.Q. moves and will maintain liaison Officer with latter AAA

10th September 1918.

G.X.963. Warning Order AAA Attack on CHAPEL HILL did not succeed this morning AAA 110th Inf. Bde. will relieve 64th Inf. Bde. tonight AAA 110th Inf. Bde. will also be prepared to advance under a barrage and occupy the YELLOW LINE from CHAPEL HILL to Southern Div. Boundary AAA On relief 64th Inf. Bde. will move to EQUANCOURT Trench System with one Battn. about SOREL LE GRAND AAA

21 Div.
G. 989.

REPORT ON OPERATIONS FROM 4th SEPT. to 16th SEPT.
1918.

4th September, 1918.

Orders were issued for the Division to relieve the 38th Division in the line, the 62nd Inf. Bde. being the leading Brigade, with 64th Inf. Bde. in support and 110 Inf. Bde. in Reserve. (Order No.224 and G.X.806 and G.X.808).

Instructions received from Corps that operations on a large scale would not be undertaken for the present. The enemy rear-guards, however, were to be engaged and pressed by our advanced guards and every opportunity taken of gaining ground.(Corps G.247).

5th September, 1918.

12.40 p.m. Orders issued for the 64 Inf. Bde. to relieve the 113th and 115th Inf. Bdes., 38th Division, in the trench system U.5. U.11 U.17.a. and U.10. 110 Inf. Bde. were to move to the area West of SAILLY SAILLISEL. (Order No.224a).

3.30 p.m. Divisional Headquarters closed at M.9.c.70.05 and opened at LES BOEUFS. (T.3.d.4.4).

6.50 p.m. Orders issued for active patrolling to be carried out during the night and the following day. If enemy resistance showed signs of slackening, the 62 Inf. Bde. were to push forward advanced guards and be prepared to follow with remainder of the Brigade. The advance would be continued until the objective W.22.c.0.4 - REVELON - W.10.Central was reached, when orders for a fresh advance would be issued from Divisional Headquarters. The 62 Inf. Bde. were not to engage in a serious attack unless instructions were issued from Divisional Headquarters to that effect. The 64 Inf. Bde. were to be prepared to hold the line ST. MARTINS WOOD to LE MESNIL - en - ARROUAISE, but efforts were to be concentrated on keeping troops fresh. 110 Inf. Bde. were to remain in their present position. (Order No.225).

/6th Sept.......

6th September, 1918.

6.15 a.m. The relief of the 38th Division was complete and G.O.C. 21st Division assumed command of the sector. The line taken over ran V.9.a.7.2 - V.15.a.3.1 - V.14.c.2.5 - V.20.a.0.0. The enemy was inactive, but there was slight gas shelling of valley near MANANCOURT and ETRICOURT.

8.5 a.m. Left Battalion 62 Inf. Bde. reported that the enemy still held EQUANCOURT TRENCH. Touch had been obtained with troops on the left.

10.30 a.m. The line now ran V.3.d.3.2 - V.9.a.5.0 - V.15.a.3.1 - V.14.c.2.6 - V.20.a.0.0. Owing to troops of the 12th Division having withdrawn from FAUCON TRENCH this trench had been occupied by the Right Battalion, 62 Inf. Bde. and an unconfirmed report stated that touch had been gained with 12th Division about V.22.b.7.1.

1 p.m. Situation. 62 Inf. Bde. reported that their right Battn. was established in trenches V.22.b. & d. and were believed to be in trenches in V.16.d. Patrols of the Left Battalion were in EQUANCOURT WOOD.

1.15 p.m. Report received that EQUANCOURT Village and Wood were now occupied by our troops.

2 p.m. Two Mobile Newton Mortars were ordered to proceed to 62 Inf. Bde. under whose orders they would act. (G.X.856).

3.10 p.m. Situation. Right Battalion, 62 Inf. Bde., were holding trenches in V.23.b. & d. and V.17.d. Left Battalion was in trenches V.17.a.0.5 and along trench system V.11.a. & c. Touch had been gained with 12th Division on right. No definite opposition had been encountered.

3.45 p.m. Orders were issued to the 64 Inf. Bde. to move one Battalion to the high ground East of ETRICOURT. As soon as the 62 Inf. Bde. had cleared the trench system running through V.10. to V.22 the 64 Inf. Bde. were to move two Battalions up to this line, ready to occupy it in depth, one Battalion remaining West of the Canal. (G.X.864).

/4.35 p.m....

4.35 p.m. Situation. Right Battalion, 62 Inf. Bde. had reached the line of the road V.23.b.3.1 to V.18.c.1.9 with advanced guard pushing on to SOREL LE GRAND. The left Battalion had encountered opposition from the tranches V.11.b. and a. but this opposition was being dealt with.

5.15 p.m. Report received from the Corps Cavalry Troop, timed 4.5 p.m., that the 2nd Linc. Regt. had a patrol in SOREL LE GRAND, and that the 1st Linc. Regt. was pushing round the North of FINS.

8 p.m. Orders issued to the 62 Inf. Bde. to continue the advance on the following day, the main guard moving forward at 6 a.m.
Objectives :-
(1) Brown Line W.22.c. - W.16.Central - W.10.a.0.0 - W.9.a.8.9.
(2) Northern end of PEIZIERE - VAUCELLETTE FARM - CHAPEL CROSSING.
64 Inf. Bde. to move forward by stages until the EQUANCOURT TRENCH SYSTEM was occupied, when further orders would be issued. The 110 Inf. Bde. to remain in present position. (D.O.226).

10.15 p.m. Situation. Line ran, Spur in W.19.a. & c. SOREL LE GRAND inclusive. Touch had been gained with 17th Division in V.6.d. Situation in FINS was uncertain.

7th September, 1918.

12.45 a.m. FINS had been definitely captured and was being heavily gas shelled by the enemy.

5.15 a.m. With the exception of the gas shelling of FINS, the enemy were inactive during the night.

8.40 a.m. Report from 62 Inf. Bde. timed 8.30 a.m. stated that the left Battalion was advancing through W.8 and W.9, apparently without opposition. Right Battalion was echeloned in rear owing to troops on right not commencing the advance until 8 a.m. No news of progress of this Battalion had yet been received, but hostile M.G. fire had been heard.

9.45 a.m. Orders were issued to the effect that when the 62 Inf. Bde. had occupied the whole of the first objective, the 64 Inf. Bde. were to move one Battalion to occupy SOREL LE GRAND. When the reserve Battalion 62 Inf. Bde. had moved forward from first objective, the 64 Inf. Bde. were to send one Battalion to W.8.Central and another to about W.20.a. & c. keeping one Battalion in SOREL LE GRAND. When 62 Inf. Bde. had gained the whole of the

/second....

second objective, the 64 Inf. Bde. were to dispose their troops so as to be able to occupy the first objective in case of need, or to take up the advance on the following day. The 110 Inf. Bde. were warned that they would probably move to ground East of the Canal du Nord during the evening. (G.X.894).

10 a.m. Report received from the 62 Inf. Bde. timed 9.45 a.m. that the right Battalion held the ridge W.20.a. & c. but were held up by M.G. fire coming from about W.26.d. The left Battn. of the 12th Division held the ridge W.25. and were also held up by M.G. fire. The left Battalion 62 Inf. Bde. had reached W.9.Central and had been ordered to push on to REVELON RIDGE. Enemy had been seen retiring out of HEUDECOURT.

12 Noon. Divisional Headquarters closed at LES BOEUFS and opened at LE MESNIL EN ARROUAISE (U.5.c.3.2).

4 p.m. 110 Inf. Bde. were ordered to move to bivouacs in the area between Canal du Nord and a line running North and South through LE MESNIL en ARROUAISE before dark tonight. (G.X.899).

The reserve M.G. Coy. were ordered to reconnoitre positions in trench system V.22.b. - V.16.b. & d. - W.11.a. & c. These positions were to be occupied before dark. (G.X.900).

4.5 p.m. The 64 Inf. Bde. were ordered to move one Battalion to the neighbourhood of SOREL LE GRAND. (G.X.901).

4.25 p.m. 62 Inf. Bde. reported the situation at 1 p.m. as under :-

Right Battalion were in W.27.b. Left Battalion had been reported by the Corps Cavalry to be on the general line W.9.Cen. to railway North of HEUDECOURT. HEUDECOURT was reported to have been captured.

4.50 p.m. Situation. Right Bn. 62 Inf. Bde. held trenches in W.23.a. & c. with advanced posts in W.22.d. Left Battalion held trenches in W.9.b. and W.10.c. and was advancing to the attack on REVELON RIDGE. The right Battalion was advancing to the spur W.23.Central in order to cover the left flank of the 12th Division.

8 p.m. Orders issued for the 62 Inf. Bde. to send forward advanced guards at 6 a.m. tomorrow to try and capture the second objective. If the enemy's resistance had slackened, advanced guards were to be supported, but no serious attack

/was.......

was to be undertaken without reference to Div. H.Q. 94th and 95th Bdes. R.F.A. were placed under the orders of 62 Inf. Bde. Artillery and Machine Guns were to be freely used for harassing fire. 64 and 110 Inf. Bdes. would remain in their present positions but the 64 Inf. Bde. were to carry out the necessary reconnaissances with a view to relief of 62 Inf. Bde. on the night 8th/9th. (D.O.227).

8th September, 1918.

5.40 a.m. Situation unchanged during the night. There was spasmodic shelling throughout the night of roads, tracks and villages in the forward area. Hostile night bombing squadrons were very active.

8.45 a.m. Situation: Enemy held RAILTON - REVELON - W.10.Central. 1st Linc. Regt. had an encounter with an enemy patrol near RAILTON, in which four prisoners were captured. Enemy attempted to raid one of our posts at 5.30 a.m. but was repulsed before entering our lines.

9.45 a.m. Owing to the enemy putting down a very heavy barrage on the Division on our left, the 62 Inf. Bde. called on the leading Battalion of the 64 Inf. Bde. to form a defensive flank facing North in case of necessity. (G.X.919).

10.50 a.m. Situation. The right Battalion 62 Inf. Bde. attacked at 7.30 a.m. in conjunction with 58th Division on right and captured the KNOLL at W.23.Central with little opposition. The Battalion was moving on the second objective, the trench line W.24.c. - W.23.d. which objective was also later reported as captured. Troops were pushed down railway through W.24.c. & d. to connect with left of 58th Division who were believed to have captured PEIZIERE. This village, however, was not captured.

12.20 p.m. Trenches in W.23.Central and W.21.a & c. were being consolidated. RAILTON was being mopped up and a few prisoners had been taken.

1.10 p.m. Situation. REVELON FARM was reported captured and Battalions had been pushed forward to GENIN WELL COPSE. Heavy M.G. fire was being encountered from LOWLAND SUPPORT.

/2.30 p.m.

2.30 p.m. Report received from 62 Inf. Bde. that their troops had worked along the railway at W.24.d. but had been driven back by a counter-attack. They also reported that PEIZIERE was strongly held by the enemy.

10.10 p.m. Orders issued to the 64 Inf. Bde. to attack tomorrow at 4 a.m. in conjunction with the 17th Division on their left. The objectives were CHAPEL HILL and high ground in W.11.d. After capture of these objectives, the 62 Inf. Bde. were to push patrols to VAUCELLETTE FARM, which was to be occupied in absence of resistance. The 110 Inf. Bde. were to have two Battalions in the vicinity of, and ready to occupy, EQUANCOURT TRENCH SYSTEM by 6 a.m. tomorrow morning. The third battalion was to move to the neighbourhood of SOREL LE GRAND. The 62 Inf. Bde. would be withdrawn gradually under orders of Div. H.Q. to MANANCOURT and ETRICOURT and to ground just East of Canal. (D.O.228).

9th September, 1918.

5.30 a.m. Situation. Very little activity during the night. Enemy harassed RAILTON Cross roads with Artillery. No news had yet been received from the attacking Battalions.

7 a.m. 64 Inf. Bde. reported that the first objective in W.11.d. had been captured, but this report had not been confirmed. The enemy were heavily shelling RAILTON and REVELON.

8.10 a.m. Situation. Owing to GENIN WELL COPSE No.2 not having been held by our troops during the night it had to be taken by the attacking troops this morning, and consequently these troops lost the barrage. The line now reported ran W.18.c.9.9 along rly. to W.17.b.4.8. thence along LOWLAND SUPPORT to Northern Divl. Boundary.

Three Machine Guns and some prisoners were captured.

4.30 p.m. Situation remained unchanged. There was some hostile shelling of back areas.

5 p.m. 64 Inf. Bde. reported that they were continuing the attack at 5.30 p.m. in order to gain the final objectives.

/8 p.m....

8 p.m. 64 Inf. Bde. were ordered that unless attack delivered at 5 p.m. was successful, the attack would be continued in conjunction with 17th Division at 4 a.m. the following day. The objectives would be CHAPEL HILL thence along CAVALRY TRENCH and LOWLAND TRENCH to junction with 17th Division at W.12.a.0.0. At 5.15 a.m. the 58th Division on the right were attacking EPEHY and PEIZIERE at which hour the 64 and 110 Inf. Bdes. were to advance and occupy the YELLOW LINE under a creeping barrage. In view of this the 110 Inf. Bde. would be relieving the 62 Inf. Bde. in the Brown Line and at KNOLL W.23.Central during the night. 110 Inf. Bde. were also to be prepared to occupy REVELON FARM and GENIN WELL COPSE No.1 if vacated by forward move of troops of 64 Inf. Bde. On relief, 62 Inf. Bde. was to move to the EQUANCOURT - ETRICOURT Area. (D.O.229).

10th September, 1918.

6.35 a.m. Situation. Heavy shelling of trench system W.24.a. & c. during the night. No news had yet been received of the attack. There was heavy rain and wind during the night.

10.40 a.m. Report received from 64 Inf. Bde. that the attack on CHAPEL HILL and high ground in W.11.d. was not successful. No details had yet been received.

11.30 a.m. Warning order issued that the 110 Inf. Bde. would relieve the 64 Inf. Bde. during the night. The 110 Inf. Bde. was also to be prepared to advance under a barrage and occupy the Yellow Line from CHAPEL HILL to Southern Divisional Boundary. On relief, the 64 Inf. Bde. would move to the EQUANCOURT TRENCH SYSTEM with one Battalion about SOREL LE GRAND. (G.X.693).

7.30 p.m. Orders issued for the 110 Inf. Bde. to advance under a barrage and make good the whole of the Yellow Line within the Divisional Sector. 110 Inf. Bde. would also relieve the 64 Inf. Bde. in the line. (D.O.230).

11.25 p.m. 64 Inf. Bde. reported that a patrol of the 15th Durham L.I. had reached point W.18.c.4.7 where they encountered heavy M.G. fire from both sides. Patrol reported the Yellow Line to be occupied in W.18.c. and W.24.a.

/11th Sept. ......

11th September, 1918.

5.20 a.m. Situation. The attack by the 110 Inf. Bde. started at 3 a.m. and the objectives were now reported as captured, but this report not yet confirmed. Enemy retaliation was slight in the forward area, but heavy on back area, where all valleys were being gassed. The relief of the 64 Inf. Bde. by the 110 Inf. Bde. was complete at 2.45 a.m.

12.30 p.m. Report received from the 110 Inf. Bde. giving situation as follows. One Coy. in trench system from W.23.d.85.30 to W.24.c.45.95. One Platoon in trench system W.24.a.6.2, one Coy. W.18.c.9.3 to W.18.c.9.6. Hostile counter-attack from direction of CHAPEL HILL had been repulsed. This trench system was being heavily shelled by the enemy and the dispositions of the remaining troops could not be ascertained.

2.15 p.m. 110 Inf. Bde. were informed that gas would be projected on CHAPEL CROSSING and VAUCELLETTE FARM between 1.30 a.m. and 2.30 a.m. Sept. 12th. (G.X.5).

2.15 p.m. Brigades were ordered to send all Cavalry and Cyclists attached to them to concentrate in EMRICOURT where they would be under the orders of the 62 Inf. Bde. (G.X.6.).

4.30 p.m. Situation. Line ran W.23.d.8.0 along line of trenches W.18.c.8.9 where a small gap still existed. Line was continued from W.18.a.8.4 along LOWLAND SUPPORT to Northern Divl. Boundary. Touch had been gained on both flanks. Endeavours were being made to clear up the situation in the gap. Enemy trench mortars were active from LOWLAND TRENCH, but were being engaged by Stokes mortars.

12th September, 1918.

12.30 a.m. Report received from the 110 Inf. Bde. that the 1st Bn. Wilts. Regt. had been unable to gain touch with the 7th Leic. Regt. in the Yellow Line. The patrol had been attacked with M.G. fire and bombed by the enemy who were holding a strong post about W.18.a.8.4

6 a.m. Situation during the night unchanged. Gas was successfully projected at 1.30 a.m. Practically no hostile retaliation.

/11.30 a.m.

11.30 a.m. Situation. No activity on the right Battalion front. Left Battalion front was heavily shelled from W.17.b.9.9 to W.11.c.8.6 between 5 a.m. and 7 a.m. At 6 a.m. the enemy attempted to bomb down trench leading to our line at W.11.c.8.6. but were repulsed. Touch had not yet been obtained between 7th Leic. Regt. and 1st Wilts. Regt.

6 p.m. Situation unchanged during the day. At 2 p.m. the enemy attempted to raid the post at W.17.b.6.9 but was repulsed before entering our line.

13th September, 1918.

5.25 a.m. The situation remained quiet and unchanged during the night. Touch had now been gained between the 7th Leic. Regt. and the 1st Wilts. Regt., the enemy pocket which had existed between these two Battalions being cleared up.

9 a.m. 110 Inf. Bde. caught a deserter who stated that the enemy would make an attack on our present line on CHAPEL HILL at 10 a.m. The attack would be accompanied by flammenwerfer. This attack was carried out.

1.5 p.m. 110 Inf. Bde. were informed that gas would be projected on to the railway cutting W.35.b.95.70 between 1.30 a.m. and 2.30 a.m. 14th instant. (G.X.23).

2 p.m. Report received from 110 Inf. Bde. timed 12.30 p.m. that the enemy attacked with flammenwerfer at 10 a.m. and obtained a temporary footing in our line at the trench junction W.11.c.8.6. He was immediately counter-attacked and driven out, 12 men and 1 M.G. being captured. The enemy's losses were reported as being very heavy. Our line was intact and in touch on both flanks. None of our men were missing. The enemy attack was accompanied by heavy Artillery and Trench Mortar bombardment.

The situation for the remainder of the day remained unchanged. There was no enemy activity.

14th September, 1918.

5.25 a.m. There was no change in the situation during the night which passed quietly. An enemy bombing aeroplane was brought down in our lines at 10.30 p.m., the Officer Pilot being captured.

/9.5 a.m......

9.5 a.m. Report received from the 110 Inf. Bde. that preceded by a Trench Mortar bombardment about 20 of the enemy attempted to enter our line at W.18.a.7.4 but were entirely repulsed by rifle and Lewis Gun fire.

4.30 p.m. Situation. Up to 1 p.m. the enemy artillery was fairly active on back areas, but after that hour there was practically no fire.

15th September, 1918.

5.15 a.m. Situation during the night remained unchanged. Enemy Artillery was comparatively quiet but increased slightly at 4 a.m. Some hostile trench mortar fire on the front line in the right sector.

4 p.m. Orders issued that the 110 Inf. Bde. would be relieved by the 19th Inf. Bde. in the line tonight 15th/16th instant. On relief, the 110 Inf. Bde. would move to ETRICOURT and MANANCOURT. The Coys. of the 21st Bn. M.G.C. in the line would not be relieved. (D.O.231).

5.36 p.m. Situation remained unchanged except for some shelling of HEUDECOURT. Our Artillery carried out the usual harassing fire.

16th September, 1918.

2.20 a.m. The relief of the 110 Inf. Bde. by the 19th Inf. Bde. was complete and command of the sector passed to the G.O.C. 33rd Division.

5.15 a.m. The enemy opened a bombardment of the area V.9.c. & d. V.15, V.16.c. & d. where the 62 and 64th Inf. Bdes. were bivouaced, with H.E. and gas. The bombardment ceased at 5.45 a.m. A few casualties were caused.

During the above operations, the following prisoners were captured by the Division.

Officers.	O.R.
5	246

21st DIVISION.

Summary of Casualties from Sept. 4th - 16th (inclusive). 1918.

UNIT.	Killed.		Wounded.		Missing.		TOTAL.	
	Off.	O.R.	Off.	O.R.	Off.	O.R.	Off.	O.R.
62nd Inf. Brigade.								
12/13th North Fus.	-	13	8	125	-	18	8	156
1st Lincoln Regt.	-	8	4	32	-	-	4	40
2nd Lincoln Regt.	-	12	4	65	-	6	4	83
62nd T.M. Batt.	-	-	-	4	-	-	-	4
Total.	-	33	16	226	-	24	16	283
64th Inf. Brigade.								
1st East Yorks Regt.	1	5	3	37	4	134	8	176
9th K.O.Y.L.I.	4	6	6	88	-	17	10	111
15th Durham L.I.	2	18	6	168	-	86	8	272
64th T.M. Batt.	-	-	-	2	-	-	-	2
Total.	7	29	15	295	4	237	26	561
110th Inf. Brigade.								
Headquarters.	-	-	-	-	-	-	-	-
6th Leicester Regt.	-	1	1	21	-	2	1	24
7th Leicester Regt.	-	10	3	74	-	18	3	102
1st Wilts Regt.	-	3	3	34	-	7	3	44
110th T.M. Batt.	-	-	-	1	-	-	-	1
Total.	-	14	7	130	-	27	7	171
14th North Fus (P).	-	-	-	-	-	-	-	-
21st Bn M.G.C.	-	5	3	25	-	1	3	31
Divl. Artillery.								
94th Brigade RFA.	-	-	-	1	-	-	-	1
95th Brigade RFA.	-	-	1	13	-	-	1	13
Total.	-	-	1	14	-	-	1	14
Div. Engineers.								
97th Field Coy RE.	-	-	-	7	-	-	-	7
98th Field Coy RE.	-	-	-	3	-	-	-	3
126th Field Coy RE.	-	-	-	-	-	-	-	-
Total	-	-	-	10	-	-	-	10
R. A. M. C.								
Regt M.O.	1	-	-	-	-	-	1	-
63rd Field Amb.	-	-	-	4	-	-	-	4
64th Field Amb.	-	1	-	1	-	-	-	2
65th Field Amb.	-	2	-	9	-	-	-	11
Total.	1	3	-	14	-	-	1	17
Chaplains Dept.	-	-	1	-	-	-	1	-
TOTAL.	8	84	43	714	4	289	55	1087

--------0--------

21 Div.
G. 997.

REPORT ON OPERATIONS FROM 17th to 20th September 1918.

Map 57.c. S.E. 1/20,000.

Divisional Order No.233. issued for the attack on the enemy's positions on September 18th. The 62nd Inf. Bde. were ordered to capture VAUCELLETTE FARM and the line of ridge through X.19. and X.20.c. The 110th Inf. Bde. on the right and the 64th Inf. Bde. on left were to pass through the 62nd Inf. Bde. and attack and capture the line BEET Trench, MEUNIER Trench, MEATH Post and LIMERICK Post.

17th September 1918.

5.50 a.m. There was no change in the situation during the night. The enemy continually shelled the FINS - HEUDECOURT Road. Hostile bombing aeroplanes dropped bombs around MANANCOURT, EQUANCOURT and SOREL LE GRAND, which places were also occasionally shelled by H.V. guns.

6.10 a.m. The relief of the 19th Inf. Bde. 33rd Division, by the 62nd Inf. Bde. was complete and G.O.C. 21st Division assumed command of the Sector.

Except for desultory enemy shelling in the forward area and occasional H.V. shelling of MANANCOURT and ETRICOURT, the day passed quietly. There was no change in the situation.

18th September 1918.

5.15 a.m. Situation during the night remained unchanged. The enemy fired a few gas shells into the HEUDECOURT Valley.

6.15 a.m. Situation at 6 a.m. Verbal report received by the 62nd Inf. Bde. stated that the left Battalion had gained the first objective, i.e., CAVALRY SUPPORT. Very little hostile retaliation to our barrage.

7.10 a.m. The 62nd Inf. Bde. reported verbally that the whole of the first objective had been gained on the Divisional front.

/8 a.m.........

8 a.m. Situation 7.45 a.m. The whole of the second objective of the 62nd Inf. Bde. had been captured, except the extreme right at about X.26.a.5.9. where the situation was not yet known. The attack of the 64th Inf. Bde. on the final objective had started to time, but no news as to progress had yet been received.

8.45 a.m. The Cyclist Squadron attached to the Division was ordered to report to H.Q., 64th Inf. Bde. as soon as possible. (G.X.233 and 234).

9.10 a.m. 64th Inf. Bde. were ordered to communicate with Divisional Headquarters before using the Cyclists as the situation on the right of the 62nd Inf. Bde was not clear. Until the situation was satisfactory, the cyclists would be at the disposal of the 62nd Inf. Bde. to be used on their right flank. (G.X.236 and 239).

9.30 a.m. Situation 9 a.m. Situation as regards 62nd Inf. Bde. remained unchanged. Touch had been gained with the 58th Division on the right at X.19.c.2.0. but no news yet received as to touch in PLANE Trench. Touch had also been gained with the 17th Division on the left near VAUCELLETTE FARM. Both 110th and 64th Inf. Bdes. had passed through to the attack on the final objectives up to time.

10.25 a.m. Situation at 10.15 a.m. The 58th Division reported that their troops in POPLAR Trench stated that the 6th Leicestershire Regt. were well on ahead. No reports had yet been received from either the 64th or 110th Inf. Bdes, but F.O.O's reported the advance appeared to be going well and prisoners were coming in.

10.50 a.m. Pigeon message received from 15th Durham Light Infantry timed 8.30 a.m. stated that they had occupied RACKET Trench and Copse in X.13.b.

11.30 a.m. Left Battalion 64th Inf. Bde. report timed 10.40 a.m. stated that the Support Trench to MEUNIER Trench had been captured and prisoners and guns taken. One 10.5 c.m. battery had been captured with teams complete. No definite report had been received from the right Brigade, but our

/troops......

troops had been seen nearing MEATH Post and to be held up by heavy M.G. fire from LIMERICK Post.

11.30 a.m. The 62nd Inf. Bde. reported that touch had now been gained with the 58th Division at X.20.c.2.0.

11.45 a.m. The Cyclists were now placed at the disposal of the 64th Inf. Bde. for exploitation (G.X.245).

11.55 a.m. The Div. Cav. Troop was ordered to move at once to Headquarters 64th Inf. Bde. where they would come under the orders of that Brigade and be used for the exploitation of VILLERS GUISLAIN (G.X.246 and 247).

Situation 11.45 a.m. The right Brigade reported that steady progress was being made towards the final objective, but no touch could be gained with the 12th Division on the right and heavy M.G. fire was coming from LARK SPUR. The Left Battalion during the advance met a heavy counter-attack in LINNET VALLEY. Prisoners were taken and the advance resumed.

12.30 p.m. Report received from the left Battalion, 64th Inf. Bde. timed 10.25 a.m. that they had captured the whole of BERT Trench at 9 a.m. and held it with Platoon Posts from X.8.d.7.1. to X.8.a.5.4. They also held a portion of GUISLAIN Trench in X.8.d. Officer patrols had been pushed forward towards VILLERS GUISLAIN. Casualties were slight.

12.55 p.m. The 62nd Inf. Bde. were ordered to place one Coy. of their left Battalion at the disposal of the 64th Inf. Bde. who were to use this Coy. to relieve a Coy. of their Reserve Battalion. (G.X.252).

2.30 p.m. Situation. On right Brigade front MEATH LANE and MEATH POST believed to be occupied. The situation on the extreme right was obscure and further attacks on LIMERICK Post in conjunction with the 12th Division were being made.

3.30 p.m. 110th Inf. Bde reported that constant Machine Gun fire and sniping were coming from enemy pocket in X.25. Central.

Situation 3 p.m. 64th Inf. Bde. held the whole of the final objectives from left Boundary to LEITH WALK in X.15.d. 110th Inf. Bde. continued the line from MEATH POST (exclusive) then PARRS Trench to LIMERICK LANE. Situation on the extreme right was still obscure. Troops who had captured

/MEATH.....

MEATH Post earlier in the day had been heavily counter-attacked and forced to withdraw.

4.40 p.m. Report from 64th Inf. Bde. timed 3.40 p.m. stated that the enemy counter-attacked the left of the 9th K.O.Y.L.I. in BEET Trench about 2.30 p.m. Troops had been forced back slightly. The situation was quickly restored by an immediate counter-attack and the whole line regained.

5.35 p.m. 62nd Inf. Bde. were ordered to place the Coy. of the 1st Lincolnshire Regt. detailed to hold RACKET Trench at the disposal of the 64th Inf. Bde, to replace one Coy. 15th Durham Light Infantry. who had been used to reinforce the left flank (G.X.262).

7.30 p.m. Situation. 64th Inf. Bde. unchanged, with defensive flank from X.15.d.8.9. to X.15.c.Central, where the line was continued by the 110th Inf. Bde. to X.21.a.5.6. - MEATH LANE - Road in X.20.b. and d. The Division on right reported enemy to be still in POPLAR Trench, CHESTNUT AVENUE and CULLEN Post.

8 p.m. Orders issued for the 110th Inf. Bde. to relieve the 62nd Inf. Bde. in PLANE Trench during the night. The 62nd Inf. Bde. were to hold the VAUCELLETTE FARM Ridge from the Div. Southern boundary to SKITTLE ALLEY inclusive, taking over the N. portion of this line from the 17th Division. 64th Inf.Bde. were to hold the final objective and to use all their resources for this purpose. 62nd Inf. Bde. were to place one Battn. at the disposal of the 64th Inf. Bde. for the purpose of holding supporting position West of BEET FACTORY (X.14.a. The R.E. and Pioneers were to construct and wire a line of Posts on the general line PLANE Trench, Spur X.20.a. West of Factory, FIVES Trench. 110th Inf. Bde. were to be prepared to carry out an attack on LIMERICK Post the following morning. (Order No.234).

19th September 1918.

6 a.m. Situation. The enemy counter-attacked the 110th Inf. Bde. in Area X.21.a. at about 4.15 p.m. on the 18th inst,

/but.......

but was repulsed. During the night the enemy forced the 64th Inf. Bde. to withdraw from LEITH WALK in X.15.d. Northwards up MEUNIER TRENCH to about X.15.b.3.7. A counter-attack by the 64 Inf. Bde. to restore the situation was being made. Counter-preparation was fired at 4.45 a.m. and finished at 5.10 am. Considerable hostile M.G. fire throughout the night from LIMERICK POST.

3.30 p.m.
Orders issued for the relief of the Division by the 33rd Div. On relief 110 Inf. Bde. were to move to the area ETRICOURT and MANANCOURT. 62 Inf. Bde. to the area West and South West of LE MESNIL EN ARROUAISE. 64 Inf. Bde. to LES BOEUFS. (D.O.235).
The situation during the day remained unchanged with very little hostile activity.

5.45 p.m.
Under orders from Corps, the command of the Artillery covering the right sector would pass to the G.O.C. 33rd Division on completion of relief. (Corps G.668).

9.40 p.m.
64 Inf. Bde. were ordered to hand over the command of the Cyclist Squadron to the 98th Inf. Bde. on completion of the relief. (G.X.317).

20th September, 1918.

4.40 a.m.
The relief of the Division by the 33rd Division was complete and the command passed to G.O.C. 33rd Division.
Prisoners and guns captured during the above operations were :-

		Officers.	O.R.
Prisoners		27	667
Guns	...	15	

Telegrams to accompany REPORT ON OPERATIONS from
17th to 20th September 1918.

18th September 1918.

G.X.233. Cyclists being sent to you for use either as mobile reserve or exploitation purposes.

G.X.234. Report with your troop to General Edwards at 64th Inf. Bde. H.Q. in Sunken Road, W.22.c. as soon as possible AAA You should assemble troop some spot West of W.22.c. and proceed to Bde. H.Q. yourself for orders.

G.X.236. Reference G.X.233. AAA Situation on right of 62nd Inf. Bde. not yet clear AAA Communicate with Div. H.Q. before using Cyclists AAA If communication not possible, communicate with 62nd Bde. AAA Cyclists will be at disposal of 62nd Inf. Bde. for use on their right if required. AAA If 62nd Inf. Bde. satisfied as to situation on right Cyclists will be used by you in accordance with G.X.233.

G.X.239. Cyclists have been sent to report to 64th Inf. Bde. AAA They are placed under your orders until the situation on your right is clear AAA When situation is clear Cyclists revert to 64th Inf. Bde AAA

G.X.245. Cyclists will now be used by 64th Inf. Bde. for exploitation AAA

G.X.246. Cavalry Troop has been ordered to report your H.Q. forthwith AAA Troop to be used for exploitation of VILLERS GUISLAIN.

G.X.247. Move at once to H.Q. 64th Inf. Bde. in sunken road W.22.c. AAA On arrival you will come under orders of 64th Inf. Bde. and will be used for exploitation of VILLERS GUISLAIN.

G.X.252. 62nd Inf. Bde. will place one Coy. of their left Battn. at disposal of 64th Inf. Bde AAA If required, 64th Inf. Bde. will use this Coy. to relieve a Coy. of their Reserve Battn AAA 64th Inf. Bde. will inform 62nd Inf. Bde. if Coy. is used AAA

G.X.262. One Coy 1st Lincoln Regt. detailed to hold RACKET Trench, is placed at disposal of 64th Inf. Bde. to replace one Coy. 15th D.L.I. used to reinforce left Flank AAA

19th September 1918.

G.668. from Corps. Reference G.650 today AAA Command of artillery covering right Sector will pass on completion of infantry relief when command of sector will pass from G.O.C. 21 Div. to G.O.C. 33 Div AAA C.R.A. 21 Div, will move to 33 Div H.Q. and remain for 24 hours with C.R.A. 33 Div AAA

G.X. 317. 64th Inf. Bde will hand over command of Cyclist Squadron to 98th Bde. to-night AAA On completion of relief Cyclist Sqdn. will come under orders of 33 Div AAA

21st DIVISION.

Summary of Casualties Sept 17th - 20th 1918 (inclusive).

UNIT.	Killed.		Wounded.		Missing.		TOTAL.	
	Off.	O.R.	Off.	O.R.	Off.	O.R.	Off.	O.R.
62nd Inf. Brigade.								
12/13th North Fus.	-	5	2	72	-	11	2	88
1st Lincoln Regt.	1	7	-	55	-	14	1	76
2nd Lincoln Regt.	1	5	2	52	-	14	3	71
62nd T.M. Batt.	-	-	-	-	-	-	-	-
Total.	2	17	4	179	-	39	6	235
64th Inf. Brigade.								
1st East Yorks R.	2	11	3	68	1	38	6	117
9th K.O.Y.L.I.	1	15	3	57	-	31	4	103
15th Durham L.I.	-	11	2	49	-	15	2	75
64th T.M. Batt.	-	-	-	-	-	-	-	2
Total.	3	37	8	174	1	84	12	295
110th Inf. Brigade.								
Headquarters.	-	1	-	1	-	-	-	2
6th Leicester Regt.	1	15	4	72	-	2	5	89
7th Leicester Regt.	-	7	-	52	-	1	-	60
1st Wilts Regt.	-	15	5	85	-	14	5	114
110th T.M. Batt.	-	1	-	3	-	-	-	4
Total.	1	39	9	213	-	17	10	269
14th North Fus (P).	-	2	-	14	-	-	-	16
21st Bn M.G.C.	1	5	4	28	-	2	5	35
Divl. Artillery.								
94th Brigade RFA.	-	-	-	8	-	-	-	8
95th Brigade RFA.	-	-	-	2	-	-	-	2
21st D.A.C.	-	-	-	12	-	-	-	12
Total.	-	-	-	22	-	-	-	22
Div. Engineers.								
97th Field Coy RE.	-	-	-	3	-	-	-	3
98th Field Coy RE.	-	-	-	5	-	-	-	5
126th Field Coy RE.	-	-	-	2	-	-	-	2
Total.	-	-	-	10	-	-	-	10
21st Div.Sig.Coy.	-	2	-	3	-	-	-	5
222nd Emp. Coy.	-	-	-	1	-	-	-	1
T O T A L.	7	102	25	644	1	142	33	888

----------0---------

With Sept. diary

S E C R E T.

21 Div.
G. 42.

SUMMARY OF OPERATIONS for period Sept. 26th to Oct. 10th.1918.

Ref: Sheet 57.C. S.E.) 1/20,000.
57.C. S.W.)

Orders were issued for the Division to relieve the 17th Division in the left Sector, V Corps front, on night 25th/26th instant. 110 Inf. Bde. relieving the 51st Inf. Bde. on the right and the 62 Inf. Bde. relieving the 50th Inf. Bde. on the left The 64th Inf. Bde. relieving the 52nd Inf. Bde. in support.(D.O.236

In conjunction with operations to the North, the 21st Division was ordered :-

(a) To capture AFRICAN TRENCH from Q.31.a.6.5 to the Northern Divisional Boundary.

(b) To advance along the QUENTIN RIDGE and capture GONNELIEU at the same time as the 33rd Division on the right attacked VILLERS GUISLAIN. (D.O.237).

September 26th, 1918.

3.5 a.m. The relief of the 17th Division was complete and command of the Sector passed to G.O.C., 21st Division.

The situation throughout the night was quiet except for slight hostile shelling of back areas including a few gas shells.

4.50 p.m. Situation remained unchanged throughout the day. There was intermittent shelling of SOMME ALLEY, GAUCHE ALLEY, CHAPEL HILL and W.12.d., chiefly with 5.9".

September 27th, 1918.

At Zero hour, 7.52 a.m., in conjunction with the attack, 'K' Special Coy. R.E. successfully discharged 110 oil drums into the Western outskirts of GOUZEAUCOURT.

9.30 a.m. 62 Inf. Bde. reported that the right Coy. had reached their objective and were holding strong post in sunken road at Q.35.a.8.8. The situation on the left was not yet known.

/10.15 a.m......

10.15 a.m. R.A.F. Observer reported our troops in strength at Q.29.c.90.50. Returning wounded also reported our troops on objective. Enemy were reported at Q.29.c.80.75. and Q.29.a.85.20. These were being dealt with by Stokes Mortars.

11.30 a.m. 62nd Infantry Brigade report timed 11.15 a.m. stated that three Coys. left Battalion attacked AFRICAN Trench at 7.52 a.m. The right and centre Coys. gained their objective but the left Coy. was held up by enfilade Machine Gun fire from the North. The Centre Coy. had worked Northwards up AFRICAN Trench and gained the remainder of the objective where a block had been established on the Divisional Boundary. No touch had been gained with the 5th Division on the left and it was understood that their right Battalion had been held up.

12 noon. Divisional Headquarters closed at U.5.c.3.2. and reopened at V.4.b.2.5.

5 p.m. Situation remained unchanged during the day. The enemy intermittently shelled the Divisional front.

Brigades were informed that the operation ordered in Para 1(b) of Divisional Order No.237 would not take place tonight, but would probably take place on the night 28th/29th September (G.498).

28th September 1918.

5.10 a.m. During the night the enemy put down a heavy bombardment with Artillery and Trench Mortars on AFRICAN Trench and subsequent counter-attack forced our troops to withdraw. The 62nd Inf. Bde. now held their original line from Q.35.a.5.4. to Q.29.c.0.1. where they were in touch with the 5th Division.

10.40 a.m. The 62nd Infantry Brigade reported that the enemy had evacuated AFRICAN Trench as far North as the Divisional Boundary and that patrols were pushing forward towards GOUZEAUCOURT.

11.35 a.m. Orders issued to the effect that 110th Infantry Brigade were to occupy the line GREEN LANE, GREEN SWITCH, should they meet with no resistance and to get in touch with the 5th Division at R.26.a.9.1. When this line had been made

11 a.m. Report received from the 62nd Inf. Bde. that patrols of the 1st Linc. Regt. had reached trench running from Q.36.c.0.0 to road Q.36.a.0.2. and found it clear of the enemy. The patrol proceeded to the W. edge of GOUZEAUCOURT & met with no opposition

good, patrols were to be sent to the BROWN Line (line of road X.3.a. - R.33.c. and a.) but no advance in force was to be made until touch had been established with the 5th Division on the left. Should patrols still report no resistance, 110th Infantry Brigade would occupy the BROWN Line and send patrols to the GREEN Line (ROSE TRENCH - RIBBLE TRENCH R.35). As soon as 110th Inf. Bde. had occupied GREEN LANE, GREEN SWITCH, and their patrols had reached the BROWN Line, 62nd Infantry Brigade were to assemble in GOUZEAUCOURT VALLEY (G.X.515).

1 p.m. 62nd Infantry Brigade reported a group of enemy snipers located in Quarry R.31.c.9.7. who were being dealt with.

3.10 p.m. 62nd Infantry Brigade reported that left Battn. had reached R.35.a.5.9. without opposition and had located party of enemy in FLAG RAVINE R.20.a.

4.35 p.m. Situation. Our troops occupied GREEN LANE and R.A.F. Observer reported that GREEN SWITCH as far North as R.26.a.6.0. was also occupied.

6.15 p.m. 21st Battalion Machine Gun Corps were ordered to send the two Companies 17th Battn. Machine Gun Corps attached to them for barrage work back to rejoin their own Unit. (G.X.526.).

7.30 p.m. Orders issued for the attack on the GREEN and BROWN Lines early the following morning. 110th Infantry Bde. were to attack on the right with 62nd Infantry Brigade on the left. Two Tanks were placed at the disposal of each Brigade. One Machine Gun Coy. was also detailed to accompany each Brigade (Div. Order No. 238).

9.10 p.m. Situation at 9 p.m. Line ran VILLERS TRENCH X.2.a.5.3. along GREEN LANE, GREEN SWITCH TO R.26.a.4.0. Enemy heavily shelled the Eastern edge of GAUCHE WOOD at 8.30 p.m.

10.20 p.m. Ref. Order No. 238, instructions were issued that when the GREEN Line had been captured patrols were to be sent forward to the Canal. If no opposition was met with the C.R.E was to begin making arrangements to bridge the Canal (G.X.536)

/11.25 p.m.....

11.25 p.m. The two supply tanks were placed under the orders of the 62nd Infantry Brigade (G.X.547).

September 29th, 1918.

1.30 a.m. Report received from 110th Inf. Bde. timed 12.20 a.m. giving the situation as follows :- 6th Leicestershire Regt. held VILLERS Trench X.2.a.8.0. thence N.W. along VILLERS Trench GREEN LANE to cross roads R.31.d.9.1. where they were in touch with the 7th Leicestershire Regt. Line was continued N.W. along road thence North along GREEN LANE, GREEN SWITCH to cross Roads R.26.c.4.0.

5 a.m. Situation during the night remained unchanged. The attack started at 3.30 a.m. but no details had yet been received.

7.15 a.m. Situation. 110th Infantry Brigade position was obscure, but attack apparently held up by heavy Machine Gun fire from R.32.c. and also from the direction of the CEMETERY X.2.d. No reports yet received from the 62nd Infantry Brigade.

8 a.m. No change on the 110th Infantry Brigade front. The 62nd Infantry Brigade had been held up along the whole Brigade front West of GONNELIEU, which place was strongly held by the enemy with many Machine Guns. 62nd Infantry Brigade were now reorganizing in GREEN SWITCH. Considerable hostile Artillery and Machine Gun fire had been encountered.

9.20 a.m. 64th Infantry Brigade were ordered to hold two Battalions in readiness to move at quarter of an hours' notice to occupy LOWLAND TRENCH, HEATHER TRENCH and AFRICAN TRENCH within Divisional Boundaries. (G.X.556).

10 a.m. Report received from 110th Infantry Brigade timed 9 a.m. stated that the right Coy. 6th Leicestershire Regt held the CEMETERY X.2.d.9.9. - CROSS POST - Road junction X.2.b.65.20. thence N.E. for about 100 yards along the Sunken Road. This Coy. was in touch with the 33rd Division on the right. Remaining Coys. of this Battalion were along LANCASHIRE TRENCH, GREEN LANE to about R.31.d.5.2. A party was bombing down VILLERS TRENCH to gain touch with the forward Coy. near the Cemetery. 7th Leic. Regt. were established

/in.........

in GREEN LANE from R.31.d.5.2 to about R.31.d.Central whence line was continued along GREEN SWITCH. Attack had been held up by heavy Machine Gun fire from R.32.c. and VILLERS GUISLAIN.

Situation of 62 Inf. Bde. was unchanged. The enemy held RESERVE LINE and GIN AVENUE in strength.

<u>10.50 a.m.</u> 110 Inf. Bde. were ordered to place one Battalion at the disposal of the 62nd Inf. Bde. This Battalion was to move at once to the vicinity of Quarry R.25.d. Battalion would be used to advance along the BANTEUX SPUR. 62 Inf. Bde. were to send as much of the Brigade as could quickly be made available round the North of GONNELIEU towards R.28.Central and to get in touch with the right of the 5th Division at that place. 110 Inf. Bde. were to take over the defence of GREEN SWITCH as far North as R.26.c.3.0. (G.X.562).

<u>11.10 a.m.</u> 64 Inf. Bde. were ordered to move one Battalion forthwith to area Q.35.c - W.5.a. On arrival this Battalion was to be prepared either to hold AFRICAN TRENCH, HEATHER TRENCH within Divisional Boundaries or to concentrate quickly and move either North or South of GOUZEAUCOURT followed by remainder of Brigade to exploit success. (G.X.564).

The Cyclist Squadron was transferred from the 110 Inf. Bde. to the 62 Inf. Bde. and were ordered to move to 62 Inf. Bde. H.Q. as soon as possible. (G.X.565).

<u>12.10 p.m.</u> Situation at 12 noon. Two Battalions 62 Inf. Bde. moving through R.20 and R.21 with objective BANTEUX SPUR supported by one Battalion 110 Inf. Bde. The Third Battalion, 62 Inf. Bde., was working round the North of GONNELIEU.

<u>2.50 p.m.</u> 64 Inf. Bde. were ordered to move another Battalion to area Q.35.c. W.5.a. the third Battalion to remain in Q.32. (G.X.573).

<u>4.35 p.m.</u> Situation on Divisional Front unchanged. The Battalions of the 62 Inf. Bde. which were moving to the North of GONNELIEU were now in the following positions :- One Battalion in FERN TRENCH with right on road at R.21.c.7.0. Troops of the 5th Division were also in this trench. One Battalion in NEWPORT TRENCH and third Battalion in Sunken Road R.19.b. Enemy held JAM TRENCH and LA VACQUERIE Road in strength. Some enemy Machine Guns were still in LA VACQUERIE.

<u>9.5 p.m.</u> Instructions received from the Corps that the Division was to re-organise and rest during the 30th September. The Div. was to be prepared to follow up the enemy on any sign of a retirement. All enemy trenches and positions would be kept under intense harassing fire. (V Corps G.180).

10.10 p.m. Orders issued to the effect that active patrolling was to be carried out during the night. Should GONNELIEU and Brown Line be entered by Patrols without resistance, they were to be at once occupied in force and patrols pushed on to the Green Line. Should this line be found empty, it was to be occupied and patrols pushed on to the Canal. All available Heavy Artillery and Field Howitzers were to bombard GONNELIEU from 4.5 a.m. to 5 a.m. 64 Inf. Bde. were ordered to remain in their present positions until further orders. (D.O.239).

September 30th, 1918.

5.20 a.m. Situation remained unchanged during the night, with very little hostile activity. The 62 Inf. Bde. reported that the Reserve Line was very strongly held by the enemy at 4.50 a.m.

10 a.m. Owing to 5th Division reporting that they had patrols in GONNELIEU and BANTEUX, 62 Inf. Bde. were ordered to send patrols through the 5th Division area so as to enter GONNELIEU from the North. These patrols were to be supported by stronger bodies. 110 Inf. Bde. were to send patrols to the Brown Line and to reinforce them as soon as VILLERS GUISLAIN was occupied by the 33rd Division. 62 Inf. Bde. were to send one Battalion round the North of GONNELIEU to work down GLASGOW and PRESTON TRENCHES with objective Green Line and Southern slopes of BANTEUX SPUR. (G.X.594).

10.50 a.m. 62 Inf. Bde. report timed 10.15 a.m. stated that one Battalion had gone through GONNELIEU and occupied Brown Line as far South as KITCHEN CRATER. Another Battalion was working round the North of GONNELIEU towards the Green Line, the third Battalion being in support. 110 Inf. Bde. reported that the Cemetery at X.2.d.9.9 was still strongly held.

11.50 a.m. 110 Inf. Bde. had occupied the Brown Line and were pushing on towards the Green Line, to which line the 62 Inf. Bde. were also advancing.

12.10 p.m. 110 and 62 Inf. Bdes. as soon as the Green Line had been made good were to send forward strong fighting patrols to the Canal to seize crossings and establish bridge-heads on the Eastern Bank. 64 Inf. Bde. were to move to area just West of QUENTIN RIDGE forthwith and to be prepared on receipt of orders to advance through the leading Brigades, to cross the Canal and occupy the HINDENBURG

/LINE.....

LINE between MANCOURT FARM and BANTOUZELLE (both exclusive). The Cyclist Squadron would be transferred from 62 Inf. Bde. to 64 Inf. Bde. when latter Brigade took up the advance. (D.O.240).

6 p.m. Patrols had now reached the West bank of the Canal but were prevented from crossing the Canal by Heavy Machine Gun fire from the Eastern bank. All bridges had been destroyed.

7.30 p.m. 110 and 62 Inf. Bdes. were ordered to continue to hold the Green Line and to push out patrols who were to try and cross the Canal by any available crossings. Should any bridges be found repairable, and if hostile fire permitted, the R.E. were to construct crossings. Such crossings were to be guarded by posts on the Western bank in order to prevent the enemy blowing them up. 64 Inf. Bde. were to remain in their present positions. (D.O.241).

10.20 p.m. Situation for the remainder of the day remained unchanged. The enemy were reported to be holding the trench line S.2.c. & a. to M.31.d. & b. The bridge at M.31.b.1.1 blew up just as our patrol was about to cross.

1st October, 1918.

5.25 a.m. The situation remained unchanged. Slight hostile shelling of the forward area at intervals during the night.

10 a.m. Patrols during the night reported that no enemy had been encountered on the West bank of the Canal. One German who had been left behind in HONNECOURT was captured. BANTOUZELLE was held by the enemy but in what strength could not be determined.

4.50 p.m. Situation remained unchanged throughout the day. Slight hostile Artillery and Machine Gun fire on area West of Canal.

2nd October, 1918.

During the night 62 Inf. Bde. succeeded in getting one bridge across the Canal South of BANTEUX but all attempts to pass troops over this bridge were stopped by heavy Rifle and Machine Gun fire from the Eastern bank.

Later in the day this bridge was destroyed by a direct hit from an enemy Trench Mortar.

Situation on the Divisional front remained unchanged.

/3rd Oct.

3rd October, 1918.

Situation remained unchanged. All attempts to cross the canal were stopped by heavy Machine Gun fire.

Orders issued for the 110 Inf. Bde. to extend their left during the night 3rd/4th October, and take over the front now held by 62 Inf. Bde. On relief, 62 Inf. Bde. to withdraw to the area Q.34, Q.35, W.4, W.5. (D.O.242).

12.30 p.m. The M.G.Coy. attached to 64 Inf. Bde. were ordered to reconnoitre defensive positions on the QUENTIN RIDGE. These positions were only to be occupied in case of hostile attack. (E.X.662).

6 p.m. In conjunction with the attack being made in a Northerly direction by the 50th Division from LE CATELET, the Divisional Artillery and Machine Gun Battalion were ordered to keep the HINDENBURG LINE under steady continuous fire whilst these operations were in progress. 110 Inf. Bde. were to keep touch with the enemy by means of patrols endeavouring to cross the canal by means of rafts. As soon as the 110 Inf. Bde. had gained bridge-head on East bank, 64 Inf. Bde. were to be prepared to cross the Canal and establish themselves in the HINDENBURG LINE within Divisional Boundaries. The Cyclist Squadron was placed under orders of 64 Inf. Bde. (D.O.243).

4th October, 1918.

During the day and night the situation remained unchanged. Patrols were unable to cross the canal owing to hostile fire. There was slight hostile shelling of BANTEUX SPUR throughout the day.

Under orders from Corps two extra Mobile Newton Mortars were placed at the disposal of the Division. (V Corps C.T.283).

5th October, 1918.

5.5 a.m. Situation remained unchanged during the night. Practically no enemy activity.

12.5 p.m. Owing to all indications pointing to the fact that the enemy had withdrawn opposite the Corps front, and R.A.F. Observers reporting the HINDENBURG LINE deserted, 110 Inf. Bde. were ordered to establish a bridge-head round the Eastern outskirts of BANTOUZELLE under cover of which the C.R.E. was to construct bridges to take Infantry in fours. As soon as this objective

/had......

had been gained, 110 Inf. Bde. were to seize a more extended bridge-head as follows :- ARNOULD QUARRY - C.T. through M.33.a. and M.27.d. - HINDENBURG SUPPORT LINE from M.27.d.3.5 to M.27.b.0.3, thence via RED FARM to Canal. Fighting patrols were then to be sent to HINDENBURG SUPPORT LINE between RANCOURT FARM exclusive and M.27.d. As soon as patrols had reached this line, 110 Inf. Bde. were to occupy it. 64 Inf. Bde. were to move the heads of leading Battalions to BANTEUX forthwith and to start crossing canal as soon as 110 Inf. Bde. had gained the larger bridge-head. 64 Inf. Bde. would then pass through the 110 Inf. Bde. with the following objectives :- HINDENBURG SUPPORT LINE if not already captured by the 110 Inf. Bde. Line of road MONTECOUVEZ FARM - BONNE ENFANCE FARM within Divisional Boundaries. When latter objective had been made good, patrols were to be sent to the MASNIERES - BEAUREVOIR TRENCH SYSTEM to ascertain if it was occupied by the enemy or not. 62 Inf. Bde. were ordered to move to area R.28.c. & d. R.29.c. & d. R.24. as soon as vacated by 110 and 64 Inf. Bdes. (D.O.244).

<u>2.40 p.m.</u> 110 Inf. Bde. reported that the larger bridge-head had been gained and their patrols had been seen in M.33.d. and M.34.c. Troops of the Division on the right had been seen in and about RANCOURT FARM.

<u>3 p.m.</u> Divisional Headquarters closed at V.4.b.3.5 and opened at W.11.c.5.8.

<u>4.30 p.m.</u> The HINDENBURG SUPPORT LINE had been captured within the Divisional Boundaries. Patrols had been pushed on to the line MONTECOUVEZ FARM - BONNE ENFANCE FARM, from both of which hostile Machine Gun fire was coming and also from Copse M.36.c. Touch had been gained with troops on the right. Troops on the left were reported to be on the line M.23.c. - M.17.d.

64 Inf. Bde. reported that 15th Battalion, Durham Light Infantry were crossing the Canal and Cyclists had reached M.34.Cen. at 3 p.m. and reported enemy Machine Gun in GRATTE PANCHE FARM. At 3.15 p.m. this farm was seen to be on fire.

<u>5 p.m.</u> 64 Inf. Bde. reported that Cyclists had reached M.35.b.2.9 but were encountering M.G. fire from both flanks. Dismounted patrol was being sent out.

<u>5.30 p.m.</u> 64 Inf. Bde. were now passing through 110 Inf. Bde. on their way to the line MONTECOUVEZ FARM - BONNE ENFANCE FARM.

/7.15 p.m.....

7.15 p.m. Report from Cyclists timed 4 p.m. stated BONNE ENFANCE FARM clear of enemy. Machine Gun fire was still coming from the direction of MONTECOUVEZ FARM.

Two bridges at R.36.c.9.9 and R.36.c.9.8 had now been completed for Infantry in fours and pack animals.

8.45 p.m. Orders issued for the advance to be continued on the 6th October, 64 Inf. Bde. acting as Advance Guard Brigade.

Objectives as follows :-

(a) Line of road M.33.d. & b. - HAUT FARM - HURTEBISE FARM.

(b) WALINCOURT Village and high ground N.18.a. patrols being pushed forward into SORVAL CHATEAU and SELVIGNY.

Touch was to be gained if possible on both flanks at the conclusion of each bound, but the advance was not to be delayed for this purpose. 78th Bde. R.F.A. would come under the direct orders of 64 Inf. Bde. 110 Inf. Bde. would act as Supporting Brigade and would move to the line MONTECOUVEZ FARM - BONNE ENFANCE FARM as soon as the 64 Inf. Bde. had completely passed over the MASNIERES - BEAUREVOIR TRENCH SYSTEM. 62 Inf. Bde. would be reserve Brigade and was to move to the HINDENBURG SUPPORT LINE as soon as the 110 Inf. Bde. was clear of this line. The policy for the 64 Inf. Bde. was to manoeuvre the enemy out of any positions he might be holding without engaging the Brigade in a frontal attack on a strong position. (D.O.245).

10.50 p.m. Cyclists reported the enemy still holding MONTECOUVEZ FARM. No further reports had been received as to the situation of the 64 Inf. Bde.

Two bridges at the lock M.25.d.8.6 had been completed to carry Infantry in fours. One of these bridges was capable of taking field guns. Six other bridges had been completed for Infantry only.

6th October, 1918.

5.20 a.m. 64 Inf. Bde. held the line BONABUS FARM exclusive to BONNE ENFANCE FARM inclusive. Enemy still held MONTECOUVEZ FARM. Very little hostile activity during the night.

/8 a.m.....

8 a.m. 64 Inf. Bde. reported that MONTECOUVEZ FARM had been captured. Our troops were also reported to be entering BEAUREVOIR LINE in T.2.a. but this report was not yet confirmed.

11.30 a.m. 64 Inf. Bde. reported the situation at 10 a.m. as follows :- The Right Battalion had two Coys. in sunken road T.1.b. - N.31.c. One Coy. MONTECOUVEZ FARM. One Coy. in support M.36.c. Left Battalion one Coy. along road N.25.a., one Coy. BONNE ENFANCE FARM. Two Coys. in trench line M.29.b. & d. Right Battalion was endeavouring to work down sunken road T.2.c. but was meeting with heavy opposition.

11.55 a.m. In conjunction with the attacks to be made by Divisions on the right, 64th Inf. Bde. were ordered to attack and occupy ANGLES CHATEAU at Dusk, the 110 Inf. Bde. being ordered to place one Battalion at the disposal of 64 Inf. Bde. to protect the right flank. These orders were afterwards cancelled.

5.15 p.m. Situation. Right Battalion 64 Inf. Bde. remained unchanged. Troops of the 64 Inf. Bde. who were occupying BONNE ENFANCE FARM were withdrawn from the buildings owing to hostile shell fire and now held sunken road M.30.b. & d.

9 p.m. Under instructions received from V Corps 2 Coys. 17th Bn. M.G.C. were placed at the disposal of the Division for barrage work. (V Corps G.389).

10.30 p.m. Right Battalion 64 Inf. Bde. now held trench line T.1.c.5.5 to T.1.b.8.5. Otherwise there was no change in the situation.

7th October, 1918.

5.30 a.m. Situation remained unaltered during the night with very little enemy activity. Touch had been gained with the 38th Division on the right.

9.30 a.m. Situation unchanged. Patrols reported that the BEAUREVOIR LINE was strongly held and the wire to be in good condition. Attempts to extend Northwards along the trench from T.1.b.8.5 were strongly resisted and no progress made.

7.30 p.m. Orders issued for the attack on the enemy's positions to be continued on Oct. 8th, the objectives of the Division being as follows :-

(a) ANGLES CHATEAU to trench N.33.a.1.6.

(b) Trench N.33.a.1.6 - HAUT FARM - HURTEBISE FARM.

(c) WALINCOURT and high ground N.18.a.

The attack on the first objective was to be carried out by the 64th Inf. Bde. on the right and the 110 Inf. Bde. on the left, Zero hour would be 1 a.m. The attack on the second objective would be carried out by the 110 Inf. Bde., Zero hour being 5.15 a.m. The attack on the third objective would be carried out by the 62nd Inf. Bde., Zero hour being 8 a.m. After the capture of the third objective, the 62nd Inf. Bde. was to send out patrols to the Eastern edge of GARD WOOD - SORVAL CHATEAU - SELVIGNY Village. The Cyclist Squadron was placed at the disposal of the 62nd Inf. Bde. for this purpose. Should SELVIGNY be found unoccupied, reconnoitring patrols were to be pushed out towards CAULLERY. (D.O.246).

Situation remained unchanged throughout the remainder of the day. Enemy shelled MONTECOUVEZ and BONNE ENFANCE FARMS.

October 8th, 1918.

5 a.m. 64 Inf. Bde. reported that the BEAUREVOIR LINE had been occupied but no news yet received of further progress. Wounded Coy. Comdr. from the 110th Inf. Bde. stated that he had been wounded about 200 yards from the objective. Touch had been gained on both flanks. Hostile shelling during the assembly of the troops was negligible.

8 a.m. Divisional Headquarters closed at REVELON FARM and opened at M.32.b.7.1.

9 a.m. Both 64th and 110th Inf. Bdes. reported the first objective had been captured. 64 Inf. Bde. were in touch with the 38th Division at ANGLES CHATEAU. 110 Inf. Bde. reported the assembly and forming up of troops for the second attack was carried out successfully and troops had moved off well under the barrage. ARDISSART FARM had been captured. Many prisoners were reported coming in.

9.15 a.m. 110 Inf. Bde. reported second objective had been captured and the 62nd Inf. Bde. were passing through on their way to the third objective. There was considerable hostile shelling of the BEAUREVOIR LINE.

/9.40 a.m.

9.40 a.m. 64 Inf. Bde. and 110 Inf. Bde. were ordered to collect all available troops less one Battalion each to be ready on receipt of orders, to advance in support of 62nd Inf. Bde. Each Brigade was to keep one Battalion and 8 Machine Guns as garrison of the first and second objectives. (G.A.102).

10.45 a.m. No report had yet been received as to the progress of the 62nd Inf. Bde. The situation in ANGLES CHATEAU was not yet clear, as some enemy still appeared to be in the building. These were being 'mopped up'. Troops in HAUT FARM reported that the enemy could be seen retiring Eastwards and that hostile Artillery was also being withdrawn.

12.20 p.m. The 62nd Inf. Bde. line ran ANGLE WOOD inclusive - trench line through N.28.b. & d. to about N.22.c.8.4. Gap existed from this point to about N.21.b. whence line was believed to run through HURTEBISE COPSE - but this was not yet confirmed. Hostile field guns were firing from N.23.d.3.2 and were being engaged by our forward sections. The situation at ANGLES CHATEAU had been cleared up and our troops were in touch with 113th Inf. Bde. in the Quarry T.3.b.

1.30 p.m. Situation on right was unchanged. Further advance out of ANGLE WOOD was stopped owing to intense M.G. fire from MALINCOURT. The left Battalion of the 62nd Inf. Bde. had reached N.16.c. where touch had been gained with 37th Division. Patrols were being pushed across the stream and towards high ground N.18.a. but were meeting with considerable opposition, especially from GUILLEMIN FARM. 110 Inf. Bde. were ordered to be prepared to attack GUILLEMIN FARM and the high ground N.18.a. during the afternoon, probable Zero Hour being about 5 p.m. As a preparatory measure, two Battalions were to be moved forthwith to area West of BRISEUX WOOD (G.X.808).

3.5 p.m. 62 Inf. Bde. reported that the whole of the NAUROY - AUDIGNY LINE within Divisional Boundaries had been captured. Touch had been gained on both flanks. Enemy were seen to be limbering up guns in N.35.c. These were engaged by L.G. fire and casualties inflicted.

3.35 p.m. 64 Inf. Bde. were ordered to move one Battalion forthwith to ANGLE WOOD where it came under the orders of 62nd Inf. Bde. It would be used to assist 62nd Inf. Bde. in their advance on WALINCOURT. (G.X.813).

/5.20 p.m.....

5.20 p.m. The West edge of WALINCOURT and sunken road N.17.b. & d. were strongly held by enemy Machine Guns and further progress without a barrage was impossible. Attack would be re-newed with a barrage at 6 p.m.

11 p.m. Orders issued to the effect that when the 17th Division had passed through the 62nd Inf. Bde. on the 9th October, Brigades were, on orders being received from Division, to concentrate and re-organise in the following areas :-

62 Inf. Bde. ... In Squares N.17, 23 and 29.
64 : : ... : : N.28, 27 and 32.
110 : : ... : : N.22, 21 and 20.

The 17th and 21st Divisional Artilleries would come under order of G.O.C., 17th Division as soon as that Division had passed through the 62nd Inf. Bde. (G.X.827).

The Cyclist Squadron was transferred to 17th Division (G.X.830).

9th October, 1918.

1.10 a.m. 62 Inf. Bde. reported the situation at 11 p.m. 8th Oct. to be as follows :- Line ran N.29.d.9.5 along sunken road N.9.b.5.7 - N.23.Central - thenoe to stream N.22.b.5.4 - thence along stream to N.16.Central. Posts had been established along the N.W. edge of MILL WOOD and also on the W. outskirts of WALINCOURT. The enemy was shelling all sunken roads in N.29. . and N.23. and also WALINCOURT with gas shell. GUILLEMIN FARM was strongly held by the enemy.

During the day the 62nd Inf. Bde. concentrated in WALINCOURT and the 64th and 110th Inf. Bdes. re-organised their Battalions in the present positions.

10th October, 1918.

9.5 a.m. 64 Inf. Bde. were ordered to move to billets in WALINCOURT. (G.X.864).

12.40 p.m. 110 Inf. Bde. were ordered to move during the afternoon to billets in CAULLERY. (G.X.869).

3.5 p.m. Divisional Headquarters closed M.32.b.7.1 and opened in WALINCOURT.

The following prisoners and guns were captured during these operations :-

	Officers.	O.R.	Guns.
Sept. 26th - Oct. 10th. ...	14	802.	5

Copy of Telegrams to accompany 21st Division Summary of Operations for period 26.9.18 to 10.10.18.

28th September, 1918.

G.X.526. 2 Coys. 17th M.G.Bn. attached to you will rejoin their own Battalion forthwith.

G.X.536. Ref: Order No.238. When Green Line objective has been captured patrols will be sent forward to the Canal. Reports will be rendered as to whether opposition is met. If no opposition C.R.E. will begin arrangements to bridge canal.

G.X.547. Supply tank will be under orders of 62nd Inf. Bde.

29th September, 1918.

G.X.556. Hold two Bns. in readiness to move at ¼ of an hours' notice to occupy LOWLAND TRENCH, HEATHER AND AFRICAN TRENCHES within Divl. Boundaries.

G.X.562. 110 Inf. Bde. will place one Bn. at disposal of 62 Bde. Bn. to move at once to vicinity of Quarry R.25.d. pushing reconnaissance ahead through R.20 - R.21. Object of reconnaissance to find covered approach for Bn. to GOUZEAUCOURT - CAMBRAI Road, from which advance can be made on BANTEUX SPUR. Bn. detailed by 110 Inf. Bde. will send Officer to report 62 Bde. H.Q. Q.35.a.5.6. 62 Inf. Bde. will establish report centre at Station R.31.a.9.9 to which reconnaissance sent out by Bn. of 110 Bde. will send reports. 62 Bde. will send as much of his own Bde. as can quickly be made available round N. of GONNELIEU towards R.28.Central and to get touch with right of 5th Division there. 110 Bde. will take over GREEN SWITCH as far N. as R.26.c.3.0.

G.X.564. 64 Bde. will move one Bn. forthwith to area Q.35.c. W.5.a. On arrival Bn. will be prepared either to hold AFRICAN TRENCH HEATHER TRENCH within Divl. Boundaries or to concentrate quickly and move either N. or S. of GOUZEAUCOURT followed by remainder of Bde. to exploit success.

G.X.565. Cyclist Squadron will be transferred forthwith from 110 Bde. to 62 Bde. O.C. Squadron to report 62 Bde. at once and Squadron to move to 62 Bde. H.Q. as soon as possible.

G.X.573. In confirmation of G.X.564 64 Bde. will move another Bn. to area about Q.35.c. W.5.a. ~~ix~~ and will maintain remaining Bn. in Q.32. 64 Bde. will report on completion of move.

G.180 from V Corps.

G.172 is cancelled. 33rd and 21st Divs. will re-organise and rest their troops tomorrow rectifying their present front line where necessary. They will be prepared to immediately follow up the enemy and take prisoners on any signs of a retirement. The enemy's trenches on the Corps front will be kept under a constant bombardment. The G.O.C. 21st Div. will inform Corps H.Q. as soon as the situation is such as to allow of his pushing into GONNELIEU so that until this time the Village may be kept under bombardment.

/30th Sept...

<u>30th September, 1918.</u>

<u>G.X.694.</u> 5th Div. report they have patrols in GONNELIEU and BANTEUX. 62 Bde. will push patrols round through 5th Division area so as to enter GONNELIEU from North. These patrols to be supported by stronger bodies. If GONNELIEU occupied by us patrols to work down Reserve Line and KITCHEN STREET to join hands with 110 Inf. Bde. 110 Inf. Bde. will send patrols to BROWN LINE and reinforce them when VILLERS GUISLAIN is occupied by 33rd Div. 62 Bde. will send one Bn. round N. of GONNELIEU to work down GLASGOW and PRESTON TRENCHES with objective GREEN LINE and Southern slopes of BANTEUX SPUR getting touch with 5th Div. on left.

<u>3rd October, 1918.</u>

<u>G.X.662.</u> The M.G.Coy. attached 64th Bde. will reconnoitre defensive positions on QUENTIN RIDGE. These positions will not be occupied except in case of hostile attack.

<u>4th October, 1918.</u>

<u>G.T.282. from T.M.O. V Corps.</u> Two more Mobile Newton Mortars being sent your Division 6th instant.

<u>6th October, 1918.</u>

<u>G.389 from V Corps.</u> Ref: G.376 of today. Two Coys. 17th and ~~21st~~ 33rd M.G.Bns are alotted 21st and 38th Divs. respectively for barrage purposes. Details as regards their temporary attachment to be arranged direct between Divns.

<u>8th October, 1918.</u>

<u>G.A.102.</u> 64 and 110 Bdes. will each collect all available troops less one Bn. each ready on receipt of orders to advance in support of 62 Bde. 64 and 110 Bdes. will leave one Bn. and 8 M.Gs each to garrison RED LINE. Dividing line between Brigades HAUT FARM incl. to 64 Bde. thence via road running Westwards to N.26.d.1.5. 64 and 110 Bdes. will each report as soon as one Bn. is ready to move forward.

<u>G.X.808.</u> 110 Bde. will be prepared to attack GUILLEMIN and high ground N.18.a. this afternoon. Probable Zero about 17.00 hrs. As preparatory measure two Bns. will be moved forthwith to area W. of MALSSUX WOOD. Completion of move to be reported.

<u>G.X.813.</u> 64 Bde. will move one Bn. forthwith to ANGLE WOOD where it will come under the orders of 62 Bde. It will be used to assist 62nd Bde. in their advance on WALINCOURT. C.O. to report 62 Bde. H.Q.

<u>G.X.807.</u> The ~~xxBde.~~17th Div. will pass through the 62 Bde. early tomorrow morning and resume the advance. When the 17th Div. have passed through orders will be issued to Bdes. to concentrate and re-organise in the following areas :- 62 Bde. in squares N.17, 23 & 29. 64 Bde. in Squares N.28, 27 and 32. 110 Inf. Bde. Squares N.22, 21 and 20. M.G.Coys. re-organise with affiliated Bdes. Cyclists will re-organise with 62 Bde. and will not be transferred without further orders. 17th and 21st D.As come under orders G.O.C. 17th Div. on completion of relief.

/G.X.820.....

G.X.830. Under orders from Corps the Squadron N.I.H. will be transferred to 17th Divisiom from 05.20 hours tomorrow.

10th october, 1918.

G.X.864. Your Bde. will move this morning to Billets in WALINCOURT

G.X.869. 110 Bde. will move this afternoon to Billets in CAULLERY.

- - - - - - - - - - - - - - - - -

War Diary

App I

TELEGRAM.

URGENT OPERATIONS PRIORITY	Words	
	Sent.	
	[illegible]..................m	
	TO..................	
	BY..................	

BUMA	RORU	5th Corps.	15th Sqn.R.A.F.
BURA	JEKU	5th Corps R.A.	Div.Cyclist Coy.
RUVE	JEMU	17th Div.	Div. Cav. Troop.
WUMA	FOLO	42nd Div.	
JENU	A/Q	38th Div.	

/ 1st / AAA

JEZU Order No.221. AAA The 4th and 5th Corps are carrying out a series of operations tomorrow September 2nd AAA In conformity with verbal instructions already given AAA RUVE will capture SUGAR FACTORY N.24.Central AAA at 2 a.m. Artillery barrage will come down on line N.24.a.1.7. to N.18.d.1.3. and will lift at 2.12 a.m. AAA Barrage will move at rate of 100 yds. in 4 minutes until line N.24.d.0.1. to O.19.c.0.6. is reached where it will form protector for 8 minutes and then cease AAA After capture of SUGAR FACTORY RUVE will push force not to exceed one Coy. to about O.19.d.Central with object of preventing withdrawal of garrison of LE TRANSLOY AAA In conjunction with main attack to be delivered later in morning BURA will capture LOBDA COPSE AAA 17th Div. will be attacking ROCQUIGNY crossing Main Road just S.E. of LE TRANSLOY at 6.15 a.m. AAA 42nd Div. will be attack VILIERS AU FLOS and pushing on towards BARASTRE with Zero hour 5.15 a.m. AAA Artillery barrage for BURAS attack will come down on the line N.18.d.2.0. to N.18.b.2.6. AAA Barrage will move at rate of 100 yds in 3 minutes until line O.19.b.0.5 O.13.d.5.0. O.13.d.6.9. is reached, where it will form a protector for 9 minutes and then cease AAA After capture of LOBDA COPSE BURA will effect junction with 42nd Div. at Cross Roads O.13.a.2.4. AAA When 42nd Div. move forward to their 2nd Objective BURA will establish post at O.13.b.4.0. and will send patrol to get in touch with 42nd Div. at O.13.b.9.1. AAA BURA will also establish line from LOBDA COPSE to SUGAR FACTORY and get in touch with RUVES force in O.19.d.Central. AAA O.C. M.G.Battn. will arrange M.G. barrages to co-ordinate with artillery barrages AAA Artillery arrangements other than detailed above will appear in Artillery orders AAA Contact Aeroplane will call for flares at daylight and subsequently at odd hours 7 a.m. 9 a.m. etc. AAA ACKNOWLEDGE AAA Addsd. recipients JEZU Order No. 220.

(Margin annotations: "At 5.15 am"; "lift at 5.18 am and")

JEZU

H.W. Lamblyn

8.15 p.m.

Lieut.Col. G.S.

War Diary

TELEGRAM

App II

URGENT
OPERATIONS
PRIORITY

Words

Sent
At.................m
By..................
To..................

BUMA	RORU	5th Corps	15th Sqn R.A.F.
BURA	JEKU	5th Corps R.A.	Div. Cyclist Coy.
RUVE	JEMU	17th Div.	Div. Cav Troop.
WUMA	FOLO	42nd Div.	
JENU	A/Q	38th Div.	

/ 2nd / AAA

JEZU Order No. 222 AAA 17 Div. are holding general line O.32. central. O.19.b. and d. central. LABDA COPSE AAA 42 Div. are holding line O.13.b.3.1. thence Eastern edge of VILLERS-AU-FLOS to high ground in O.8.central. AAA These Divs. will be advancing on ROCQUIGNY and BARASTRE to-night or to-morrow morning AAA JEZU comes into Corps Reserve AAA RUVE will relieve forward Bn. of BURA to-night September 2nd/3rd AAA RUVE will then hold SUGAR FACTORY and LABDA COPSEmaintaining touch with 42 Div. at O.13.b.3.1. AAA RUVE will also garrison defences of BEAULENCOURT AAA RUVE will maintain at least one Bn. in Bde. Reserve in Valley West of main BAPAUME - PERONNE Road AAA BURA including HOWI will be prepared to hold general line N.22.central. N.10.central. AAA Bde. will be disposed between this line and LUISENHOF FARM Road AAA BUMA will move to area near LES BOEUFS this evening AAA One M.G. Coy will remain affiliated to each Bde. AAA R.E. Pioneers etc. will remain in present accommodation AAA Further orders will be issued as regards Div. Arty. AAA Completion of movements and reliefs will be reported by wire to JEZU H.Q. AAA Acknowledge AAA Added recipients JEZU Order No.221.

JEZU.

6.15 p.m.

H W Franklyn

Lieut.-Col., G.S.

File.

TELEGRAM.

URGENT OPERATIONS PRIORITY HHM.	Words --- Sent At..............m By.............. To..............	

BUMA	RORU	5th Corps.	15th S₄n R.A.F.
BURA	JEKU	5th Corps R.A.	Div. Cav. Troops.
RUVE	JEMU	17th Div.	Div. Cyclist Coy.
WUMA	FOLO	42nd Div.	
JENU	A/Q	38th Div.	

/ 3rd / AAA

JEZU Order No. 223 AAA General line reached by our Troops is Eastern edge VAUX WOODS to Railway West of YTRES AAA Probable enemy line of resistance is CANAL de L'ESCAUT to BANTEUX and HINDENBURG LINE AAA Corps will continue the advance tomorrow to the general line W.22.Central - Q.32.d. AAA JEZU will remain in Corps Reserve AAA BUMA Group will move to area about O.20 and O.21. tomorrow 4th inst. so as to clear LE TRANSLOY by 10 a.m. AAA BUMA will establish observation posts in the Trench System East of ROCQUIGNY as soon as vacated by 17th Div and will be prepared to hold this line between O.35 c.O.O. and O.16.c.O.O. in case of necessity AAA Following distances will be maintained on line of march AAA 200 yds between Coys. and 500 yds between Battns. AAA BUMA will notify JEZU position of new H.Q. as soon as possible tomorrow AAA RUVE and BURA will probably not move but BURA will be ready to move at one hour's notice AAA Div.Cav. and Div. Cyclists will remain in present positions ready to move at one hour's notice AAA 'Q' will issue orders for move of BUMAS Transport AAA Acknowledge AAA Addsd. recipients JEZU Order No.222.

JEZU

10.25 p.m.

HHMacdougall. Major
Lt.-Col. G.S.
for.

File.

TELEGRAM.

PRIORITY.	Words. Sent At..............m. By................ To................	

BUMA	RORU	5th Corps.
BURA	JEKU	5th Corps R.A.
RUVE	JEMU	17 Div.
WUMA	FOLO	38 Div.
JENU	A/Q.	15 Sqn. R.A.F.

/ 4 / AAA

JEZU Order No. 224. AAA 38th Div. and 17th Div. are reported at 7 p.m. to have troops across CANAL DU NORD but not yet across EQUANCOURT Trench System AAA JEZU will relieve 38th Div. tomorrow Sept. 5th AAA BUMA Group will relieve advanced guard Brigade Group 38th Div. AAA BURA will relieve supporting Brigade and RUVE reserve Brigade AAA BUMA will keep in touch with situation of leading Brigade TOMORROW AAA If advance during Sept. 5th is carried across NURLU - FINS Road BUMA will move to vicinity of CANAL DU NORD during afternoon AAA BURA Group will move tomorrow morning to reach West of SAILLY SAILLISEL by 1 p.m. and have dinners there AAA Any orders for BURA will be sent to BUMA H.Q. O.31.b.3.3. after 11 a.m. AAA RUVE Group will be prepared to move at one hour's notice after 9 a.m. AAA Distances for Infantry on march 500 yards between Battns. and 200 yds. between Coys AAA Div. Cav. and Cyclists and two Sections GILE have been ordered to report BUMAS H.Q. tomorrow morning and will come under BUMAS Orders AAA 21 Div. Arty. reverts to JEZU AAA Orders for move of Units not mentioned above will be issued later AAA Div. H.Q. closes LE SARS 2.30 p.m. and opens LES BOEUFS same hour AAA ACKNOWLEDGE AAA Addsd. all concerned.

JEZU

7.45 p.m.

[illegible signature]

Lt.-Col. G.S.

File.

TELEGRAM.

URGENT OPERATIONS PRIORITY 64th and 110 Bdes. HH	Words. Sent. At.............. To.............. By..............	

BUMA 'Q'
BURA 38th Div.
RUVE vth Corps.

GX. 822. / 5th / AAA

Ref. JEZU Order No. 224 AAA BURA Group will relieve 113 and 115 Brigades in Trench System U.5. U.11. U.17.a. and U.10. this afternoon. AAA Both these Brigades are very weak AAA Exact positions occupied by 38th Div. need not be taken up AAA Woods and Valleys are full of gas and will be avoided AAA BURA H.Q. will be established at 113 Bde. H.Q. U.8.a.5.5. from 3 p.m. AAA Leading troops BURA will cross main LE TRANSLOY - SAILLY SAILLISEL Road at 3.30 p.m. AAA Movement by Platoons. AAA BURA will wire exact position of Battns. on completion of relief AAA Dispositions of 113 and 115 Brigades by wire for BURA only AAA RUVE will move to area W. of SAILLY SAILLISEL AAA Starting point LE TRANSLOY SUGAR FACTORY at 4.30 p.m. AAA RUVE H.Q. will be established at 115 Bde. H.Q. U.14.a.0.4. from 5 p.m. AAA Added BUMA BURA RUVE reptd to 'Q' 38th Div 5th Corps.

JEZU

12.40 p.m.

H Craufurd(?)

Lt. Col.G.S.

File

TELEGRAM

URGENT
OPERATION
PRIORITY
TO 62nd
BRIGADES
Priority
remain-
der. HLG.

Words

Sent
At.................m
To.................
By.................

BUMA	RORU	5th Corps.	15th Sqn R.A.F.
BURA	JEKU	5th Corps R.A.	
RUVE	~~JENU~~ JEMU	12th Div.	
WUMA	FOLO	17th Div.	
JENU	A/Q	38th Div.	

/ 5th / AAA

JEZU Order No. 225 AAA Situation remains as already issued to Brigades AAA BUMA will carry out active patrolling during tonight and tomorrow AAA If resistance of enemy opposite Div. front shows signs of slackening BUMA will push forward advanced guard and prepare to follow with remainder of Bde AAA Advance will continue until objective W.22.c.0.4. - REVELON - W.10.Central is reached when orders for fresh advance will be issued from Div. H.Q. AAA BUMA will NOT engage in serious attack unless fresh instructions are issued AAA Successive Bde. Report Centres will be established by Div. Signals whenever further advance is made at Cross Roads V.14.b. AAA Cross Roads V.18.c. AAA HEUDECOURT SQUARE AAA Sunken Road W.18.c.8.2. AAA BURA will be prepared to hold line St.MARTINS WOOD - LE MESNIL-EN-ARROAISE but as counter-attack by enemy across CANAL DU NORD is unlikely efforts will be concentrated on keeping troops fresh AAA RUVE will remain as at present AAA BURA and RUVE will not advance without orders from Div. H.Q. AAA 21st Div. Arty. takes over from 38th Div. Arty. tonight AAA 62nd Div. Arty. remains covering Sector AAA ACKNOWLEDGE AAA Addsd. all concerned.

JEZU

6.50 p.m.

H L Tracklyn.

Lt. Col. G.S.

✓ File.

TELEGRAM

URGENT
OPERATIONS
PRIORITY

62nd Bde
HGF.

Words
Sent At..................m To................... By...................

BUMA	RORU	5th Corps.	15th Sqn. R.A.F.
BURA	JEKU	5th Corps R.A.	
OVE	JEMU	12th Div.	
WUMA	FOLO	17th Div.	
JENU	A/Q	38th Div.	

/ 6th / AAA

21 Div. Order 226 AAA Situation at 7.30 p.m. AAA 12 Div. hold V.29. with troops in Cutting V.30. AAA 17th Div. are reported to hold trench P. 36.b and d. and V.6. b and d. AAA 62nd Bde. hold NURLU - FINS Road in V.23 and V.17. with advanced troops in SOREL-LE-GRAND AA Position about FINS uncertain AAA 62nd Brigade group will continue advance tomorrow AAA Main guard will move forward at 6 a.m. AAA 1st Objective Old BROWN Line W.22.c. W.16.Central W.10.a.0.0. W.9.a.8.9. AAA 2nd Objective Northern end of PEIZIERE -VAUCELLETTE FARM - CHAPEL CROSSING AAA 64th Brigade Group will move forward by stages already ordered until EQUANCOURT trench system is occupied when further orders will be issued AAA 110th Brigade group will remain in present position AAA Next bound when ordered will be to area just East of CANAL DU NORD AAA Reserve M.G. Coy. will assemble V.20 a and b. by 8 a.m. tomorrow and will maintain Officer at report centre V.14.b.8.3. AAA Div. H.Q. will move to U.5.c.3.2. at an hour to be notified later. AAA ACKNOWLEDGE AAA Added recipients Order No. 225.

JEZU

8 p.m.

H.L. Franklyn

Lt. Col. G.S.

File.

TELEGRAM.

Urgent Operations Priority to 64th Bde ~~and M.G.Bn.~~ [initials]	Words Sent At..............m To............... By...............	

BUMA WUMA FOLO.
BURA RORU
RUVE 'Q'

GX. 894 / 7th / AAA

Reference 21 Div Order No. 226 AAA When BUMA has occupied whole of 1st Objective BURA will move one Battn. to occupy SOREL LE GRAND AAA When BUMAS Reserve BN. moves forward from 1st objective BURA will move one Battn to about W.8.Central and another to about W.20.a and c. maintaining one Battn. in SOREL AAA When BUMA reports whole of 2nd objective captured BURA will dispose Brigade so as to be able to occupy 1st objective in case of need or to take up advance tomorrow AAA RUVE will probably move to ground E. of CANAL DU NORD this evening so all preparations should be made AAA Reserve M.G. Coy. will move via EQUANCOURT to about V.17.d. forthwith AAA This Coy. will move in future when leading Brigade H.Q. moves and will maintain liaison Officer with latter AAA Acknowledge.

JEZU

9.45 a.m.

H.Kaulback[?]
Lt. Col G.S.

War Diary

App. 8

TELEGRAM.

URGENT OPERATIONS PRIORITY to 62nd Bde 64th " H.Q.	Words .... Sent At.................m To................ By................	

BUMA	RORU	5th Corps.	15th Sqn R.A.F.
BURA	JEKU	5th Corps R.A.	
RUVE	JEMU	12th Div.	
WUMA	FOLO	17th Div.	
JENU	A/Q	38th Div.	

/ 7th / AAA

JEZU Order No. 227. Reports tend to show that enemy is holding line Q.35. - W.5. - W.11. - CHAPEL HILL - VAUCELLETTE FARM - PEIZIERE in some strength AAA Third Corps hold SAULCOURT - GUYENCOURT - W.28.Central AAA 17th Div. hold trench line W.3. Q.32. AAA 62nd Bde. hold general line of BROWN Line W.22.c. W.9.b. AAA 62nd Bde. will send forward advanced guards at 6 a.m. tomorrow to try and make good second objective AAA If enemy's resistance has slackened advanced guards will be supported AAA No serious attack will be undertaken without reference to Div. H.Q. AAA Brigadier 62nd Bde. will support his advanced guards with 94 and 95 Bdes R.A. which are placed under his orders AAA M.Gs. will be freely used firing from the high ground on each flank AAA Reserve M.G. Coy. will be used by 62nd Bde. for this purpose AAA Arty and M.Gs. will be very freely used for harassing AAA 64th and 110th Bdes. will remain as at present AAA 64th Bde. will carry out necessary reconnaissances with a view to relieving 62nd Bde. tomorrow night AAA 110th Bde. will reconnoitre EQUANCOURT trench system with a view to future occupation AAA ACKNOWLEDGE AAA Addsd recipients JEZU Order No. 226.

JEZU

8 p.m.

H L Franklyn

Lt.Col. G.S.

War Diary.

TELEGRAM

URGENT OPERATIONS PRIORITY TO 62nd and 64th Bdes. 110 "	Words. Sent At............... To............... By...............	app 9

BUMA	RORU	5th Corps.	15th Sqn R.A.F.
BURA	JEKU	5th Corps R.A.	
RUVE	JEMU	17th Div.	
WUMA	FOLO	38th Div.	
JENU	A/Q	58th Div.	

/ 8th / AAA

21st Div. Order No. 228. AAA 58th Div. hold YELLOW Line E.5.b. & d. W.29.b & d. AAA 17 Div hold trench line W.3. Q.32 with outposts in front AAA 62 Bde. Held YELLOW Line W.24.c. Knoll at W.23.Central REVELON Farm with patrol in GENIN WELL COPSE No.2. AAA 64 Bde. will attack tomorrow at 4 a.m. in conjunction with 17 Div on their left AAA 58 Div will not be attacking tomorrow but will keep PEIZIERE under heavy bombardment from 4 a.m. to 4.15 a.m. and from 5.15 a.m. to 6 a.m. AAA Objectives for 64 Bde. are CHAPEL HILL and high ground in W.11.d. AAA 17 Div are attacking HEATHER SUPPORT and HEATHER TRENCH as far South as W.5.c.7.1. and W.5.d.1.2. respectively AAA After capture of objectives 17 Div. will work down these two trenches to obtain touch with 64 Bde. on Div. Boundary AAA Barrage for CHAPEL HILL attack opens at Zero on line W.18.b.0.1. W.18.a.2.9. lifts at Zero plus 15 and moves at 100 yards in 4 minutes to line W.18.b.7.8. W.12.c.9.5. then jumps to Rly. X.13.a.8.6. X.7.a.0.2. for 6 minutes and bursts of fire until Zero plus 60. AAA Barrage for W.11.d. attack opens on line W.18.a.2.8. W.17.a. 7.8. lifts at Zero plus 15 mins. and moves at rate of 100 yds. in 4 minutes until line W.12.c.2.4. W.11.a.7.4. is reached and then stops AAA Other artillery arrangements in Arty. Orders AAA Reserve M.G.Coy. is transferred from 62 to 64 Bde and will be used for barrage work and harassing fire AAA After capture of CHAPEL HILL 64 Bde will push patrols towards VAUCELLETTE FARM which will be occupied in absence of resistance AAA 110 Bde. will have 2 Battns. in vicinity of and ready to occupy EQUANCOURT Trench System by 6 a.m. tomorrow AAA Remaining Battn. will move to neighbourhood of SOREL LE GRAND AAA 62 Bde. will be withdrawn gradually under orders from Div.H Q. to MANANCOURT and ETRICOURT and ground just East of CANAL AAA Acknowledge. AAA Added. all concerned.

JEZU

10.10 p.m.

H. Gaechlyn

Lt. Col. G.S.

War Diary

App 10

TELEGRAM

URGENT OPERATIONS PRIORITY TO BDES.	Words Sent At..............m To.............. By..............	

BUMA	RORU	5th Corps.	15th Sqn R.A.F.
BURA	JEKU	5th Corps R.A.	
RUVE	JEMU	17th Div	
WUMA	FOLO	38th Div.	
JENU	A/Q	58th Div.	

/ 9th / AAA

21st Div. Order No. 229 AAA 58th Div. hold YELLOW LINE up to W.23.d.8.0. AAA 17 Div hold HEATHER SUPPORT from W.11.a.5.0. northwards AAA 64 Bde. holds trench from W.18.b.0.3. along LOWLAND SUPPORT to junction with 17 Div.AAA Following attacks will take place tomorrow AAA 64 Bde will unless attack delivered at 5.30 p.m. succeeded attack in conjunction with 17 Div at 4 a.m. AAA Objective of 17 Div. LOWLAND AND HEATHER TRENCHES AAA Objective of 64 Bde. CHAPEL HILL thence along CAVALRY TRENCH and LOWLAND TRENCH to junction with 17 Div. at W.12.a.0.0. AAA 58 Div. will attack EPEHY and PEIZIERE at 5.15 a.m. AAA At same hour 64 Bde. and 110 Bde. will advance under a creeping barrage and occupy YELLOW LINE AAA 64 Bde. from CHAPEL HILL to RAILTON - VAUCELLETTE FARM Road exclusive. AAA 110 Bde. from this Road inclusive to Southern Div. boundary where touch must be obtained with 58 Div. AAA When PEIZIERE is reported captured by 58 Div 110 Bde. will detail parties to work along RAILTON - PEIZIERE Rly. occupying "T" heads and join up with 58 Div. at Bridge W.30.a.9.7. AAA At 5.45 a.m. barrage will come down on line W.18.d.4.7. X.13.a.0.3. and will creep South-Eastwards until clear of VAUCELLETTE FARM AAA 64 Bde. will detail patrols to follow barrage down CAVALRY TRENCH and CAVALRY SUPPORT AAA Progress down these trenches will be made good by blocks AAA If and when VAUCELLETTE FARM is entered 64 Bde. will send garrison to occupy it AAA M.Gs. and Stokes Mortars will be freely used to assist consolidation of final objectives and help to resist counter-attacks AAA All above barrages will move at rate of 100 yds in 4 minutes AAA Details of lifts and of Heavy Arty. support will appear in Arty. orders AAA 64 Bde will arrange M.G. barrages for attack Reserve M.G.Coy being placed at their disposal AAA 110 Bde. will relieve 62 Bde. in BROWN LINE and at Knoll W.23.Central tonight under arrangements between Brigadiers AAA 110 Bde. will be prepared to occupy REVELON FARM and No.1. Copse if vacated by forward move of troops of 64 Bde AAA On relief 62 Bde to MANANCOURT - ETRICOURT Area AAA ACKNOWLEDGE AAA Addsd recipients Order 228.

JEZU

8 p.m.

H. Lauchlan [signature]

Lt.Col.G.S.

War Diary

TELEGRAM

Urgent operations priority to 64 & 110 Bdes

HWF

Words	
Sent	
At.............m	App 11
To.............	
By.............	

BUMA RORU 5th Corps 15th Sqn R.A.F.
BURA JEKU 5th Corps R.A.
RUVE JEMU 17th Div.
WUMA FOLO 38th Div.
JENU A/Q 58th Div.

/ 10th / AAA

21 Div

Order No. 230. AAA 58th Div. are reported to hold TOTTENHAM POST and WOOD FARM otherwise position of flank Divs. remains unchanged AAA 64 Bde. line is as given in Order No. 229 of yesterday AAA 110 Bde will advance under a barrage and make good the whole of the YELLOW LINE within the Div. Sector tonight affecting junction with 58 Div on Southern Boundary AAA Barrage will come down on line W.23.d.5.4. to W.17.d.6.6. will lift at Zero plus 10 minutes and advance at rate of 100 yards in five minutes until line W.24.d.5.4. to W.18.d.6.6. is reached and remain stationary here for 10 minutes and then cease AAA Other artillery arrangements in artillery orders AAA 110 Bde will use Reserve M.G. Coy. for barrage and this Coy. will now come under their orders AAA 110 Bde. will relieve 64 Bde. in line tonight AAA After relief 64 Bde. will be accommodated in and about EQUANCOURT Trench System with one Battn. near SOREL AAA Letter on policy for immediate future follows AAA Acknowledge AAA Added recipients JEZU Order 229.

JEZU

7.30 p.m.

H L Gamblyn

Lt.Col. G.S.

War Diary

TELEGRAM

URGENT OPERATIONS PRIORITY TO 64 and 110 BDES	Words Sent. At..................m To.................. By..................	App 12

BUMA RORU 5th Corps 15th Sqn R.A.F.
BURA JEKU 5th Corps R.A.
ZUVE JEMU 17th Div.
WUMA FOLO 38th Div.
JENU A/Q 58th Div.

G.X. 963. / 10th / AAA

Warning Order AAA Attack on CHAPEL HILL did not succeed this morning AAA 110 Bde. will relieve 64 Bde tonight AAA 110 Bde. will also be prepared to advance under a barrage and occupy the YELLOW LINE from CHAPEL HILL to Southern Div. Boundary AAA On relief 64 Bde. will move to EQUANCOURT Trench System with one Battn about SOREL LE GRAND AAA ACKNOWLEDGE AAA Added recipients JEZU Order No. 229.

JEZU

11.20 p.m.

A.H. Macdougall. Major.
for
Lt. Col. G.S.

TELEGRAM.

URGENT
OPERATIONS
PRIORITY to
110th and
19th Inf.Bdes.

Words.

Sent.
At.....................m
To.....................
By.....................

App B

DADE	JESO	V Corps H.A.
BASU	ZOHO	17th Div.
VUFE	ZODU	33rd Div.
LODE	A/Q.	38th Div.
ZOKI	A.P.M.	15th Sqn. R.A.F.
ZUFA	V Corps.	19th Inf. Bde.
ZEJU	V Corps R.A.	58th Div.

15 K

ZOWU Order No.231 AAA VUFE (110 Bde) will be relieved by HASA (19 Bde) in the line tonight 15th/16th instant under arrangements to be made between Brigadiers concerned AAA On relief VUFE will take over accommodation vacated by HASA AAA Coys. of ZEJU will not be relieved AAA 2 Sections SULU at present attached to VUFE will revert to ZOKI at 8 p.m. today AAA No movement will take place before dark AAA Completion of relief will be reported to these Headquarters AAA Command of Sector passes to GOQE on completion of relief AAA Ack AAA Adsd all concerned

ZOWU

4 p.m.

[signature] Capt.
for Lt. Col. G.S.

TELEGRAM.

URGENT
OPERATIONS
PRIORITY TO
62nd Bde. D.M.G.C.
33rd Div.17th.Div.

HHM Major for Lt Col

Words.

Sent.
At.............m
To.............
By.............

app 14

DADE	JESO	
BASU	ZOHO	Vth Corps H.A.
VUFE	ZODU	17th Div.
LODE	A/Q	33rd Div.
ZOKI	A.P.M.	38th Div.
DUFA	5th Corps.	15th Sqn R.A.F.
ZEJU	5th Corps R.A.	19th Inf. Bde.
		58th Div.

/v 16th / AAA

21st Div. Order No. 232 AAA 62nd Bde. will relieve the right half of 19th Bde. 33rd Div. in the line on the night 16/17 inst under arrangements to be made by Brigadiers AAA 19th T.M.Bty. will remain in line under 62 Bde. AAA On completion of relief Northern Div. Boundary will be W.18.Central - V.17.Central - V.11.a.1.0. - thence West along railway AAA O.C. 21 M.G.Bn. will arrange direct with O.C. 17 M.G.Bn. for relief of M.Gs. North of new boundary AAA 64 Bde. will clear all troops from the trenches and EQUANCOURT village North of the Railway by 6 p.m. 16 inst AAA Completion of reliefs will be reported to Div.H.Q. AAA Acknowledge AAA Added. recipients Div. order No.231.

ZOWU

HHMacdougall. Major
for
Lt.Co. G.S.

APP 15

22

SECRET. Copy No..........

21st DIVISION ORDER No.233.

Ref. Map.Sheet 57.c.S.E.
1/20,000. 16th September 1918.

1. The enemy is holding the general line CHAPEL HILL, VAUCELLETTE FARM, PEIZIERE, EPEHY, in considerable strength but, it is believed, in little depth.

2. (a) The Vth Corps is attacking on a date which has been comminicated to those concerned and at a Zero hour which will be notified later, in conjunction with the Fourth Army and other Armies to the South.

(b) The 58th Division (173rd Brigade on left) will be attacking on our right during first phase of operations, i.e., up to and including capture of POPLAR TRENCH. The 12th Division (37th Infantry Brigade on left) will be attacking on our right from POPLAR TRENCH to the RED LINE and to the exploitation line (marked blue on map).

(c) The 17th Division will be attacking on our left and will include FIVES TRENCH in their objective.

3. (a) The 21st Division will capture successively the BROWN, GREEN and RED lines (see Map).

(b) The 62nd Infantry Brigade will capture the BROWN and GREEN lines.

(c) The 110th Infantry Brigade on the right and the 64th Infantry Brigade on the left will capture the BROWN line. RED

(d) The 110th Infantry Brigade will exploit, with previously detailed Companies, up to the BLUE line, to protect the left flank of the 12th Division, under arrangements to be made between the B.G.C. 110th Infantry Brigade and the B.G.C. 37th Infantry Brigade.

(e) The 64th Infantry Brigade will exploit up to the BLACK line (One or more Coys. being definitely detailed for this purpose), with the idea of rounding up prisoners and capturing material. When this has been done, Units detailed for exploitation will return to the RED line.

(f) Immediately after the 110th Infantry Brigade has passed through the 62nd Infantry Brigade, this latter Brigade will collect one Battalion into Divisional Reserve in the neighbourhood of LINNET VALLEY.

(g) There will be a pause of 18 minutes on the BROWN line and of 15 minutes on line of road running from POPLAR TRENCH to TARGELLE TRENCH and thence by BEET FACTORY (see Barrage Map). The length of pause on the GREEN line will be notified later.

/4.........

4. Liaison posts will be established with neighbouring Units as follows :-

(a) Between 62nd Infantry Brigade and 173rd Infantry Brigade at X.20.c.2.0.

(b) Between 62nd Infantry Brigade and 17th Division at S.E. Corner of BIRCH TREE COPSE X.13.b.3.1.

(c) Between 110th Infantry Brigade and 37th Infantry Brigade at X.22.c.4.3. and X.23.c.5.5.

(d) Between 64th Infantry Brigade and 17th Division at junction of BEET TRENCH and CHAPEL STREET.

(e) Between 110th Infantry Brigade and 64th Infantry Brigade at junction of MEUNIER TRENCH and LEITH WALK.

These Liaison posts will be joint posts and will consist of one Platoon found by each Unit concerned.

5. Five Brigades of Field Artillery will support the attack of the 21st Division, in addition to Heavy Artillery, of these, three Brigades will support the attack of the 62nd Infantry Brigade and all five Brigades of the 110th and 64th Infantry Brigades.

Barrage tables will be issued separately.

Other Artillery arrangements will appear in Artillery Orders.

6. The attack of the 62nd Infantry Brigade will be supported by a barrage fired by :-

Three Coys. of 21st Battalion Machine Gun Corps.

Two " 33rd. " " " "

The attack of the 110th Infantry Brigade will be supported by a barrage of One Machine Gun Company and of the 64th Infantry Brigade by the barrage of 8 Machine Guns.

Each Infantry Brigade will have one Machine Gun Company to cover its advance by direct fire and to assist in consolidation.

Orders for the above will be issued to all concerned by O.C., 21st Battalion Machine Gun Corps.

7. (a) 8 Stokes Mortars of the 19th Brigade are placed at the disposal of the 62nd Infantry Brigade for a hurricane bombardment at Zero.

(b) One Supply Tank is allotted to 110th Infantry Brigade and one Supply Tank to 64th Infantry Brigade. These tanks will be used in the first instance for carrying forward Stokes Mortars and ammunition for use in the RED line.

/8......

8. The O.C. 15th Squadron R.A.F. will be arranging for a contact aeroplane to call for flares as early as possible after daylight and subsequently at odd hours (i.e., 7 a.m., 9.am, 11 a.m., etc.)

RED flares will be used.

Flares will be lit by the foremost troops at the above hours or at any other hour, when called for by the contact aeroplane, sounding a Klaxon Horn.

The aeroplane signal to denote the assembly of enemy to counter-attack is the dropping of a Red Smoke Bomb over the place where the enemy is seen.

9. Headquarters will be established as follows :-

(a) Divisional Headquarters ..LE MESNIL en ARROUAISE.

(b) 62nd Infantry Brigade Headquarters .. W.21.c.0.0.

(c) 110th Infantry Brigade H.Q. in first instance at W.21.c.0.0. and subsequently at W.18.d.0.2.

(d) 64th Infantry Brigade Headquarters in first instance at Railway Cutting W.23.b. and subsequently at W.18.c.7.5.

10. Watches will be synchronized by an Officer from Divisional Headquarters between 7 p.m. and 8 p.m. on Z. minus 1 day.

11. Acknowledge.

Lieut.Colonel.
General Staff.
21st Division.

Issued through Signals at

	Copy No.		Copy No.
62nd Inf. Bde.	1	A.P.M.	12
64th : :	2	Vth Corps.	13-14.
110th : :	3	Vth Corps R.A.	15
C.R.A.	4	Vth Corps H.A.	16
C.R.E.	5.	12th Div.	17
Pioneers.	6	17th Div.	18
D.M.G.C.	7	33rd Div.	19
Signals.	8	58th Div.	20
A.D.M.S.	9	15th Sqn R.A.F.	21
Train.	10.	War Diary	22
A/Q	11.	File	23

APPENDIX A.

ASSEMBLY ARRANGEMENTS.

1. The 62nd Infantry Brigade will take over from 19th Infantry Brigade on the night 16th/17th September.

On relief 19th Infantry Brigade will withdraw to the MANANCOURT - ETRICOURT Area.

2. (a) On the Y/Z night, the 62nd Infantry Brigade will close up into assembly positions on the YELLOW line.

(b) The 110th and 64th Infantry Brigades will assemble immediately in rear of the 62nd Infantry Brigade.

(c) The B.G.C., 62nd Infantry Brigade will inform the B.Gs.C. 110th and 64th Infantry Brigades of the positions to be taken up by his rearmost troops.

3. The 110th Infantry Brigade will move to assembly positions by the cross-country tracks A1, A2. A3.

The 64th Infantry Brigade will move by cross-country tracks B1, B2. B3.

These tracks must be reconnoitred previously by at least one Officer from Each Coy. Maps showing how the tracks run will be supplied by the C.R.E.

The 110th and 64th Infantry Brigades will not cross the NURLU-FINS road before 8 p.m.

No other troops will be allowed to use these tracks on Y/Z night.

4. The assembly of all Brigades must be completed by 5 a.m. on Z day and the fact reported to Divisional Headquarters by wiring the Code Word "SMITH".

Appendix "B" to 21st Division Order No. 233.

ARTILLERY ARRANGEMENTS.

1. Artillery Support.
The 94th, 72nd and 315th Brigades will be grouped under Lieutenant-Colonel Boyd for the immediate support of the 62nd and 110th Infantry Brigades.
The 95th and 2nd New Zealand Brigades will be grouped under Lieutenant-Colonel Phillips for the immediate support of the 64th Infantry Brigade.

2. Liaison.
During the first part of the operations, Lieutenant-Colonel Boyd will be with G.Os.C. 62nd and 110th Infantry Brigades at Brickyard W.21.c.1.2. If the G.O.C., 110th Infantry Brigade goes forward, he will send an Officer and two Signallers with him.
Lieutenant-Colonel Phillips will be with G.O.C. 64th Infantry Brigade at W.28.b.1.9. If the G.O.C., 64th Infantry Brigade goes forward, he will send an Officer and two Signallers with him.

3. Communications.
21st Division Signals will be responsible for communications from Brickyard, W.21.c.1.2 and from W.28.b.1.9 back to Divisional Artillery Headquarters. If Brigadiers move forward, they will be responsible for communications from their Liaison Officers back to the Artillery Brigade Commanders at these points.
Artillery Brigades are laying separate Artillery lines forward from these points to the Infantry forward report centres.

4. Information.
Two Artillery Officers with Signallers are being sent forward with the 110th Infantry Brigade attack and two with the 64th Infantry Brigade attack. They will be given a "roving commission" and will send back all information by the Artillery wires from the Infantry forward report centres. Visual signalling will also be arranged.

5. Barrages.
Copies of the barrage map have been issued to all concerned. The lines show the lifts of the 18-pdr. shrapnel barrage.
For the 62nd Infantry Brigade attack, all the 18-pdrs. will fire shrapnel on these lines.
For the 64th and 110th Infantry Brigade attacks, 2/3rds of the 18-pdrs. will fire shrapnel on these lines, and 1/3rd of the 18-pdrs. will fire H.E. 100 yards beyond.
All 18-pdr. barrages will include 10% of smoke.
4.5" Howitzers will be employed on smoke barrages and with H.E. on strong points and sunken roads 300 yards in front of 18-pdr. shrapnel barrage.
6" Howitzers and 60-pdrs. will be employed on counter-battery work, and on strong points 500 yards in front of 18-pdr. shrapnel barrage.
The 18-pdr. shrapnel barrage will be at the rate of 3 rounds per gun per minute while the Infantry are advancing - 1 per minute during protection barrages, quickening up to 4 per minute for 2 minutes before the next advance begins, as a signal to the Infantry to get up close under the barrage.

6. Exploitation.
Barrages for exploitation will be arranged by Brigadiers direct with their affiliated Artillery Brigade Commander.

7. Artillery Orders.
Detailed Artillery Orders have been issued to all concerned.

Appendix "C" to 21st Division Order No. 233.

CONSOLIDATION OF OBJECTIVES AND WORK OF R.E. & PIONEERS.

1. Both the Red and Green Lines, after capture, will be consolidated in depth.

Existing trenches will normally be avoided; Platoon posts will be dug well in front of the Red and Green Lines and these can eventually be joined up to form an outpost line; supporting troops and local reserves will dig themselves in in rear of the trenches forming the objectives.

2. A line of Strong Points will be constructed as follows :-

X.21.c.1.1.	X.14.b.2.2.
X.21.c.1.9.	X.14.a.5.5.
X.21.a.1.6.	X.8.c.7.1.
X.15.c.1.2.	X.8.c.2.3.
X.14.d.7.7.	X.7.d.7.2.

Simultaneously with the construction of the Strong Points, a continuous belt of wire, to cover them, will be begun.

This work will be carried out by two Field Coys. R.E. and two Companies, 14th Bn. Northumberland Fusiliers (Pioneers) immediately after dark on 'Z' day.

All the necessary R.E. reconnaissance and the bringing up of the required material will be carried out by daylight.

The works in the 110th Infantry Brigade area will be carried out under the supervision of the O.C. 98th Field Coy. R.E. and of those in the 64th Infantry Brigade area under the O.C. 97th Field Coy. R.E.

These Officers will keep the two Brigadiers concerned acquainted with the progress of the work.

The posts will be taken over as soon as sufficiently complete by Infantry Garrisons.

4. One Company Pioneers will be detailed to put the RAILTON - PEIZIERE and the RAILTON - VAUCELLETTE FARM Roads into a state of repair.

Appendix "D" to 21st Division Order No.233.

I N T E L L I G E N C E.

The Divisional Intelligence Officer will be at the Divisional P. of W. Cage, V.18.c.1.9 to interrogate prisoners.

He will be in direct communication with Divisional Headquarters by telephone.

All maps, papers, documents and soldbucher (paybooks) will be collected by Brigades from enemy dead, and forwarded to the Divisional Intelligence Officer at the P. of W. Cage.

Identity discs will be left on the dead.

Papers will not be collected from prisoners.

All documents found in dug-outs will be forwarded to the Divisional Intelligence Officer.

Brigades will wire (priority) to Divisional Headquarters the Regiments and Divisions to which the first batch of prisoners belong, and will subsequently wire any new identifications.

Two Military Mounted Police will be attached to each Brigade Headquarters to escort prisoners from Brigade Headquarters to the Divisional P. of W. Cage.

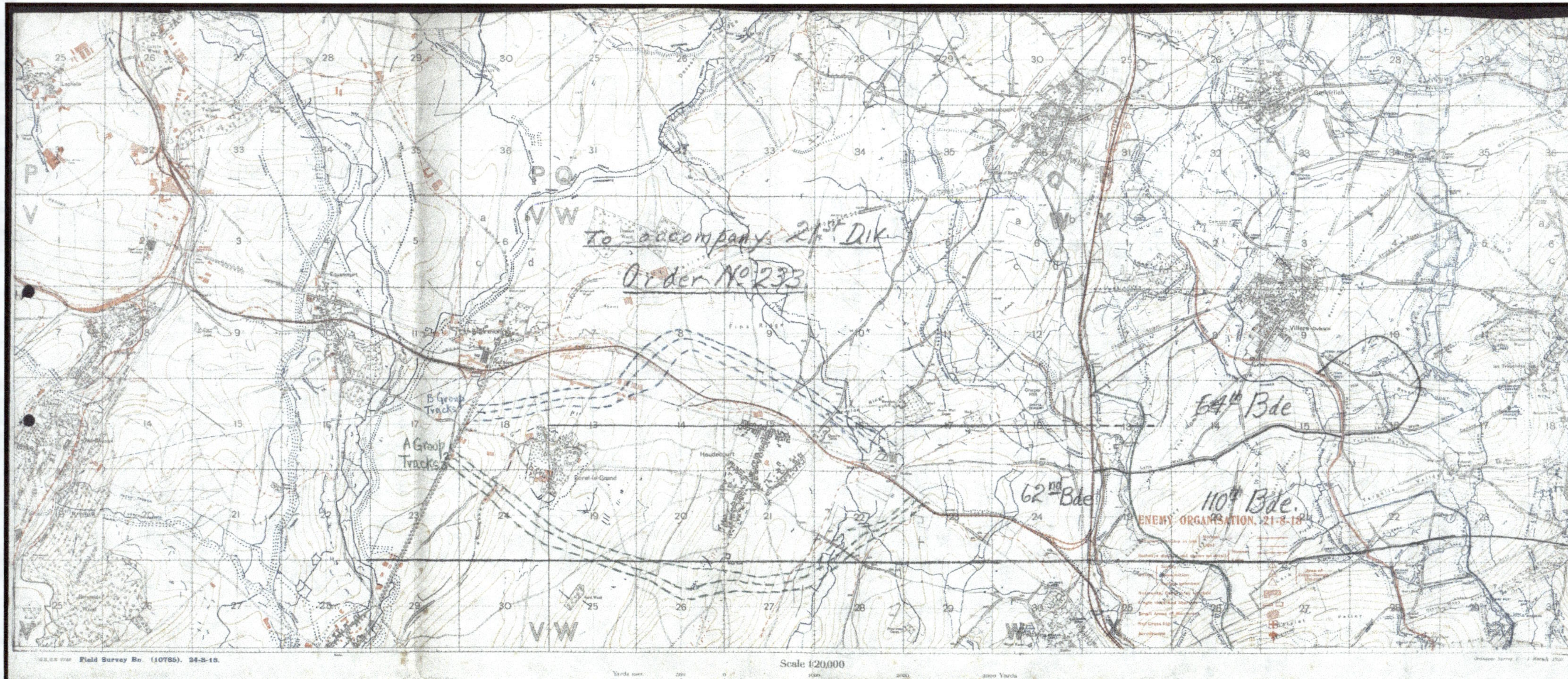
To accompany 21st Div
Order No 233
64th Bde
110th Bde.
62nd Bde
B Group Tracks
A Group Tracks
ENEMY ORGANISATION. 21-8-18
Villers-Guislain
Fins Ridge
Heudecourt
Sorel-le-Grand
Field Survey Bn. (10765). 24-8-18.
Scale 1:20,000

SECRET.

Copy No.......

22

21st Division Order No.237.

Ref: Map 57.C. S.E. 1/20,000.

26th September, 1918.

1. In conjunction with operations to the North, the 21st Division will :-

(a) Capture AFRICAN TRENCH from trench junction Q.35.a.6.5 to the Northern Divisional Boundary.

(b) Advance along QUENTIN RIDGE and capture GONNELIEU at the same time that the 33rd Division on the right attacks VILLERS GUISLAIN.

2. The date for attack (a) and the probable date for attack (b) have been communicated to all concerned. The Zero hour for each will be notified later.

3. (a) The attack on AFRICAN TRENCH will be carried out by one Battalion, 62nd Infantry Brigade supported by one Brigade R.F.A. and 12 - 6" Newton Mortars.

This attack will be made in conjunction with the 13th Infantry Brigade (5th Division) on the left.

(b) The ground for 300 yards East of AFRICAN TRENCH will be cleared of the enemy by specially detailed parties, after which these parties will return to the trench.

(c) Details of an indirect Machine Gun Barrage will be notified separately.

4. (a) The attack along QUENTIN RIDGE will be carried out by the 64th and 110th Infantry Brigades.

(b) One Battalion 64th Infantry Brigade on the right and the 110th Infantry Brigade on the left will capture successively the dotted Green and Red lines, after which two Battalions 64th Infantry Brigade will pass through the 110th Infantry Brigade and take GONNELIEU Village, connecting with the 5th Division who will be attacking FUSILIER and CEMETRY RIDGES from the N.W.

(c) The 64th Infantry Brigade will make good the Brown line as a final objective.

(d) The 110th Infantry Brigade will detail parties to "mop up" the Quarry in R.31.c. and the loop trench in R.31.b.

"Green Switch" and "QUENTIN ALLEY" will be held as a defensive flank against GOUZEAUCOURT, until this latter place has been captured.

GREEN LANE and GREEN SWITCH will also be held as a supporting line to the final objective.

/(e)......

(e) After the capture of VILLERS TRENCH the 64th Infantry Brigade, when they renew their advance, will arrange to leave a garrison in it connecting with the 33rd Division on the right and the 110th Infantry Brigade on the left.

5. After the capture of the Brown Line orders may be received for the exploitation of success to the Green Line. If GOUZEAUCOURT has been cleared and sufficient notice is received, this exploitation will be carried out by the 62nd Infantry Brigade; otherwise orders will be issued for one Battalion 110th Infantry Brigade on the right and one Battalion 64th Infantry Brigade on the left to undertake this operation.

6. The 62nd Infantry Brigade will keep constant touch with the enemy in GOUZEAUCOURT (particularly at Zero plus two hours) by means of patrols and will be prepared to reinforce these patrols and occupy the village if the enemy shows signs of evacuating it.

Liaison will be arranged by 62nd Infantry Brigade with the two Newton Mortar Batteries which will be bombarding GOUZEAUCOURT so that their fire can be stopped earlier than Zero plus two hours, if required. (see Para 9).

7. Liaison Posts will be established as follows :-

(a) Between 64th Infantry Brigade and 33rd Division at the Cemetery X.2.d.9.9 and on the Boundary in GLASS STREET.

(b) Between 64th Infantry Brigade and 5th Division at road junction R.27.a.9.1.

These Liaison Posts will be joint posts and will consist of one platoon found by each Unit concerned.

8. (a) Four Brigades R.F.A. will support the attack along QUENTIN RIDGE.

Barrage Tables will be issued separately.

(b) Heavy Artillery to support the attack will be :-

3 Batteries 6" Howitzers.
1 Battery 8" :
1 : 9.2" :
1 : 60 pdrs.

(c) The tasks of the Heavy Artillery will be to bombard the Red Line and GONNELIEU until the approach of the Infantry.

(d) When it becomes necessary to lift off GONNELIEU, all except 1 - 6" Howitzer Battery and the 60-pdr. Battery will be engaged on counter-battery work. The 6" Howitzer Battery will fire on BANTEUX SPUR and the 60-pdr. Battery on the area round TURNER CRATER (R.34.d.).

9. (a) 18 - 6" Newton Mortars will bombard GOUZEAUCOURT, particularly the Eastern outskirts from Zero till Zero plus two hours.

/(b)....

(b) 6 Newton Mortars will put down a hurricane bombardment on the trenches in R.31.d. from Zero to Zero plus 4 minutes and will then lift and join in the bombardment of GOUZEAUCOURT.

10. (a) 1½ Machine Gun Companies will cover the advance of the 64th and 110th Infantry Brigades by an indirect barrage.

(b) Two Machine Gun Companies will engage the area between the main Railway and GOUZEAUCOURT from Zero till Zero plus two hours.
One Machine Gun Company is allotted to 64th Infantry Brigade and one Company to 110th Infantry Brigade for consolidation purposes.

(c) Eight Machine Guns will remain with the 62nd Infantry Brigade.

11. Four Tanks will assist the advance along QUENTIN RIDGE and the capture of GONNELIEU. They will afterwards rally West of the Village and will be prepared to assist the troops detailed to make an immediate counter-attack against GONNELIEU, should this be necessary.

12. The O.C. 15th Squadron, R.A.F. will be arranging for contact aeroplanes to call for flares during daylight. The call for flares will be the sounding of a Klaxon Horn.
RED flares will be used.
Only the foremost troops will light flares when the aeroplane calls.
The aeroplane signal to denote the assembly of enemy to counter-attack is the dropping of a red smoke bomb over the place where the enemy is seen.

13. Watches will be synchronised by an Officer from Divisional Headquarters between 5 p.m. and 6 p.m. on the evening before each attack.

14. A C K N O W L E D G E.

H. H. Laughlyn

Lieut.Colonel,
General Staff,
21st Division.

Issued at 9am to :-

	Copy No.		Copy No.
62 Inf. Bde.	1	A.P.M.	12
64 : :	2	5th Div.	13
110 : :	3	17th Div.	14
C.R.A.	4	33rd Div.	15
C.R.E.	5	38th Div.	16
Pioneers.	6	V Corps.	17 - 18
D.M.G.C.	7	V Corps R.A.	19
Signals.	8	V Corps H.A.	20
A.D.M.S.	9	B Coy.Tanks.	21
Train.	10	War Diary.	22
A/Q.	11	File.	23
		15 Sqn RAF	24

S E C R E T.

21 Div.
G. 467.

All recipients of Divl. Order No.237.

The following amendments and addenda will be made to 21st Division Order No.237 :-

Para 5 will be amended to read :-

"As soon as the protective barrage lifts, previously detailed fighting patrols will advance with the object of capturing prisoners and feeling their way towards the Green Line. If these patrols do not meet with resistance, they will be supported and the Green Line made good, if possible.

If patrols meet resistance there is no question of attacking the Green Line, but a properly organised operation will be arranged by the Divisional Commander to take place at a later date. This operation will probably be carried out by the 62nd Infantry Brigade; in any case fresh orders for this operation will be issued."

Add new sub-para (c) to para 7 :-

"(c) Between 110th Infantry Brigade and 1st Devons (Right Battalion, 5th Division) at R.26.a.8.1 where reserve line crosses main road."

H L Knaublyn.

Lieut.Colonel,
General Staff,
21st Division.

26.9.18.

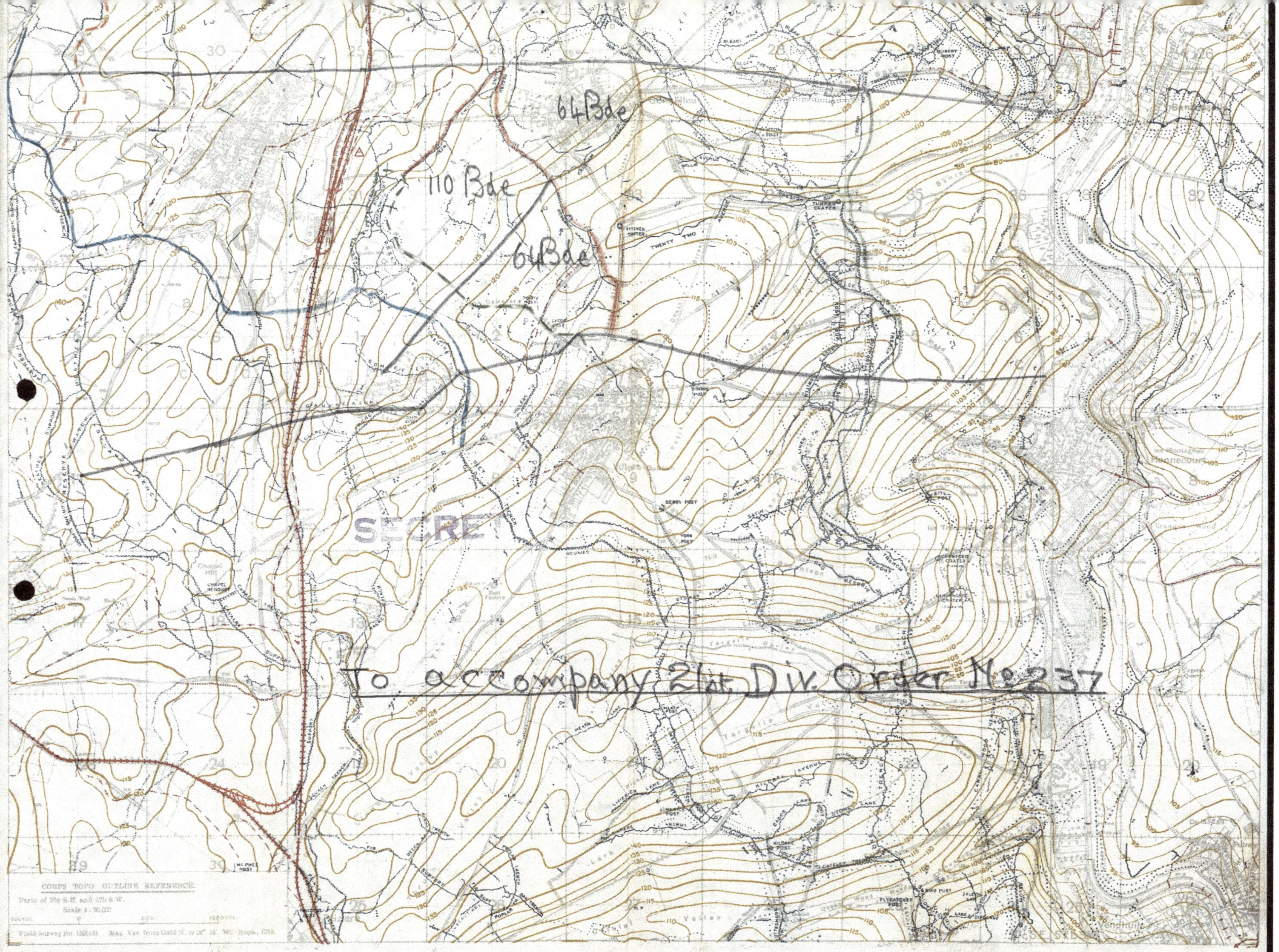
64 Bde
110 Bde
64 Bde
SECRET
To accompany 21st Div. Order No 237
CORPS TOPO OUTLINE REFERENCE
Scale 1:20,000

MESSAGE FORM.

TO.. No...........

1.—I am at..

NOTE.—Either give map reference or mark your position by a X on a map or trace.

2.—My Line runs..

3.—My Platoon/Company is at.................................... and is consolidating.

4.—My Platoon/Company is at.................................... and has consolidated.

5.—Am held up (*a*) by wire at ....

(*b*) at..............................by M.G. at ....

6.—Enemy holding strong point...

7.—I am in touch with..........................on Right/Left at..............................

8.—I am not in touch with......................on Right/Left at..............................

9.—Am in need of :...

....

10.—Counter attack forming at...

11.—I estimate my present strength at......................rifles.

12.—Add any other useful information here :—

Time..............m.

Date..............................1918.

Name..

Platoon..............................

Company..........................

Battalion ....

(a) Carry no maps or papers which may be of value to the enemy.
(b) Give no information if captured, except the following, which you are bound to give :— Name and Rank.
(c) Collect all captured maps and papers and send them in at once.

APPENDIX A

ASSEMBLY AND PRELIMINARY ARRANGEMENTS.

1. As early as possible after dark on Y/Z night :-

(a) The 62nd Infantry Brigade will relieve the 110th Infantry Brigade as far East as the Main Railway Line (inclusive).

(b) The 64th Infantry Brigade will relieve the Right Battalion of the 110th Infantry Brigade as far West as the inter-Brigade Boundary shown on the Map issued with Order No. 237.

2. The 110th Infantry Brigade will arrange to vacate LOWLAND and HEATHER TRENCHES and LOWLAND and HEATHER Support by 10.30 p.m. on Y/Z night,

3. The 64th Infantry Brigade will have no troops East of the Main Railway Line before Zero, except the Battalion detailed to capture the Green dotted and Red Lines.

4. The C.R.E. will mark out two tracks for the 64th Infantry Brigade leading from LOWLAND Trench East of QUENTIN REDOUBT.

Appendix 'B'.

ARTILLERY ARRANGEMENTS.

1. ARTILLERY SUPPORT.
The following Field Artillery Brigades will cover the advance along QUENTIN RIDGE :-

78th Bde.
79th :
121st :
122nd :

2. LIAISON.
(a) The 78th and 122nd Field Artillery Brigades will maintain a joint liaison Officer with the 64th Inf. Bde. H.Q.

(b) The 79th and 121st Field Artillery Brigades will maintain a joint liaison Officer with the 110th Inf. Bde. H.Q.

3. BARRAGES.
(a) The barrage up to and including the protective barrage beyond the Red Line will move at the rate of 100 yards in four minutes and subsequently (i.e. through GONNELIEU Village) at the rate of 100 yards in six minutes.

(b) All lifts will be by 100 yards at a time except in the Village, when lifts will be 50 yards every 3 minutes.

(c) Up to and including the protective barrage beyond the Red Line an 18-pdr. Battery in each Brigade will fire H.E. 100 yards in advance of shrapnel barrage. The other two Batteries will fire shrapnel with 10% smoke.

(d) When the barrage is lifting through GONNELIEU, all Batteries will fire H.E. only.

Appendix 'C'.

INTELLIGENCE.

The Divisional Intelligence Officer will be at the Divisional P. of W. Cage, Quarry W.16.c. to interrogate prisoners.

He will be in direct communication with Divisional Headquarters by telephone.

All Maps, papers, documents and Soldbucher (paybooks) will be collected by Brigades from enemy dead, and forwarded to the Divisional Intelligence Officer at the P. of W. Cage.

Identity discs will be left on the dead.

Papers will not be collected from prisoners.

All documents found in dug-outs will be forwarded to the Divisional Intelligence Officer.

Brigades will wire (Priority) to Divisional Headquarters the Regiments and Divisions to which the first batch of prisoners belong, and will subsequently wire any new identifications.

Two Military Mounted Police will be attached to each Infantry Brigade Headquarters to escort prisoners from Brigade Headquarters to the Divisional P. of W. Cage.

---

21 Div. Communications. 27·9·18

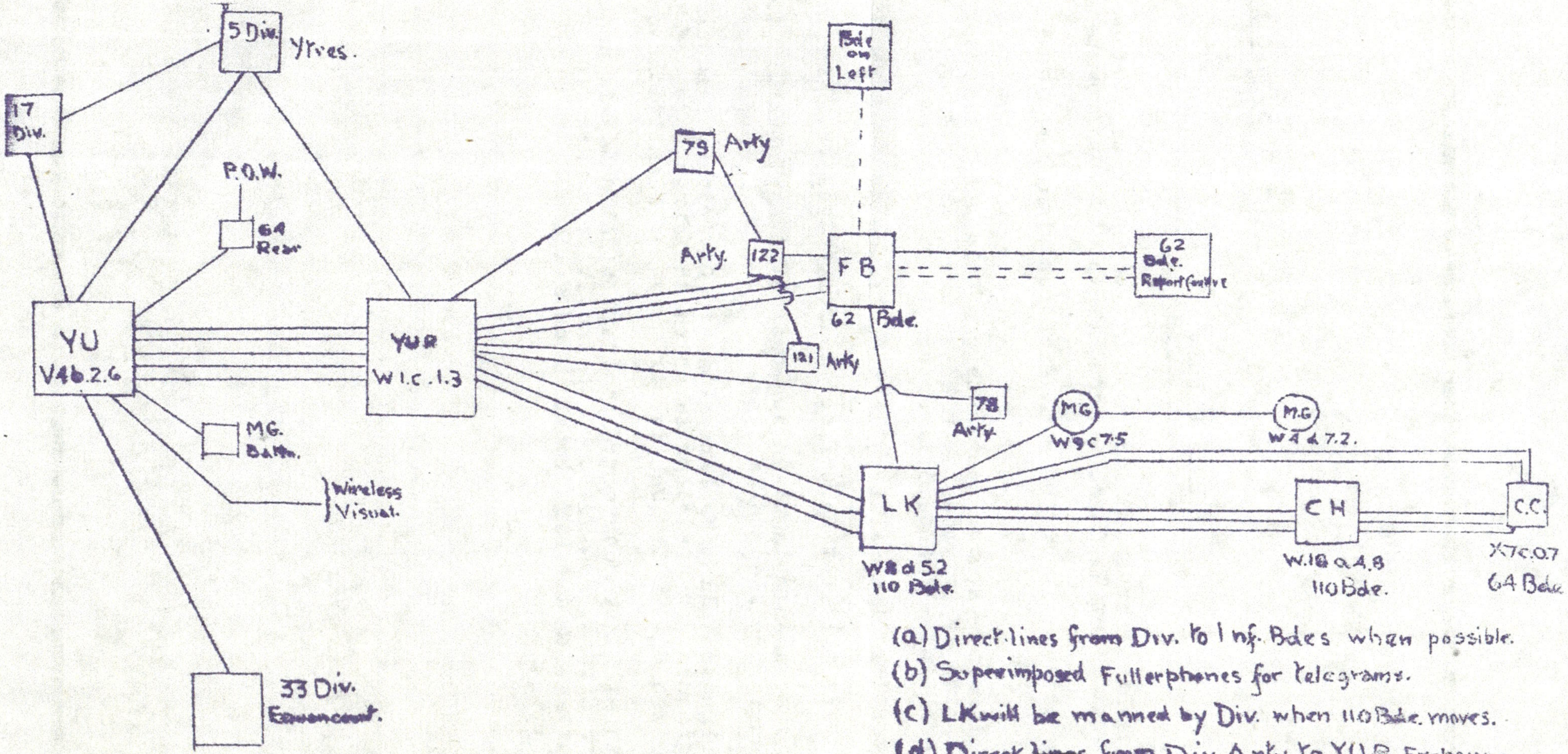

(a) Direct lines from Div. to Inf. Bdes when possible.

(b) Superimposed Fullerphones for telegrams.

(c) LK will be manned by Div. when 110 Bde. moves.

(d) Direct ~~lines~~ pair from Div. Arty. to YUR. Exchange (not for messages)

Appendix 'G'.

T A N K S.

1. Four Tanks of 'B' Company, No.11 Tank Battalion will co-operate in the attack along QUENTIN RIDGE on GONNELIEU.

2. Tanks will assemble after dark on September 27th in X.7.a. South-West of GAUCHE WOOD.
They will move from their assembly position so as to advance with the Infantry under the barrage.

3. (a) One Tank will move South of GAUCHE WOOD straight to the Cemetery X.2.d.9.9, thence, when the barrage lifts, via the Red Line and South East of GONNELIEU.

(b) The other three Tanks will move West of GAUCHE WOOD and will follow the routes, already notified to all concerned.

4. When GONNELIEU has been captured and "mopped up", all four Tanks will assemble West of the Village and will establish a report centre at R.26.d.0.1, where Red Line crosses road. The Infantry Commander on the spot, if he requires the services of the Tanks for a counter-attack on GONNELIEU can get in touch with them at this spot.

Appendix 'H'.

MISCELLANEOUS.

1. Light Signals.

(a) S.O.S. Signal for V Corps ~~will remain~~ Green/Red/Green.

(b) S.O.S. Signal for IV Corps on our left is Red/Green/Red.

(c) Coloured Very lights will be used as follows :-

(i) Red. By the foremost Infantry to denote the position they have reached. This signal must be freely used.

(ii) Green. As a signal to our Artillery to lengthen range.

2. Tools.

Battalions of the 64th Infantry Brigade detailed to capture the Brown Line will carry a good proportion of tools. The tools to be carried by other Battalions will be cut down to the minimum. The exact numbers of tools per Battalion will be arranged by Brigadiers.

3. Distinctive Marks.

The following will wear a knot of white tape on the left shoulder strap :-

(a) The Right Battalion of the 64th Infantry Brigade (detailed to attack Green dotted and Red Lines).

(b) The 4th King's Regiment (Left Battalion 33rd Div.).

(c) The Battalion of the 110th Infantry Brigade detailed to capture the Red Line.

(d) The Left Battalion 64th Infantry Brigade detailed to capture GONNELIEU.

(e) The 1st Devons (Right Battalion 5th Division).

4. Pass-word.

The pass-word to be used by the Right of the 5th Division and the left of this Division so as to ensure recognition will be the word "THRUSH".

5. Thinning out.

After the 64th Infantry Brigade have passed through troops of 110th Infantry Brigade who have captured the Red Line, all troops of 110th Infantry Brigade (less 1 Company) will be withdrawn from the Red Line. This Company will not withdraw until relieved by the 64th Infantry Brigade.

The actual village of GONNELIEU will, as far as possible, be kept clear of troops, once it has been captured and "Mopped up".

PTO

6. <u>Headquarters</u>.

Divisional Headquarters will be at V.4.b.2.5.

64th Infantry Brigade H.Q. .. X.7.c.0.7.

110th : : : .. W.18.a.3.8.

---

app 20

TELEGRAM.

URGENT
OPERATIONS
PRIORITY TO

Bdes
HG

Words

Sent.
At..............
To..............
By..............

DADE	LODE	33rd Div.
BASU	ZEJU	5th Corps.
VUFE	5th Div.	15th Sqn. R.A.F.

G.X.5151 / 28 / AAA

IVth Corps report that enemy have withdrawn from their front AAA DADE has occupied AFRICAN TRENCH and is pushing patrols towards GOUZEAUCOURT AAA If patrols sent out by VUFE meet no resistance VUFE will occupy line GREEN LANE GREEN SWITCH getting touch with 5th Division at R.26.a.9.1 AAA When this line made good by VUFE patrols will be sent to BROWN LINE but no advance in force until touch established with 5th Division on left AAA When 5th Division have occupied FUSILIER RIDGE and if patrols still report no resistance VUFE will make good BROWN LINE and send patrols to GREEN LINE AAA In addition to above VUFE will send one special reconnoitring patrol at once to KITCHEN CRATER and another to GONNELIEU to report if enemy occupy these places or not AAA When VUFE has occupied GREEN LANE GREEN SWITCH and when patrols have reached BROWN LINE DADE will assemble Brigade in GOUZEAUCOURT VALLEY assuming that GOUZEAUCOURT is found empty AAA DADE will be prepared on receipt of orders to move through VUFE and occupy GREEN LINE AAA BASU will be at half hours' notice to move AAA Ack AAA Added all concerned

---

H C Franklyn

ZOWU
11.35 a.m.

Lieut.Colonel,
General Staff,

app 21

TELEGRAM.

Words

Sent.

DRLS.
S.&R. 5th Div
33rd "

At....................
To....................
By....................

DADE	JESO	33rd Div.	15th Sqn. R.A.F.
BASU	ZOHO		
VUFE	DUFA	V Corps.	Cyclist Troop.
LODE	A/Q.	V Corps R.A.	
ZOKI	5th Div.	V Corps H.A.	
ZEJU		'B' Coy. Tanks.	

- / 28th / AAA

ZOWU Order No.238 AAA Enemy have withdrawn opposite Vth and IVth Corps fronts but to what extent is not yet known AAA ZOWU has been ordered to capture BROWN and GREEN LINES early tomorrow morning AAA VUFE will attack on right and DADE on left AAA Dividing line between Brigades R.31, R.33, R.36.Central AAA 33rd Division will be attacking VILLERS GUISLAIN and GREEN LINE in conjunction with us AAA 5th Division will be attacking FUSILIER and CEMETERY RIDGES and subsequently BANTEUX AAA Two Tanks will work with VUFE and two Tanks with DADE AAA The former rendezvous X.8.a.1.9 and latter R.25.d.2.0 about 11 p.m. AAA Right pair Tanks will work via Cemetery X.2.d. KITCHEN CRATER TURNER CRATER and clear GREEN LINE AAA Left pair Tanks work round each side GONNELIEU and down GLASGOW TRENCH and prepared to deal with BANTEUX SUPPORT if Infantry in difficulties AAA All Tanks rally KITCHEN CRATER after operations where available for immediate counter-attack AAA Artillery starting line for barrage X.2.d.3.5 to R.26.d.3.8 AAA Barrage moves 100 yards in six minutes to BROWN LINE and 100 yards in four minutes from BROWN to GREEN LINE AAA Barrage will be amended and added to according to most Easterly line reached by Infantry this evening AAA Barrage Tables issued to Brigades show other details AAA One M.G.Coy. will accompany each Brigade AAA Unless otherwise detailed Barrage for attack on BROWN LINE will come down at 3.30 a.m. and for attack from BROWN to GREEN LINE at 5.50 a.m. AAA Ack AAA Addsd all concerned

H. Glanville(?)

ZOWU
7.30 p.m.

Lieut.Colonel,
General Staff.

app 22

TELEGRAM.

URGENT OPERATIONS
PRIORITY to 3 Bdes.

Words

Sent.
At....................
To....................
By....................

DADE	JESO	V Corps.
BASU	ZOHO	V Corps R.A.
VUFE	DUFA	V Corps H.A.
LODE	A/Q.	15 Sqn. R.A.F.
ZOKI	5th Div.	Divl. Cyclists Troop.
ZEJU	33rd Div.	

- / 29th / AAA

ZOWU Order No.239 AAA Owing to success of both flanks today it appears probable that the enemy will withdraw shortly from our immediate front AAA Active patrolling will be carried out by VUFE and DADE tonight AAA If GONNELIEU and BROWN LINE are entered by patrols without resistance either tonight or tomorrow they will at once be occupied in force and patrols pushed on to GREEN LINE AAA If GREEN LINE is occupied by patrols this line will also be occupied in strength and patrols pushed down towards CANAL AAA Boundary between Brigades Sunken Road at R.26.c.3.0 - R.32.Central - R.34.Central - R.36.Central AAA Patrolling must be carried out by strong fighting patrols and minor resistance must be overcome AAA Patrols must be sent out at least once every hour and be particularly active just before Dawn AAA All available heavy Artillery and Field Howitzers will bombard GONNELIEU from 4.5 a.m. to 5 a.m. and then Cease AAA DADE will inform Div. H.Q. by 3 a.m. if bombardment is not to take place owing to their being in occupation of village AAA Any barrage required by Brigades for patrols to work under will be arranged with affiliated Artillery AAA DADE will have call on 122 Brigade as well as 79th Brigade for this purpose AAA BASU will remain in present positions till further orders AAA Ack AAA Adsd all concerned

---

ZOWU
10.10 p.m.

H.L. Knaresbrough
Lieut.Colonel,
General Staff.

app 23

TELEGRAM.

Urgent Operations Priority to 3 Bdes. HCT	Words / Sent. At............... To............... By...............

DADE	JESO	V Corps.
BASU	ZOHO	V Corps R.A.
VUFE	DUFA	V Corps H.A.
LODE	A/Q.	15 Sqn. R.A.F.
ZOKI	5 Div.	Divl. Cyclist Troop.
ZEJU	33 Div.	

\- / 30th / AAA

ZOWU Order No.240 AAA Prisoners state that enemy will withdraw to distance of 4 kilo-metres East of Canal AAA When GREEN LINE has been made good on Divl. Front DADE and VUFE will send forward to Canal sieze crossings and establish bridgeheads on East bank AAA BASU will move to just West of QUENTIN RIDGE forthwith and will be prepared on receipt of orders to advance through VUFE and DADE cross Canal and occupy HINDENBURG LINE between RANCOURT FARM and BANTOUZEELE both exclusive AAA Report Centres will be established by Div. Signals at KITCHEN CRATER TURNER QUARRY successiv ARNOLD QUARRY AAA DADE will transfer Cyclists in R.32c to BASU when latter takes up advance AAA Adsd all concerned AAA Ack

---

H. C. Franklyn

ZOWU
12.10 p.m.

Lieut.Colonel,
General Staff.

app 24

TELEGRAM.

URGENT OPERATIONS PRIORITY to 3 Bdes.	Words Sent At.................. To.................. By..................

HWT

DADE	JESO	V Corps.
BASU	ZOHO	V Corps R.A.
VUFE	DUFA	V Corps H.A.
LODE	A/Q.	15th Sqn.R.A.F.
ZOKI	5th Div.	Div. Cyclist Troop.
ZEJU	33rd Div.	

- / 30th / AAA

ZOWU Order No.241 AAA VUFE on right and DADE on left will continue to hold GREEN LINE AAA Front line to be held thinly and Brigades disposed in depth AAA BASU will remain in present positions AAA Patrols will be sent to Canal bank tonight accompanied by R.E. AAA If any bridges are found to be repairable and hostile fire permits R.E. will carry out repairs protected by Infantry patrol on East bank AAA Risk of heavy casualties will NOT be run AAA If any bridges are found intact or are repaired by R.E. post will be established on West bank to cover bridge with fire and so prevent demolition by enemy AAA If patrols can cross canal they will work towards HINDENBURG LINE to report if enemy hold this line or not AAA All troops East of GREEN LINE except those detailed to guard Bridges or to occupy tactical points selected by Brigadiers will be withdrawn before daylight AAA Troops to be rested as much as possible tonight and tomorrow unless situation changes AAA Ack AAA Adsd all concerned

H L Knatchbull

ZOWU
7.30 p.m.

Lieut.Colonel,
General Staff.

Copp 26

21 Div.
G. 731.

Report on examination of Prisoners of 44th Reserve Division captured at BEAULENCOURT on morning of 1st September, 1918.

ORDER OF BATTLE. North to South. 206 R.I.R.
208 :
205 : (3rd Battn).

The 2nd Battalion 208 R.I.R. from HAPLINCOURT relieved 3rd Battalion 205 R.I.R. South of BEAULENCOURT last night, the relief being complete about 10 p.m. A returning guide of the 205 R.I.R. was captured behind BEAULENCOURT in our attack at 2 a.m., and it is therefore probable that the 3rd Battn 205 R.I.R. did not proceed as far as HAPLINCOURT on account of the alarm. The Battalion H.Q. 3rd Battn. 205 R.I.R. was in the SUGAR FACTORY, N.24.Central.

Battalions in the Outpost Line appear to have had three Coys. in front with one Coy. in Support for counter-attack. Coys. were very weak, the strongest being 80 men, whilst one Coy. was said to be only 13 strong.

Prisoners were taken from the following Units :-

208 R.I.R.	No.
2nd M.G.Coy.	5
3rd :	5
6th Coy.	33
10th :	10
11th :	15
12th :	6
4th :	20
1st :	2
2nd :	1
9th :	11
5th :	4

Unit	No.
205 R.I.R. 10th Coy.	1
208 M.W. Det.	1
44th Res F.A.R.	3
206 R.I.R. 8th Coy.	9
347th I.R. 7th Coy.	4

The Coy. Commanders of the 11th, 4th and 9th Coys. 208th R.I.R. were also captured.

Total captures so far counted, 3 Officers, 130 Other Ranks, 2 - 77 mm guns, 2 light Minenwerfer, 30 Machine Guns and other material.

BEAULENCOURT POSITION.

According to the three captured Coy. Commanders, the orders were to hold the position which they occupied yesterday, there being no question of a further immediate withdrawal, though that might come eventually.

There appear to have been 3 Coys. of 208th R.I.R. in the forward outpost line 500 yards West of BEAULENCOURT, each Coy. holding a Sector compatible with its strength, one strong Coy (strength about 80) said to have a front of 400 yards. One Coy. was in close support. The Battalion front was about 1,200 yds.

The main line of resistance lay between BEAULENCOURT and VILLERS AU FLOS. The line was not a trench line, the men being in the open 300 yards in front of old trench in N.12.d.

South of BEAULENCOURT the outpost line was apparently held in the same manner as that round the West end of the Village. The 2nd Battn. of the 208th R.I.R. took over the old positions of the 3rd Battn. 205th R.I.R. whose support line was said to have been very thin indeed, with the support Coy. 500 yards West of the SUGAR FACTORY in N.24.Central.

ANTI-TANK GUNS AND MINENWERFER.

Up to the evening of the 31st August there were four Anti-tank 77 mm guns in the Sector of the 208th R.I.R. but two of these are stated to have been withdrawn on the night 31st August/1st September. The remaining two were captured. One had received a direct hit and was practically destroyed and the other was damaged. An Officer explained the withdrawal of the two guns by the suggestion that an attack was suspected and that the principle of distribution of forces in depth would be fulfilled by withdrawal of two guns to position in rear of the main line of resistance.

There were also 4 light minenwerfer for anti-tank purposes and a similar procedure in the withdrawal of two had been followed. Two were captured.

GENERAL.

Prisoners' statements are in agreement that the direction of our attack was a surprise, and in the darkness and confusion the advantage lay with the attackers.

The examination of some 30 prisoners including 3 Coy. Commanders left the impression that whilst a certain depression existed, there was a strong element not only trusting in their Higher Command, but holding also a belief in the possibility of final victory for the German Army or at worst a satisfactory Peace by Agreement.

The information from prisoners is scanty and must not be too readily accepted. The customary knowledge of dispositions usually displayed by a prisoner taken in trench warfare was lacking.

21st Division.

1/9/18.

-:-:-:-:-:-:-:-:-:-:-:-:-:-:-:-:-:-

App 27

War Diary

TELEGRAM.

	Words.	
	Sent At.............. To.............. By..............	

BUMA JENU A/Q A.P.M.
BURA MOVI JEKU Div. Cav Troop.
RUVE FOLO JEMU Div. Cyclist Coy.
WUMA RORU Camp.Comdt.

Gx765 1 2 1 aaa

The following from General SHUTE 5th Corps begins AAA My warmest congratulations to you on your operations of the last few days AAA Please convey my appreciation and thanks to all under your command for the rapid and thorough manner in which they carried out the many and difficult tasks assigned to them AAA The great results obtained by the Division were due to the skill of the Commander and the dash of the men AAA Ends.

JEZU

7.40 p.m.

H.H. Macdougall. Major
General Staff.

App 28

War Diary.

21st Division.

Report on examination of Prisoners of War captured 2nd September 1918.

Coys. Engaged.

The following Coys. suffered most severely in prisoners :-

205th R.I.R.	10th Coy.	
206th R.I.R.	7th Coy.	18 Prisoners were taken from this Coy. including the Coy. Commander.
208th R.I.R.	1st Coy.	16 Prisoners.
	3rd Coy.	17 Prisoners.
	5th Coy.	28 Prisoners.

The Coy. Commanders of the 1st, 3rd, 5th and 6th Coys. of this Regiment were also captured.

A number of men from the Divisional Pioneer and Minenwerfer Coys. were also captured, these Units having been thrown into the line as ordinary Infantrymen.

49th Reserve Division.

By midnight 1st/2nd September the 226th R.I.R. had taken up a position in close support of the 206th and 208th R.I.R's (44th Res. Div.) between VILLERS AU FLOS and LE TRANSLOY. The statements of all prisoners taken from the 226th R.I.R. agree that considerable confusion and disorganization existed in the Sectors of the 206th and 208th R.I.R.

Although the men of the 226th R.I.R. are undoubtedly exhausted through recent hurried movements by rail and march route, some of them having had less than 2 hours sleep in the last 4 days, they make a good impression and are undoubtedly a good Division. The Colonel in Command of 226th R.I.R. is much beloved.

Reliefs.

Coy. Orderly of a Platoon Commander of the 170th R.I.R. captured this morning stated that runners with the Regtl. Transport told him that guides of the 56th Division were at the Transport and that the 52nd Division was to be relieved by the 56th Division, probably on the night 2nd/3rd.

By mid-day one man of the 226th R.I.R. 49th Reserve Division from the LANGEMARCK Sector had been taken. Further prisoners were taken later, their statements are in agreement that the 49th Reserve Div. was relieved at LANGEMARCH on night 26th/27th August. The 226th R.I.R. was relieved by a Bavarian Regt No.22. The rear party of returning guides of the 226th R.I.R. stated that just after the completion of the relief a raid was made by the Belgians on the incoming Bavarian Div, 40 prisoners being taken.

REGIMENTS IDENTIFIED UP TILL 5 p.m. 2nd SEPTR.

44th R.D	208th R.I.R.	87 O.R.	49th Res. Div.	226 R.I.R.	1 O.R.
	206th R.I.R.	33 O.R.	52nd Div.	170 I.R.	1 O.R.
	205th R.I.R.	12 O.R.			
	44th R. F.A.R.	7 O.R.			
	244th M.W. Abt.	2 O.R.			

General Impressions.

44th Res. Division. From the statements of prisoners as regards casualties (at least 20 per Coy. in the last 5 days) exclusive of the number of prisoners taken, it is practically certain that the 206th and 208th Regts. are at present of no fighting value until rested and reinforced. A marked feature of the operations has been the large percentage of Officers captured, especially Coy. Commanders. The Division has been retained in line until exhausted and losses have reduced its fighting value to a dangerously low level.

Short conversations with Officers gained no information of Military importance. It is remarked that they have a growing belief that the British Armies are worn down to a grade below that of which they would be capable of striking a decisive blow and the quality of the troops is markedly different to those taken in 1917. They say that the same remarks apply to their own troops and opinion now inclines to the belief that owing to the lack of experience and training the Americans are only "cannon fodder", and that eventually the Allies will come to negotiations for a Peace by agreement. All Officers expressed the greatest admiration of and confidence in LUDENDORFF. HINDENBURG was not mentioned.

Total captures 2nd September, 16 Officers, and 150 Other Ranks (approx).

2/9/18.

War Diary

SECRET.

21 Div.
G. 985

App 79

62nd Inf. Bde.
64th : :
110th : :
C.R.A.
C.R.E.
D.M.G.C.
'Q'
Signals.

POLICY FOR IMMEDIATE FUTURE.

1. As soon as the YELLOW LINE has been made good and junction effected with the 58th Division about W.24.d.8.0. and with the 17th Division about W.11. Central, the general policy is :-

(a) To keep touch with the enemy, so that advantage may be taken of any weakening of resistance.

(b) To make all preparations for subsequent operations, which will probably be on a more extended scale than those carried out recently.

(c) To harass the enemy with all available means.

(d) To improve the defences in the Divisional Sector.

2. As regards (a), constant patrolling will be carried out and if any opportunity presents itself of improving our position in the CHAPEL HILL area, it will be taken advantage of.
Fighting patrols will be used in likely places (e.g. along Railway in W.24.d. and along Sunken Road W.18.d.) for rounding up prisoners.

3. As regards 1(b), information will be communicated to those immediately concerned.

As regards 1(c), Stokes Mortars, Machine Guns and Artillery will be freely used both by day and night to harass the enemy's communications, centres of resistance and of accommodation.

Details as to Gas-projector attacks will be issued later.

4. As regards 1(d) :-

Infantry Garrisons will deepen the trenches where necessary and repair the wire entanglements.

The C.R.E. will detail :-

(a) One Field Coy. R.E. to make REVELON FARM into a strong point for a garrison of one Coy.

(b) One Field Coy. R.E. will be employed on renovating the BROWN LINE.

/(c).......

(c) One Coy. Pioneers will wire CAVALRY SUPPORT and LOWLAND SUPPORT.

(d) One Coy. Pioneers will construct strong points in the EQUANCOURT Trench System.

5\. (a) The forward Brigade will be responsible for the defence of the Sector up to and including the BROWN LINE.

(b) The Supporting Brigade (less 1 Battalion) will be responsible for the defence of the GREEN LINE (EQUANCOURT System), & will be ready to occupy it at one hour's notice.
The B.G.C. forward Brigade will have the call on one Battalion supporting Brigade (located near SOREL LE GRAND) for counter-attacking to regain any portion of the BROWN LINE or for forming a defensive flank either to the East or West of this line. Except in case of great urgency, this Battalion will not be used without reference to Divisional Headquarters.

(c) The Brigade in the ETRICOURT - MANANCOURT Area will be in Divisional Reserve.

H.H. Fraulelyn[?] Lieut Col

General Staff.
21st Division.

10th September 1918.

"C" Form.

MESSAGES AND SIGNALS.

Army Form C. 2123.
(In books of 100.)

No. of Message 84

Prefix ___ Code ___ Words ___	Received.	Sent, or sent out.	Office Stamp.
£ s. d.	From VVC	At ___ m.	EGO 30.IX.18
Charges to Collect	By Scott	To 2h	
Service Instructions		By	
urgent Operations Priority			

Handed in at 21 Div Office 10 3a m. Received 10 15a m.

TO 5 Corps (1)

*Sender's Number	Day of Month	In reply to Number	AAA
GX 594	30		

5th	Div	report	they
have	patrols	in	GONNELIEU
and	BANTEUX	aaa	DADE (62 Inf Bde)
will	push	patrols	round
through	5TH	Div	area
so	as	to	enter
GONNELIEU	from	North	aaa
These	patrols	to	be
supported	by	stronger	Bodies
aaa	If	GONNELIEU	occupied
by	us	patrols	to
work	down	Reserve	Line
and	KITCHEN	STREET	to
join	hands (110 Inf Bde)	with	VUFE (110 Inf Bde)
aaa	VUFE	will	send
patrols	to	BROWN	LINE
and	reinforce	them	when

FROM
PLACE & TIME

*This line should be erased if not required.

(37802) Wt. W14832/M1523. [E 930]. 100,000 Pads—3/17. M.R.Co.,Ltd. Forms C./2123.

"C" Form.

Army Form C. 2123.
(In books of 100.)

MESSAGES AND SIGNALS. No. of Message

Prefix Code Words | Received. From By | Sent, or sent out. At m. To By | Office Stamp. 30.IX.18 ...APHS

£ s. d.

Charges to Collect

Service Instructions

Handed in at Office m. Received. m.

TO

II

Sender's Number	Day of Month	In reply to Number	AAA
GX 594			

VILLERS	GUISLAIN	is	occupied
by	33rd	Div	aaa
DADE	will	send	one
Bn	Round	north	of
GONNELIEU	to	work	down
GLASGOW	and	PRESTON	TRENCHES
with	objective	GREEN	LINE
and	southern	slopes	of
BANTEUX	Spur	getting	touch
with	5th	Div	on
Left	aaa	ack	

1221 Adl

FROM
PLACE & TIME 21 Div 10 am

*This line should be erased if not required.

(27802) Wt. W14832/M1523. [E 930]. 100,000 Pads—3/17. M.R.Co.,Ltd. Forms C./2123.

App 30

S.

REPORT ON THE EXAMINATION OF PRISONERSOF WAR OF 2nd Coy and 9th Coy. 403rd I.R. CAPTURED IN W.24.a and c. on 11th September 1918.

INTELLIGENCE.

The YELLOW SUPPORT LINE in W.24.a. was held by one outpost Coy of 403 I.R. as far as the Railway at W.24.a.3.0. and part of another Coy. South of the Railway to fill a gap between the 403rd I.R. and a Jaeger Regt. of the Alpen Korps to the South.

Practically the whole of the outpost Coy. was captured and part of the one South of the Railway.

Prisoners vary slightly, though mostly state there were Four L.M.Gs. with the outpost Coy.

There were no troops known of between the outpost Coy. and the main line of resistance, which was CAVALRY SUPPORT in X.19, with the exception of some connecting links (locality uncertain) consisting of pairs of men. The main line was held with 3 Coys. in CAVALRY SUPPORT, including one Heavy M.G. Coy. with its guns on the side of the railway. From midnight approximately up to broad daylight the troops in CAVALRY SUPPORT were supported by 3 more Coys in or round CRICKET TRENCH. Order of Battle is 401 I.R, 402 I.R. 403 I.R. reading from North to South.

WIRE.

New wire has been put out during the last few days on the W. side of CAVALRY SUPPORT in X.19. but this was stated to be very ineffective up till the 9th inst, which was the last date on which the troops captured had done any work there. In a Sector of CAVALRY SUPPORT occupied by the M.G.Coy. between the two short communication trenches in X.19.a. leading towards the Railway, no work on the wire had been done, as the Machine Gunners did not take kindly to the work.

MINEFIELD.

The old anti-tank minefield is still stated to be intact.

SUPPORTS.

The supports which moved up into CRICKET TRENCH in the night were located during the day in the triangle of sunken roads in X.14.b, c & d.

DEMOLITIONS. No information was obtained as to the preparation of dug-outs for destruction.

COOKERS.

The Field Kitchens came at one time to the junction of the Cross Roads at X.13.d.6.1. but on account of shelling later took up a position about X.14.c.4.2. The last time the cookers were visited by any of the men, they were brought through VILLERS GUISLAIN to about X.14.a.6.5.

MORALE.

The men of the best morale were those who operated the L.M.Gs. though theirs could not be called good. The ordinary Infantry were generally only too pleased to be captured, and most had faith in the expectation of good treatment on this side.

Among those of fair morale there is still a lingering hope and belief that HINDENBURG has something up his sleeve, or at any rate a peace by agreement could be arranged.

ORDERS.

The orders current were those usual to an outpost Coy. They were to hold up the attack as long as possible, giving warning to the main line, and in the event of overwhelming superiority, to fall back on to the main line.

13th September 1918.

21st Division.
Headquarters.

App 21

REPORT ON EXAMINATION OF PRISONERS OF THE 401st AND 402nd I.Rs, 201st DIVISION CAPTURED ON THE MORNING OF THE 13th SEPTEMBER, 1918.

ORDER OF BATTLE.

From the statements of prisoners the Order of Battle opposite this front appears to be unchanged, the ALPINE KORPS being still in the EPEHY Sector and the 6th Cavalry Division in the GOUZEAUCOURT Sector.

402nd I.R.

One prisoner from this Regt. deserted to us yesterday morning in W.18. giving warning of an impending attack which later materialised. This prisoner's Company was in W.18.d. in CAVALRY SUPPORT and was ordered yesterday morning to leave their position on the left flank of the Regt. and proceed to the right flank of the Regt. in CAVALRY TRENCH on CHAPEL HILL, their light M.Gs. and other equipment being left in their regular Sector. The Coy. was then to attack in conjunction with other Coys. and also with the 401st I.R. to regain CAVALRY SUPPORT and LOWLAND SUPPORT in W.18. and W.11, the Cavalry on their right also co-operating.

DISPOSITIONS.

Previous information was confirmed with regard to the Coys. occupying the dug-outs immediately North of CHAPEL CROSSING in the Railway Crossing at X.7.c.1.5., the Support Battn. of the Regt. occupying FIVES TRENCH and CRICKET TRENCH.

401st I.R.

Prisoners of this Regt. belong to the 7th Coy. and confirm the intention of the attack as stated by the deserter, though the exact line to be finally taken up was not known to them. There was only one Officer in their Coy. who was later to have given them further instructions.

DISPOSITIONS.

The 2nd Battn. was billeted when in Support, in a large dugout with at least 3 entrances, in the sunken Road in W.6.d. and 12.b. This dug-out is about 30 steps deep, the steps being very high and contains all 4 Coys. of the Support Battn. together with the T.M.Coy. which co-operated also in the attack.

TRENCH MORTARS.

From prisoners statements there appear to have been four Medium Trench Mortar emplacements in the Sunken Road in W.12.b. and at least two others close to seven tall trees at W.12.b.4.8. Each Trench Mortar had 100 rounds for the barrage yesterday morning and when the operation was finished, it was understood that the guns were to be taken away again.

METHOD OF ATTACK.

From the statements of a few prisoners captured, the attack was made with from two to three Flamenwerfers per Coy, each Flamenwerfer being accompanied by a man with a Light Machine Gun, the attacking troops following in Artillery formation, one Section behind another.

COOKERS.

The cookers for the 2nd Battn, 401st. I.R. were brought up into the Sunken Road in W.12.b. and 6.d.

ORDERS.

Whilst in Support, the 2nd. Battn. in the event of an alarm, was to man the trenches in W.6.d. Beyond this, there appear to have been no special orders prevalent, though prisoners stated that fresh attacks, accompanied by tanks are expected daily, and troops in Support and in Reserve are always ready to 'stand-to' at short notice.

RAILHEAD.

The Railhead for the 201st Division is at WALINCOURT. One man from hospital in NAMUR was detrained here on the night of the 11th/12th inst.

GENERAL.

The deserter stated that when he came over to us, it was his intention subsequently to return to his Section and get them to come over as well, but in the meantime, it having become too light, he thought it too dangerous.

/He.........

He stated he was quite sure that they would ~~ha~~ all have willingly deserted with him. The prisoners of the 7th Coy. 401st I.R. stated that in the attack they reached their objectives and their orders were to form a defensive flank at W.11.c.6.8. and then to gain touch with the Cavalry on their right, but owing to the Cavalry having failed to advance, they found themselves in the air, and as soon as our counter-attacking troops appeard up the Sunken Road in W.11.c.5.9. they seized this opportunity of surrendering.

A considerable number of prisoners have now been examined from every Regt. in the 201st Division. Most of them said that they surrendered readily and the moral of the Division appears throughout to be very low.

14.9.1918.

Headquarters.
21st Division.

App 38

S E C R E T.

21 Div.
G. 396.

PROCEEDINGS OF CONFERENCE HELD AT DIVISIONAL HEADQUARTERS, 23rd SEPT. 1918.

Present :-
B.G.C., 62nd Inf. Bde.
B.G.C., 64th " "
O.C. 110th " "
C.R.A.
C.R.E.
D.M.G.C.
A.A.&Q.M.G.
O.C.Signals.

1. The Divisional Commander explained the situation and the reasons for the Division again going into the line in relief of 17th Division.

2. The Divisional Commander said that he did not intend that the 64th Infantry Brigade, which would be in support, to take over the dispositions at present held by support Brigade, 17th Div. The dispositions of the 64th Infantry Brigade would be as follows :-

1 Battalion ... V.3.
1 " ... Q.32.
1 " ... V.6.

3. Combing out.
The Divisional Commander wished Brigadiers to go into the question of combing out all men at present employed in transport lines, band etc. He said that he wished every man who is not essential for transport etc. to be available to take his place in the line.

4. Attack on Strong Points.
The Divisional Commander said that the Corps Commander had pointed out that most of the casualties suffered by the 33rd Division in their recent attacks had been caused through Brigades attacking strong points by driblets instead of forming a proper plan by which strong points could be attacked with sufficient force using trench mortars etc.

5. Gas.
The area which the Division is taking over has been subjected to a certain amount of gas shelling during the last few days. The Divisional Commander wished Brigadiers to ensure that proper gas discipline is observed.

6. Tracks.
B.Gs.C. 62nd and 64th Inf. Bdes. pointed out that the tracks laid out for recent operations crossed sunken roads in such a way that in wet weather it was extremely difficult for troops to get up the banks. The C.R.E. said he would take this matter in hand.

7. The B.G.C. 64th Inf. Bde. considered that, when one Brigade had to leap-frog through another Brigade in the attack, it was advisable to detail a Company from the Reserve Battalion to mop up any points that might not have been cleared by the first attacking Brigade in order that the troops making the second attack should not be delayed. This method was employed by the 64th Inf. Bde. in the recent attack and was fully justified. The Divisional Commander agreed.

/8.......

8. The B.G.C. 62nd Inf. Bde. suggested that when all three Brigades were taking part in an attack, the Division should lay down in orders the times for marching to the assembling positions and also the time by which the assembly of each Brigade was to be completed. The Divisional Commander agreed.

9. Communications.

The Divisional Commander considered that during recent operations communications had not been entirely satisfactory.

O.C. Signals said that this was not due to Brigades but entirely to technical faults which he hoped had now been rectified. He suggested that only Infantry and Artillery Brigades, M.G.Companies and the liaison Heavy Artillery Brigade should be allowed to use Divisional Exchanges. Instructions will be issued on this point.

In order to lessen the traffic on telephone and telegraph lines, it was suggested that Divisional and Brigade Operation Orders should be sent by D.R.

B.G.C. 62nd Inf. Bde. said that he found communication with flank Brigades was very difficult during recent operations.

The Divisional Commander said that during moving warfare it would be impossible to lay lateral lines for this purpose and that the Corps Cyclists attached to Brigades should be used for this purpose.

B.G.C. 64th Inf. Bde. said that during recent operations the three lines laid from Division to Brigades were too close together and that one shell broke them all. O.C. Signals said that this matter had been taken up.

10. Greatcoats.

Brigadiers were adverse to taking greatcoats into the line. The A.A.& Q.M.G. said that leather jerkins would be available tomorrow and Brigadiers said that they would like them issued.

The Divisional Commander said that in his opinion it was essential that everything should be done for the men's comfort in the present case but that he left the matter entirely in the hands of Brigadiers.

A.H. Macdougall. Major
for Lt. Col.

23.9.18.

General Staff,
21st Division.

Appx 33

S E C R E T.

21 Div.
G. 587.

62nd Inf. Bde.	D.M.G.C.	Signals.
64th : :	"Q"	
110th : :	A.D.M.S.	
C.R.A.	A.P.M.	
C.R.E.	Cyclist Sqn.	

FORECAST OF FUTURE POLICY.

The following forecast is given as a guide only :-

1. The Corps on our right with IInd American Corps is to cross the Canal today and capture GOUY and LE CATELET, after which the Australian Corps will pass through and take BEAUREVOIR, the American Corps forming a defensive flank from GOUY through S.23. Central to the Canal at S.13.d.

2. On the completion of this operation the 38th Division will cross the Canal and relieve the Americans holding the defensive flank.

3. Meanwhile, the 33rd Division will push forward its right and bridge the Canal between VENDHUILLE and HONNECOURT, and relieve the left Brigade 38th Division.

4. The 38th Division will then capture LA TERRIERE. The remainder of 33rd Division will cross the Canal and occupy the general line LA TERRIERE - HONNECOURT (both inclusive).

5. By this time the IVth Corps on our left should have captured BANTEUX and BANTOUZEELE and the 21st Division should be on the GREEN Line.

6. When the above situation or something akin to it has arisen, the 21st Division will cross the Canal and occupy the HINDENBURG LINE between RANCOURT FARM and BANTOUZEELE both exclusive.
The 33rd Division will assist this operation by attacking Northwards towards S.3. and S.4.Central, should any resistance be met with.

7. The C.R.E. is making arrangements to construct bridges over the Canal at :-

S.1.d.4.9.
S.1.b.9.4.
M.31.b.2.2.

and to provide means for an Infantry party to be thrown across to cover the bridging operations.

/8........

8. The forward Divisional boundaries will be issued shortly on a Map.

9. It is not possible yet to allot tasks to Brigades, but it is probable that after the capture of the GREEN Line by the 62nd and 110th Infantry Brigades the 64th Infantry Brigade will take over the Divisional front with the 110th Infantry Brigade in Support and 62nd Infantry Brigade in Reserve.

10. The route of supply for the Division will be :-

FINS - GOUZECOURT - VILLERS GUISLAIN or GONNELIEU to BANTOUZELLE.

H.L. Greenhalgh Lieut Col

29th September 1918.

General Staff.
21st Division.

War Diary.

TELEGRAM.

URGENT OPERATIONS PRIORITY	Words Sent At..............m By.............. To..............	APP 3

BUMA	RORU	5th Corps.	15th S.n R.A.F.
BURA	JEKU	5th Corps R.A.	Div. Cav. Troops.
RUVE	JEMU	17th Div.	Div. Cyclist Coy.
WUMA	FOLO	42nd Div.	
JENU	A/Q	38th Div.	

/ 3rd / AAA

JEZU Order No. 223 AAA General line reached by our Troops is Eastern edge VAUX WOODS to Railway West of YTRES AAA Probable enemy line of resistance is CANAL de L'ESCAUT to BANTEUX and HINDENBURG LINE AAA Corps will continue the advance tomorrow to the general line W.22.Central - Q.32.d. AAA JEZU will remain in Corps Reserve AAA BUMA Group will move to area about O.20 and O.21. tomorrow 4th inst. so as to clear LE TRANSLOY by 10 a.m. AAA BUMA will establish observation posts in the Trench System East of ROCQUIGNY as soon as vacated by 17th Div and will be prepared to hold this line between O.35 c.O.O. and O.16.c.O.O. in case of necessity AAA Following distances will be maintained on line of march AAA 200 yds between Coys. and 500 yds between Battns. AAA BUMA will notify JEZU position of new H.Q. as soon as possible tomorrow AAA RUVE and BURA will probably not move but BURA will be ready to move at one hour's notice AAA Div.Cav. and Div. Cyclists will remain in present positions ready to move at one hour's notice AAA 'Q' will issue orders for move of BUMAS Transport AAA Acknowledge AAA Addsd. recipients JEZU Order No.222.

JEZU

10.25 p.m.

H.H. Macdougall. Major
for Lt.-Col. G.S.

TELEGRAM.

War Diary.

App VI

	Words.	
PRIORITY.	Sent At..............m. By............... To...............	

BUMA	RORU	5th Corps.
BURA	JEKU	5th Corps R.A.
RUVE	JEMU	17 Div.
WUMA	POLO	38 Div.
JENU	A/Q.	15 Sqn. R.A.F.

/ 4 / AAA

JEZU Order No. 224. AAA 38th Div. and 17th Div. are reported at 7 p.m. to have troops across CANAL DU NORD but not yet across EQUANCOURT Trench System AAA JEZU will relieve 38th Div. tomorrow Sept. 5th AAA BUMA Group will relieve advanced guard Brigade Group 38th Div. AAA BURA will relieve supporting Brigade and RUVE reserve Brigade AAA BUMA will keep in touch with situation of leading Brigade tomorrow AAA If advance during Sept. 5th is carried across NURLU - FINS Road BUMA will move to vicinity of CANAL DU NORD during afternoon AAA BURA Group will move tomorrow morning to reach West of SAILLY SAILLISEL by 1 p.m. and have dinners there AAA Any orders for BURA will be sent to BUMA H.Q. O.31.b.3.3. after 11 a.m. AAA RUVE Group will be prepared to move at one hour's notice after 9 a.m. AAA Distances for Infantry on march 500 yards between Battns. and 200 yds. between Coys AAA Div. Cav. and Cyclists and two Sections GILE have been ordered to report BUMAS H.Q. tomorrow morning and will come under BUMAS Orders AAA 21 Div. Arty. reverts to JEZU AAA Orders for move of Units not mentioned above will be issued later AAA Div. H.Q. closes LE SARS 2.30 p.m. and opens LES BOEUFS same hour AAA ACKNOWLEDGE AAA Addsd. all concerned.

JEZU

7.45 p.m.

H. Lauchlye

Lt.-Col. G.S.

TELEGRAM.

URGENT OPERATIONS PRIORITY 64th and 110 Bdes. HW	Words. Sent. At.............. To.............. By..............	

BUMA 'Q'
BURA 38th Div.
RUVE vth Corps.

GX. 822. / 5th / AAA

Ref. JEZU Order No. 224 AAA BURA Group will relieve 113 and 115 Brigades in Trench System U.5. U.11. U.17.a. and U.10. this afternoon. AAA Both these Brigades are very weak AAA Exact positions occupied by 38th Div. need not be taken up AAA Woods and Valleys are full of gas and will be avoided AAA BURA H.Q. will be established at 113 Bde. H.Q. U.8.a.5.5. from 3 p.m. AAA Leading troops BURA will cross main LE TRANSLOY - SAILLY SAILLISEL Road at 3.30 p.m. AAA Movement by Platoons. AAA BURA will wire exact position of Battns. on completion of relief AAA Dispositions of 113 and 115 Brigades by wire for BURA only AAA RUVE will move to area W. of SAILLY SAILLISEL AAA Starting point LE TRANSLOY SUGAR FACTORY at 4.30 p.m. AAA RUVE H.Q. will be established at 115 Bde. H.Q. U.14.a.0.4. from 5 p.m. AAA Added BUMA BURA RUVE reptd to 'Q' 38th Div 5th Corps.

JEZU

H.C. Trangbley

12.40 p.m.

Lt. Col.G.S.

War Diary.

TELEGRAM

URGENT
OPERATION
PRIORITY
TO 62nd
BRIGADES
Priority
remainder.

Words

App. 5

Sent
At..................m
To..................
By..................

BUMA	RORU	5th Corps.	15th Sqn R.A.F.
BURA	JEKU	5th Corps R.A.	
RUVE	~~XXXXX~~ JEMU	12th Div.	
WUMA	FOLO	17th Div.	
JENU	A/Q	38th Div.	

/ 5th / AAA

JEZU Order No. 225 AAA Situation remains as already issued to Brigades AAA BUMA will carry out active patrolling during tonight and tomorrow AAA If resistance of enemy opposite Div. front shows signs of slackening BUMA will push forward advanced guard and prepare to follow with remainder of Bde AAA Advance will continue until objective W.22.c.0.4. - REVELON - W.10.Central is reached when orders for fresh advance will be issued from Div. H.Q. AAA BUMA will NOT engage in serious attack unless fresh instructions are issued AAA Successive Bds. Report Centres will be established by Div. Signals whenever further advance is made at Cross Roads V.18.c. AAA HEUDECOURT SQUARE AAA Sunken Road W.18.c.8.2. AAA BURA will be prepared to hold line St.MARTINS WOOD - LE MESNIL-EN-ARROAISE but as counter-attack by enemy across CANAL DU NORD is unlikely efforts will be concentrated on keeping troops fresh AAA RUVE will remain as at present AAA BURA and RUVE will not advance without orders from Div. H.Q. AAA 21st Div. Arty. takes over from 38th Div. Arty. tonight AAA 62nd Div. Arty. remains covering Sector AAA ACKNOWLEDGE AAA Addsd. all concerned.

JEZU

6.50 p.m.

H.L. Knaebbyn [signature]

Lt. Col. G.S.

War Diary

TELEGRAM

URGENT
OPERATIONS
PRIORITY

62nd Bde

HLF.

	Words	
	Sent At.................m To................. By.................	app 6

BUMA	RORU	5th Corps.	15th Sqn. R.A.F.
BURA	JEKU	5th Corps R.A.	
RUVE	JEMU	12th Div.	
WUMA	FOLO	17th Div.	
JENU	A/Q	38th Div.	

/ 6th / AAA

21 Div. Order 226 AAA Situation at 7.30 p.m. AAA 12 Div. hold V.29. with troops in Cutting V.30. AAA 17th Div. are reported to hold trench P. 36.b and d. and V.6. b and d. AAA 62nd Bde. hold NURLU - FINS Road in V.23 and V.17. with advanced troops in SOREL-LE-GRAND AA Position about FINS uncertain AAA 62nd Brigade group will continue advance tomorrow AAA Main guard will move forward at 6 a.m. AAA 1st Objective Old BROWN Line W.22.c. W.16.Central W.10.a.0.0. W.9.a.8.9. AAA 2nd Objective Northern end of PEIZIERE -VAUCELLETTE FARM - CHAPEL CROSSING AAA 64th Brigade Group will move forward by stages already ordered until EQUANCOURT trench system is occupied when further orders will be issued AAA 110th Brigade group will remain in present position AAA Next bound when ordered will be to area just East of CANAL DU NORD AAA Reserve M.G. Coy. will assemble V.20 a and b. by 8 a.m. tomorrow and will maintain Officer at report centre V.14.b.8.3. AAA Div. H.Q. will move to U.5.c.3.2. at an hour to be notified later. AAA ACKNOWLEDGE AAA Added recipients Order No. 225.

JEZU

8 p.m.

HLGranklyn

Lt. Col. G.S.

War Diary

TELEGRAM.

App 9

Urgent Operations Priority to 64th Bde ~~and M.G.Bn.~~ AHG	Words Sent At..............m To.............. By..............	

BUMA WUMA FOLO.
BURA RORU
RUVE 'Q'

GX. 894 / 7th / AAA

Reference 21 Div Order No. 226 AAA When BUMA has occupied whole of 1st Objective BURA will move one Battn. to occupy SOREL LE GRAND AAA When BUMAS Reserve BN. moves forward from 1st objective BURA will move one Battn to about W.8.Central and another to about W.20.a and c. maintaining one Battn. in SOREL AAA When BUMA reports whole of 2nd objective captured BURA will dispose Brigade so as to be able to occupy 1st objective in case of need or to take up advance tomorrow AAA RUVE will probably move to ground E. of CANAL DU NORD this evening so all preparations should be made AAA Reserve M.G. Coy. will move via EQUANCOURT to about V.17.d. forthwith AAA This Coy. will move in future when leading Brigade H.Q. moves and will maintain liaison Officer with latter AAA Acknowledge.

JEZU

9.45 a.m.

A H Grantley
Lt. Col. G.S.

TELEGRAM.

URGENT
OPERATIONS
PRIORITY TO

Bdes
HG

Words

Sent.
At..............
To..............
By..............

DADE	LODE	33rd Div.
BASU	ZEJU	5th Corps.
VUFE	5th Div.	15th Sqn. R.A.F.

G.X.515 / 28 / AAA

Ivth Corps report that enemy have withdrawn from their front AAA DADE has occupied AFRICAN TRENCH and is pushing patrols towards GOUZEAUCOURT AAA If patrols sent out by VUFE meet no resistance VUFE will occupy line GREEN LANE GREEN SWITCH getting touch with 5th Division at R.26.a.9.1 AAA When this line made good by VUFE patrols will be sent to BROWN LINE but no advance in force until touch established with 5th Division on left AAA When 5th Division have occupied FUSILIER RIDGE and if patrols still report no resistance VUFE will make good BROWN LINE and send patrols to GREEN LINE AAA In addition to above VUFE will send one special reconnoitring patrol at once to KITCHEN CRATER and another to GONNELIEU to report if enemy occupy these places or not AAA When VUFE has occupied GREEN LANE GREEN SWITCH and when patrols have reached BROWN LINE DADE will assemble Brigade in GOUZEAUCOURT VALLEY assuming that GOUZEAUCOURT is found empty AAA DADE will be prepared on receipt of orders to move through VUFE and occupy GREEN LINE AAA BASU will be at half hours' notice to move AAA Ack AAA Added all concerned

---

H C Franklyn

ZOWU
11.35 a.m.

Lieut.Colonel,
General Staff,

TELEGRAM.

Words

Sent.

DRLS.
S.&R. 5th Div
33rd " H.A.

At....................
To....................
By....................

DADE	JESO	33rd Div.	15th Sqn. R.A.F.
BASU	ZOHO		
VUFE	DUFA	V Corps.	Cyclist Troop.
LODE	A/Q.	V Corps R.A.	
ZOKI	5th Div.	V Corps H.A.	
ZEJU		'B' Coy. Tanks.	

\- / 28th / AAA

ZOWU Order No.238 AAA Enemy have withdrawn opposite Vth and IVth Corps fronts but to what extent is not yet known AAA ZOWU has been ordered to capture BROWN and GREEN LINES early tomorrow morning AAA VUFE will attack on right and DADE on left AAA Dividing line between Brigades R.31, R.33, R.36.Central AAA 33rd Division will be attacking VILLERS GUISLAIN and GREEN LINE in conjunction with us AAA 5th Division will be attacking FUSILIER and CEMETERY RIDGES and subsequently BANTEUX AAA Two Tanks will work with VUFE and two Tanks with DADE AAA The former rendezvous X.8.a.1.9 and latter R.25.d.2.0 about 11 p.m. AAA Right pair Tanks will work via Cemetery X.2.d. KITCHEN CRATER TURNER CRATER and clear GREEN LINE AAA Left pair Tanks work round each side GONNELIEU and down GLASGOW TRENCH and prepared to deal with BANTEUX SUPPORT if Infantry in difficulties AAA All Tanks rally KITCHEN CRATER after operations where available for immediate counter-attack AAA Artillery starting line for barrage X.2.d.3.5 to R.26.d.3.8 AAA Barrage moves 100 yards in six minutes to BROWN LINE and 100 yards in four minutes from BROWN to GREEN LINE AAA Barrage will be amended and added to according to most Easterly line reached by Infantry this evening AAA Barrage Tables issued to Brigades show other details AAA One M.G.Coy. will accompany each Brigade AAA Unless otherwise detailed Barrage for attack on BROWN LINE will come down at 3.30 a.m. and for attack from BROWN to GREEN LINE at 5.50 a.m. AAA Ack AAA Addsd all concerned

---

H.C.Franklyn
Lieut.Colonel,
General Staff.

ZOWU
7.30 p.m.

TELEGRAM.

URGENT OPERATIONS
PRIORITY to 3 Bdes.

Words

Sent.
At....................
To....................
By....................

DADE	JESO	V Corps.
BASU	ZOHO	V Corps R.A.
VUFE	DUFA	V Corps H.A.
LODE	A/Q.	15 Sqn. R.A.F.
ZOKI	6th Div.	Divl. Cyclists Troop.
ZEJU	33rd Div.	

- / 29th / AAA

ZOWU Order No.239 AAA Owing to success of both flanks today it appears probable that the enemy will withdraw shortly from our immediate front AAA Active patrolling will be carried out by VUFE and DADE tonight AAA If GONNELIEU and BROWN LINE are entered by patrols without resistance either tonight or tomorrow they will at once be occupied in force and patrols pushed on to GREEN LINE AAA If GREEN LINE is occupied by patrols this line will also be occupied in strength and patrols pushed down towards CANAL AAA Boundary between Brigades Sunken Road at R.26.c.3.0 - R.32.Central - R.34.Central - R.36.Central AAA Patrolling must be carried out by strong fighting patrols and minor resistance must be overcome AAA Patrols must be sent out at least once every hour and be particularly active just before Dawn AAA All available heavy Artillery and Field Howitzers will bombard GONNELIEU from 4.5 a.m. to 5 a.m. and then Cease AAA DADE will inform Div. H.Q. by 3 a.m. if bombardment is not to take place owing to their being in occupation of village AAA Any barrage required by Brigades for patrols to work under will be arranged with affiliated Artillery AAA DADE will have call on 122 Brigade as well as 79th Brigade for this purpose AAA BASU will remain in present positions till further orders AAA Ack AAA Adsd all concerned

---

H. Knatchbull-Hugessen [signature]

ZOWU
10.10 p.m.

Lieut.Colonel,
General Staff.

TELEGRAM.

Words

Urgent
Operations
Priority to
3 Bdes. HLF

Sent.
At...............
To...............
By...............

DADE	JESO	V Corps.
BASU	ZOHO	V Corps R.A.
VUFE	DUFA	V Corps H.A.
LODE	A/Q.	15 Sqn. R.A.F.
ZOKI	5 Div.	Divl. Cyclist Troop.
ZEJU	33 Div.	

- / 30th / AAA

ZOWU Order No.240 AAA Prisoners state that enemy will withdraw to distance of 4 kilo-metres East of Canal AAA When GREEN LINE has been made good on Divl. Front DADE and VUFE will send forward to Canal sieze crossings and establish bridgeheads on East bank AAA BASU will move to just West of QUENTIN RIDGE forthwith and will be prepared on receipt of orders to advance through VUFE and DADE cross Canal and occupy HINDENBURG LINE between RANCOURT FARM and BANTOUZEELE both exclusive AAA Report Centres will be established by Div. Signals at KITCHEN CRATER TURNER QUARRY successiv ARNOLD QUARRY AAA DADE will transfer Cyclists to BASU when latter takes up advance AAA Addsd all concerned AAA Ack in R.33c

---

HLKnoubly

ZOWU
12.10 p.m.

Lieut.Colonel,
General Staff.

TELEGRAM.

URGENT OPERATIONS
PRIORITY to
3 Bdes.

Words

Sent
At..................
To..................
By..................

DADE
BASU
VUFE
LODE
ZOKI
ZEJU

JESO
ZOHO
DUFA
A/Q.
5th Div.
33rd Div.

V Corps.
V Corps R.A.
V Corps H.A.
15th Sqn.R.A.F.
Div. Cyclist Troop.

– / 30th / AAA

ZOWU Order No.241 AAA VUFE on right and DADE on left will continue to hold GREEN LINE AAA Front line to be held thinly and Brigades disposed in depth AAA BASU will remain in present positions AAA Patrols will be sent to Canal bank tonight accompanied by R.E. AAA If any bridges are found to be repairable and hostile fire permits R.E. will carry out repairs protected by Infantry patrol on East bank AAA Risk of heavy casualties will NOT be run AAA If any bridges are found intact or are repaired by R.E. post will be established on West bank to cover bridge with fire and so prevent demolition by enemy AAA If patrols can cross canal they will work towards HINDENBURG LINE to report if enemy hold this line or not AAA All troops East of GREEN LINE except those detailed to guard Bridges or to occupy tactical points selected by Brigadiers will be withdrawn before daylight AAA Troops to be rested as much as possible tonight and tomorrow unless situation changes AAA Ack AAA Adsd all concerned

ZOWU
7.30 p.m.

H L Knoblyn

Lieut.Colonel,
General Staff.

1

TELEGRAM.

Urgent Operations Priority to 3 Bdes.	Words	
	Sent	
	At....................	
	To....................	
	By....................	

DADE	JESO	38th Div.
BASU	ZOHO	V Corps.
VUFE	DUFA	V Corps R.A.
LODE	A/Q.	V Corps H.A.
ZOKI	33rd Div.	15 Sqn. R.A.F.
ZEJU	37th Div.	Div. Cyclists.

-	/	3rd /	AAA

300 yds E of

ZOWU Order No.243 AAA The 50th Div. have reached Northern outskirts of CATELET and GOUY and are to attack high ground S.28. S.29 this evening AAA 38th Div. will then relieve them and will tomorrow attack LA TERRIERE and clear crossings for 33rd Div. at OSSUS AAA 33rd Div. will then cross Canal and form offensive flank facing North between LA TERRIERE and HONNECOURT AAA C.R.A. and M.G.Bn. will keep HINDENBURG LINE and ground between it and Canal under steady continuous fire during these operations AAA VUFE will keep touch with the enemy tonight with patrols endeavouring to pass patrols across Canal on rafts AAA Patrols to withdraw before daylight. AAA VUFE will be prepared from tomorrow inclusive as pressure from South increases to push patrols across Canal and to support them AAA C.R.E. will arrange for bridges to be thrown whenever and wherever VUFE obtains lodgement on East bank AAA BASU will be prepared to cross by these bridges or via HONNECOURT and establish themselves in HINDENBURG LINE within Div. Boundaries AAA Cyclist Sqn. comes under orders of BASU from tomorrow inclusive AAA O.C. will report BASU H.Q. during morning AAA Ack AAA Adsd all concerned.

H.C. Trambley [signature]

ZOWU
1800 hrs.

Lieut.Colonel,
General Staff.

TELEGRAM.

URGENT OPERATIONS PRIORITY to 3 Bdes.	Words Sent. At.................... To.................... By....................

DADE	JESO	38th Div.
BASU	ZOHO	V Corps.
VUFE	DUFA	V Corps R.A.
LODE	A/Q.	V Corps H.A.
ZOKI	33rd Div.	15 Sqn. R.A.F.
ZEJU	37th Div.	Div. Cyclist Troop.

\- / 5th / AAA

ZOWU Order No.244 AAA All indications show enemy have withdrawn opposite Corps front AAA Aeroplanes report HINDENBURG LINE appears deserted AAA 33rd Div. reported to have patrol in or near LA TERRIERE AAA VUFE will establish bridge-head round outskirts of BANTOUZELLE forthwith under cover of which C.R.E. will throw bridges to take Infantry in fours AAA When this objective made good VUFE will occupy more extended bridge-head as follows AAA ARNOULD QUARRY - C.T. through M.33.a. and M.27.d. - HINDENBURG SUPPORT Line from M.27.d.3.5 to M.27.b.0.3 thence via RED FARM to Canal AAA Fighting patrols will then be sent to HINDENBURG SUPPORT Line between RANCOURT FARM excl. and M.27.d. AAA This line will be occupied by VUFE as soon as made good by patrols but VUFE will continue to hold bridge-head strongly until further notice AAA BASU will move heads of leading Battns. to BANTEUX forthwith and will start crossing Canal as soon as VUFE has made good larger bridge-head AAA Objectives for BASU as follows AAA HINDENBURG SUPPORT Line from RANCOURT FARM exclusive to M.27.d. if not already made good by VUFE AAA Line of road MONTECOUVEZ FARM - BONNE ENFANCE FARM within Divl. Boundaries AAA When latter objective made good patrols will be sent to MASNIERES BEAUREVOIR Trench System to ascertain if occupied by enemy or not AAA Minor resistance must be overcome by VUFE and BASU AAA Touch must be obtained and kept with 33rd Div. AAA Care must be taken to protect left flank throughout operations until 37th Div. are up in line AAA DADE will move to area R.28.c. & d. R.29.c. & d. R.34. as soon as vacated by VUFE and BASU AAA One M.G.Coy. with each Bde. AAA Successive Report Centres will be established by Divl. Signals at ARNOULD QUARRY GRATTE PANCHE FARM and ARDISSART FARM AAA Ack AAA Addsd all concerned

---

Lieut.Colonel,
General Staff.

ZOWU
1205 hrs.

TELEGRAM.

URGENT OPERATIONS
PRIORITY to 3 Bdes.

Words

Sent.

At....................
To....................
By....................

DADE	JESO	38th Div.
BASU	ZOHO	5 Corps.
VUFE	DUFA	5 Corps R.A.
LODE	A/Q.	5 Corps H.A.
ZOKI	33rd Div.	15 Sqn. R.A.F.
ZEJU	37th Div.	

- / 5th / AAA

ZOWU Order No.245 AAA Line reached today not yet certain but we hold BONNE ENFANCE FARM-M.24.c. - M.17.d. AAA Aeroplane reports enemy seen retiring from BEAUREVOIR Line this evening AAA Advance will be resumed tomorrow Oct. 6th AAA BASU will act as advanced guard Brigade AAA First objective line of road N.33.d. & b. - HAUT FARM - HURTEBEISE FARM AAA Second objective WALINCOURT Village and high ground N.18.a. with patrols into SERVAL CHATEAU and SELVIGNY AAA Touch will be gained if possible on flanks at conclusion of each bound but advance must not be delayed for this purpose AAA 78th Bde. R.F.A. come under direct orders of BASU for tomorrow AAA VUFE will act as supporting Brigade and will move to line MONTECOUVEZ FARM - BONNE ENFANCE FARM as soon as BASU has completely cleared BEAUREVOIR front line AAA DADE will be Reserve Brigade and will move to HINDENBURG SUPPORT LINE as soon as VUFE has completely cleared this line AAA Policy for BASU will be to manoeuvre enemy out of positions he may be holding and to act vigorously without engaging Brigade in frontal attack on strong position AAA 38th Div. on our right are being directed on high ground in O.27.Central AAA Objective for 37th Div. not yet known AAA Ack AAA Adsd all concerned

---

Lieut.Colonel,
General Staff.

ZOWU
20.45 hrs.

War Diary.

General Staff.

21st Division.

October 1918.

(Report on operations attached).

Report on operations 22nd – 26th [illegible] is with Recommendations

Voe

C O N F I D E N T I A L.

W A R D I A R Y

OF

"G" Branch, Headquarters, 21st Division.

FROM:- 1st Oct. 1918. TO:- 31st Oct. 1918.

Instructions regarding War Diaries and Intelligence Summaries are contained in F. S. Regs., Part II, and the Staff Manual respectively. Title pages will be prepared in manuscript.

or

INTELLIGENCE SUMMARY.

(*Erase heading not required.*)

Place	Date	Hour	Summary of Events and Information	Remarks and references to Appendices
EQUANCOURT.				
	Oct.	1st	1 a.m. One prisoner captured near HONNECOURT. No change in the situation during the day. Enemy activity slight. Snipers and Machine Guns active from the Eastern bank of the Canal.	
	Oct.	2nd	5.30 a.m. Bridge swung across the Canal. Two men succeeded in crossing the Canal but were forced to retire in the face of heavy Machine Gun fire. Enemy snipers active throughout the operation.	
			2.35 p.m. 64th Inf. Bde. H.Q. opened at REVELON near HEUDECOURT.	
			3.30 p.m. Corps policy dictated - Rest, re-organisation, reconnaissance, patrolling and sniping by Machine Guns.	
	Oct.	3rd	9.45 a.m. All attempts to cross the Canal met by heavy Machine Gun fire. Day very quiet. Little hostile shelling.	
			9.35 p.m. 110th Inf. Bde. took over whole Divisional Front. 62nd Inf. Bde. in support and 64th Inf. Bde. in Reserve.	App I
	Oct.	4th	Slight hostile shelling of BANTEUX SPUR. Enemy very quiet. Patrols reported on two intact footbridges over Canal South of BANTEUX.	App II
	Oct.	5th	8 a.m. Enemy commenced to retire on V Corps front. 33rd Division got patrols across the Canal at HONNECOURT.	
			9 a.m. 110 Inf. Bde. succeeded in getting patrols across Canal at BANTEUX. BANTOUZELLE occupied.	
			12 Noon. HINDENBURG LINE and HINDENBURG SUPPORT LINE occupied without resistance.	App III

D. D. & L., London, E.C.
(A7883) Wt. W809/M1672 350,000 4/17 Sch. 52a Forms/C/2118/14

Instructions regarding War Diaries and Intelligence Summaries are contained in F. S. Regs., Part II. and the Staff Manual respectively. Title pages will be prepared in manuscript.

INTELLIGENCE SUMMARY.

(Erase heading not required.)

Place	Date	Hour	Summary of Events and Information	Remarks and references to Appendices
			64th Inf. Bde. crossed canal and took over from 110th Inf. Bde. as leading Brigade, with two Battalions in front line and one in support.	
			6 p.m. Our troops occupied LE CATALET - NAUROY line along Divisional front without resistance and patrols pushed forward towards MASNIERES - BEAUREVOIR line. BONNE ENFANCE Farm taken by 64th Inf. Bde. but further advance held up by heavy fire.	
	Oct.	6th.	8 a.m. MONTECOUVEZ Farm captured.	
			9.10 a.m. 110th Inf. Bde. H.Q. opened M.32.b.7.1. and 64th Inf. Bde. GRATTE PANCHE FM.	App II
			11.30 a.m. Line of 64th Inf. Bde. reported MONTECOUVEZ FARM - N.25.a. - BONNE ENFANCE FARM with advanced troops along sunken road T.2.c.	
			2.55 a.m. 21st Div. G.X.761 issued detailing orders for attack by 64th Inf. Bde. on ENGLES CHATEAU at dusk, subsequently cancelled at 4.15 p.m.	
			10.30 p.m. Right Battalion, 64th Inf. Bde. now hold trench line T.1.c.5.6. to T.1.b.8.5. otherwise no change.	
	Oct.	7th.	5 a.m. Situation unchanged - night passed quietly.	
			9.30 a.m. Patrols report BEAUREVOIR line strongly held and wire in good condition. Attempts to work Northwards along trench T.1.b.8.5. strongly resisted.	
			9.30 p.m. 21st Div. Order No.246 issued detailing attack by 21st Div. on WALINCOURT.	App I
BANTOUZELLE. M.32.b.7.1.	Oct.	8th.	8 a.m. Divisional Headquarters opened at M.32.b.7.1.	

D. D. & L., London, E.C. (A7883) Wt W809/M1672 350,000 4/17 Sch. 52a Forms/C/2118/14

Instructions regarding War Diaries and Intelligence Summaries are contained in F. S. Regs., Part II, and the Staff Manual respectively. Title pages will be prepared in manuscript.

INTELLIGENCE SUMMARY.

(Erase heading not required.)

Place	Date	Hour	Summary of Events and Information	Remarks and references to Appendices
			9.10 a.m. First objective captured by 64th and 110th Inf. Bdes. and 62nd Inf. Bde. moving through to third objective. Considerable hostile shelling of BEAUREVOIR Line.	
			9.40 a.m. 21st Division G.A.102. issued detailing 64th and 110th Inf. Bdes. to collect all available troops less one battalion each, ready to follow up advance of 62nd Inf. Bde.	
			12.20 p.m. Line of 62nd Inf. Bde. runs ANGLE WOOD (incl)-trench line N.28.b and d. to N.22.c.8.4. - HURTEBISE COPSE.	
			1.30 p.m. Situation unchanged. Left Battn. 62nd Inf. Bde. reached N.16.c. where in touch with 37th Division. Further advance impossible without barrage.	
			1.30 p.m. 21st Div. G.X.808 issued detailing 110th Inf. Bde. to be prepared to attack GUILLEMIN FARM on the afternoon and to move Battns. to BRISIEUX WOOD area preparatory to attack.	
			3.35 p.m. 64th Inf. Bde. ordered to send one Battn. to ANGLE WOOD where it was to come under orders of 62nd Inf. Bde.	
			6 p.m. 62nd Inf. Bde. attacked WALINCOURT and reached line N.29.d.9.5. - N.29.b.5.7. - N.23.Cent. thence along SARGRENAN RIVER.	
			7 p.m. Vth Corps G.458 issued detailing advance of 17th Division through 21st Div. at 5.20 a.m.	
			11 p.m. 21st Div. G.X.827 issued stating advance by 17th Division through 21st Div. and action of Division after advance by 17th Division.	

D. D. & L., London, E.C.
(A7883) Wt. W809/M1672 350,000 4/17 Sch. 52a Forms/C/2118/14

Summaries are contained in F. S. Regs., Part II. and the Staff Manual respectively. Title pages will be prepared in manuscript.

INTELLIGENCE SUMMARY.

(Erase heading not required.)

Place	Date	Hour	Summary of Events and Information	Remarks and references to Appendices
	Oct.	9th.	5.20 a.m. 17th Division advanced through 21st Division. 21st Division came into support to 17th Division.	App. VI
			10 a.m. Orders issued to Brigades to concentrate in present areas.	
			7 p.m. Vth Corps G.501 issued detailing advance of Vth Corps at 5.30 a.m. Division to maintain touch with 17th Division and regulate advance by progress of 17th Division.	
			8 p.m. Division disposed as follows :-	
			Divisional Headquarters. ... M.32.b.7.1.	
			62nd Inf. Bde. ... WALINCOURT	
			64th : : ... One Bn. WALINCOURT. 2 Bns. N.32.33.34. area. Brigade H.Q. MONTECOUVEZ FARM.	
			110th Inf. Bde. ... N.19. 20, 21 and 26 area. Brigade H.Q. MONTECOUVEZ FARM.	
WALINCOURT.	Oct.	10th.	Division resting. Locations :-	
			Divisional Headquarters. ... N.24.d.6.2.	
			62nd Inf. Bde.) 64th : :) ... WALINCOURT.	
			110th : : ... CAULLERY.	
			Divisional Commander held a Conference at Divisional H.Q. at 5 p.m.	
	Oct.11 to 18th.		Division resting, reorganizing and training in the WALINCOURT - CAULLERY area. A Conference to discuss future operations took place at Corps Headquarters at 10.30 a.m. on Octr.18th. 21st Division Instructions Series G.F. No.1. issued giving details of future operations. See appdx.	App. VII

D. D. & L., London, E.C. (A7883) Wt. W809/M1672 350,000 4/17 Sch. 52a Forms/C/2118/14

Instructions regarding War Diaries and Intelligence Summaries are contained in F. S. Regs., Part II. and the Staff Manual respectively. Title pages will be prepared in manuscript.

INTELLIGENCE SUMMARY.

(Erase heading not required.)

Place	Date	Hour	Summary of Events and Information	Remarks and references to Appendices
	Oct.	19th.	64th Inf. Bde. moved from WALINCOURT to MONTIGNY.	
	Oct.	20th.	Division in Reserve.	
	Oct.	21st.	21st Division Order No.247 issued detailing attack by 21st Division in conjunction with other operations by Third and Fourth Armies on October 23rd.	App. VIII
	Oct.	22nd.	During the day Brigades moved up to assembly positions in vicinity of INCHY and on night of 22nd/23rd 64th and 110th Inf. Bdes took over the right and left sub-Sectors of the left Sector Vth Corps front, preparatory to the attack. Relief was complete at 10.45 p.m. and G.O.C. 21st Division assumed command of the line. Divisional Headquarters moved to INCHY.	
INCHY.	Oct.	23rd.	Attack commenced at 2 a.m. The enemy put down a heavy counter-preparation at 12.15 a.m. on 110th Inf. Bde. assembly areas, inflicting casualties. In spite of this, troops moved off to time.	App. IX App. X
			6 a.m. First objective captured on Divisional front.	
			9.40 a.m. 2nd Objective captured and leading Brigades advancing on 3rd objective. Hostile Artillery and Machine Gun fire considerable.	
			11 a.m. 3rd objective reported captured and 62nd Inf. Bde. advancing through leading Brigades, VENDEGIES clear of the enemy.	
			11.50 a.m. 21st Div. G.X.151 issued detailing 64th Inf. Bde. to keep in touch with progress made by the 62nd Inf. Bde. and move one Battn. at once to F.14.a. 64th Inf. Bde. to move one Battn. to F.8.d. as soon as 62nd Inf. Bde. crossed Road running S.E. from F.8.Cent. These Brigades to be prepared to support 62nd Inf. Bde. or form defensive flank facing S.E.	

D. D. & L., London, E.C.
(A7883) Wt. W809/M1672 350,000 4/17 Sch. 52a Forms/C/2118/14

Instructions regarding War Diaries and Intelligence Summaries are contained in F. S. Regs., Part II. and the Staff Manual respectively. Title pages will be prepared in manuscript.

INTELLIGENCE SUMMARY.

(Erase heading not required.)

Place	Date	Hour	Summary of Events and Information	Remarks and references to Appendices
			12.55 p.m. 62nd Inf. Bde. captured VENDEGIES. Line reported F.14.a and b. F.8.c. F.7.b. Troops still advancing.	
			3.45 p.m. 62nd Inf. Bde. captured GREEN LINE and continuing advance on POIX.	
			5 p.m. Heavy opposition encountered in advance from GREEN LINE and attack held up on this line. Prisoners in Div. Cage 5 p.m. 15 Officers and 477 O.R.	
			5 p.m. 21st Div. G.X.162. Warning Order issued detailing resumption of advance on 24th October.	
			6 p.m. Vth Corps G.316 received detailing Corps policy and details of objectives for 24th inst.	
			5.45 p.m. Enemy counter-attacked 62nd Inf. Bde. after heavy artillery barrage on the right. Line reported to run along road F.8.b.; no change on left, which runs F.8.a.5.9. - F.8.a.1.6. - F.1.d.Central.	
			8.30 p.m. 21st Div. Order No. 248 issued giving details for resumption of attack on 24th October by 64th Inf. Bde. on right and 62nd Inf. Bde. on left.	
NEUVILLY.	Oct.	24th.	~~24th Octobers~~ 7 a.m. Left Brigade report attack progressing steadily. Right Brigade report left Battn. held up by heavy M.G.fire. Left Battn. advancing well. Hostile artillery fire very heavy.	
			8.35 a.m. First objective gained. POIX DU NORD being mopped up.	
			1 p.m. Further advance held up by intense Machine Gun fire from X.23.a. and d.	

D. D. & L., London, E.C.
(A7883) Wt. W809/M1672 350,000 4/17 Sch. 52a Forms/C/2118/14

Instructions regarding War Diaries and Intelligence Summaries are contained in F. S. Regs., Part II. and the Staff Manual respectively. Title pages will be prepared in manuscript.

INTELLIGENCE SUMMARY.

(Erase heading not required.)

Place	Date	Hour	Summary of Events and Information	Remarks and references to Appendices
			2.40 p.m. 21st Div. Order No. 249. issued detailing resumption of attack on 2nd objective by 64th Inf. Bde. on right, 62nd Inf. Bde. on left at 4 p.m. 21st Div. G.X.196 issued detailing the pushing forward of patrols after attack, to the line of ENGLEFONTAINE - LOUVIGNIES ROAD.	App XI
			7.20 p.m. Objective taken on entire Divisional front. Considerable M.G. fire encountered. Prisoners through Div. Cage today, 1 Off. 212 O.R.	
			8.15 p.m. 21st Division Order No. 250 issued detailing action to be taken by Division on 25th October.	App XII
	Oct.	25th.	9.10 a.m. Heavy shelling of POIX during the night.	
			21st Division order No. 251.issued detailing relief of 62nd and 64th Inf. Bdes. by 110th Inf Bde. 62nd Inf. Bde. to withdraw to W. of POIX and 64th Inf. Bde. to VENDEGIES area.	App XIII
			10 a.m. Divisional Headquarters opened at OVILLERS.	
			1.20 p.m. Vth Corps G.393. Warning Order issued detailing relief of 21st Division by 17th Division on 26/27th Oct.	
			2.45 p.m. Our troops reported by an aeroplane to be along road X.30.c and a. - X.24.c.	
			3.50 p.m. 21st Division Order No. 252 issued detailing action of 110th Inf. Bde. in conjunction with attack by the 33rd Division at 1 a.m.	App XIV
			7.30 p.m. 21st Division Warning Order G.X.228 issued re relief of 21st Division by 17th Division.	App XV
			12.30 p.m. Relief of 64th and 62nd Inf. Bdes. by 110th Inf. Bde. completed. 110th Inf. Bde. established an Outpost Zone by Platoon Posts as follows :- S.13.d.0.4. - X.17.d.9.9. - X.12.c.0.5. - X.11.b.0.2. - X.11.b.0.9.	

D. D. & L., London, E.C.
(A7883) Wt W809/M1672 350,000 4/17 Sch. 52a Forms/C/2118/14

Instructions regarding War Diaries and Intelligence Summaries are contained in F. S. Regs., Part II. and the Staff Manual respectively. Title pages will be prepared in manuscript.

INTELLIGENCE SUMMARY.

(*Erase heading not required.*)

Place	Date.	Hour	Summary of Events and Information	Remarks and references to Appendices
	Oct.	26th.	Considerable M.G. fire encountered. 21st Division Order No. 253. issued detailing relief of 21st Division by the 17th Division on the 26/27th October. Relief complete 10 p.m. G.O.C. 17th Division assumed command of the line. Divisional Headquarters opened NEUVILLY.	App XVI
NEUVILLY	Oct.	27th.	Division in reserve resting and disposed as follows :- Divisional Headquarters .... NEUVILLY. 62nd Inf. Bde. .... NEUVILLY. 64th : : .... INCHY. 110th Inf. Bde. .... OVILLERS & AMERVAL.	
	Oct.	28th.	Division in reserve resting and reorganizing. 21st Division Order No. 254 issued detailing the relief of the 17th Division by the 21st Division.	App XVII App XVIII
	Oct.	29th.	Relief of the 17th Division complete 9.40 p.m. G.O.C. 21st Division assumed command of the Left Sector, Vth Corps.	
	Oct.	30th.	POIX DU NORD very heavily shelled during the night.	
OVILLERS.			Divisional Headquarters opened OVILLERS 10 a.m.	
	Oct.	31st.	Area X.23. and ARBRE - DE - LA - CROIX shelled with Yellow and Blue Cros gas. POIX shelled during the afternoon. 21st Division Order No.255. issued detailing re-adjustment of Divisional and Brigade Boundaries on the night 1st/2nd November.	App XIX App XX

Instructions regarding War Diaries and Intelligence Summaries are contained in F. S. Regs., Part II, and the Staff Manual respectively. Title pages will be prepared in manuscript.

or

INTELLIGENCE SUMMARY.

(Erase heading not required.)

Place	Date	Hour	Summary of Events and Information	Remarks and references to Appendices
			21st Division Intelligence Summaries. Appendix	21
			Defensive Arrangements - Left Division, Vth Corps. :	22
			Proceedings of Conference held at Divisional Headquarters, 25th October. :	23
			Mentions of the 21st Division in the Commander in Chief's Dispatches from January to October 1918. :	24
			Report on Operations of 21st Division from 21st August to 3rd Septr. 1918. :	25
			: : : : : : : 4th Septr. to 16th Septr 1918. :	26
			: : : : : : : 17th Septr. to 20th Septr 1918. :	27
			: : : : : : : 26th Septr. to 18th Octr. 1918. :	28
			Campbell Major General Commanding 21st Division.	

D. D. & L., London, E.C.
(A7883) Wt. W809/M1672 350,000 4/17 **Sch. 52a** Forms/C/2118/14

App. I

SECRET.

Copy No. 22

21st Division Order No.242.

2nd October, 1918.

Ref: Sheet 57.C. S.E. 1/40,000.

1. The 110 Infantry Brigade will take over the front now held by the 62nd Infantry Brigade on the night 3rd/4th October.
Relief to be complete by 0200 hours.

2. On relief, 62nd Infantry Brigade will withdraw to the area Q.34, Q.35, W.4 and W.5.
62nd Infantry Brigade will report as soon as possible the proposed location of their Headquarters.

3. All details of relief will be arranged between Brigadiers

4. Machine Gun Reliefs will be arranged by O.C. 21st Battalion, Machine Gun Corps.

5. Completion of relief will be reported to Divisional Headquarters.

6. ACKNOWLEDGE.

H.H. Macdougall. Major
for.
Lieut.Colonel,
General Staff,
21st Division.

Issued through Signals at 1930 hours to :-

	Copy No.		Copy No.
62 Inf. Bde.	1	A.P.M.	12
64 : :	2	D.G.O.	13
110 : :	3	V Corps.	14 - 15
C.R.A.	4	V Corps R.A.	16
C.R.E.	5	V Corps H.A.	17
Pioneers.	6	37th Div.	18
D.M.G.C.	7	33rd Div.	19
Signals.	8	17th Div.	20
A.D.M.S.	9	15 Sqn. R.A.F.	21
Train.	10	War Diary.	22
A/Q.	11	File.	23

App 7

TELEGRAM.

Urgent Operations
Priority to
3 Bdes.

Words

Sent
At....................
To....................
By....................

DADE	JESO	38th Div.
BASU	ZOHO	V Corps.
VUFE	DUFA	V Corps R.A.
LODE	A/Q.	V Corps H.A.
ZOKI	33rd Div.	15 Sqn. R.A.F.
ZEJU	37th Div.	Div. Cyclists.

– / 3rd / AAA

ZOWU Order No.243 AAA The 50th Div. have reached Northern outskirts of CATELET and GOUY and are to attack high ground S.28. S.29 this evening AAA 38th Div. will then relieve them and will tomorrow attack LA TERRIERE and clear crossings for 33rd Div. at OSSUS AAA 33rd Div. will then cross Canal and form offensive flank facing North between LA TERRIERE and HONNECOURT AAA C.R.A. and M.G.Bn. will keep HINDENBURG LINE and ground between it and [300 Yds E of] Canal under steady continuous fire during these operations AAA VUFE will keep touch with the enemy tonight with patrols endeavouring to pass patrols across Canal on rafts AAA Patrols to withdraw before daylight. AAA VUFE will be prepared from tomorrow inclusive as pressure from South increases to push patrols across Canal and to support them AAA C.R.E. will arrange for bridges to be thrown whenever and wherever VUFE obtains lodgement on East bank AAA BASU will be prepared to cross by these bridges or via HONNECOURT and establish themselves in HINDENBURG LINE within Div. Boundaries AAA Cyclist Sqn. comes under orders of BASU from tomorrow inclusive AAA O.C. will report BASU H.Q. during morning AAA Ack AAA Adsd all concerned.

H. L. Knaubbye

ZOWU
1800 hrs.

Lieut.Colonel,
General Staff.

"C" Form — Army Form C. 2123 (In books of 100.)

MESSAGES AND SIGNALS.

No of Message............

Prefix.........Code.........Words..........

£ s. d.

Charges to Collect

Service Instructions.

Received. From .... By ....

Sent, or sent out. At .... m. To .... By ....

2W

Office Stamp. 3.X.18

Handed in at............Office.........m. Received.........m.

TO

*Sender's Number	Day of Month	In reply to Number	AAA
3 AW			

Corps	order	No	[illegible]
aaa	The	50th	Div
have	reached	northern	outskirts
of	CATELET	and	GOUY
and	are	to	attack
high	ground	S.E.	[illegible]
this	evening	aaa	38
Div	will	then	relieve
them	and	will	tomorrow
attack	LA	TERRIERE	and
clear	crossing	for	33rd
Div	at	OSSUS	aaa
33rd	Div	will	then
cross	Canal	and	form
offensive	flank	facing	north
between	LA	TERRIERE	and
HONNECOURT	aaa	CRA	and

FROM

TIME & PLACE

*This line should be erased if not required

C & R 7800. Wt. W14833/M1523 100,000. 8/17 (E930). Forms C/2123.

1912 hrs

Army Form C. 2123
(In books of 100.)

"C" Form

MESSAGES AND SIGNALS.

No of Message..............

Prefix..........Code.........Words.......... £ s d Charges to Collect	Received. From.......... By..........	Sent, or sent out. At..........m. To.......... By..........	Office Stamp.

Service Instructions.

Handed in at...................................Office..........m. Received..................m.

TO (2)

*Sender's Number	Day of Month	In reply to Number	AAA
✓	2		

MG	bn	will	keep
HINDENBURG	LINE	and	ground
between	it	and	300
yds	E	of	canal
under	steady	continuous	fire
during	these	operations	aaa
VUFE 110 Inf Bde	will	keep	touch
with	the	enemy	tonight
with	patrols	endeavouring	
to	pass	patrols	across
Canal	on	Rafts	aaa
patrol	to	withdraw	before
daylight	aaa	VUFE 110 Inf Bde	will
be	prepared	from	tomorrow
inclusive	if	pressure	from
south	weakens	to	push
patrols	across	canal	and

FROM

TIME & PLACE

*This line should be erased if not required

C & R 7800. Wt. W14832/M1523 100,000. 8/17. (E930). Forms C/2123

Army Form C. 2123
(In books of 100.)

"C" Form

MESSAGES AND SIGNALS

No of Message..........

Prefix.........Code.........Words.........	Received.	Sent, or sent out.	Office Stamp.
£ s. d. Charges to Collect	From .... By	At ....m. To .... By	
Service Instructions.			

Handed in at........ Office.......... m. Received.................m.

TO (3)

*Sender's Number	Day of Month	In reply to Number	AAA

to support them aaa RE will arrange for Bridges to be thrown wherever and whenever VUFE (110 Inf Bde) obtains lodgement on far bank aaa BASU (64 Inf B.) will be prepared to cross by these bridges or via HONNECOURT and establish themselves in HINDENBURG LINE within the boundaries aaa Exploit on coming under orders of BASU (64 Inf Bde) from tomorrow [illegible] aaa OC [illegible] will report to BASU (64 Inf Bde) during morning aaa Ack aaa Addsd all concerned

FROM

TIME & PLACE [illegible] 21 [illegible] 1800

*This line should be erased if not required

G. & R. 7800. Wt. W14832/M1528 100,000 8/17 (E930) Forms C/2123.

"C" Form. 171 Army Form C. 2123 (In books of 100.)

MESSAGES AND SIGNALS. No of Message..........

Prefix SM Code 2150 Words 94	Received From [illegible] By..........	Sent, or sent out. At..........m. To .... By..........	Office Stamp
Charges to Collect £ s d			
Service Instructions. Pty			

Handed in at.......... Office 2150 m Received 2205 m

TO 5th Corps

Sender's Number	Day of Month	In reply to Number	AAA
G X 930	5th	—	

Situation aaa Cyclists report MONTECOUVEZ FM held by Enemy 1930 aaa No other reports received aaa Following bridges completed aaa 2 bridges at Lock M25d86 one for guns one for infantry in fours aaa Latter bridge will be fit for guns tomorrow aaa 2 pontoon bridges for infantry in file aaa 2 Cork float bridges for infantry in single file aaa one trestle bridge for infantry in fours

FROM

TIME & PLACE

*This line should be erased if not required

C. & E. 7800. Wt. W14822/M1523 105,000 8/17 (E930) Forms C/2123 2515

"C" Form.

Army Form C. 2123
(In books of 100.)

MESSAGES AND SIGNALS

No of Message..........

Prefix..........Code.........Words..........

£ s d

Charges to Collect

Service Instructions.

Received
From HQ
By..................

Sent, or sent out.
At..........m.
To..........
By..........

Office Stamp.
E50 ... TELEGRAPHS

Handed in at...Office..........m Received..........m

TO (2)

Sender's Number	Day of Month	In reply to Number	AAA
34730			

aaa One repaired enemy bridge fit for infantry in front aaa All above bridges between R36 D9.8 and LOCK in BANTEUX

Q / CE } To see for return

Returned [illegible] Cyprus [illegible] 6/11

J. H. Blegman Capt for Bgde

5.10.18

CE Allen

FROM ZOWU 215th Army [illegible] ARL

TIME & PLACE 2150

*This line should be erased if not required

5/10

C. & R. 7300. Wt. W14332/M1524 100,000 2/17 (E930) Forms C/2123

App

TELEGRAM.

URGENT OPERATIONS	Words
PRIORITY to 3 Bdes.	Sent.
AHJ	At...................
	To...................
	By...................

Vufe = 110 Bde
Basu = 64 "
Dade = 62 "

DADE	JESO	38th Div.
BASU	ZOHO	V Corps.
VUFE	DUFA	V Corps R.A.
LODE	A/Q.	V Corps H.A.
ZOKI	33rd Div.	15 Sqn. R.A.F.
ZEJU	37th Div.	Div. Cyclist Troop.

- / 5th / AAA

21 Div.

ZOWU Order No.244 AAA All indications show enemy have withdrawn opposite Corps front AAA Aeroplanes report HINDENBURG LINE appears deserted AAA 33rd Div. reported to have patrol in or near LA TERRIERE AAA VUFE will establish bridge-head round outskirts of BANTOUZELLE under cover of which C.R.E. will throw bridges to take forthwith Infantry in fours AAA When this objective made good VUFE will occupy more extended bridge-head as follows AAA ARNOULD QUARRY - C.T. through M.33.a. and M.27.d. - HINDENBURG SUPPORT Line from M.27.d.3.5 to M.27.b.0.3 thence via RED FARM to Canal AAA Fighting patrols will then be sent to HINDENBURG SUPPORT Line between RANCOURT FARM excl and M.27.d. AAA This line will be occupied by VUFE as soon as made good by patrols but VUFE will continue to hold bridge-head strongly until further notice AAA BASU will move heads of leading Battns. to BANTEUX forthwith and will start crossing Canal as soon as VUFE has made good larger bridge-head AAA Objectives for BASU as follows AAA HINDENBURG SUPPORT Line from RANCOURT FARM exclusive to M.27.d. if not already made good by VUFE AAA Line of road MONTECOUVEZ FARM - BONNE ENFANCE FARM within Divl. Boundaries AAA When latter objective made good patrols will be sent to MASNIERES BEAUREVOIR Trench System to ascertain if occupied by enemy or not AAA Minor resistance must be overcome by VUFE and BASU AAA Touch must be obtained and kept with 33rd Div. AAA Care must be taken to protect left flank throughout operations until 37th Div. are up in line AAA DADE will move to area R.28.c. & d. R.29.c. & d. R.34. as soon as vacated by VUFE and BASU AAA One M.G.Coy. with each Bde. AAA Successive Report Centres will be established by Divl. Signals at ARNOULD QUARRY GRATTE PANCHE FARM and ARDISSART FARM AAA Ack AAA Addsd all concerned

H.V. Lauthlyn

Lieut.Colonel.
General Staff.

ZOWU
1205 hrs.

Army Form C. 2123
(In books of 100.)

"C" Form.

MESSAGES AND SIGNALS.

No. of Message 1837

Prefix SB Code 1210 Words 31	Received. From YU By Foster	Sent, or sent out. At ... m. To ... By ...	Office Stamp. ECO
Charges to Collect £ s. d.			
Service Instructions. PG			

Handed in at YU Office 1210 m. Received 13.35 m.

TO 5 Corps

*Sender's Number	Day of Month	In reply to Number	AAA
	5		

21st Div ZOWU	order	no	244
aaa	all	indications	show
enemy	have	withdrawn	opposite
corps	front	aaa	air reports
report	HINDENBURG LINE		appears
deserted	aaa	33rd	Div
reported	to	have	patrol
in	or	near	LA
TERRIERE aaa		110 Inf Bde VUFE	will
establish	Bridge-Head		round
outskirts of		BANTOUZELLE	further
within	cover	of	which
CRE	will	throw	bridge
to	take	infantry	in
force	aaa	when	the
objective	made	good	110 Inf Bde VUFE
will	occupy	more	extended

FROM
TIME & PLACE (Bridge)

*This line should be erased if not required

C. & R. 7800. Wt. W14832/M1523 100,000. 8/17. (E930). Forms C/2123.

1335

Army Form C. 2123
(In books of 100.)

"C" Form.

MESSAGES AND SIGNALS.

No. of Message..........

Prefix.......... Code......... Words..........	Received.	Sent, or sent out.	Office Stamp.
£ s. d. Charges to Collect	From	At .... m.	ECO -5 X 18
Service Instructions.	By	To	
		By	

Handed in at.......... Office.......... m. Received.......... m.

TO (2)

*Sender's Number	Day of Month	In reply to Number	AAA
	5.		

Bridge-head	as	follows	aaa
ARNOULD	QUARRY	CT	through
M33A	and	M27B	HINDENBURG
SUPPORT	line	from	M27B3.5
to	M27B0.3	thence	via
RED	FARM	to	Canal
aaa	Fighting	patrols	will
then	be	sent	to
HINDENBURG	SUPPORT	line	between
RANCOURT	FARM	excl	and
M27D	aaa	This	line
will	be	occupied	by
VUFE 110 Inf Bde	as	soon	as
made	good	by	patrols
but	VUFE 110 Inf Bde	will	continue
to	hold	bridgehead	strongly
until	further	notice	aaa

FROM

TIME & PLACE

*This line should be erased if not required

C. & R. 7300. Wt. W14832/M1523 100,000. 8/17. (E930). Forms C/2123

"C" Form.

MESSAGES AND SIGNALS.

Army Form C. 2121
(In books of 100.)

No. of Message..........

Prefix..........Code.........Words..........	Received.	Sent, or sent out.	Office Stamp.
£ s. d. Charges to Collect	From.......... By..........	At..........m. To.......... By..........	-9 X 18
Service Instructions.			

Handed in at.......... Office..........m. Received..........

TO (3)

Sender's Number	Day of Month	In reply to Number	AAA

BASU (64 Inf Bde) will move heads of leading Battns to BANTEUX forthwith and will start crossing canal as soon as VUFE (110 Inf Bde) has made good larger bridge head aaa Objectives for BASU (64 Inf Bde) as follows aaa HINDENBURG SUPPORT line from RANCOURT FARM exclusive to M27D if not already made good by VUFE (110 Inf Bde) aaa line of road MONTECOUVREZ FARM - BONNE ENFANCE FARM within Divl boundaries aaa when latter objective made good patrols

FROM

TIME & PLACE

*This line should be erased if not required

C. & R. 7800. Wt. W14832/M1523 100,000. 8/17 (E920). Forms C/2121.

Army Form C. 2123
(In books of 100.)

"C" Form.

MESSAGES AND SIGNALS.

No. of Message..............

Prefix.......Code.......Words.......	Received.	Sent, or sent out.	Office Stamp.
£ s. d.	From	At 8 X m.	ECO
Charges to Collect	By	To	
Service Instructions.		By	

Handded in at.......Office.......m. Received.......m.

TO (4)

*Sender's Number	Day of Month	In reply to Number	AAA
will	be	sent	to
MASNIERES	BEAUREVOIR	trench	system
to	ascertain	if	occupied
by	enemy	or	not
aaa	minor	resistance	must
be	overcome	by	VUFE 110 Inf Bde
and	BASU 64 Inf Bde	aaa	touch
must	be	obtained	and
kept	with	33rd	Div
aaa	care	must	be
taken	to	protect	left
flank	throughout	operations	
until	38	Div	are
up	in	line	aaa
DADE 62 Inf Bde	will	move	to
area	R28b	and	d
R29 b	and	d	R34

FROM

TIME & PLACE

*This line should be erased if not required

C. & R. 7800. Wt. W14832/M1523 100,000. 8/17 (E930). Forms C/2123.

Army Form C. 2123
(In books of 100.)

"C" Form.

MESSAGES AND SIGNALS.

No. of Message..........

Prefix.......... Code.......... Words..........

£ s. d.

Charges to Collect

Service Instructions.

Received.

From..........

By..........

Sent, or sent out.

At..........m.

To..........

By..........

Office Stamp.

Handed in at.......... Office.......... m. Received..........m.

TO (5)

*Sender's Number	Day of Month	In reply to Number	AAA

as	soon	as	vacated
by	VUFE (110 Inf Bde)	and	BASO (64 Inf Bde)
aaa	one	MG	coy
with	each	Bde	aaa
Successive	report	Centres	will
be	established	by	Divl
Signals	at	ARNOUD	QUARRY
GRATTEPANCHE		FARM	and
ARDISSART	FARM	aaa	ack
aaa	added	all	concd

ukf

FROM 21 Div

TIME & PLACE 1205 hrs

*This line should be erased if not required

C. & R. 7800. Wt. W14832/M1523 100,000. 8/17 (E980). Forms C/2123.

App 4

TELEGRAM.

URGENT OPERATIONS
PRIORITY to 3 Bdes.

Words
Sent.
At.....................
To.....................
By.....................

DADE	JESO	38th Div.
BASU	ZOHO	5 Corps.
VUFE	DUFA	5 Corps R.A.
LODE	A/Q.	5 Corps H.A.
ZOKI	33rd Div.	15 Sqn. R.A.F.
ZEJU	37th Div.	

- / 5th / AAA

ZOWU Order No.245 AAA Line reached today not yet certain but we hold BONNE ENFANCE FARM-M.24.c. - M.17.d. AAA Aeroplane reports enemy seen retiring from BEAUREVOIR Line this evening AAA Advance will be resumed tomorrow Oct. 6th AAA BASU will act as advanced guard Brigade AAA First objective line of road N.33.d. & b. - HAUT FARM - HURTEBEISE FARM AAA Second objective WALINCOURT Village and high ground N.18.a. with patrols into SERVAL CHATEAU and SELVIGNY AAA Touch will be gained if possible on flanks at conclusion of each bound but advance must not be delayed for this purpose AAA 78th Bde. R.F.A. come under direct orders of BASU for tomorrow AAA VUFE will act as supporting Brigade and will move to line MONTECOUVEZ FARM - BONNE ENFANCE FARM as soon as BASU has completely cleared BEAUREVOIR front line AAA DADE will be Reserve Brigade and will move to HINDENBURG SUPPORT LINE as soon as VUFE has completely cleared this line AAA Policy for BASU will be to manoeuvre enemy out of positions he may be holding and to act vigorously without engaging Brigade in frontal attack on strong position AAA 38th Div. on our right are being directed on high ground in O.27.Central AAA Objective for 37th Div. not yet known AAA Ack AAA Addd all concerned

---

H. Knobbyl(?)

Lieut.Colonel,
General Staff.

ZOWU
20.45 hrs.

367

"C" Form.

Army Form C. 2123
(In books of 100.)

MESSAGES AND SIGNALS.

No. of Message..........

Prefix SB Code 2125 Words 224 £ s d Charges to Collect	Received From YU HQ By........	Sent, or sent out. At........m. To........ By........	Office Stamp.
Service Instructions. Pty			

Handed in at YU Office 2125 m Received 2155

TO 5th Corps

*Sender's Number	Day of Month	In reply to Number	AAA
50 Div	5		

ZOWU	order	no	245
aaa	line	reached	today
not	yet	certain	but
we	hold	BONNE	ENFANCE
FM	— M24C	— M17D	aaa
aeroplane	reports	enemy	seen
retiring	from	BEAUREVOIR	line
this	evening	aaa	advance
will	be	resumed	tomorrow
at	6	aaa	BASU (25 Bde)
will	act	as	advance
guard	brigade	aaa	first
objective	line	of	road
N33D	and	B —	HAUT
FM —	HURTEBEISE	FM	aaa
Second	objective	WALINCOURT	Village
and	high	ground	N18A

FROM

TIME & PLACE

*This line should be erased if not required

C. & R. 7800. Wt. W14822/M1523 100,000 3/17 (E930) Forms C/2123

Army Form C. 2123
(In books of 100.)

"C" Form.

MESSAGES AND SIGNALS

No of Message...........

Prefix.......Code.......Words.......	Received	Sent, or sent out.	Office Stamp
£ s d	From 110	At.........m.	
Charges to Collect	By........	To........	
Service Instructions.		By........	

Handed in at...Office.......... m Received..................m

TO (2)

*Sender's Number	Day of Month	In reply to Number	AAA

with	patrols	into	SERVAL
ided CHATEAU	and	SELVIGNY	aaa
Touch	will	be	gained
if	possible	on	flanks
at	conclusion	of	each
bound	but	advance	must
not	be	delayed	for
this	purpose	aaa	78
Bde	RFA	come	under Bde
direction	orders	of	BASU, 110th Bde
for	tomorrow	aaa	VUFE
will	act	as	supporting
brigade	and	will	move
to	line	MONTECOUVEZ	FM —
BONNE	ENFANCE FM.		as
soon	as	BASU 64 Inf Bde	has

completely cleared BEAUREVOIR front

FROM

TIME & PLACE

*This line should be erased if not required

C. & R. 7800. Wt W14832/M1523 108,000 8/17 (E930) Forms C/2123

Army Form C. 2123
(In books of 100.)

"C" Form.

MESSAGES AND SIGNALS.

No of Message..........

Prefix.......Code.......Words....... £ s d	Received From 110 By	Sent, or sent out. At.......m. To .... By	Office Stamp. ECO -5.X.18
Charges to Collect			
Service Instructions.			

Handed in at...........Office.......m Received.......

TO (3)

*Sender's Number	Day of Month	In reply to Number 62 I.Bde.	AAA
line	aaa	DADE	will
be	reserve	brigade	and
will	move	to	HINDENBURG
SUPPORT	LINE	as	soon
as	DUFE 110 I Bde	has	completely
cleared	this	line 64 Inf Bde	aaa
Policy	for	BASU	will
be	to	manoeuvre	enemy
out	of	positions	he
may	be	holding	and
to	act	vigorously	without
engaging	brigade	in	frontal
attack	on	strong	position
aaa	38	Divn	on
our	right	are	being
directed	on	high	ground
in	O27	central	area

FROM

TIME & PLACE

*This line should be erased if not required

C. & R. 7300. Wt. W14832/M1528 106,000 3/17 (E930) Forms C/2123

"C" Form.

Army Form C. 2123
(In books of 100.)

MESSAGES AND SIGNALS

No of Message..........

Prefix..........Code.........Words.......... £ s d Charges to Collect	Received From 18A By..........	Sent, or sent out. At..........m. To.......... By..........	Office Stamp ECO
Service Instructions.			

Handed in at..........Office..........m Received..........m

TO (4)

*Sender's Number	Day of Month	In reply to Number	AAA
Objective	for	37th	Div
not	yet	known	aaa
ack	aaa	addsd	all
concd			

21 Div

FROM Zowu

TIME & PLACE 2045 hrs

*This line should be erased if not required

C. & R. 7800. Wt. W14838/M1528 100,000 3/17 (E930) Forms C/2123

2205

War Diary.

21 Div.
G. 786.

Report on Prisoners of War examined on 6th instant.

9th Coy. 105th I.R. 30th Division.

Only one prisoner was examined who was found in a dug-out in M.34.c. According to the statement of this prisoner, the 9th Coy., then strictly the outpost Company, as soon as they discovered that they had been left behind in the lurch, threw all their rifles and Machine Gunes into a heap in disgust, and walked back, their Officer acquiescing and laughing. After a time they fell out on the side of a track for a rest and one man got wounded by a bullet. The man examined put him in a dug-out and bandaged him up, subsequently being found by one of our patrols.

The men of this Regiment are chiefly Saxons and are of very poor moral and fighting quality.

The 9th Coy. is said to be about 50 strong.

2nd Coy. 99th I.R., 30th Division.

One Corporal of this Company stated that his Company was only 32 strong.

The Company Office which was lately in CAUDRY he believed had been ordered to VALENCIENNES and all preparations for a general retirement of at least 20 kilo-metres are being made in the back areas. A new line is being dug in the back area, which is said to consist at present of dug-outs only, and that work is in progress on wire and trenches. The line is already occupied by the new Divisions through which the Divisionsin the present line are to be withdrawn. This information was imparted to him by a Sergt.-Major who had it from an Officer. All the Sergt.-Majors are said to have been told a certain amount about general intentions, but practically nothing is said to the men or lower N.C.Os.

9th and 12th Coys. 99th I.R., 30th Div. Captured at MONTECOUVEZ FARM M.31.c.

According to these prisoners our advance was to be delayed on the BEAUREVOIR - MASNIERES Line in order to gain time in the evacuation of civilians and stores in the back areas. Several prisoners spoke of a withdrawal of 30 kilo-metres but their ideas are vague and arise from general gossip. They all say they have been told nothing.

/The.....

The BEAUREVOIR Line was held on the morning of the 6th instant by the troops composing the screen and support troops of the previous day. The line is only said to be held in Sectors with both light and heavy machine guns with the Infantry Companies. The trenches are at the most only waist deep, several prisoners saying that they were only knee deep. The wire is very strong but that at the time the gaps where tracks and roads passed through were not believed to have been blocked.

MORAL OF 30th DIVISION.

The men say that the 30th Division was once considered a very good storm Division, but from its recent heavy engagements in CHAMPAGNE, and on this front, it is now "fought out" and can now hardly be considered a storm Div.

G Swydonk Lt
for

7.10.18.

General Staff,
21st Division.

App 5
23

SECRET.

Copy No.........

21st Division Order No.246.

7th October, 1918.

Ref: Map 1/20,000, 57.B. S.W.

1. The Third and Fourth Armies have been ordered to attack the enemy opposite their fronts on 8th October, 1918.

2. The 21st Division will attack with :-

(a) First Objective ... GREEN LINE.

(b) Second Objective ... RED LINE.

(c) Third Objective ... BLUE LINE.

3. (a) The 38th Division will be attacking on the right of the 21st Division with :-

First Objective ... VILLERS OUTREAUX.

Second Objective ... MALINCOURT - WALINCOURT MILL - 0.25.Central.

(b) The 37th Division will be attacking on the left of the 21st Division with :-

First Objective ... BEAUREVOIR - MASNIERES Trench System.

Second Objective ... Ridge running Northwards from BURTEBISE FARM.

Third Objective ... BRISEUX WOOD.

Fourth Objective ... High ground in 0.11.b.

(c) The 38th Division will advance from their first to the second objective at 0800 hours.

(d) The 37th Division will push straight on to their third objective after the capture of the second objective (0638 hours) and from the third to the fourth objective at 1000 hours.

4. (a) The attack on the first objective will be carried out by the 64th Infantry Brigade on the right and the 110th Infantry Brigade on the left.
The Inter-Brigade Boundary is shown "BLACK" on map.
Zero for this attack will be at 0100 hours.

(b) The attack on the second objective will be carried out by the 110th Infantry Brigade.
Zero for this attack will be 0515 hours.

(c) The attack on the third objective will be carried out by the 62nd Infantry Brigade.
Zero for this attack will be 0800 hours.

/(d).......

(d) After the capture of the third objective, the 62nd Infantry Brigade will send patrols :-

i. To the Eastern edge of GARD WOOD.

ii. SORVAL CHATEAU.

III. SELVIGNY Village.

The Cyclist Squadron, which is placed at the disposal of 62nd Infantry Brigade, should be used for this purpose. Standing Patrols will remain in the above places if found unoccupied, and Reconnoitring Patrols pushed on towards CAULLERY.

5. Liaison Posts will be established as follows :-

(a) Between 64th Infantry Brigade and 38th Division at Road Junction T.3.a.9.1.

(b) Between 110th Infantry Brigade and 37th Division at HURTEBISE FARM.

(c) Between 62nd Infantry Brigade and 37th Division at bend in Sunken Road N.12.c.0.5.

(d) Between 62nd Infantry Brigade and 38th Division at STAR Roads O.25.Central.

These Liaison Posts will be joint posts and will consist of One Platoon found by each Unit concerned.

6. (a) Five Field Artillery Brigades will support the attack of the 21st Division.

(b) Barrage Tables will be issued separately.

(c) Targets for Heavy Artillery will appear in Artillery Orders.

(d) The Village of WALINCOURT and the high ground in N.18. will be kept under smoke from 0800 hours till the approach of the 62nd Infantry Brigade necessitates lifting.

(e) The 94th Brigade R.F.A./will come under the direct orders of the B.G.C., 62nd Infantry Brigade for the attack on the third objective and will not take part in the barrage for this attack.

7. (a) Three Machine Gun Companies will put down a barrage for the attack on the second objective.

(b) One Machine Gun Company will support the advance of the 62nd Infantry Brigade by direct fire from the ridge in N.27 and N.21.

(c) One Machine Gun Company is allotted to each Infantry Brigade for consolidating objectives, when gained.

/8.......

8. Six Tanks (Mark V*) will assist in the attack; of these :-

(a) Four Tanks will assist the advance of the 110th Infantry Brigade on the second objective.

(b) Two Tanks will be available for 64th Infantry Brigade after daylight, for clearing up ANGLES CHATEAU area, if this has not already been done.

(c) On the completion of these tasks Tanks will rally by pairs at each of the following places :-

ARDISSART FARM.
Rd. junc. N.26.a.8.9.
Rd. junc. N.20.c.4.9.

All six Tanks will advance from these places with the supporting troops of the 62nd Infantry Brigade, as they pass through and will be used for clearing up "pockets" of the enemy during the advance to the third objective.

9. The 15th Squadron, R.A.F. will be calling for flares as soon as possible after daylight and subsequently at 0900, 1100 hours etc.

10. Divisional Headquarters will close at REVELON FARM at ~~0700~~ 0900 October 8th and will re-open at M.32.b.7.1 at the same hour.

11. A C K N O W L E D G E.

J.H. Franklyn

Lieut.Colonel,
General Staff,
21st Division.

Issued at 1930 hrs. through
Signals to :-

	Copy No.		Copy No.
62 Inf. Bde.	1	A.P.M.	12
64 : :	2	17th Div.	13
110 : :	3	37th Div.	14
C.R.A.	4	38th Div.	15
C.R.E.	5	33rd Div.	16
Pioneers.	6	V Corps,	17 - 18
D.M.G.C.	7	V Corps R.A.	19
Signals.	8	V Corps H.A.	20
A.D.M.S.	9	'B' Coy. 11th Bn.Tanks.	21
Train.	10	15th Sqn.	22
A/Q.	11	War Diary.	23
		File.	24

APPENDIX 'A'.

ASSEMBLY ARRANGEMENTS.

1. The 64th Infantry Brigade will move all troops, detailed to take part in the attack on the first objective South of the Inter-Brigade Boundary, as soon as possible after dark tonight, October 7th.

2. All troops of 64th and 110th Infantry Brigades taking part in the operations will be East of the NAUROY Trench Line by 11.59 hours, October 7th, so as to allow the 62nd Infantry Brigade to assemble in this line.

3. Tanks will move up so as to arrive at rendezvous just west of MONTECOUVEZ FARM by 02.00 hours, October 8th. They must not reach this point before 0100 hours.

4. Brigade Headquarters will be established as follows :-

64th Inf. Bde.	...	S.5.b.9.5.
110th : :	...	GRATTE PANCHE FARM.
62nd : :	...	- ditto - (in 1st instance).
62nd : :	...	ARDISSART FARM (later).

5. (a) When 110th Infantry Brigade advance to second objective, the 64th Infantry Brigade will occupy the BEAUREVOIR Trench System, thus vacated, as far North as N.32.a.2.8.

(b) After the capture of the second objective, the 110th Infantry Brigade will take over the high ground as far South as ANGLES CHATEAU (inclusive) from the 64th Infantry Brigade, under arrangements to be made between Brigadiers concerned.

(c) After the capture of the second objective, the 64th Infantry Brigade will keep Units as concentrated as possible, so as to be ready, on receipt of orders, to move forward to support the 62nd Infantry Brigade as soon as the RED LINE is definitely captured, All garrisons of line as now held may be withdrawn.

APPENDIX "B".

With reference to 21st Divisional Order No.246.

DIVISIONAL.

1. Divisional Communications will be as on the attached diagram from 0800 hours.

2. Divisional Headquarters remains at REVELON till ~~0700~~ 0800 hours. While there, the lines are extended back and the wireless system is connected to the Division by visual.

3. All Artillery Brigades will attach Orderlies to the Infantry Brigade at GRATTE PANCHE FARM or later at ARDISSART FARM if more convenient. These will deliver telegrams received by Morse.

BRIGADE.

4. Lines will be arranged in each case on the Report Centre principle.

5. Visual is being arranged as a second means of communication.

6. Pigeons.
Six pigeons have already been sent to the 64th Infantry Brigade.
Six birds are also being allotted to the 62nd and 110th Infantry Brigades.
Arrangemants have been made to provide a small message book in each basket.

7. Wireless Loop-sets.
Two loop-sets are allotted to each Brigade for use as required.

8. Popham Panels will be taken by Battalions of the 62nd Infantry Brigade.

MACHINE GUNS.

9. The Machine Gun Battalion is connected to the advanced Divisional Exchange.

10. The Lines Officer is arranging to connect up all Companies to Infantry Brigade or Centre Exchanges.

Divisional Communications after 8'0" AM 8/10/18.

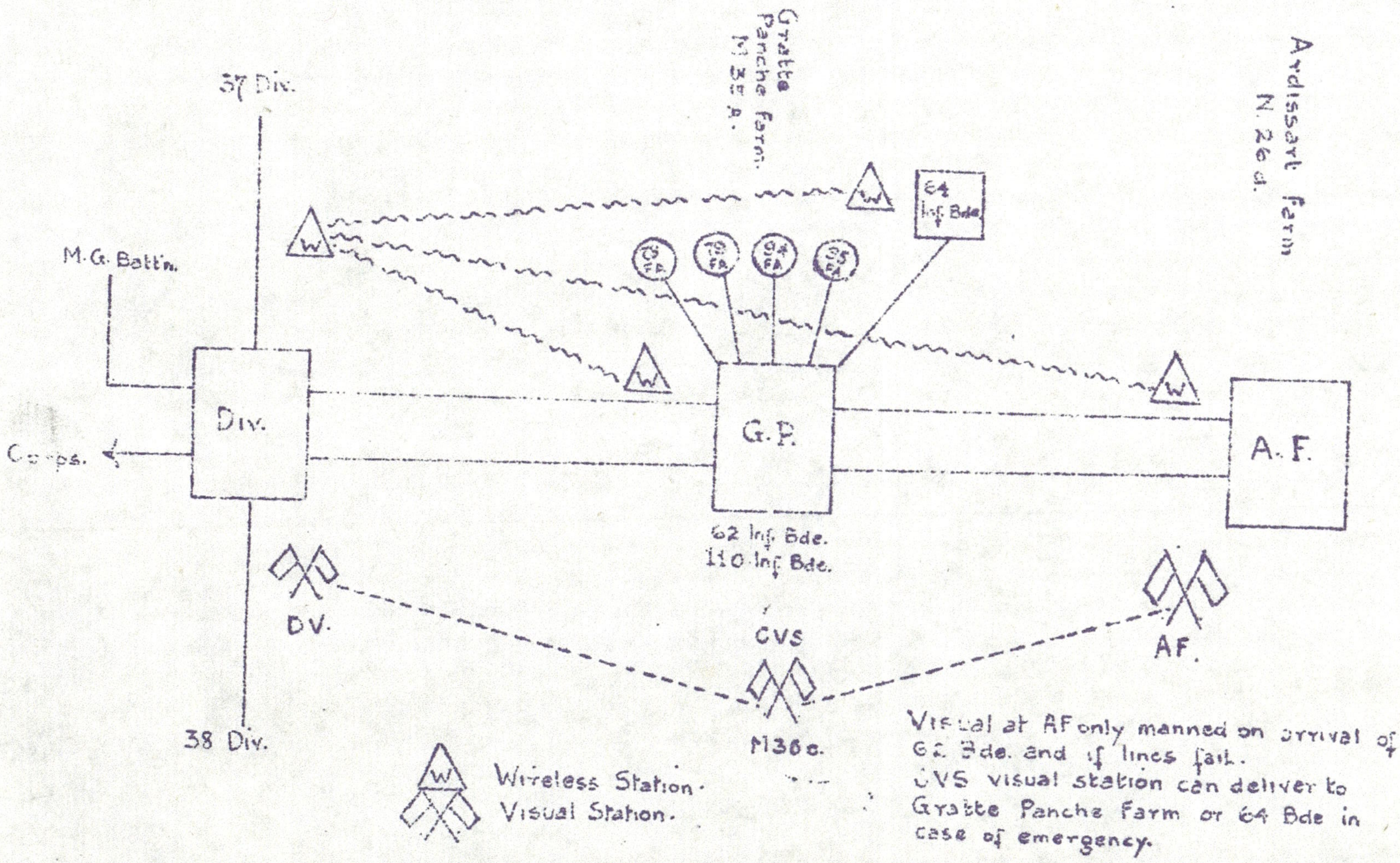

1
20,000

FRANCE

EDITION 5. C

TRENCHES REVISED FROM
INFORMATION RECEIVED UP TO 21-9-18.

SHEET 57B S.W.

SIGNAL.

URGENT OPERATIONS — Words.

PRIORITY TO Three — Sent.

Brigades and C.R.E.

AHM

To..................
By..................
At..................

DADS LOHN 'Q'
BASU ZOAI ZOZU
VUFE ASJU ZORO.

G.X. 827. / 6th / AAA

The 17th Division will pass through xxx DADS early tomorrow morning and resume the advance AAA When the 17th Div. have passed through orders will be issued to Brigades to concentrate and re-organise in the following areas AAA DADS in Squares N.17, 23 and 29 AAA BASU Squares N.26, 27 and 32 AAA VUFE Squares N.28, 31 and 33 AAA M.G.Coys. reorganise with affiliated Brigades AAA Cyclists will re-organise with DADS and will NOT be transferred without further orders AAA 17th and 21st D.As come under orders of G.O.C. 17th Div. on completion of relief AAA ACK AAA Addsd DADS, BASU VUFE ASJU reptd LOHN ZOAI 'Q' ZOZU and ZORO

A H Macdougall Major
for
Lieut.Colonel,
General Staff.

ZORO
23.00 hrs.

App 7

War Diary

S E C R E T.

21 Div.
G. 46.

@ 62 Inf, Bde. A.D.M.S. 18th October, 1918.
@ 64 : : "Q"
@ 110 : : A.P.M.
@ C.R.A. @ Signals.
@ C.R.E. @ D.M.G.C.
Pioneers.

21st Division Instructions for forthcoming Operations - Series G.F. No.1.

Ref: Maps 1/20,000.
Sheets 57.B. S.W. & N.E.
51.A. S.E.

---

1. The enemy is holding that portion of NEUVILLY on the right bank of the River SELLE, the Railway and the road immediately West of it, also the high ground in K.17, 11, 10 and 3.
   It is believed that this position is strongly held, but that in rear there is little in the way of defences and very few troops available to hold them.

2. (a) The Third Army, with V Corps on the right, has been ordered to attack the enemy on Sunday, October 20th, at an hour which has been notified to those concerned.

   (b) The Fourth Army will not co-operate in this attack.

   (c) The V Corps will be attacking with 38th Division on the right and 17th Division on the left. The objectives are shown on attached Map.

3. At a date and hour to be notified later, but not before Dawn on October ~~21st~~ 22nd, the 33rd Division on the right and the 21st Division on the left will pass through the 38th and 17th Divisions respectively and renew the attack; the objectives for this second attack have not yet been decided.

4. The 64th Infantry Brigade will attack on the right and the 110th Infantry Brigade on the left.
   The 62nd Infantry Brigade will be in Divisional Reserve. The inter-Brigade Boundary is shown on attached Map.

5. Five Brigades of Field Artillery will be available to cover the attack; of these, one Brigade will be put under the orders of B.Gs.C., 64th and 110th Infantry Brigades. respectively.

6. One Machine Gun Company will be affiliated to each of the two leading Brigades.

7. Such Cyclists and Mobile Trench Mortars as are available will be divided equally between the 64th and 110th Infantry Brigades.

/8.........

8. The following moves will take place on October 19th and 20th :-

(a) On October 19th, 64th Infantry Brigade and one M.G. Coy. will move to MONTIGNY. (Head not to reach MONTIGNY before ~~5~~ 7 p.m.).

(b) On October ~~20th~~ 21st, 64th and 110th Infantry Brigades (each with one M.G.Coy.) will move to just East and North of INCHY respectively.
(Dividing line between Brigades during halt :- Main INCHY - NEUVILLY Road).

62nd Infantry Brigade will move to just West of INCHY or to MONTIGNY (depending on time of Zero on October ~~21st~~ 22nd).

Times for these moves will be notified later.

(c) At Zero, October ~~21st~~ 22nd, the 64th and 110th Infantry Brigades will be East of the River SELLE, the leading troops of 62nd Infantry Brigade will be just West of River SELLE.

(d) Divisional Headquarters will close at WALINCOURT and open at INCHY about Noon on October ~~20th~~ 21st.

H E Franklyn Lieut-Col

General Staff,
21st Division.

Copies to :-

17th Division.
33rd Division.
V Corps.
V Corps R.A.
V Corps H.A.

Maps issued to those marked @

S E C R E T.

21st DIVISION INSTRUCTIONS FOR FORTHCOMING OPERATIONS.

SERIES G.F. No.2

Information concerning ground East of the SOLESMES - FOREST Road in the vicinity of the Divisional Boundaries.

ENEMY DEFENCES.

Trench Lines.

(a). Small excavations have been made at 57.b. E.11.a.4.8. - E.11.a.7.7. - E.11.a.8.9.

(b) A new trench line has been dug from 57.b. E.22.c.8.9. - E.22.d.4.4. to E.29.a.6.5, also the beginnings of a trench from 57.b. E.23.c.8.1. to E.29.a.9.8.

(c) The beginnings of a shell holed line can be seen from E.15.d.5.3. to E.22.a.2.4. probably linking up with the trench line at E.22.c.8.9.

(d) There appears to be a Post in the West bank of the Road at E.28.d.3.5.

(e) Old practice trenches are visible on the . CHAMPS DE MANOEUVRES S. of LE QUESNOY 51.M. 31.a.

(f) From aeroplane photographs, wire and short lengths of trench appear on the E. bank of the HARPIES River in the vicinity of VENDEGIES.

(g) The sunken roads and banks S.W. of Forest have been organized for defence and occupation.

DEMOLITIONS.

A crater has been blown beside the road at 51.A. X.10.a.7.6.

RIVERS.

Civilians found in HAUSSY state that the River HARPIES is about 6 feet deep . On the other hand, civilians in the Corps area state that the average depth is 1 metre. It is stated to be 1 metre wide except for 500 yards at CHATEAU DE BOIS-LE-DUC, where it is 4 metres wide.

The following streams are stated to be more than 3' to 4' wide, but in no case do they exceed 12' in width in the Forest de MORMAL area. The banks are solid and not more than 3' to 4' high :-

RIEUX CARNOY	12' wide, 1'6" deep.
LA RHONELLE	12' wide, 3' of water.
LE RUISSEAU de l'EGAILLON	12' wide, 3' of water.

ROADS.

(a) FOREST - OVILLERS. Sunken from last house out of FOREST for 100 metres. Banks are 6 m. high. Condition good.

(b) NEUVILLY - FOREST ROAD. In good condition. From K.9.a.5.8. East for 1 kilometre the banks are 5 - 6 m. high.

(c) MONTAY - ENGLEFONTAINE. 1st Class Road. Not in very good repair. Metalled; pave through villages.

The road from AMERVAL to OVILLERS is bad; from OVILLERS to VENDEGIES fair.

MISCELLANEOUS.

The light railway from SOLESMES to ETROEUNGT has been dismantled and the rails laid in the FORET de MORMAL.

East of a rough line MAGINGHIEN - BAZUEL - BOUSIES - BEAUDIGNIES the country becomes extremely close, covered with small pastures and plantations, surrounded by thick hedges. There are many scattered farms, many ditches, few sunken roads and infrequent areas of open country. According to a French escaped Prisoner of War, many of the hedges in JOLIMETZ- POIX DU NORD area are interwoven with wire, or have grown up around an old wire fence. They are serious obstacles. The paper map which will be issued to all concerned tonight contains all information obtained from aeroplane photographs.

H.E. Lachlyle
Lieut.-Colonel.
General Staff.,

19th October 1918.

W.D.

SECRET.

21st DIVISION INSTRUCTIONS FOR FORTHCOMING OPERATIONS.

Series G.F.No.3. 21st Oct. 1918.

COMMUNICATIONS.

A. **BRIGADE COMMUNICATION CENTRES.**

1\. (i) Cellar of house on North side of road at K.2.c.3.2. To be established by Division by 17.00 hrs on 22nd instant. To be known as N.V.

(ii) North East corner of Copse at E.29.a.2.2. To be established by 110th Inf. Bde. as early as possible. To be known as A.M.

(iii) On road between Chateau and Village of VENDEGIES AU BOIS at F.13.b.1.8. To be established by 110th Inf. Bde. as early as possible. To be known as V.G.

(iv) Road just N.W. of Spinning Mill about F.3.a.8.2. To be established by 62nd Inf. Bde. as early as possible. To be known as P.X.

2\. The personnel for A.M. and V.G. together with a Cable Detachment under an Officer will report to Signal Officer, 110 Inf. Bde. by the evening of the 22nd instant.
Linesmen, instruments and a proportion of the operators for P.X. will be collected from N.V. by the 62nd Inf. Bde. when they pass there. The Cable Detachment will be taken on from V.G.
In addition, the 64th Inf. Bde. will lay a light cable line from their own resources between N.V. and A.M. and V.G. The 62nd Inf. Bde. will do the same between V.G. and P.X.

3\. Two horse D.Rs who are to be stationed at each Report Centre for the transmission of messages between Centres, when lines are down, will report or be collected at the same time as the remainder of the centre parties.

4\. Brigade Centres will be marked by a Signal flag with a Divisional Sign superimposed. Orderlies will be attached by Infantry & Artillery Brigades and M.G.Coys. in accordance with 21 Div. G.970 of 14.10.18.

5\. The Division will have three heavy lines to A.M. by Zero Plus 320 and to V.G. by Zero Plus 612.

/B......

B. DIVISIONAL WIRELESS AND VISUAL.

1. The Divisional Visual Station (call D.V.) will be in J.18.a. and later when Division moves, in K.3.a. The Divisional Visual Transmitting Station (call Q.C.) will be on high ground in E.22.a. by Zero plus 60.
Infantry and Artillery Brigades have instructions about obtaining touch with one of these.

2. The Main Divisional Wireless Station will be established in K.3.b. by 12.00 hrs. on 22nd instant. This will be in touch with N.V. by line and with Division by wireless.
The 110th Inf. Bde. is responsible for the erection of wireless at A.M. The 62nd Inf. Bde. at V.G. and P.X.

C. BRIGADE - BATTALION COMMUNICATIONS.

1. Battalion Report Centres.
Brigade Centres, while in front of the leading Brigade, though manned by Divisional men, function as Battalion Report Centres.
3,000 yards, the distance between Brigade Report Centres, is too large a bound for Battalion Report Centres. The 64th Inf. Bde. will establish one Battalion Report Centre between N.V. and A.M. and one between A.M. and V.G. at points to be arranged mutually between Brigadiers 64th and 110th Inf. Bdes.
At these points the light and heavy cable lines laid by the 64th and 110th Inf. Bdes. respectively will be brought together as for a Brigade Centre and a loop-set will be installed. Unlike Brigade Centres, these intermediate centres will only be kept open as exchanges as long as actually required by the Brigades concerned. While open, they will be marked by a signal flag.

2. Loop-sets.
One front loop-set is allotted to each of the 64th and 110th Inf. Bdes. to be used with one of their leading Battalions. One front loop-set is allotted to a Divisional Artillery F.O.O.
Three rear loop-sets are allotted for installation at the combined Battalion Report Centres of 64th and 110th Inf. Bdes. They will be used and moved by

/agreement.....

agreement between the Brigades. All loop-sets and personnel except that with the F.O.O. will be taken over by the 62nd Inf. Bde. on passing through.

3. Runners.
Battalion Report Centres will be used as Runner and Linesmen posts.

4. Visual.
Visual will be arranged by Brigade Signal Officers according to the situation.

5. Popham Panels.
Brigades and Battalions will carry their panels and will wherever possible put them out near their Headquarters.

6. Message Rockets.
All message rockets asked for have been supplied to Brigades. Definite receiving stations for each objective must be laid down in orders and men detailed to watch for them.

7. Pigeons.
Only 12 Pigeons are available and these are allotted at the 62nd Inf. Bde.

MACHINE GUN COMMUNICATIONS.

Machine Gun Coys. and Battalion H.Q. will connect themselves to the nearest Centre or Brigade. Orderlies will be in attendance for messages. 48 message rockets have been supplied for Section and Company communication.

W.D

SECRET.

21st DIVISION INSTRUCTIONS FOR FORTHCOMING OPERATIONS.

Series G.F.No.4.

21st October, 1918.

ARRANGEMENTS for R.E. and PIONEERS.

1. One Section R.E. will be attached to each Infantry Brigade. These Sections should move well forward in their respective Brigade Areas, so that there may be no loss of time in preparing improvised bridges over streams such as the River HARPIES.

2. One Field Coy. R.E. (less 1 Section) will follow up 62nd Inf. Bde. and will repair the road bridges over the River SELLE at :-

F.13.d.5.3.
F.13.a.9.6.
F.7.c.6.7.

so as to allow these bridges to be used by Field Artillery and First Line Transport.

3. Two Field Coys. R.E. (each less 1 Section) will be held in readiness to construct strong points to assist the defence of either the Red or Green Lines, or both.

These strong points will be located as follows :-

Red Line.	F.19.c.4.4.	E.24.b.5.3.
	E.18.d.6.1.	E.18.d.1.1.
	E.18.a.8.6.	E.17.d.7.8.
Green Line.	F.9.c.0.2.	F.9.a.3.4.
	F.8.b.5.7.	F.8.a.6.6.
	F.2.c.7.8.	F.1.d.8.9.

4. The Pioneer Battalion will be employed on repairing roads; efforts will be concentrated on the road which runs NEUVILLY - K.10.b. - AMERVAL - OVILLERS - VENDEGIES.

The Pioneer Battalion will cross the CAMBRAI - BERTRY Railway at Zero plus 2 hours and proceed straight to their work.

SECRET. 21st Div. A.1237/65.

21st DIVISION INSTRUCTION FOR FORTHCOMING OPERATIONS.

SERIES G.F. No.5.

1. **FIRST LINE TRANSPORT.**

(a) First Line Transport will in the first instance move with Units.

(b) When Units move forward 'B' Echelon First Line Transport will concentrate as follows :-

62nd Inf.Bde.	J.28.a. & c.
64th "	J.16.
110th "	J.23.
21st M.G.Battn.	J.28.b. & d.
14th N.Fusrs (P)	J.26.
Field Coys. R.E.	J.26.
63rd Field Ambulance.	CAULLERY.
65th Field Ambulance.	J.21.a.

(c) Pack trains will be organised by Brigadiers as usual.

2. **21st DIVISIONAL TRAIN.**

21st Div.Train will move on Oct. ~~21st~~ 22nd to the neighbourhood of TRONQUOY. Moves will be timed so as not to interfere with the movements of Brigades; otherwise no restrictions as to time and route.

3. **S.A.A.SECTION, D.A.C.**

(a) S.A.A.Section D.A.C., will move to Square P.1.b. on afternoon of Oct. ~~21st~~ 22nd. Time of move will be notified later.

(b) S.A.A.Section will send 5 L.G.S.Wagons to report to each Inf.Brigade this afternoon rationed for consumption Oct.20th.

4. **AMMUNITION.**

(a) A.R.P. (Gun) is at J.25.d.5.8.

(b) Fireworks & Grenades required to be carried on the man will be issued to Brigades at INCHY on Oct. ~~21st~~ 22nd.

(c) 17th Div. S.A.A. & Grenade Dump is at ~~J.27.c.8.2.~~ J.23.c.2.6
A forward dump will be established at K.2.b.3.1.
These dumps may be drawn on by this Division after Zero.

5. **WATER.**

(a) There are waterpoints at INCHY, MONTIGNY, J.33.b.2.6., J.26.b.7.3. & J.26.b.3.7.

17th Division are arranging for supply and policing of waterpoints which will be prepared on the River SELLE. C.R.E., 21st Division will assist C.R.E., 17th Division as required.

(b) Brigades will report water supplies in areas captured by them and will prevent them being polluted.
A.D.M.S., will arrange for water to be tested.

6. **ROADS.**

The following roads will be repaired. No dumps, ammunition refilling points, or supply refilling points, will be made on these roads:-

MONTAY - ENGLEFONTAINE by 33rd & 38th Divisions.

NEUVILLY, AMERVAL, OVILLERS, VENDEGIES - Railway South of NEUVILLY, POIX, ENGLEFONTAINE, BASSEVILLE (S.E. of LE QUESNOY) by 17th & 21st Divisions.

7. **TRAFFIC CONTROL.**

17th Division will be responsible for Traffic Control up to the line FOREST - E.23.b., and 21st Division East of this Line.

8. **STRAGGLER POSTS.**

D.A.P.M., will arrange for a line of Straggler Posts to be in position by Zero hour on the LE CATEAU - SOLESMES road.

Stragglers Collecting post K.9.a.2.7.

9. **PRISONERS OF WAR CAGE.**

Prisoners of War cage will be established at K.9.a.2.7. at Zero hour.

10. **CIVILIANS.**

Brigades will report as early as possible the number of civilians in Villages captured by them. O.C., 21st Div. Train will arrange to feed these civilians, and D.A.P.M. will arrange to prevent them leaving the Villages.

G. Acland Troyte

Lt.Colonel.
A.A. & Q.M.G.,
21st Division.

H.Q., 21st Division.
19th October 1918.

Distribution:-

62nd Inf.Bde	M.G.Battn.	M.T.Coy.
64th "	A.D.M.S.,	Div.Reception Camp.
110th "	Div.Train.	Camp Commandant.
Div.Artillery.	D.A.P.M.	Salvage Officer.
C.R.E.	S.A.A.Sec. D.A.C.	17th Division.
14th N.Fusrs (P)	Signal Coy.	33rd Division.

W.D.

SECRET.

21st DIVISION INSTRUCTIONS FOR FORTHCOMING OPERATIONS.

Series G.F.No.6.

21st October, 1918.

ASSEMBLY ARRANGEMENTS.

1. Preliminary moves, prior to relieving the 17th Division in the line on the night 22nd/23rd October, will be carried out as follows on October 22nd.:-

(a) 110 Inf. Bde. will march to halt area North of INCHY, head to pass Northernmost house in CAULLERY at 09.30 hours.
Route - LIGNY - AUDENCOURT.

(b) 62 Inf. Bde. will march to bivouacs West of INCHY, head to pass present Div. H.Q. at 10.30 hours.
Route - SELVIGNY - CAULLERY - LIGNY - AUDENCOURT.

(c) 64 Inf. Bde. will march to halt area East of INCHY, head to pass house, O.6.c.8.2 at 11.15 hours.

Note. All moves will be by Companies at 50 yards interval, with 200 yards between Battalions.

2. The relief of the 52nd Inf. Bde. plus 2 M.G.Coys. 17th Division in the line will be carried out as under on the night 22nd/23rd instant. Relief to be complete as soon as possible after dark.

(a) 64 Inf. Bde. plus one M.G.Coy. will relieve the right half of the 52nd Inf. Bde. Leading troops of 64th Inf. Bde. will leave their halt area at 17.00 hours.

(b) 110 Inf. Bde. plus one M.G.Coy. will relieve the left half of the 52nd Inf. Bde. Leading troops 110th Inf. Bde. will cross the River SELLE at 17.00 hours.

(c) The Battalion, 50th Inf. Bde. at present along the road through K.3.Central, will not be relieved, but will commence withdrawing at 17.00 hours.

(d) H.Q. 52nd Inf. Bde. are at K.8.a.1.3.

/Note.....

<u>Note</u>. The high ground J.24. & K.19 is under observation by the enemy from about L.19.
The area round RAMBOURLIEUX FARM, K.13 and K.14.a. & c. is most often shelled by the enemy.

3. The roads East of INCHY and bridges over the River available for the move of 64th and 110th Inf. Bdes. for the relief of the 52nd Inf. Bde. are allotted as under :-

(a) 64 Inf. Bde. - Roads S.E. of the direct INCHY - NEUVILLY Road (exclusive).
Bridges S.E. of the Village of NEUVILLY (exclusive).

(b) 110 Inf. Bde. - All other roads and bridges in the Divisional Area.

4. All roads and bridges East of INCHY will be clear of troops, 17th Division, from 02.00 hours October 23rd.
All traffic, 17th Division, moving Westwards has been ordered to give way to traffic moving Eastwards.

5. Completion of relief will be reported to Div. H.Q.

6. Command of the Sector passes to G.O.C. 21st Division on completion of/relief.
Inf.

7. 64th and 110th Inf. Bdes. will notify Div. H.Q. as soon as possible the proposed position of their Brigade H.Q. after completion of relief.

H.M. Macdougall Major for Lt. Col.
General Staff,
21st Division.

21.10.18.

To :- All recipients of G.F. Series.

W.D.

S E C R E T.

21st DIVISION INSTRUCTIONS FOR FORTHCOMING OPERATIONS.

Series G.F.No.7.

21st October, 1918.

M I S C E L L A N E O U S.

1. Light Signals.

The following light signals will be used :-

(a) Red Very Lights ... to signify "We are here."

(b) Green Very Lights .. to intimate to the Artillery to lengthen range.

(c) Red Flares .. As a signal to denote the position of our leading Infantry to contact aeroplanes.

The S.O.S. signal is a rifle grenade bursting into Green/Red/Green.

2. Reports.

Brigades will render hourly situation reports to Div. H.Q. In the absence of any special information, negative reports will be sent.

. Marking of H.Q.

(a) Attention is called to the necessity of marking all Headquarters with a distinctive flag.

(b) The signal for Report Centres established by Divisional Signals will be a blue and white signal flag with the Divisional sign in blue and white on it.

[signature]

General Staff,
21st Division.

Escarmain
Haussy
Vertain
Romeries
Vertigneul
Neuville
Haut de l'Arbrisseau
Ghissignies
Salesches
ENEMY ORGANISATION 12-10-18
Solesmes
Grand Champ
Beaurain
Vendegies
Vendegies au Bois
Poix-du-Nord
Briastre
Ovillers
Vendegies Wood
Amerval
Richemont
Croix
Bousies
Neuvilly
Forest
SECRET
Montay
Pommereuil
LE CATEAU

War Diary

SECRET. Copy No. 24

Ref: Maps 1/20,00

Sheets 57.B.

"C"
MESSAGES AND

Prefix SM Code 2350 Words 20	Received. From PGD By
Charges to Collect	At
Service Instructions	To
	By

Handed in at 9u Office 2350 m. Received 0004 m.

TO 5th Corps

*Sender's Number.	Day of Month.	In reply to Number.	AAA
GX119	21/10/18		

Cancel paras 1 and 2 of 21st divn Order 247 dated 21st inst

FROM
PLACE & TIME 21 Divn 2350 0020

*This line should be erased if not required.

(19629) W1528/M1970. 300,000 Pads. 4/17. McC. & Co., Ltd. (E1213).

~~1. The~~ ... operatio... October... concerne...

~~2. The~~ ~~the righ~~... ~~for thes~~... ~~21st Div~~...

3. (a) not ... wil...

(b) the ...

4. The ... V Corps ... successi...

5. (a) ... 110th Infantry Brigade ... Red Dotted Line, Red Line, and Green Dotted Line.

(b) After the capture of the Green Dotted Line, the 110th Infantry Brigade will establish posts beyond VENDEGIES Village so as to assist the advance of the 62nd Infantry Brigade.

(c) The 62nd Infantry Brigade will pass through the two leading Brigades and capture the Green and Brown Lines.

(d) After the capture of the Brown Line, the 62nd Infantry Brigade will exploit through and beyond the BOIS DE GLAGEON.

The Cyclist Squadron, which is placed at the disposal of the 62nd Infantry Brigade, should be used for this purpose.

/6.........

SECRET.   Copy No.......24

21st Division Order No. 247.

21st October, 1918.

Ref: Maps 1/20,000.

Sheets 57.B. N.E., 51.A. S.E.

~~1. The Third and Fourth Armies, in conjunction with other operations, have been ordered to attack the enemy on October 23rd, at an hour which has been notified to all concerned.~~

~~2. The V Corps will be attacking with 38th Division on the right and 17th Division on the left. The objectives for these operations were given in the Map accompanying 21st Division G.F.No.1.~~

3. (a) On October 23rd, at an hour which has been notified to all concerned, the Third and Fourth Armies will renew the attack.

(b) The 33rd Division will attack on the right and the 37th Division on the left of the 21st Division.

4. The 21st Division will be the left Division of the V Corps and will attack in a North Easterly direction with successive objectives :-

(a) Red Dotted Line.
(b) Red Line.
(c) Green Dotted Line.
(d) Green Line.
(e) Brown Line.

5. (a) The 64th Infantry Brigade on the right and the 110th Infantry Brigade on the left will capture the Red Dotted Line, Red Line, and Green Dotted Line.

(b) After the capture of the Green Dotted Line, the 110th Infantry Brigade will establish posts beyond VENDEGIES Village so as to assist the advance of the 62nd Infantry Brigade.

(c) The 62nd Infantry Brigade will pass through the two leading Brigades and capture the Green and Brown Lines.

(d) After the capture of the Brown Line, the 62nd Infantry Brigade will exploit through and beyond the BOIS DE GLAGEON.

The Cyclist Squadron, which is placed at the disposal of the 62nd Infantry Brigade, should be used for this purpose.

/6..........

6. Liaison Posts will be established as follows :-

(a) Between 64th and (19th Inf. Bde.) 33rd Division.
On Red Dotted Line at Corner of Fence E.30.c.7.5.
On Red Line : : : : F.19.c.8.5.
On Green Dotted Line : : : F.19.b.9.9.

(b) Between 62nd Inf. Bde. and (19th Inf. Bde) 33rd Div.
On Green Line at road junction F.9.c.8.5.

Between 62nd Inf. Bde. and (100th Inf. Bde.) 33rd Div.
On Brown Line at LES TUILERIES road junction.

(c) Between 110th Inf. Bde. and 37th Division.
On Red Line at Corner of Fence E.12.c.6.0.

(d) Between 62nd Inf. Bde. and 37th Division.
On Brown Line at SALESCHES Station.

Liaison Posts will be joint posts and will consist of one Platoon found by each Unit concerned.

7. (a) Five Field Artillery Brigades will support the attack of the 21st Division.

(b) Four Field Artillery Brigades will support the advance of the 64th and 110th Infantry Brigades.
The Barrage will consist of two thirds of the 18 pdrs. firing shrapnel with 10% smoke, and one third of the 18 pdrs. firing H.E. 100 yards in advance of the shrapnel barrage.
4.5" Howitzers and Heavy Artillery will deepen the barrage in advance of the 18 pdrs., special attention being paid to sunken roads and the outskirts of villages.

(c) 4.5" Howitzers will fire smoke on the general line of the River HARPIES during the advance of the 64th and 110th Infantry Brigades from the Red Line.

(d) The 94th Bde. R.F.A. is placed under the orders of the B.G.C., 62nd Infantry Brigade to support his attack. This Brigade will not be employed with barrages detailed in sub-para (b) above.

(e) Six Mobile Trench Mortars are placed at the disposal of the 62nd Infantry Brigade.

8. (a) One and a half Machine Gun Companies will support the advance of the 64th and 110th Infantry Brigades with an indirect Machine Gun Barrage.

(b) One Machine Gun Company will be affiliated to each Infantry Brigade. Eight Guns of the Company allotted to 62nd Infantry Brigade will not join this Brigade until after firing the barrage detailed in sub-para (a).

(c) These Machine Gun Companies are to be used for offensive action i.e. supporting the advance by direct fire as well as for consolidation purposes.

/9.....

9. Two Tanks are allotted to the 64th Infantry Brigade and one Tank to 110th Infantry Brigade for the purpose of clearing the Village of OVILLERS.

One Platoon of Infantry will be detailed to accompany each Tank.

After OVILLERS has been 'mopped up' Tanks will rally at the Chateau F.13.a.

10. The 15th Squadron, R.A.F. will be calling for flares as soon as possible after daylight and subsequently at 09.00, 11.00 hours etc.

11. Divisional Headquarters will be at INCHY during the first stages of the operations, subsequently moving to about K.2.b.2.2, and then along the general line of the Brigade Report Centres (detailed in 21st Division G.F.No.3).

12. A c k n o w l e d g e.

H.C.Grambleyn

Lieut.Colonel,
General Staff,
21st Division.

Issued at 13.30 hrs. through
Signals to :-

	Copy No.		Copy No.
62 Inf. Bde.	1	V Corps.	14 - 15
64 : :	2	@ V Corps R.A.	16
110 : :	3	@ V Corps H.A.	17
C.R.A.	4	@ 17th Div.	18
C.R.E.	5	33rd Div.	19
@ Pioneers.	6	37th Div.	20
D.M.G.O.	7	@ 38 Div.	21
Signals.	8	@ 15 Sqn.R.A.F.	22
@ A.D.M.S.	9	11th Tank Bn.	23
Train.	10	War Diary.	24
@ A/Q.	11	File.	25
A.P.M.	12.	5th Division	26.
@ D.G.O.	13		

@ Map showing objectives follows.

War Diary

SECRET.

21 Div.
G. 104.

All recipients of Div. Order No.247.

The following amendments will be made to 21st Division Order No.247 :-

Para 3 (b) will be amended to read :-

"The 33rd Division will attack on the right of the 21st Division and the 5th Division on the left of the 21st Division as far as the Green Dotted Line, where the 37th Div. will pass through and continue the attack on our left."

Para 5 (d) will be amended to read :-

"After capture of the Brown Line, 62nd Inf. Bde. will exploit as far as the road running South Eastwards from GHISSIGNIES through Squares X.11, X.17, and a Reconnoitring Patrol will be sent into LOUVIGNIES - LEZ - QUESNOY.

The Cyclist Squadron, which is placed at the disposal of the 62nd Inf. Bde. will be used for this purpose."

Add to para 5 sub-para (e) :-

"As soon as the Red Line has been captured, the 64th and 110 Inf. Bdes. will each re-organise one Battalion so that assistance may be sent to the 62nd Inf. Bde. if required at a later period.

After the capture of the Green Dotted Line, the 64th Inf. Bde. will re-organise and concentrate a second Battalion. The two Battalions thus re-organised will be prepared in case of need to form a defensive flank between the Spur in F.19.c. and the River HARPIES in F.16.d.

If these Battalions are not required to form this defensive flank, they will move forward so as to occupy the Green Line as soon as this line is vacated by the 62nd Inf. Bde.

The 110th Inf. Bde. will take over the S.E. portion of the Green Dotted Line from the 64th Inf. Bde. The Battalion 64th Inf. Bde. thus relieved, will move forward in support of remainder of Brigade.

/The......

TELEGRAM.

Words.

URGENT OPERATIONS
PRIORITY 3 Bdes.

HWH

At....................
To....................
By....................

DADE	LODE	ZEJU	ZODU	17 Div.	15 Sqn R.A.F.
BASU	ZOKI	A/Q.	V Corps.	33 Div.	
VUFE	DUFA	ZORO	5 Div.	37 Div.	

- / 25 / AAA

ZOWU Order No.252 AAA In conjunction with operation by 33rd Div. VUFE will establish outpost zone tonight in front of present line AAA Fighting patrols will be sent forward under creeping barrage to establish Platoon Posts approximately in following places AAA S.13.d.0.4 X.18.b.9.4 X.18.b.7.6 X.11.d.8.8. X.11.b.5.4 X.11.b.1.9 AAA Barrage will come down at 01.00 hours Oct. 26th on line S.19.b.0.7 to X.11.b.0.5 will pause for 8 minutes and then advance at 100 yards in 4 mins. until 300 yards clear of posts given above and then cease AAA At Dawn Reconnoitring Patrols will be sent forward to line of orchards S.W. and South of LOUVIGNIES AAA If no enemy encountered action detailed in ZOWU Order No.250 of yesterday will be adopted AAA If enemy encountered Reconnoitring Patrols will be withdrawn AAA Relief of BASU and DADE must be completed by 23.59 hours so as to facilitate above operation AAA Whole Cyclist Squadron comes under VUFE after relief AAA Ack AAA Adsd all concerned

---

H.H. Lambidge

ZOWU
15.50 hrs.

Lt.Col.

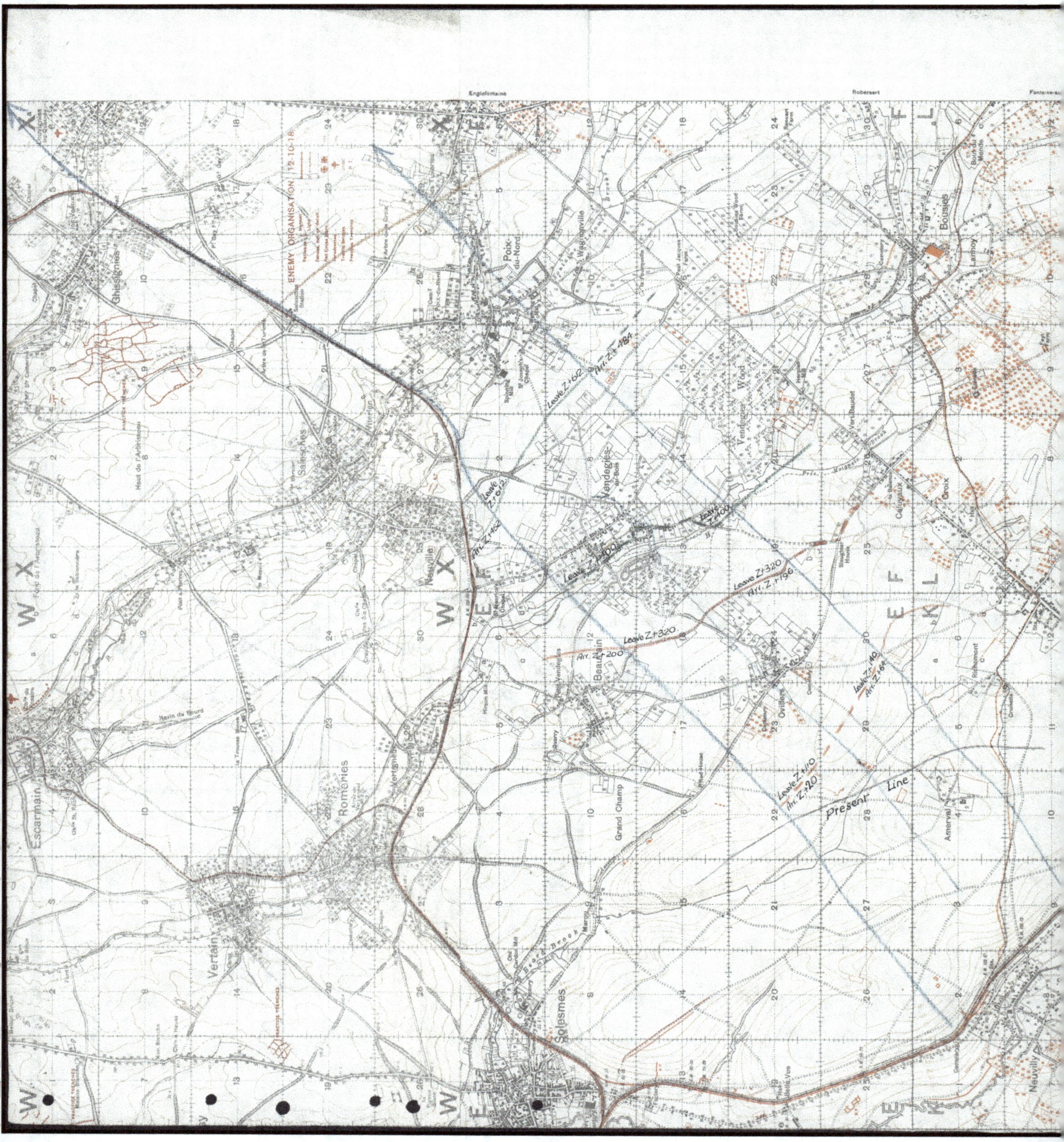

Englefontaine
Robersart
ENEMY ORGANISATION 12-10-18
Poix-du-Nord
Vendegies Wood
Vendegies-au-Bois
Bousies
Salesches
Neuville
Beaurain
Ovillers
Grand Champ
Romeries
Vertain
Escarmain
Solesmes
Amerval
Neuvilly
Present Line
Leave Z+320
Arr. Z+196
Leave Z+110
Arr. Z+20

"C" Form.

Army Form C. 2123.
(In books of 100.)

MESSAGES AND SIGNALS. 307

No. of Message ....

Prefix SB Code 1700 Words 205	Received. From Fu By Cps	Sent, or sent out. At ... To ... By ...	Office Stamp. E 23 X. 18 ... SIGNALS
Charges to Collect			
Service Instructions Pty			

Handed in at Fu Office 1700 m. Received 2000 m.

TO 5th Corps.

* Sender's Number	Day of Month.	In reply to Number	AAA
GX 162	23		

ZOWU 21 Div	warning	order	aaa
advance	will	be	resumed
tomorrow	by	ZOWU 21 Div	aaa
objective	line	of	road
X21A9.0	GRAND	GAYFARM	to
halt	X11A5.5	aaa	Right
Div	boundary	from	X2.9
cent	to	cross	roads
S3c8.7	aaa	left	Div
boundary	from	X6A0.2	M31B3.0
M26B5.0	M21C3.0	aaa	Inter-
-Brigade	boundary	POIX	SPINNING
MILL	to	road	junction
X23D1.4	just	inclusive	to
right	Brigade	thence	straight
line	to	X22D6.5	South
of	road	to	X17B3.1

FROM
PLACE & TIME

* This line should be erased if not required.

9310—W.528—100,000—10/5/17—E.P.Co.—(E1213).

Service Instructions

"C" Form.

MESSAGES AND SIGNALS.

Army Form C. 2123.
(In books of 100.)

No. of Message

Prefix ... Code ... Words ... £ s. d. Charges to Collect Service Instructions	Received. From ... By Cps	Sent, or sent out. At ... m. To ... By ...	Office Stamp. E 28.X.18 SIGNALS

Handed in at ... Office 1700 m. Received ...

TO (2)

*Sender's Number	Day of Month.	In reply to Number	AAA
GX162			

thence straight line to ~~X~~ ~~and~~ M33C0.8 aaa 64 Bde BASU will attack on right and 62nd Bde DADE on left aaa jumping off line depends on progress of 62 Bde DADE today aaa after capture of objective advance guards will be sent forward to make as much ground as possible towards JOLIMETZ-LE QUESNOY road aaa cancelling previous instructions basu will now take over GREEN line on right Brigade front and 110 Bde VUFE on

FROM

PLACE & TIME

* This line should be erased if not required.

9310—W.528—100,000—10/5/17—E.P.Co.—(E1213).

Army Form C. 2123.
(In books of 100.)

"C" Form.

MESSAGES AND SIGNALS.

No. of Message

Prefix Code Words	Received.	Sent, or sent out.	Office Stamp
£ s. d.	From	At m.	E 23.X.18 C.1 ARMY SIGNALS
Charges to Collect	By Cpo	To	
Service Instructions		By	

Handed in at Office m. Received 2000 m.

TO (3)

* Sender's Number	Day of Month.	In reply to Number	AAA
G162			

Left	Brigade	front .	as
soon	as	vacated	by
62 Bde DADE	aaa	64 Bde BASU	All
push	forward	troops	to
protect	right	rear	of
DADE 62 Bde	during	latters	advance
today	and	will	take
over	right	Brigade	front
from	62 Bde DADE	on	final
line	reached	tonight	aaa
110 Bde VIFE	will	be	disposed
tonight	between	Green	line
inclusive	and	Red	line
exclusive	and	will	be
in	Div	Reserve	tomorrow
aaa	Further	orders	later
acknowledge			

FROM 21 Divn

PLACE & TIME 1700

Ack

* This line should be erased if not required.

2018

9310—W.528—100,000—10/5/17—E.P.Co.—(E1213).

"C" Form.

(In books of 100.)

MESSAGES AND SIGNALS.

No. of Message

Prefix SB Code 1905 Words 24	Received. From YU By Bn	Sent, or sent out. At m. To By	Office Stamp.
Charges to Collect £ s. d.			
Service Instructions Pty			

Handed in at YU Office 1905 m. Received 2012 m.

TO 5 Corps

*Sender's Number	Day of Month.	In reply to Number	AAA
Gx11.9	23		

Ref	ZOWU	warning order	
Gx 162	inter	Bde Boundary	
for	Rd	Junc	X28d1.4
Road	Rd	Junc	X28c1.4

FROM PLACE & TIME: 21 Lhan

2010

* This line should be erased if not required.

9310—W.528—100,000—10/5/17—E.P.Co.—(E1213).

"C" Form.

MESSAGES AND SIGNALS.

Army Form C. 2123. (In books of 100.)

No. of Message

Prefix ... Code ... Words ... £ s. d.	Received.	Sent, or sent out.	Office Stamp.
Charges to Collect	From	At ... m.	
Service Instructions Urgent Opns Pty	By	To	
		By	

Handed in at ... Office 2100 m. Received 21.53 m.

TO 5 Corps G

Sender's Number	Day of Month.	In reply to Number	AAA
21 Div	23		

ZOWU	order	no	248
aaa	Ref	warning	order
GX162	of	today	aaa
advance	is	being	continued
tomorrow	aaa	33rd	Div
attack	LANDRECIES - LE		QUESNOY
Road	aaa	37	Div
attack	high	ground	north
of	GHISSIGNIES	aaa	BASU 64 IB
on	right	and	DADE 62 IB
on	left	will	attack
with	first	objective	line
of	Road	from	X29C7.7
to	X21B7.1	aaa	second
objective	line	of	road
from	~~X29C7.7 to~~		~~X21B7.1~~
[illegible]			

FROM

PLACE & TIME

* This line should be erased if not required.

9310—W.528—100,000—10/5/17—E.P.Co.—(E1213).

Army Form C. 2123.
(In books of 100.)

"C" Form.

MESSAGES AND SIGNALS.

No. of Message

Prefix ___ Code ___ Words ___	Received.	Sent, or sent out.	Office Stamp.
£ s. d.	From	At ___ m.	23 X 15
Charges to Collect	By	To	TELEGRAPH
Service Instructions		By	

Handed in at YO Office ___ m. Received ___ m.

TO (2)

* Sender's Number	Day of Month.	In reply to Number	AAA
Rd	June	X24a90	GRAND
GAY	FARM	to	HALT
XIIa55	aaa	advance	to
first	objective	under	barrage
aaa	NO	barrage	for
advance	beyond	first	objective
aaa	Artillery	starting	line
300	yards	in	advance
of	road	F9c66	F2a35
aaa	barrage	dwells	on
starting	line	for	8
minutes	and	then	advances
at	rate	of	100
yards	in	4	minutes
aaa	Protector	Beyond	first
objective	for	8	minutes
and	then	ceases	aaa

FROM

PLACE & TIME

* This line should be erased if not required.

9310—W.528—100,000—10/5/17—E.P.Co.—(E1213).

Army Form C. 2123.
(In books of 100.)

"C" Form.
MESSAGES AND SIGNALS.

No. of Message ....

Prefix ...... Code ...... Words ...... £ s. d. Charges to Collect	Received From ...... By	Sent, or sent out. At ...... m. To ...... By	Office Stamp.

Service Instructions

Handed in at ...... Office ...... m. Received ...... m.

TO (3)

*Sender's Number | Day of Month. | In reply to Number | AAA

No Barrage for right
Brigade through village of
POIX DU NORD aaa
BASU 64 Bde will pick up
Barrage on far side
of village aaa advance
through village will be
calculated at rate of
100 yards in 4
Minutes aaa Reserve Coy
Machine Guns will barrage
400 yards ahead of
artillery aaa one M4
Coy remains with each
Brigade aaa 95th Bde
R.F.A. will support advance
from first to second

FROM
PLACE & TIME

* This line should be erased if not required.

9310—W.528—100,000—10/5/17—E.P.Co.—(E1213).

"C" Form.

MESSAGES AND SIGNALS.

Army Form C. 2123.
(In books of 100.)

No. of Message

Prefix ____ Code ____ Words ____	Received.	Sent, or sent out.	Office Stamp.
£ s. d.	From	At ____ m.	TELEGRAPHS
Charges to Collect	By	To	
Service Instructions		By	

Handed in at ____ Office ____ m. Received ____ m.

TO

* Sender's Number	Day of Month.	In reply to Number	AAA
	23		

objectives	and	keep	liaison
with	64th BASD	and	62 DIVADE
HQ	aaa	Second	objective
will	be	consolidated	in
depth	when	captured	aaa
liaison	post	with	33rd
Div	at	Rd	June
X2ua9.0	and	with	37th
Div	on	Rly	at
X5C9.5	aaa	after	capture
of	objectives	all	three
Divs	will	send	advance
guards	forward	to	make
good	outpost	ZONE	aaa
33	Div	to	FUTOY
and	JOLIMETZ	aaa	37th
Div	to	east	of

FROM

PLACE & TIME

* This line should be erased if not required.

9310—W.528—100,000—10/5/17—E.P.Co.—(E1213).

Prefix ______ Code ______ Words ______

£ s. d.

Charges to Collect

Service Instructions

Received. From V By Bm

Sent, or sent out. At ______ m. To ______ By ______

Office Stamp. PHS

Handed in at ______ Office ______ m. Received 2153 m.

TO (5)

* Sender's Number	Day of Month.	In reply to Number	AAA
	7/3		

LE	QUESNOY	aaa	Objective
for 2nd Bde	ZOWU	adv	Guards
on	JOLIMETZ	-LE	QUESNOY
Road	aaa 110 Bde	VUFE	will
act	as	adv	guard
leading	troops	crossing	green
line	at	07.00	hours
and	advancing	through	BASU 64
and 62 Bde	DADE	after	capture
of	second	objective	aaa
9th	Bde	R.F.A.	will
support	advance	of	VUFE 110 Bde
aaa	most	important	for
VUFE 110 Bde	to	protect	right
of	37th	Div	during
advance	aaa	ack	aaa
addsd	all	concerned	

FROM 21 Divn

PLACE & TIME 2100

Noted

* This line should be erased if not required.

9310—W.528—100,000—10/5/17—E.P.Co.—(E1213).

War Diary.

App 9

TELEGRAM

Words

Urgent
operations
priority to
Brigades.

Sent.

To......................
At......................
By......................

DADE	LODE	ZEJU	ZODU	17 Div.	5th Corps.
BASU	ZOKI	A/Q	5th Div.	37 Div.	
VUFE	DUPA	ZOHO	33 Div.	15th Sqn.	

G.X. 162 / 23 / AAA

Zowu Warning Order AAA Advance will be resumed tomorrow by ZOWU AAA Objective Line of road X.24.a.9.0. GRAND GAY FARM to Halt X.11.a.5.5. AAA Right Div. Boundary from X.29.Cent. to Cross Roads S.3.c.8.7. AAA Left Div. Boundary from X.6.a.0.2. M.31.b.3.0. M.26.b.5.0. M.21.c.3.0. AAA Inter-brigade boundary POIX SPINNING MILL to road junction X.28.d.1.4. (X.28.c.1.4) just inclusive to right Brigade thence straight line to X.22.d.6.5. South of Road to X.17.b.3.1. thence straight line to M.33.c.0.8. AAA BASU will attack on right and DADE ON LEFT AAA Jumping off line depends on progress of DADE today AAA After capture of objective advance guards will be sent forward to make as much ground as possible towards JOLIMETZ - LE QUESNOY Road AAA Cancelling previous instructions BASU will now take over GREEN line on right Brigade front and VUFE on left Brigade front as soon as vacated by DADE AAA BASU will push forward troops to protect right rear of DADE during latters advance today and will take over right Brigade front from DADE ON final line reached tonight AAA VUFE will be disposed tonight between GREEN Line inclusive and RED line exclusive and will be in Div. Reserve tomorrow AAA Further orders later. ACknowledge.

ZOWU
1200

H. H. Hanbury? Lieut-Col
General Staff.
21st Division.

War Diary.

App 10

TELEGRAM.
Words

URGENT OPERATIONS
PRIORITY 3 Bdes.
D.M.G.C. H.G. Lt Col

To....................
At....................
By....................

DADE	ZOKI	ZEJU	ZODU	17 Div.	V Corps.
BASU	LODE	A/Q.	5 Div.	37 Div.	
VUFE	DUFA	ZOHO	33 Div.	15 Sqn. R.A.F.	

- / 23 / AAA

ZOWU Order No.248 AAA Ref. Warning Order G.X.162 of today AAA Advance is being continued tomorrow AAA 33rd Div. attack LANDRECIES - LE QUESNOY Road AAA 37 Div. attack high ground North of GHISSIGNIES AAA BASU on right and DADE on left will attack with first objective line of road from X.29.c.7.7 to X.21.b.7.1 AAA Second objective line of road from rd. junc. X.24.a.9.0 GRAND GAY FARM to Halt X.11.a.5.5 AAA Advance to first objective under barrage AAA No barrage for advance beyond first objective AAA Artillery starting line 300 yards in advance of road F.9.c.6.6 F.2.a.3.5 AAA Barrage dwells on starting line for 8 minutes and then advances at rate of 100 yards in 4 minutes AAA Protector beyond first objective for 8 minutes and then ceases AAA No barrage for right Brigade through Village of POIX DU NORD AAA BASU will pick up barrage on far side of village AAA Advance through village will be calculated at rate of 100 yards in 4 minutes AAA Reserve Coy. Machine Guns will barrage 400 yards ahead of Artillery AAA One M.G.Coy. remains with each Brigade AAA 95th Bde. R.F.A. will support advance from first to second objectives and keep liaison with BASU and DADE H.Q. AAA Second objective will be consolidated in depth when captured AAA Liaison post with 33rd Div. at rd. junc. X.24.a.9.0 and with 37th Div. on rly. at X.5.c.9.5. AAA After capture of objectives all three Divs. will send advanced guards forward to make good outpost zone AAA 33 Div. to FUTOY and JOLIMETZ AAA 37th Div. to East of LE QUESNOY AAA Objective for ZOWU Adv. Guards main JOLIMETZ - LE QUESNOY Road AAA VUFE will act as Adv. Guard leading troops crossing Green Line at 07.00 hours and advancing through BASU and DADE after capture of second objective AAA 95th Bde. R.F.A. will support advance of VUFE AAA Most important for VUFE to protect right of 37th Div. during advance AAA Ack AAA Addsd all concerned

H.L. Franklyn Lieut Col

ZOWU 20.30 hours General Staff,

File.

"A" Form.

MESSAGES AND SIGNALS.

Army Form C. 2121.
(In pads of 100.)

No. of Message ....

Prefix .... Code .... m.	Words.	Charge.	This message is on a/c of:	Recd. at .... m.
Office of Origin and Service Instructions.	Sent		.... Service.	Date ....
	At .... m.			From ....
	To			
	By		(Signature of "Franking Officer.")	By ....

TO

[illegible]	[illegible]	17 Div.	V Corps.
[illegible]	[illegible] 5 Div.	37 Div.	
[illegible]	[illegible] 33 Div.	15 Sqn.	

Sender's Number.	Day of Month.	In reply to Number.	
* G.X.169.	23		AAA

Ref. [illegible] Warning Order G.X.16[illegible] Inter-Bde. Boundary for rd. junc. X.28.d.1.4 read rd. junc. X.28.c.1.4.

From [illegible]
Place
Time

The above may be forwarded as now corrected.

Censor.

(Z) (Sgd) G.[illegible] Capt.

Signature of Addressor or person authorised to telegraph in his name.

* This line, except **AAA**, should be erased if not required.

Wt. W 3253/P511. 500,000 Pads. 1/18. B. & S. Ltd. (E2389.)

"A" Form.
MESSAGES AND SIGNALS.

Army Form C. 2121.
(In pads of 100.)
No. of Message

Prefix........Code........m. | Words. | Charge.
Office of Origin and Service Instructions.
4 p. 11

Sent
At........m.
To
By

This message is on a/c of: War Diary Service.
(Signature of "Franking Officer.")

Recd. at........m.
Date
From
By

TO					
DADE	LODE	ZEJU	ZODU	17 Div.	15 Sqn.
BASU	ZOKI	A/Q.	5 Div.	37 Div.	R.A.F.
VUFE	DUFA	ZOHO	33 Div.	V Corps.	

Sender's Number.	Day of Month.	In reply to Number.	
* G.X.249.	24		AAA

ZOWU Order No.249 AAA BASU on right and DADE on left will attack and capture second objective this afternoon AAA Arty comes down at 16.00 hours on line 300 yards in front of LES TUILERIES - SALESCHES Road on right Bde. front and about 400 yards in front of this road on left Bde. front AAA Exact Arty starting line has been given to those concerned AAA Barrage lifts at 16.12 and advances at rate of 100 yards in 3 mins until 300 yards beyond objective and then ceases AAA Heavy Arty will bombard objective and orchards West of objective from Zero till safety compels lift AAA H.A. then lifts on to high ground 500 yards beyond objective for 20 mins and then ceases AAA Ack

From ZOWU
Place
Time 14.40

The above may be forwarded as now corrected.
Censor.

(Z) (Sgd) H.E.F. Lt.Col.
Signature of Addressor or person authorised to telegraph in his name.

* This line, except AAA, should be erased if not required.

Wt. W 3253/P511. 500,000 Pads. 1/18. B. & S. Ltd. (E2380.)

App 17

War Diary

URGENT
OPERATIONS
PRIORITY 3 Bdes.

Sent
At..................
To..................
By..................

DADE	LODE	ZEJU	ZODU	17 Div.	V Corps.
BASU	ZOKI	A/Q.	5 Div.	37 Div.	
VUFE	DUFA	ZOHO	33 Div.	15 Sqn. R.A.F.	

G.M. / 24 / AAA

ZOWU Order No.250 AAA It is considered possible that the enemy may withdraw from opposite our front tonight AAA BASU and DADE will send out patrols at Dawn to search ground between our present front line and line of orchards about 1,000 yards N.E. of it AAA If no enemy encountered these patrols will be supported and patrols sent on again to line of road through CROIX ROUGE and into LOUVIGNIES AAA If still no enemy encountered DADE and BASU will NOT be required to send patrols further AAA VUFE will have two Coys. between Brown Line and POIX inclusive by 07.00 hrs. tomorrow Oct. 25th AAA Remainder of Bde. will be disposed in depth and obtain as much rest as possible until leading Coys. are ordered to move AAA VUFE will keep close touch with situation through BASU and DADE H.Q. AAA If patrols report no enemy on this side of line of orchards VUFE will order leading Coys. to advance and take over work of patrolling from DADE and BASU AAA These two Coys. will patrol by bounds and will support patrols on conclusion of each bound AAA VUFE will support leading Coys. by remainder of Bde. making good as first objective line of JOLIMETZ - LE QUESNOY Rd. AAA When this road made good patrols will be sent forward to Railway but no further advance except by patrols until ordered from Div. H.Q. AAA If BASU and DADE encounter enemy it is not the Divl. Comdr's intention to make ground by fighting AAA Divs. on flanks will be taking similar action AAA One Bde. R.F.A. will be held in readiness and come under orders of VUFE if latter moves forward AAA One Troop Cyclists will be sent to report to each Bde. about 08.00 tomorrow and will be used to get touch with the enemy if Inf. patrols fail to do so AAA Div. H.Q. closes NEUVILLY 10.00 and re-opens OVILLERS same hour AAA Ack

ZOWU.
22.15 hrs.

H. C. Hamblyn [signature]
Lieut.Col.

War Diary.

17/10/13

TELEGRAM

Urgent operations priority to Bdes.

Words.

Sent.
At..................
To..................
By..................

DADE	LODE	ZEJU	ZODU	17 Div.	15th Sqn.R.A.F.
BASU	ZOKI	A/Q	5th Corps.	33rd Div.	
VUFE	DUFA	ZOHO	5th Div.	37th Div.	

- / 25 / AAA

ZOWU order No.251 AAA If VUFE does not pass through DADE and BASU today VUFE will relieve DADE and BASU tonight 25/26 inst AAA Details will be arranged between Brigadiers AAA On relief DADE will withdraw to the area between the BROWN and GREEN lines both exclusive AAA BASU will withdraw to the area between the GREEN line and VENDEGIES both inclusive AAA DADE will be prepared to hold the BROWN line or to form a defensive flank facing S.E. AAA BASU will be prepared to hold the GREEN line AAA DADE will hold two Battns. in readiness to move at quarter hours notice and BASU will hold one Battan. ready to move at half hours notice AAA Reserve M.G. Coy. will be disposed for the defence of the GREEN line AAA Completion of relief will be reported to ZOWU AAA Ack.

ZOWU
0910.

H. Hardingwell. Major
for Lt. Col.

War Diary

App 14

TELEGRAM.

Words.

URGENT OPERATIONS
PRIORITY 3 Bdes.

HWJ

At......................
To......................
By......................

DADE	LODE	ZEJU	ZODU	17 Div.	15 Sqn R.A.F.
BASU	ZOKI	A/Q.	V Corps.	33 Div.	
VUFE	DUFA	ZOHO	5 Div.	37 Div.	

- / 25 / AAA

ZOWU Order No.252 AAA In conjunction with operation by 33rd Div. VUFE will establish outpost zone tonight in front of present line AAA Fighting Patrols will be sent forward under creeping barrage to establish Platoon Posts approximately in following places AAA S.13.d.0.4 X.18.b.9.4 X.18.b.7.6 X.11.d.8.8. X.11.b.5.4 X.11.b.1.9 AAA Barrage will come down at 01.00 hours Oct. 26th on line S.19.b.0.7 to X.11.b.0.5 will pause for 8 minutes and then advance at 100 yards in 4 mins. until 300 yards clear of posts given above and then cease AAA At Dawn Reconnoitring Patrols will be sent forward to line of orchards S.W. and South of LOUVIGNIES AAA If no enemy encountered action detailed in ZOWU Order No.250 of yesterday will be adopted AAA If enemy encountered Reconnoitring Patrols will be withdrawn AAA Relief of BASU and DADE must be completed by 23.59 hours so as to facilitate above operation AAA Whole Cyclist Squadron comes under VUFE after relief AAA Ack AAA Adsd all concerned

H H Trawbridge

ZOWU
15.50 hrs.

Lt.Col.

Army Form C. 2123.
(In books of 100.)

"C" FORM.

MESSAGES AND SIGNALS.

No. of Message..........

Prefix.........Code.......Words.........	Received.	Sent, or sent out.	Office Stamp.
£ s. d.	From..............	At..........m.	25. X. 18. [illegible] SIGNALS
Charges to Collect	By..............	To..........	
Service Instructions		By..........	

Handed in at..........................Office..........m. Received..........m. 1836

TO [illegible] October 1918.

* Sender's Number.	Day of Month.	In reply to Number.	~~AAA~~
21 Div	25		

ZOWU	[illegible]	No.	252
[illegible]	[illegible]	[illegible]	will
[illegible]	[illegible]	33	[illegible]
VIIFE 1109	[illegible]	[illegible]	outpost
ZONE	tonight	in	front
of	present	line	[illegible]
holding	[illegible]	will	be
[illegible]	[illegible]	[illegible]	keeping
[illegible]	to	[illegible]	platoons
posts	approximately	on	following
[illegible]	[illegible]	S 18 d 0.4	X 18 b 9.4
X 18 b 1.6	X 11 d 8.8	X 11 b 5.4	X 11 b 1.4
[illegible]	barrage	will	[illegible]
[illegible]	at	01.00	[illegible]
[illegible]	26th	on	line
S 19 b 0 7	to	X 11 b 0.5	will
[illegible]	for	8	minutes

FROM	and then
PLACE & TIME	

* This line should be erased if not required.

(3866.) Wt. W528/M1970. 100,000 Pads. 3/17. H. W. & V., Ld. (E. 1213.)

Army Form C. 2123.
(In books of 100.)

"C" FORM.

MESSAGES AND SIGNALS.

No. of Message..............

Prefix.......Code.......Words.......	Received.	Sent, or sent out.	Office Stamp.
£ s. d. Charges to Collect	From........ By........	At........m.	25 X.18 SIGNALS
Service Instructions		To........ By........	

Handed in at..............................Office..............m. Received..............m.

TO 5 Corps (?)

*Sender's Number.	Day of Month.	In reply to Number.	AAA
	25		

advance	at	100	yards
in	4	mins	until
300	yards	east	of
[illegible]	given	above	and
then	[illegible]	[illegible]	at
[illegible]	consolidating	[illegible]	will
be	[illegible]	[illegible]	the
line	of	[illegible]	SW
and	South	of	LOUVIGNIES
[illegible]	of	the	enemy
encountered	action	detailed	in
21 Div	order	No.	200
of	[illegible]	will	be
adopted	[illegible]	if	enemy
encountered	[illegible]	[illegible]	patrols [illegible]
be	withdrawn	and	[illegible]
of	BASU	and	DADE

FROM 64 Inf Bde 62 Inf Bde

PLACE & TIME

* This line should be erased if not required.

(3866.) Wt. W528/M1970. 100,000 Pads. 5/17. H. W. & V., Ld. (E. 1213.)

Army Form C. 2123.
(In books of 100.)

"C" FORM.

MESSAGES AND SIGNALS. No. of Message..........

Prefix.........Code.......Words.........	Received.	Sent, or sent out.	Office Stamp.
£ s. d.	From..................	At...............m.	DZ 25. X. 18
Charges to Collect	By..................	To..................	SIGNALS
Service Instructions		By..................	

Handed in at...Office..............m. Received..............m.

TO [illegible] (8)

* Sender's Number.	Day of Month.	In reply to Number.	AAA

must be completed by
23.30 hours so as
to facilitate above operation
and whole cyclist squadron
[illegible] under VIII C [illegible]
[illegible] [illegible] [illegible]
[illegible] are concerned

110 Inf Bde
Noted.

FROM [illegible] 15.50 [illegible]

PLACE & TIME

* This line should be erased if not required.

(3866.) Wt. W528/M1970. 100,000 Pads. 5/17. H. W. & V., Ld. **(E. 1213.)**

War Diary.
App 15

SECRET.

Words

To....................
At....................
By....................

DADE LODE ZEJU ZODU
BASU ZOKI A/Q JESO
VUFE DUFA ZOHO

GX. 228. / 25 / AAA

Warning Order AAA ZOWU less LODE will be relieved by 17th Division less Arty tomorrow and night 26/27 inst AAA DADE and BASU will be relieved by 50 and 51 Inf. Bdes. respectively AAA Reliefs to be complete by 1530 hrs AAA VUFE will be relieved by 52 Inf. Bde. AAA On relief BASU to INCHY DADE to NEUVILLY VUFE to OVILLERS and AMERVAL AAA 3 Coys ZEJU will be billeted with affiliated Bdes AAA ZEJU H.Q. and Res. Coy. to NEUVILLY AAA ZOKI will arrange reliefs of Field Coys.R.E. and DUFA AAA Added DADE, BASU, VUFE, ZEJU, ZOKI repeated LODE, DUFA, A/Q, JESO, ZOHO, ZODU.

ZOWU.
1930.

A F Macdougall Major.
for Lt. Col
General Staff.

War Diary

SECRET.

Copy No. 25

Ap/10.18

21st DIVISION ORDER NO. 253.

Ref. Sheets 57.b. and 51.a.
1/40,000.

26th October 1918.

1. The Division (less Artillery) will be relieved by the 17th Division (less Artillery) today and night 26/27th October, in accordance with attached table.

2. All details of relief will be arranged between Brigadiers.

3. Reliefs of Field Coys. R.E., Pioneers and Field Ambulances, will be arranged between Cs.R.E. and A.Ds.M.S.

4. Machine Gun reliefs will be arranged between Os.C. 21st and 17th Machine Gun Battalions.

5. Completion of relief will be reported to Divisional Headquarters.

6. Command of the Sector and the Artillery in it will pass to G.O.C., 17th Division on completion of the Infantry relief.

7. Divisional Headquarters close at OVILLERS and open at NEUVILLY at 1600 hrs, October 26th, 1918.

8. Acknowledge.

A.C. Lauchlyn

Lieut.-Colonel.
General Staff.
21st Division.

Issued through Signals at 13.30

	Copy No.		Copy No.
62nd Inf. Bde.	1	21st Bn.M.G.C.	11
64th " "	2	D.G.O.	12
110th " "	3	Train.	13
C.R.A.	4	21st M.T.Co.	14
C.R.E.	5	5th Corps.	15-16
Pioneers.	6	Vth Corps.H.A.	17
'Q'	7	Vth Corps. R.A.	18
Signals.	8	17th Div.	19
A.D.M.S.	9	33rd Div.	20
A.P.M.	10	37th Div.	21
		38th Div.	22
		15th Sqn R.A.F.	23
		O.C.'D' Sqdn.N.I.H.	24
		War Diary.	25
		File.	26.

TABLE TO ACCOMPANY 21st DIVISION ORDER NO. 253.

Serial No.	Unit.	From.	To.	Relieved by.	Route.	Remarks.
1.	62nd Inf. Bde.	Support.	NEUVILLY	50th Inf. Bde.	CROSS COUNTRY TRACKS.	Relief to be complete by 15.30 hrs.
2.	64th Inf. Bde.	Reserve.	INCHY	51st Inf. Bde.		
3.	110th Inf. Bde.	Line.	OVILLERS & AMERVAL.	52nd Inf. Bde.		Relief not to commence before dark.
4.	21st Bn.M.G.C.	Line.	2 Coys NEUVILLY. 1 Coy. INCHY. 1 Coy. OVILLERS or AMERVAL. H.Q. NEUVILLY.	17th Bn.M.G.C.		"

Notes.

A. All movement by day will be by Platoons at 100 yards interval and all precautions will be taken against observation by enemy aircraft.

B. When troops have to march on roads, they will move in file. Transport moving by road will adhere to traffic routes laid down.

"A" Form

Army Form C. 2121
(In pads of 100.)

MESSAGES AND SIGNALS.

No. of Message..........

Prefix..........Code..........m. Office of Origin and Service Instructions	Words	Charge.	This message is on a/c of:	Recd. at......m.
App 7	Sent At ....m. To .... By		18K Service. War Diary (Signature of "Franking Officer")	Date.......... From .... By..........

TO				
	DADE	ZOKI	JESO	ZOHO
	BASU	LODE	Q	
	VUFE	ZEJU	ZODU	

Sender's Number.	Day of Month.	In reply to Number.	AAA
GK 301	28		

ZOWU	will	relieve	17th
Divn	tomorrow	and	tomorrow
night	aaa	DADE	will
be	in	support	leaving
present	billets	at	1200
hrs	aaa	BASU	will
be	in	Reserve	leaving
present	billets	at	0900
hrs	aaa	VUFE	will
be	in	front	line
leaving	present	billets	at
1530	hrs	aaa	Orders
follow			

From ZOWU
Place
Time 1440

The above may be forwarded as now corrected. (Z) [signature] Major

Censor. Signature of Addressor or person authorised to telegraph in his name

* This line should be erased if not required.

Order No 1625 Wt. W3253/ P 511 27/2 H. & K., Ltd. (E. 263/

War Diary. 25

App 18

S E C R E T.

Copy No......

21st Division Order No.254.

Ref: Maps 57.B. and 51.A. 1/40,000.

28th October, 1918.

1. The Division (less Artillery) will relieve the 17th Division (less Artillery) in the Left Sector of the V Corps front on October 29th and night 29th/30th October, 1918, in accordance with the attached Table.

2. All details of relief will be arranged between Brigadiers.

3. Boundary between 62nd and 110th Infantry Brigades will be :-
X.28.c.0.2 - X.22.d.6.5 - thence along road (inclusive to 62nd Inf. Bde.) to X.17.b.3.2 - S.7.b.0.0.

4. (a) Field Coys. R.E. and Pioneer reliefs will be arranged between Cs.R.E.
Field Coys. R.E., 21st Division, will not leave present billets until 15.30 hours October 29th.

(b) Field Ambulance reliefs will be arranged between A.Ds.M.S.
Field Ambulances, 21st Division, will move with the Infantry Brigades to whom they are attached.

5. Machine Gun reliefs will be arranged between Os.C. 21st and 17th Battalions, Machine Gun Corps.

6. Completion of reliefs will be reported to Divisional Headquarters.

7. Command of the Sector and the Artillery in it will pass to the G.O.C. 21st Division on completion of the Infantry relief.

8. Divisional Headquarters close at NEUVILLY and open at OVILLERS at 16.00 hours October 29th.

9. A c k n o w l e d g e.

for [signature] Capt
Lieut.Colonel,
General Staff,
21st Division.

Issued through Signals
at 19.30 hrs. to :-

	Copy No.		Copy No.		Copy No.
62 Inf. Bde.	1	A.D.M.S.	9	17th Div.	18
64 : :	2	D.A.P.M.	10	33rd Div.	20
110 : :	3	D.M.G.O.	11	37th Div.	21
C.R.A.	4	D.G.O.	12	38th Div.	22
C.R.E.	5	Train.	13	Sqn R.A.F.	23
Pioneers.	6	21 M.T.Coy.	14	Div.Cyclists.	24
"Q"	7	V Corps.	15 - 16	War Diary.	25
Signals.	8	V Corps H.A.	17	File.	26
		V Corps R.A.	18	Div. Rec.Camp	27

Table to accompany Divisional Order No.254.

Serial No.	Unit.	From.	To.	Starting Point.	Time.	In relief of.	Route.	Remarks.
1.	64 Inf. Bde.	INCHY.	VENDEGIES. (Reserve).	Level crossing J.22.b.95.70.	09.00.	51st Inf. Bde.	NEUVILLY - OVILLERS - VENDEGIES - POIX.	Relief to be complete by 13.00.
2.	62 Inf. Bde.	NEUVILLY.	POIX.	Rly. bridge K.9.a.5.8.	12.00.	50th Inf. Bde.		Relief to be complete by 17.00.
3.	110 Inf.Bde.	OVILLERS & AMERVAL.	Line Right.	House at E.24.a.9.8.	15.30.	52nd Inf. Bde. Right Half.		-
4.	62 Inf. Bde.	POIX.	Line Left.	-	-	52nd Inf. Bde. Left Half.		Bde. H.Q. remain at H.Q. 50th Inf. Bde.
5.	21st Bn.M.G.C.	NEUVILLY, INCHY and AMERVAL.	Line.	-	-	17th Bn. M.G.C.		Coys. to move with Bdes. to which they are affiliated.
6.	F.Coys. R.E.	NEUVILLY.	Line.	Rly. bridge K.9.a.5.8.	15.30.	F.Coys. R.E. 17th Division.		-

Notes. (a) All movement East of VENDEGIES will be by Platoons at 100 yards interval.
All precautions will be taken against observation by enemy aircraft.

(b) Attention is directed to 21st Div. G.285 dated 27.10.18. reference movement on roads. These instructions will be strictly complied with.

(c) Transport moving by road will adhere to traffic routes laid down.

War Diary.

App 19

TELEGRAM.

Words.

Sent
At ....
To ....
By ....

DADE	ZOKI	ZOHO	DODU	V Corps H.A.	38th Div.
BASU	DUFA	D.A.P.M.	M.T.Coy.	17th Div.	15 Sqn.
VUDE	Q	ZEJU	V Corps.	33rd :	Div.Cyclists.
LODE	JESO	D.G.O.	V Corps R.A.	37th :	Div.Rec.Camp.

G.X. 334 - 29th. AAA

Advanced Div. report centre opens OVILLERS 19.00 hrs. Oct. 29th. AAA Div. H.Q. open OVILLERS 10.00 hrs. Oct. 30th. AAA Addsd recipients Order No. 254.

Z O W U

17.30 hrs.

A.F. Macdougall. Major.

Major G.S.

War Diary

SECRET.

Copy No. 25

App 20.

21st DIVISION ORDER NO.255.

Ref. 57.A, S.E. & 51.S.W.
1/20,000.

31st October 1918.

1. The Divisional and Brigade Boundaries will be readjusted on the night 1st/2nd November, as under :-

Northern Divisional Boundary.

X.10.d.6.0. - thence due East along grid line between X.11. and X.17, S.8 and S.14, etc.,

Southern Divisional Boundary.

X.24.c.0.0. - S.26.b.0.9. - T.25.a.0.4.

Inter-Brigade Boundary.

X.18.a.6.0. - X.17.d.6.0. - ARBRE de la CROIX (inclusive to 110th Infantry Brigade) - thence original boundary.

2. The following reliefs will be carried out on the night 1st/2nd November :-

(a). The 110th Infantry Brigade will extend its right to the new Divisional Right Boundary, relieving troops of the 38th Division.

(b). 62nd Infantry Brigade will extend its right to the new Inter-Brigade Boundary, relieving troops of the 110th Infantry Brigade.

(c). All troops of the 62nd Infantry Brigade North of the new Divisional Left Boundary will be relieved by the 37th Division.

/3.........

3. All details of relief will be arranged between Brigadiers concerned.

4. No reliefs will commence before 18.00 hrs. November 1st, and will be complete by 04.00 hrs. November 2nd.

5. Completion of reliefs will be reported to Divisional Headquarters.

6. ACKNOWLEDGE.

A.H. Macdougall Major

Lieut.-Colonel.
General Staff.
21st Division.

Issued through Signals at 19.30 hrs to

	Copy No.		Copy No.
62nd Inf. Bde.	1	Vth Corps.	15-16.
64th " "	2	Vth Corps H.A.	17
110th " "	3	Vth Corps R.A.	18
C.R.A.	4	17th Div.	19
C.R.E.	5	37th Div.	20
Pioneers.	6	38th Div.	21
"Q"	7	15th Sqn.R.A.F.	22
Signals.	8	Div.Cyclists.	23
A.D.M.S.	9	Div,Rec.Camp.	24
D.A.P.M.	10	War Diary.	25
D.M.G.C.	11	File.	26
D.G.O.	12		
Train.	13		
21st M.T.Coy.	14		

GENERAL STAFF, V CORPS.
No. G.S. 518/2
Date 30.10.18

S E C R E T.

21 Div.
G. 329.

V Corps.

Reference V Corps No. G.S.518 dated 28th October,1918.

1. (a) I do not consider it advisable to risk an attack by night (when there is no moon) in the very enclosed country now in front of us.

(b) An attack at dawn is feasible, but is generally expected.

(c) I think 10.00 hours is unnecessarily late, as there would be four hours of daylight during which E.A. might discover an unusual number of our troops in the forward area. Moreover, on the timing given in G.S.518, the operation (including the final pause) would not be complete till 16.00 hours, which is rather late if any continuation of the operation is contemplated.

(d) I consider 08.00 hours a suitable zero hour. This will allow most of the assembly to be done before light, and unless it is an exceptionally clear morning there should not be much risk of detection by aeroplanes

2. As regards pauses, I am of opinion that there should be a halt of one hour on the first objective and half an hour on the second objective, for the following reasons -

(a) On the assumption that the attack is being made on a three Brigade front, it will take half an hour to "leap-frog" each of the two Battalions concerned in each Brigade.

(b) If the attack is made in daylight, it will not be possible to close up units in the normal way before zero. The leading troops of the "second" Battalions would therefore have a lot of ground to make up between zero and the time at which they were due to take up the advance. It would not be safe to allow less than an hour for this. During this hour the "third" Battalions could close up to normal distance and so would not require more than half an hour's pause, when it came to their turn to "leap-frog".

3. I entirely agree that all advances should, if possible, be made under an Artillery barrage. The important thing is to start off after each pause with a really thick barrage, even if afterwards, owing to ammunition difficulties, it is necessary to let the barrage die away almost to nothing.

4. As regards the pace of the barrage, I am inclined to think that 100 yards in six minutes is too slow for an attack by daylight if the going is firm: such a slow rate is apt to make the advance sticky.

/Except......

Except in certain portions of the "FORET de MORMAL" where the undergrowth and trees are known to be very thick and where special arrangements for a slow barrage could be made, I consider 100 yards in four minutes would be a suitable pace.

5. For an attack by daylight a larger quantity of smoke than usual would be required, particularly at zero. It is essential that this should be guaranteed before a daylight attack is finally decided upon.

6. I strongly suggest that our low-flying aeroplanes should be active between 06.00 hours and 08.00 hours daily between now and the day fixed for the attack, so as to discourage low-flying E.A. from operating between those hours.

D. Campbell

Major-General

29th October, 1918. Commanding 21st Division.

War Diary
App 21

21st Division.

No.1.

Intelligence Summary for period 0600 2nd to 0600 3rd Oct. 1918.

PATROLS.

The ground between the front line and the Canal was actively patrolled during the 24 hours.

All attempts to cross the Canal were met by very heavy Machine Gun fire from the Eastern bank.

MOVEMENT.

House at M.26.a.10.70 was seen to be a centre of movement. Three Machine Guns were concentrated on it and later several wounded were seen to be carried away on stretchers.

Several parties on the hillside between BANTOUZELLE and HONNECOURT were dispersed by Machine Gun fire.

ARTILLERY.

Our Own. Active throughout the day. At 1155 hours an explosion was caused at RED FARM and several direct hits were observed on RANCOURT FARM.

Hostile. Shelled GAUCHE WOOD, GONNELIEU, VILLERS GUISLAIN and 22 RAVINE.

Very slight gas shelling of X.5.a. during the night.

GENERAL.

Two very good approaches to the Canal Bank are reported at M.31.b.3.7 and M.31.b.2.3.

J. Pocock. for Capt. R.G.A.

3.10.18.

Lt-Col. General Staff,
21st Division.

10

21st DIVISION.

No.2.

SUMMARY OF INFORMATION from 0600 3rd to 0600 4th Octr.1918.

PATROLS. Officer's patrol left FIFE TRENCH at X.5.a.55.45. at 2345 hrs and proceeded Eastwards. When near Sunken Road X.5.b.8.5. hostile M.G. fire was opened from direction of S.2.Cent. and from HONNECOURT. Enemy appeared to be holding line in M.31.b. and d. and M.32.c. in some strength.

Patrols from left sub-Sector during night report heavy M.G. fire from two guns at about M.31.a.0.1. and enemy Posts at M.25.c. 9.5. and 9.3.

MOVEMENT. Very little movement observed.

ARTILLERY.

(Our Own.) Continuously active. HINDENBURG LINE bombarded. RED FARM, RANCOURT FARM, QUARRY S.10.b. and Sunken Road S.10.a. among targets engaged.

(Hostile). Quiet during the day; more active during evening and night. GONNELIEU shelled with heavy calibre, 0945, and R.33.c. at intervals.

GOUZEAUCOURT shelled with H.V. gun at 1005.

Occasional shelling round area R.34.Central.

At 1800 hrs 30 to 40 4.2" were fired on right Battn. front.

During the night areas R.27 and R.30.c. intermittently shelled with 105 mm. and 77 mm and some gas shell.

Enemy light guns shelled dump found at R.36.c.6.9. and frequently shelled road R.30.c.0.4. to 9.4. between 0300 and 0600 this morning.

Some heavy howitzer shells dropped in BANTEUX.

H.V. gun accurately shelled Cross roads at R.25.d.1.2. at intervals during the day.

TRENCH MORTARS.

(Hostile). At about 2100 hrs. BANTEUX shelled with light trench mortars but silenced by our heavy artillery. M.26.d.45.80. suspected as position of Trench Mortar.

MACHINE GUNS.

Enemy M.G. located at M.31.d.60.85.

J. Pocock for Capt. R.G.A.

4th October 1918.

Lt-Col. General Staff.
21st Division.

War Diary

21st DIVISION.

SUMMARY OF GENERAL INFORMATION 6th OCTOBER 1918.

DIVISIONAL FRONT. - was approximately as follows at 6 p.m. :-

M.30.b. - N.25.c. - N.31.a. - T.1.b.

LEFT FLANK DIVISION. - M.23.d.9.1. - M.24.a.8.8. - M.17.b.Cent. -

M.11.d.1.5.

RIGHT FLANK DIVISION. - T.19.b. - T.13.Cent. - T.7.Cent. -

T.1.Cent.

OTHER FRONTS.

On morning of 6th October, 2nd Australian Division captured MONTBREHAIN with 500 prisoners. Many enemy reported killed and our Tanks did great execution. During 6th October Third Army advanced 3,000 to 6,000 yards on 11,000 yards front.

The greater part of DOUAI has been set on fire by the enemy.

The French have advanced their lines N. and E. of RHEIMS to a depth of 5 to 10 kilometres on a 45 kilometre front.

The french have taken SAPIGNEUL and BRIMONT.

Prisoners taken in PALESTINE since 19th September now total over 71,000, amongst them 3,200 Germans and Austrians 4 Turkish Divisional Commanders and the Commander of the MANN Garrison. The Arabs claim a further 8,000.

Information from prisoners captured by the Division on 6th inst:-

Prisoners stated that the line is to be gradually withdrawn to a line approximately 20 kilometres East of the HINDENBURG Line, probably the LE CATEAU - ST SOUPLET. They state that the BEAUREVOIR Line is not strongly held. The majority of the trenches are only waist deep with uncompleted dugouts. Company strengths about 50, with 4 to 5 L.M.Gs.

GENERAL. During the month of Sept. . 311,218 American troops have landed in Europe, 153246 of which are in France.

There have been uproarious scenes in the Austrian Parliament. When the Premier announced Austria's loyalty to Germany, a tremendous uproar arose among the CZECHS, who shouted "Away with Germany and the Kaiser".

App 22 War Diary

SECRET.

21 Div.
G. 230.

62nd Inf. Bde.
64th " "
110th " "
C.R.A.
C.R.E.
Pioneers.
D.M.G.O.
"Q"
Signals.

DEFENSIVE ARRANGEMENTS.
Left Division, V Corps.

1. Owing to the fact that the front of the Right Division faces East and the front of the Left Division faces N.E. the angle thus formed is particularly susceptible to counter-attack from the East. It is, therefore, necessary to maintain a defensive flank on the right of the Left Divisional Sector.

This flank will run from LES TUILLERIES approximately along the Spur from X.29.Central to the road at X.23.a.6.6.. The right of the Right Battalion holding the front line will also be bent back, roughly along the inter-Divisional Boundary.

2. DISTRIBUTION OF INFANTRY.

The Three Brigades will be distributed in depth, one behind the other.

(a). The leading Brigade will hold the line of the road X.24.c.9.0. - X.11.a.5.6. with two Battalions in depth. An outpost line, consisting of Platoon Posts, will be held approximately 800 yards in advance of this road. The Third Battalion of the leading Brigade will be disposed in rear of the right front Battalion and as far back as the road running N.W. from LES TUILLERIES (inclusive). This Battalion will be prepared to form a defensive flank facing East and N.E. within the above limits.

(b). The Support Brigade will be disposed with :-

(i) One Battalion about X.22., ready to hold the Brown Line between the road at X.22.d.6.4. and the left Divisional Boundary.

(ii) One Battalion about X.27. ready to deliver an immediate counter-attack Eastwards if called upon by B.G.C. leading Brigade. One . . Company of this Battalion with four Machine Guns will be disposed about X.28.d. ready to hold the Spur from X.28.b.9.3. to the River.

(iii) One Battalion in POIX ready to occupy Brown line between right Divisional Boundary and Road at X. 22.d.6.4., if Reserve Battalion Leading Brigade moves forward from it.

P.T.O.

(c). The Reserve Brigade will be disposed with one Battalion about the Green Line, ready to hold this line and also to form a defensive flank along the Spur running from F.9.Central N.E. to the River. The remainder of the Brigade will be in VENDEGIES and ready to support the forward Battalion.

3. DISPOSITION OF MACHINE GUNS.

(a) One Company affiliated to leading Brigade for holding position in depth.
Half Company affiliated to leading Brigade for the special purpose of protecting the right flank.

(b) One Company affiliated to Support Brigade.

(c). One Company affiliated to Reserve Brigade.

(d). Half Company as permanent garrison to Green Line.

4. CONSOLIDATION.

(a). The following strong points have been constructed by the R.E. Each strong point is/designed for a garrison of one Platoon :-

X.24.c.1.8. X.28.d.5.8.
X.23.d.3.3. X.22.d.8.1.
X.17.a.3.3. X.28.a.2.5.
X.10.d.9.1. X.22.c.1.3.

(b). The following strong points are in hand:-

X.11.c.3.0. X.22.c.5.9.

(c). The following strong points are proposed :-

X.29.b.2.4. X.23.d.3.3.
X.23.a.8.3.

(d). A wire belt is being erected by the Pioneers in front of the road X.24.a.9.0. - X.11.a.5.6.
Work starts from the Southern end tonight October 25/26th.

5. As it has been found that recent counter-attacks, delivered by the enemy have not been delivered with great determination, it must be impressed on the Commanders of local reserves that they must meet such counter-attacks by charging with the bayonet.

H.G. Franklyn Lieut Col
General Staff.
21st Division.

25th October, 1918.

Copies to :- Vth Corps.
17th Div.
33rd Div.
37th Div.
38th Div.

App 23 War Diary

SECRET.

21 Div.
G. 321.

Proceedings of Conference held at Divisional Headquarters, 28th Oct. 1918.

Present :-

B.G.C. 62 Inf. Bde.
B.G.C. 64 : :
B.G.C. 110 : :
C.R.A.
A.A.Q.M.G.
D.M.G.C.
O.C.Signals.

1. **Relief of 17th Division.**

The G.O.C. said that he had decided to take over the front line with two Brigades, the 110th Infantry Brigade being on the right and the 62nd Infantry Brigade on the left.

2. **Barrages.**

B.G.C. 64th Infantry Brigade considered that in the present form of warfare it was better to have a brrage only for about the first 1,000 yards of an advance and then barrage should gradually die away, the troops continuing the advance without it. By this means he considered that objectives could be more distant, and that the advance would be carried out more rapidly. The B.G.C. 62nd Infantry Brigade considered that no definite rule could be laid down, and that when he had to pass through another Brigade he would prefer that Brigade to have a barrage the whole way to hoi objective as he considered troops were more likely to get their objective with a barrage. The Divisional Commander said that this question was worth considering. The C.R.A. also agreed especially as he thought the enemy would have more strength in front owing to the enclosed nature of the country that we were now passing through.

The point was raised that troops were liable at night to get into our own barrage owing to them thinking the superimposed H.E. barrage, being more visible than the shrapnel barrage, was the one to follow. It was agreed that the H.E. barrage should be continued as it was of great value.

3. **Rate of Advance.**

B.G.C. 64th Infantry Brigade considered that in the recent attacks the whole rate of advance was too slow, caused chiefly by the very long halts on objectives. The Divisional Commander agreed but said that these halts had to take place in order to comply with the rate of advance of Corps on either flank.

4. **Pace of Barrage.**

The Divisional Commander asked Brigadiers if they had any points which they wished to raise with reference to the recent memorandum issued on this subject. There were no points raised.

5. **Smoke.**

Brigadiers agreed that smoke in the barrage was useful, both by day and night, but considered that the amount to be used should depend on the direction of the wind. The C.R.A. said that this point would be borne in mind in future.

6. **Gas.**

Now that our guns fired a certain amount of shell filled with a very volatile gas, the Divisional Commander asked

/Brigadiers....

Brigadiers whether they thought troops should be told or not. B.Gs.C. 64th and 110th Infantry Brigades were of opinion that troops should not be told. B.G.C. 62 Infantry Brigade thought that troops should be warned that they would probably encounter gas after the attack had started but that gas was innocuous and was only fired to induce the enemy to wear gas masks. The Divisional Commander said that he was inclined to tell the troops but only if there was sufficient time to explain the situation fully to them.

7. The Divisional Commander asked the C.R.A. what was the probable minimum time that would be taken for the Artillery to fire a new barrage if the guns had advanced 2,000 yards. The C.R.A. said that, provided the going was good, and guns could get across country, he considered there would be a delay of about 2 hours. This delay was due to the insufficient training of present personnel.

The Divisional Commander considered that when Brigades and Batteries had to move forward, they should move to forward positions of readiness during the time the Brigade or Battery Commander was reconnoitring for new positions, so that there would be practically no delay in the Battery moving to the new position as soon as it had been decided on. The C.R.A. said that this matter would be gone into.

8. Reconnaissance of the Infantry Situation.

Brigadiers considered that Artillery Officers relied too much on getting news from Brigade Headquarters instead of finding out the situation for themselves, the consequence being that Infantry Brigade Headquarters became flooded out with Artillery Officers. The Divisional Commander agreed and thought that Artillery Officers should make more use of Mounted Orderlies to ascertain the situation. The C.R.A. agreed.

9. Tools.

B.G.C. 62 Infantry Brigade said that in the recent attacks each Battalion took two pack animals carrying 80 shovels with them. These were found to be invaluable. B.Gs.C. 64th and 110th Infantry Brigades agreed that this was the best method.

10. Communications.

It was agreed that the Brigade going through the Brigades attacking the first objectives should be responsible for laying the Divisional cable to the report centre immediately in rear of these objectives.

The question of Brigades laying light cable would be considered and instructions issued on the subject.

11. Machine Guns.

The Divisional Commander considered that whenever it was possible Machine Guns should fire indirect barrages. After the first attack the firing of these barrages was purely a question of the supply of ammunition.

Brigadiers all agreed that the Machine Gun Companies attached to Brigades did very good work during the recent attacks.

12. Administrative.

(a) First Line Transport has now been divided into 'A' and 'B' Echelons.

/B.G.C.....

B.G.C. 110th Infantry Brigade said that he had sub-divided 'A' Echelon placing a proportion of it directly under the Battalion Commander, the remainder being under Brigade control. He found that this method worked extremely well during the recent attacks.

The Divisional Commander considered that Battalion Commanders should have the fighting limbers under their own control but that by day limbers could not, as a rule, go further forward than Brigade Headquarters. Beyond Brigade Headquarters pack animals would have to be used. This was agreed to.

B.G.C. 64th Infantry Brigade considered that the transport lines for Echelon 'B' were too far behind. The A.A. & Q.M.G. said that this was a question of supply of water, but that as water in the area we were now passing through was more plentiful, transport lines would be placed as far forward as the situation permits.

(B) Burials.

B.G.C. 64th Infantry Brigade considered that troops in rear e.g. Artillery, Kite Balloon Sections etc. should bury all corpses lying in their immediate area. He thought that recent orders issued on this subject prevented this from being carried out.

The Divisional Commander said that this question would be taken up with the Corps.

(C) Traffic Control.

B.G.C. 64 Infantry Brigade suggested that in view of the recent orders issued by the Corps reference troops moving across country, cross country tracks should be marked out. The Divisional Commander agreed.

The Divisional Commander considered that Traffic Control Posts should be got forward quicker and should go as far forward as limbers normally went. The A.A. & Q.M.G. said that this matter would be taken up with the A.P.M.

13. Transport with Troops.

The Divisional Commander said that if Brigadiers considered that it was a tactical move, Companies could march with their own Lewis Gun Limbers, but that all other transport should move together in rear of the Battalion.

14. R.E.

Brigadiers agreed that the Section of R.E. attached to each Brigade during the recent operations had done good work and were invaluable.

Strong Points. The Divisional Commander said that the orders were for the R.E. to construct the strong points and then hand them over to the Infantry. Some doubt existed as to whether the strong points made during the recent operations had been so handed over and the Divisional Commander wished Brigadiers and the C.R.E. to go into this matter and to report to Div. H.Q.

Horses and Transport.

The Divisional Commander again emphasised the necessity for Battalion Commanders to use their horses in the present operations. However, he wished to impress on everyone the necessity of taking as much care as possible of horses owing to their scarcity and to the difficulty of getting remounts.

/The Divisional...

The Divisional Commander said that he was not satisfied with the turnout of the transport taking into consideration the fact that the Division had recently been 12 days out of the line.

16. Consolidation.

The Divisional Commander said that the tendency at present was to crowd too many troops into the front line instead of defence in depth. The policy he laid down was that the front line should be held by posts, with strong bodies of men in suitable positions in rear ready to counter-attack to retake the front line, should it be captured by the enemy. He considered that a buffer of about 500 yards in depth was sufficient.

A H Macdougall Major.
for H. Col.
General Staff,
21st Division.

29.10.18.

Distribution.

62 Inf. Bde.
64 " "
110 " "
C.R.A.
C.R.E.
"Q"
D.M.G.C.
Signals

App 14 War Diary.

MENTIONS OF THE 21st DIVISION IN THE COMMANDER-IN-CHIEF'S DISPATCHES FROM JANUARY TO OCTOBER, 1918.

-----------------oOo-----------------

April 24th, 1918.

"During the first two days of the enemys offensive S. of Arras, the 21st Division maintained its positions at EPEHY against all assaults and only withdrew from the village under orders when the progress made by the enemy to the S. rendered such a course necessary. Before this Division withdrew it inflicted great loss on the enemy and the German Official reports acknowledge the bitterness of the fighting.".

April 30th, 1918.

"8.34 p.m. Following a bombardment of great intensity, the French and British positions from the neighbourhood of METEREN to ZILLEBEKE LAKE were violently attacked this morning by large hostile forces. Attacks were made also upon the Belgian positions N. of YPRES.

Fighting of great severity developed rapidly on the whole Allied front.

The 25th, 49th and 21st British Divisions completely repulsed every attempt made by the enemy to enter their position and despite the constant succession of determined attacks in great strength, maintained their line intact."

May 2nd 1918.

"Please inform the G.O.C. and Officers and men of the 21st Division that the share taken by them in the recent fighting N. of the LYS, following so closely upon their gallant action on the battle front S. of ARRAS, reflects credit alike on their Division and upon the British Army. I thank them for the great courage and devotion they have already displayed and am confident that any further test which the future may bring will be met by them with the same unflinching resolution".

May 29th 1918.

"On our right the 21st Division in touch with our Allies, held their battle positions throughout the day and successfully withstood the enemy's attempts to advance."

P.T.O.

September 14th 1918.

"The 21st Division which on March 21st distinguished itself in the defence of EPEHY, was in line opposite BEAUCOURT on August 21st, capturing BEAUCOURT. During the following days it advanced with great gallantry over the SOMME Battlefield, overcoming stiff resistance in the neighbourhood of LE SARS and EAUCOURT L'ABBAYE".

September 19th, 1918.

"North of PEIZIERE, the 21st Division attacked over the Northern portion of the Sector defended by it with so much gallantry on March 21st and 22nd. Having captured its old front trenches, together with the strong point known as VAUCELLETTE FARM and beaten off a hostile counter-attack, it pushed forward more than a mile beyond this line, capturing several hundred prisoners and a German Battery complete with teams in the course of its advance".

October 9th, 1918.

"In the centre, Welsh and English troops of the 38th and 21st Divisions broke through the German defence system known as the "BEAUREVOIR- MASNIERES Line" and captured MALINCOURT and the trench line West of WALINCOURT. Obstinate resistance was met with from strong bodies of the enemy with M.Gs. in VILLERS OUTREAUX. After a period of hard fighting, Welsh troops gained possession of the Village".

October 24th 1918.

"English troops of the 25th Division had hard fighting in BISHOP'S WOOD (E. of LE CATEAU) and made good progress through it. East County troops of the 18th Division advancing to a depth of $3\frac{1}{2}$ miles captured BOUSIES. English and Scottish Battalions of the 21st and 33rd Divisions, secured the crossings of the HARPIES at VENDEGIES WOOD and captured VENDEGIES Village".

Headquarters.
30th October 1918.

General Staff.
21st Division.

War Diary

TELEGRAM.

Words

Sent

at ....

To ....

By ....

D[illegible]E	ZOKI	ZOLO	ZODU	V Corps H.A.	38 Div.
BASU	DUFA	D.A.P.M.	M.T.Coy.	17th Div.	15 Sqn.
VUFE	"Q"	ZEJU	V Corps.	33rd Div.	Div.Cyclists.
LODE	JESO	D.G.O.	V Corps H.A.	37th Div.	Div.Rec.Camp.

SX 29 AAA

[illegible]f. para 8 ZOWU Order No.254 AAA Div. H.Q. will not move until further orders AAA Adsd all recipients Order No.254

ZO[illegible]

14.00

A.H. Macdougall. Major.

Major.
G.S.

21 Div.
G. 748.

REPORT ON OPERATIONS AUGUST 21st to SEPTEMBER 3rd, 1918.

Reference Maps Sheets
57.B. D. and C. 1/40,000.

On August 19th orders were received from V Corps that the Division would take part in an attack on the enemy's lines in conjunction with the Corps on either flank, the Division being ordered to carry out an attack on BEAUCOURT and the Sunken Road R.3.a.3.2 (Div. Order No.205).

On August 20th, Divisional Headquarters closed at RAINCHEVAL and opened at ACHEUX.

August 21st, 1918.

12 Midnight. The enemy commenced a heavy area bombardment with gas shell on Q.6.c. and Q.11.b. This bombardment lasted about three quarters of an hour.

5.45 a.m. The 62nd Infantry Brigade advanced to the attack on BEAUCOURT and Sunken Road R.3.a.

7.45 a.m. The 62nd Infantry Brigade reported that they had captured BEAUCOURT and had reached the railway embankment South of the Village. About 90 prisoners had been captured, our casualties being reported as very slight. Our troops were also well on the way to the Sunken Road in R.3.a.

8.25 a.m. 1 N.C.O. and 12 men of the V Corps Cyclist Regiment were ordered to report to the 64th Infantry Brigade Headquarters to assist in exploitation. (G.X.449).

9.30 a.m. The 2nd Linc. Regiment held the line of the railway embankment from R.9.d.0.3 to R.8.c.0.5 with patrols working down the MIRAUMONT ROAD. A post had been established at R.7.d.4.8. Patrols of the 12/13 North'd Fus. had passed through BEAUCOURT on their way to the Blue Line South of the River ANCRE. About 120 prisoners so far counted.

10.20 a.m. The 62nd Infantry Brigade were ordered as soon as the Brown Line (R.3.a.) was captured, to move two Companies to the line of the River ANCRE from R.4.c.6.7 to R.4.a.0.5. Picquets were to be placed on all bridges over the ANCRE. Patrols were also to be pushed forward into the S.W. outskirts of MIRAUMONT. The 64th Infantry Brigade were to place two Companies at the disposal of the 62nd Infantry Brigade to act as Brigade Reserve. (G.X.452).

10.30 a.m. Orders received from Corps to hold the 64th Infantry Brigade in readiness to move along the BEAUCOURT - MIRAUMONT ROAD, cross the River ANCRE in R.3. & 4 and to move via BATTERY VALLEY so as to threaten THIEPVAL from the rear. (V Corps G.396).

11.50 a.m....

11.50 a.m. Situation. Our troops were reported by the Royal Air Force to be on the line R.3.c.7.3 - R.3.c.4.8 - R.3.a.2.0 - R.2.b.9.6. Touch gained with troops on left. The 110th Infantry Brigade were unable to cross the ANCRE owing to very strong opposition, the enemy holding the West bank with Machine Guns.

12.20 p.m. The 62nd Infantry Brigade were ordered to attack and capture the remainder of the Brown Line. The 64th Infantry Brigade, less portion already South of the ANCRE, were ordered to assemble about R.1 and R.2. If the 62nd Infantry Brigade should fail to capture the Brown Line, the 64th Infantry Brigade were then to carry out this operation. On the Brown Line being captured, the 64th Infantry Brigade were to cross the ANCRE and move up SIXTEEN ROAD through R.16.a. & c. on to the Green Line with left flank guard along BOOM RAVINE. (Div. Order No.206).

(Owing to events detailed below, this turning movement could never be put into operation).

1.20 p.m. One Battalion 110 Infantry Brigade was placed at the disposal of the 64 Infantry Brigade. (G.X.455).

3.25 p.m. Owing to IRLES having not yet been captured, and, in consequence of this, the 42nd Division on the left having not yet entered MIRAUMONT, the 64th Infantry Brigade were ordered to take special precautions regarding their Eastern flank after crossing the ANCRE. The 62nd Infantry Brigade were to make every endeavour to throw bridges across the ANCRE between BEAUCOURT and GRANDCOURT, in order to give the 64th Infantry Brigade an alternative line for withdrawal in case of necessity. The 64th Infantry Brigade were to send patrols towards GRANDCOURT after crossing the ANCRE to connect with 62nd Infantry Brigade and also to cover bridge-heads. (G.X.460).

3.40 p.m. 110 Infantry Brigade report that the 6th Leic. Regt. had two patrols just across the ANCRE Q.18.d.4.6 and Q.13.c.7.9. Both patrols were unable to make further advance owing to enemy fire.

3.50 p.m. 110 Infantry Brigade were ordered to hold another Battalion in readiness to join 64th Infantry Brigade. (G.X.641).

The 64 Infantry Brigade were ordered to relieve two Companies 62 Infantry Brigade in R.14.a. & b. during the night, these Companies to come under orders of 62 Infantry Brigade. 1st Wilts Regt. were to remain with 64th Infantry Brigade but were not to be used except in case of emergency. Brigades were to improve and if possible increase the present crossings over the ANCRE with the aid of attached R.E. Sections. (Div. Order No.209).

5.5 p.m. 110 Infantry Brigade reported that the 6th Leic. Regt. were heavily fired at as soon as the ANCRE at R.13.a.3.7 was crossed. LOGGING TRENCH and LOGGING LANE were reported as being strongly held by the enemy.

6 p.m. Under orders from Corps, the Division was ordered to consolidate the final objective from the ANCRE at BAILLESCOURT FARM to R.3.a.0.8 with one Brigade, touch to be maintained with 42nd Division on left. One Brigade was to be in position to support the front Brigade or to re-new the offensive across the ANCRE at short notice. The 3rd Brigade was to be in position South and West of BEAUMONT HAMEL. (V Corps G.241).

/7.20 p.m.....

7.20 p.m. Situation at 7 p.m. 62nd Infantry Brigade attacked at 2 p.m. with objective R.4.c.5.6. to R.4.a.0.5. The attack was held up by Machine Gun and Artillery fire. The attack was renewed with 6 Companies about 4 p.m. and was successful. Two Companies 62nd Infantry Brigade crossed the ANCRE at 4 p.m. and gained the Blue Line from LITTLE TRENCH to R.14.b.8.3. The dispositions of 62nd Infantry Brigade were as follows :-

Two Companies from R.4.c.4.8. along road to R.3.a.9.9. where touch had not been gained with 42nd Division. Two Companies between Brown and Yellow Lines and Two Companies on Blue Line. Four Companies about R.2.c. and Two Companies in BEAUCOURT.

8.30 p.m. Orders issued for 62nd Infantry Brigade to maintain their present dispositions and to gain touch with 42nd Division. The two Companies in BEAUCOURT were to be relieved by one Company at present at R.4.c. and were then to be withdrawn into Reserve. 64th Infantry Brigade were to establish Bridgeheads over the ANCRE at selected points between R.4.d.3.4. and R.1.a.1.9. connecting with 62nd Infantry Brigade at R.4.a.5.1. 62nd Infantry Brigade to form Bridgeheads from R.9.a.1.9. to BEAUCOURT inclusive. 110th Infantry Brigade to form Bridgeheads from BEAUCOURT (exclusive) to MILL BRIDGE in area Q.6, Q.12, R.1 and R.7. One Battalion 110th Infantry Brigade to remain attached to 64th Infantry Brigade (Div. Order No.208).

10.40 p.m. Situation unchanged. Heavy hostile Machine Gun fire coming from MIRAUMONT. Prisoners so far counted 3 Officer, 156 Other Ranks.

10.50 p.m. Orders issued to the 64th Infantry Brigade that the two rear Battalions of that Brigade and One Battalion 110th Infantry Brigade attached, were not to move forward without reference to Divisional Headquarters (G.X.476).

11.58 p.m. All Brigades and Divisional Artillery were warned that owing to the trend of hostile movement during the evening having been towards MIRAUMONT and ACHIET LE GRAND, hostile counterattack was possible either tonight or tomorrow morning. The action of the two rear Battalions of the 64th Infantry Brigade and the attached Battalion 110th Infantry Brigade, would, therefore, be defensive until further orders. At dawn tomorrow 110th Infantry Brigade were to endeavour to push Patrols across the ANCRE and gain the Blue Line. As soon as the Blue Line was consolidated patrols were to be pushed forward to the Red Line. (GX.477).

22nd August 1918.

3.52 a.m. Report received from 64th Infantry Brigade that the bridges at R.9.b.6.7. and R.3.d.9.2. were in good condition. The 97th Field Company R.E. had constructed a footbridge at R.9.a.9.7. over which a Platoon of the 1st East Yorkshire Regt. had crossed about 2.15 a.m. and had met with heavy Machine Gun fire from about R.9.b.2.2.

/4 a.m......

4 a.m. Enemy heavily gas shelled the area between ARTILLERY LANE and LUMINOUS AVENUE.

7.35 a.m. 62nd Infantry Brigade reported that enemy had put down a barrage on the Brown Line, which, however, only lasted about 10 minutes. No Infantry action followed.

8.45 a.m. 110th Infantry Brigade report timed 8.20 a.m. gave the situation East of the ANCRE as follows :- At 5 a.m. two Platoons were established in LOGGING TRENCH and a third Platoon was moving along CANDY LANE with objective LOGGING SUPPORT. During the night crossings over the ANCRE at Q.18.d.4.7. and Q.18.b.9.3. were made passable for Infantry.

9.40 a.m. Situation unchanged since last report. Up to about 8 a.m. there was continuous hostile shelling of forward area, but after this hour shelling became much less and very scattered. Enemy reported to be holding Railway Embankment in R.10. in strength.

9.40 a.m. 62nd Infantry Brigade were ordered to push forward Patrols from Blue Line to portion of Red Line in their area and also to GRANDCOURT. If Red Line occupied by our Patrols, 64th Infantry Brigade were to be prepared to send two Companies to garrison it (G.X.486).

10 a.m. 62nd Infantry Brigade reported that a Patrol of the 12/13th Northumberland Fusiliers was observed to be pushing South from Blue Line. No Machine Gun fire had been encountered from THIEPVAL RIDGE for the last hour. 64th Infantry Brigade reported that the Platoon of the 1st East Yorks Regt. South of the River in N.9.b. had been driven to the North of the River where they had taken up a position covering the crossing.

12.15 p.m. 110th Infantry Brigade report, timed 11 a.m. gave the situation as follows :- Bombing Party had succeeded in reaching point in LOGGING TRENCH North of the enemy Post R.13.c.1.4. This party was working in conjunction with bombing party from the South to capture this Post. A Patrol had proceeded up CANDY AVENUE to about R.19.b.35.60. and had located enemy Machine Gun at Q.13.c.9.2. which would be dealt with by Platoon which was working down LITTLE TRENCH and LUFF AVENUE.

1.30 p.m. 62nd Infantry Brigade reported that the Valley in R.1.b. and forward area was being continuously shelled by guns of all calibre. The 2nd Lincolnshire Regt. reported that their left flank was being turned in R.3.b.

4.10 p.m. Situation. 62nd Infantry Brigade unchanged. Lewis Gun Section of North Irish Horse (Corps Cyclists) sent to reinforce the left flank in R.3.b. Situation on that flank was not satisfactory owing to the 42nd Division having their right at R.2.b.5.0. 110th Infantry Brigade held the Blue Line from LUFF AVENUE inclusive to junction of LOGGING SUPPORT and CANDY AVENUE. A Platoon was being sent along CANDY AVENUE to clear COMMON LANE. Enemy Post at R.13.c.2.6. had been rushed and garrison killed. Patrols advancing to Red Line were held up by heavy Machine Gun fire in R.14.c.Central. At 3 p.m. enemy opened a very heavy barrage on Valley in R.1.b. but shelling had now died down.

/5 p.m.....

5 p.m. 110th Infantry Brigade report that LUFF AVENUE and LOGGING SUPPORT to junction of CANDY AVENUE had been captured. Touch had been obtained with the 62nd Infantry Brigade in the Blue line. Considerable Machine Gun fire was being met with from COMMON LANE. Further Platoons were being Moved up to consolidate the Blue Line and capture COMMON LANE.

6.30 p.m. Orders received from Vth Corps that one Brigade 17th Division would relieve and take over one Brigade front at present held by 110th Infantry Brigade on night of 22nd/23rd. The boundary between the 21st and 17th Divisions would be a line running from R.21.d.0.0., R.14.c.0.0., Q.12.c.6.0., thence West along grid line between Q.11. and Q.17. 17th Divisional Artillery at present under orders of C.R.A. 21st Division would revert to C.R.A. 17th Division at 4 a.m. 23rd inst. (Vth Corps G.466., R.A. 1163 and G.X.496.).

9.55 p.m. 62nd Infantry Brigade reported that at 8.15 p.m. enemy put down a barrage including smoke on the Brown Line and in the ANCRE Valley near GRANDCOURT. The enemy were reported to have attacked and to have driven back part of the garrison of the Brown line. No news received about situation in the Yellow Line, but this line believed to be intact. One Battalion 64th Infantry Brigade was holding intermediate system along ARTILLERY LANE and another Battalion was being ordered up to PUISIEUX Road to restore situation if required.

10.5 p.m. . . Orders sent to the 62nd Infantry Brigade that if any portion of the Brown Line had been lost it was to be restored by a counter-attack in conformity with an attack of 42nd Division at 2.30 a.m. August 23rd. (G.X.503).

11.15 p.m. Situation. Enemy attacked Brown Line about 8 p.m. Attack was repeated twice afterwards. Each attack was beaten off with heavy casualties to the enemy. A few enemy reached the Brown line but were immediately ejected. Our casualties were fairly heavy. Situation was now quiet.

23rd August 1918.

1.20 a.m. 110th Infantry Brigade report that ~~Platoon~~ Posts had been established at R.19.a.4.0. R.19.a.6.5., R.13.a.6.3., R.13.d.5.6., R.14.c.3.9., R.13.c.1.4., R.13.a.6.0., and one over the ST. PIERRE DIVION Caves at Q.24.b.6.1. COMMON LANE South of R.19.a.4.0. was destroyed by shell fire and not occupied by the enemy.

5 a.m. 62nd Infantry Brigade reported that the situation in the BROWN Line had been entirely restored and that touch had been gained with the 42nd Division on the left.

6.15 a.m. The relief of the 110th Infantry Brigade by one Brigade 17th Division was reported complete.

9.55 a.m. Situation unchanged. Enemy was shelling PUISIEUX Road in R.7.c. with heavy guns. Snipers and Machine Guns were active from R.15.a.

/1.30 p.m.

1.30 p.m. Situation 12 Noon. Enemy put down a heavy barrage on our front line in response to attack carried out by troops on our left. Enemy in small parties were seen going East and S.E. from R.16.c.2.3. 12/13 North'd Fus. reported that some of their men had reached BATTERY VALLEY but had to withdraw owing to hostile M.G. fire from Eastern edge of Valley.

2.50 p.m. All Lewis Gunners of North Irish Horse (Corps Cyclists) except those belonging to 'A' Squadron were ordered to rejoin their own Unit. (G.X.521 and V Corps G.511).

3.15 p.m. Orders issued for the continuation of the attack. 64 Inf. Bde. to attack at 1 a.m. with first objective Brown Line from R.20.a.9.3 to R.8.b.7.2 and second objective Red Line from R.21.d.0.0 through R.15.Central to railway at R.9.b.3.3. The 110 Inf. Bde. to attack at 5 a.m. with objective the Blue Line R.27.b.2.8 along SIXTEEN ROAD to R.4.c.5.7 with bridge-head at R.2.d.8.4. After capture of this line, exploitation to be carried out towards LE SARS and PYS. (D.O.210).

5.55 p.m. Situation. North of river unchanged. South of River our patrols were working towards the Red Line. About 100 enemy dead had been counted in front of the Brown Line as the result of the counter-attack the day before.

7 p.m. Divisional Headquarters closed at ACHEUX and opened at MAILLY MAILLET.

8.50 p.m. Divisional Order No.210 was amended as follows :- The advance to the Green Dotted Line was to be carried out as soon as possible. 64 Inf. Bde. were to advance with its left on the River ANCRE with objective Green Dotted Line in R.11.b. & d. 110 Inf. Bde. to advance in rear of 64 Inf. Bde. and connect right of 64 Inf. Bde. with 17th Division on Green Dotted Line. (G.X.529).

11 p.m. 62 Inf. Bde. were ordered to concentrate all troops less garrison of Brown Line at once, and as soon as reliable information received that MIRAUMONT had been captured, the garrison in the Brown Line was to concentrate with its own Unit. 62 Inf. Bde. was to be prepared to cross River ANCRE either by the railway bridge or the Bridge in GRANDCOURT. (G.X.535).

24th August, 1918.

12.30 a.m. Report received from 64 Inf. Bde. that the Red Line had been captured. The right flank of this Brigade appeared to be in the air and was being continually harassed by the enemy.

12.40 a.m. 62 Inf. Bde. were ordered to be prepared to concentrate in BATTERY VALLEY or valley in R.9.d. and R.15.b. (G.X.541).

1.35 a.m. 64 Inf. Bde. reported that they were firmly established on the Red Line, but owing to fighting and broken state of ground Units were somewhat dis-organised. The Brigade was being re-organised and advance would be continued to the high ground in R.11 and R.12 at about 3.30 a.m. The right flank of the Brigade was very exposed and no touch could be obtained with any other troops.

/7.10 a.m.....

7.10 a.m. 62 Infantry Brigade were ordered to concentrate their whole Brigade less the two Companies in the Brown Line, on South bank of ANCRE, in BATTERY VALLEY and R.14.a. (G.X.545).

7.40 a.m. 110 Infantry Brigade ordered to push on by easiest route possible irrespective of left of 17th Division and to get touch with right of 64th Infantry Brigade (D.O.211).

8.45 a.m. Report received from 64th Infantry Brigade that their troops had reached final objective/ on either flank and the enemy were reported as working round flanks. Line very weakly held and reinforcements were urgently required.

(in R.11.b. No touch had been gained)

9.20 a.m. Pigeon message was received from 64th Infantry Brigade timed 7.28 a.m. reporting that they were holding high ground in R.11.b. but that the enemy had completely surrounded them and were very active with Machine Guns, Snipers and Trench Mortars. Casualties appeared to be heavy. The enemy had counter-attacked both flanks but had been completely repulsed.

9.30 a.m. Situation. 64 Infantry Brigade still held high ground R.11.b. but were entirely surrounded. 110 Infantry Brigade moving forward to support the right of the 64th Infantry Brigade on Green Dotted Line. In course of the advance they successfully attacked enemy post at R.14.d.0.0 capturing three Trench Mortars and killing between 30 and 40 of the enemy.

11 a.m. Owing to the B.G.C. 64 Infantry Brigade having been wounded, B.G.C. 110 Infantry Brigade was ordered to take command of both 64th and 110th Infantry Brigades. He was ordered to take the high ground in R.11.b. & d. and when this ground had been captured the 62nd Infantry Brigade was to pass through and advance in the direction of PYS. (D.C.1).

12 Noon. R.A.F. observer reported 11.30 a.m. that our troops were still holding out in R.11.b.Central with enemy at R.10.d.8.7 and in BOOM RAVINE.

12.16 p.m. 110 Infantry Brigade were ordered to expedite their attack as much as possible in order to relieve the 64th Infantry Brigade who were still holding out on high ground R.11.b. (D.C.3).

1.25 p.m. Situation of 64th Infantry Brigade unchanged. 110 Infantry Brigade were advancing in R.16 but exact position not definitely known.

2.30 p.m. Report received from 110 Infantry Brigade timed 1.15 p.m. that they had definitely gained touch with 64th Infantry Brigade on high ground R.11.b. & d. Small parties of the enemy were still holding out in BOOM RAVINE but were being mopped up. Touch not yet gained with 17th Division on right but the 7th Leicestershire Regiment had been ordered to occupy the remainder of the Green Dotted Line from R.17.d.0.0. to Southern Divisional Boundary and to gain touch with 17th Division.

4 p.m. The high ground R.11.b and d and R.17.b and d. now occupied. The right of the Division was at R.17.d.2.2. where it was reported to be in touch with 17th Division. 62nd Infantry Brigade were moving forward to gain touch with 42nd Division at PYS.

/under.....

Under instructions received from Corps one Cavalry Troop was being allotted to this Division as Divisional Cavalry. (Corps G.567).

4.50 p.m. R.A.F. report our men seen in M.1.b and d. and R.23 about 4 p.m.

4.55 p.m. Orders issued that the Division would advance on LE SARS. 110th Infantry Brigade were to advance forthwith and capture the line M.20.b.0.3., M.15.Central. M.10.Central, patrols being sent forward to LE SARS and DESTREMONT FARM. The 62nd Infantry Brigade to concentrate on Road R.12, R.18. ready to move through 110th Infantry Brigade and take up the advance. 64th Infantry Brigade to reorganize in BOOM RAVINE (Div. Order No.212).

5 p.m. 62nd Infantry Brigade reported that 12/13th Northumberland Fusiliers had moved up into position as ordered in G.C.1. The remainder of the Brigade were moving to BOOM RAVINE.

5.45 p.m. Orders issued that if LE SARS was found empty, it was to be occupied and patrols sent on to the BUTTE DE WARLENCOURT (G.X.570).

10.40 p.m. Orders issued for the continuation of the advance on the 25th with BEAULENCOURT as objective. The advance would be carried out by 62nd Infantry Brigade who, moving through 110th Infantry Brigade, were to capture the line M.24.a.3.0., N.7.a.0.0. When this line captured, 110th Infantry Brigade would move through 62nd Infantry Brigade to line of Road N.21.d.4.0., N.9.b.6.0. Advance would then be continued by 62nd Infantry Brigade to the BAPAUME - SAILLY SAILLISEL Road, touch being obtained with the IV Corps at RIENCOURT. 64th Infantry Brigade would remain in present position as Divisional Reserve (D.O.213.).

11.25 p.m. 110th Infantry Brigade moved from GREEN DOTTED Line towards LE SARS. Otherwise situation unchanged.

25th August 1918.

8 a.m. Divisional Headquarters closed MAILLY MAILLET and opened GRANDCOURT.

9 a.m. 64th Infantry Brigade were ordered to move at once to line or Road in R.12 and R.18. Units were to remain concentrated and obtain as much rest as possible, but to be prepared to hold the line of this road in case of necessity. (G.A.1.).

9.15 a.m. Patrol from Divisional Cav. Troop reported that the enemy were holding the Wood in N.12.b. and N.7.a. with Infantry and Machine Guns.

9.30 a.m. Pigeon message received from 62nd Infantry Brigade timed 8.55 a.m. stated that the Brigade moved without difficulty to the WARLENCOURT - COURCELETTE Road, where the 1st Wiltshire Regt. were found to be 300 yards South of it in M.14.d. with two Coys. of the 6th Leicestershire Regt. on their left. The position of the remainder of the 110th Infantry Brigade had not yet been ascertained. 62nd Infantry Brigade continued the advance but were unable to reach the summit of the ridge through M.10.Central, M.15. Central, owing to heavy Machine Gun fire from LE SARS.

9.45 a.m. 62nd Infantry Brigade reported that Artillery barrage ~~had been~~ arranged on LE SARS and that advance would be continued under this fire.

/the......

The enemy were showing signs of retiring. Touch had been gained with the 17th Division on the right near COURCELLETTE, and troops of the 42nd Division on the left had been seen near LITTLE WOOD. The high ground in M.15.c. had been gained and troops were working along high ground in M.9.d. and M.10.c.

1 p.m. 62nd Infantry Brigade were instructed to carry out the task allotted to the 110th Infantry Brigade in order No.213 if latter Brigade were not ready to carry it out (D.C.5.).

1.10 p.m. Information was received from the Corps on right that the enemy were massing for counter-attack in N.9.c. and d. and N.16.a. Instructions were sent to the 60 pdrs. attached to this Division to engage this target.

1.35 p.m. Situation at 1 p.m. 62nd Infantry Brigade attacked LE SARS and captured it. The QUARRY in M.15.a. was attacked under cover of Stokes Mortars and captured, 17 Germans being killed. The BUTTE DE WARLENCOURT was also captured, 1 Officer and 30 men being taken prisoner. Touch had been gained with 63rd Division on left, but not with 17th Division on right.

2.50 p.m. 64th Infantry Brigade were ordered to be ready to move at once in view of the possibility of the enemy counter-attacking from the direction of EAUCOURT L'ABBAYE (C.A.7.). The 21st Battalion Machine Gun Corps was ordered to send its reserve Company to take up position on the road R.18, R.12. covering the Divisional front. (G.A.8.).

3.20 p.m. Situation as follows :- 62nd Infantry Brigade on line of Road M.24.a. and M.18.b. and d. touch being established with the 63rd Division on the left. At 2.15 p.m. the enemy delivered a heavy counter-attack against the right of the 62nd Infantry Brigade from the South and South East. 110th Infantry Brigade, who were on the move to pass through the 62nd Infantry Brigade were diverted to prolong the right of the former Brigade in order to gain touch with the 17th Division. The counter-attack was repulsed at 2.45 p.m. some prisoners being taken.

4 p.m. The 64th Infantry Brigade were ordered to sit easy but to be ready to move at 6 p.m. (G.A.10.).

4.30 p.m. Orders were issued to the 62nd Infantry Brigade and 110th Infantry Brigade that the Division would probably remain in its present position for the remainder of the day. The 62nd Infantry Brigade were to be prepared, however, to advance its left to keep touch with troops on its left, should they go forward. Should the 17th Division advance, and take EAUCOURT L'ABBAYE the 110th Infantry Brigade were to be prepared to carry on the advance (G.A.11.).

7.30 p.m. Orders were issued for the 62nd and 110th Infantry Brigades to hold their present positions during the night. The 64th Infantry Brigade were to move forthwith to the high ground M.15 and M.20 and to be prepared to hold this line. The reserve Machine Gun Company was to be prepared to occupy positions on the ridge R.12 R.18. At 5.30 a.m. August 26th, 64th Infantry Brigade were to take up the advance and move through the 62nd Infantry Brigade and capture the line of the Road N.21.b.6.0. - N.9.b.7.0. When the 64th Infantry Brigade had made good this objective, the 62nd Infantry Brigade were to advance to the

/SAILLY.....

SAILLY SAILLISEL - BAPAUME ROAD. The 110 Infantry Brigade as soon the 62nd Infantry Brigade advanced, were to concentrate in M.17 and would be in Divisional Reserve. One Squadron, Corps Cyclists were placed under the orders of the 64th Infantry Brigade for the first operation and the 62nd Infantry Brigade for the second. Div. Cav. Troop were ordered to work in front of the Infantry and report the situation to leading Brigade. The 95th Bde. R.F.A. were placed under the orders of the leading Brigade. (D.O.214).

10.15 p.m. In continuation of Order No.214, 62nd Infantry Brigade were to first make good, as intermediate objective, the line of the road N.19.b. & N.17.b., the advance to the further objective not being carried out without orders from Divisional Headquarter's. As soon as the 17th Division on the right commenced their advance, 110 Infantry Brigade were to concentrate in M.17. (G.X.587).

10.45 p.m. Div. Cav. Troop were ordered to withdraw to MIRAUMONT if they had not been relieved by 7.30 p.m. on the 26th instant. (G.X.589).

10.55 p.m. Message was sent to the 63rd Division stating that it was improbable that troops of that Division who were in this Divisional area would be relieved tonight. Orders had been given to the leading Brigade to extend their left on the 26th instant to the North. (G.X.588).

26th August, 1918.

5.30 a.m. Situation unchanged during the night. Some desultory shelling over forward area about 4.50 a.m.

9.25 a.m. Situation. 64th Infantry Brigade passed through 62nd Infantry Brigade but met with heavy Machine Gun fire coming from the direction of LUISENHOF FARM. No signs of troops advancing on the right flank.

10.45 a.m. Situation. 64 Infantry Brigade reported at 9.20 a.m. that their Right Battalion appeared to be approaching the objective. The left Battalion had reached the line N.7.b.5.9 to N.13.a.7.1. where they were held up by heavy Machine Gun fire. Artillery barrage was being arranged and the advance would then be continued. Hostile resistance on the Divisional front had distinctly stiffened since yesterday. The right of the 63rd Division was in rear of our left and no touch had been gained with the 17th Division on the right.

12.35 p.m. Situation. Right Battalion, 64th Infantry Brigade, gained objectives South of LUISENHOF FARM. Left Battalion was held up on the line N.13.a.5.0 - N.7.a.5.0. 64th Infantry Brigade had two Battalions in front and one in reserve with one Cyclist Squadron and one Brigade R.F.A. attached.
62 Infantry Brigade disposed in depth with leading troops in YELLOW CUT with their left on South edge of LE BARQUE.
110 Infantry Brigade in Divisional Reserve with one Battalion at EAUCOURT L'ABBAYE, one Battalion in M.17.a. and one Battalion M.14.d. and M.15.a.

/4.15 p.m....

4.15 p.m. Situation. 64 Infantry Brigade report timed 3.15 p.m. stated that the right Battalion had been forced to withdraw and now held line of Sunken Road in N.19.a. and N.19.c. Left Battalion continued this line to N.7.b.2.0. Touch had not been gained on either flank. Cyclist Squadron were in touch with enemy at M.24.c.4.4.

7.30 p.m. Situation. Enemy counter-attacked 64th Infantry Brigade at 4 p.m. but were repulsed by rifle and Lewis Gun Fire. Heavy hostile Machine Gun fire from LIGNY and LIGNY THILLOY prevented our troops from approaching LUISENHOF FARM Road. Much enemy movement had been seen in trenches N.2.b. and N.2.c.

8.30 p.m. 64th Infantry Brigade ordered to find outposts on the general line now held. 62nd Infantry Brigade were to hold YELLOW CUT as main line of resistance. 110th Infantry Brigade were to concentrate each Unit and allow the men to rest, but were also to be prepared to hold the line DESTREMONT FARM - Road Junction M.16.b.3.3. - WARLENCOURT in case of necessity. 64th Infantry Brigade were to continue the advance on the 27th inst on BEAULENCOURT and occupy as first objective, line of the road N.19.b. - N.7.b. The 110th Infantry Brigade would then advance through the 64th Infantry Brigade with objective high ground N.20.central - N.14.b.5.0. - N.8.Central. Cyclists and Div. Cavalry Troop with Mobile Newton Mortar would work with leading Brigade. 94th Brigade R.F.A. were placed under the orders of 64th Infantry Brigade and 95th Brigade R.F.A. under the orders of 110th Infantry Brigade (Div. Order No. 215.).

27th August 1918.

6.45 a.m. Situation unchanged during the night. Patrols of 64th Infantry Brigade reported the enemy occupying LIGNY THILLOY and LUISENHOF FARM at 3 a.m.

11.50 a.m. Orders were issued cancelling Order No.215 and ordering the 64th Infantry Brigade to make good LUISENHOF FARM and the line of Road for 400 yards on each side of it, throwing refused flanks back to join with flank Divisions. This operation to be carried out by patrols, garrisons being sent forward to hold ground gained. 62nd Infantry Brigade would relieve the 64th Infantry Brigade during the night 27th/28th inst, and would also continue to hold the YELLOW CUT. On relief, the 64th Infantry Brigade would withdraw to Valley M.9. 13 and 14. (GX.622).

12.30 p.m. Situation. 64th Infantry Brigade reported that leading troops had reached line of road North of LUISENHOF FARM but were being badly enfiladed by Machine Guns from THILLOY. Very little hostile shelling.

2.45 p.m. 64th Infantry Brigade were holding line as previously reported with patrols on the road in N.13.b. and d. LUISENHOF FARM was reported unoccupied. Cyclist Sqdn. had established a Post at FACTORY CORNER (N.19.d.). Enemy Machine Guns were active from about N.7.d.9.9. Owing to reports being received that the enemy were retiring South of the SOMME, Brigades were instructed to keep close touch with the enemy, especially during the night.

/6 p.m.......

6 p.m. Situation remained unchanged. Small parties of the enemy were seen during the afternoon to come down the Valley in N.5.c. towards THILLOY.

6.30 p.m. Owing to the possibility of the enemy evacuating BAPAUME during the night of 27th/28th, harassing fire by artillery was ordered to be carried out actively during the night.

10.10 p.m. 62nd Infantry Brigade were ordered to continue the advance on the 28th inst, under an Artillery barrage commencing at 5.30 a.m. with the objective high ground N.14. N.15. (D.O.216).

28th August 1918.

7.30 a.m. 62nd Infantry Brigade reported that LUISENHOF FARM and the road in N.7.d. and N.13.b. were strongly held by the enemy. Machine Gun fire was opened on both flanks of our patrol and owing to the very heavy fire from the direction of LIGNY THILLOY it had been found impossible to advance. Large numbers of the enemy were reported to be moving into THILLOY.

9.10 a.m. 62nd Infantry Brigade reported that THILLOY and Sunken Road from LIGNY THILLOY to LUISENHOF FARM still strongly held by the enemy, as was also the trench in N.9.a, c and d. The right Battalion reported no enemy could be seen on the above road from N.13.d.6.9. to N.19.a.1.3.

4.15 p.m. 110th Infantry Brigade were ordered to relieve the 62nd Infantry Brigade in the line during the night 28th/29th inst. On relief, 62nd Infantry Brigade were to take over the present dispositions and defence arrangements of 110th Infantry Brigade. The Cyclist Squadron would come under the orders of 110th Infantry Brigade on completion of relief (D.O.217.).

7.15 p.m. Orders were issued to the effect that as the 38th Division were attacking the high ground East of GINCHY on the 29th Machine Gun and Artillery barrages were to be put down on the Divisional front in order to assist this advance. 110th Infantry Brigade were to be ready to push forward advanced guards on any slackening of the enemy's resistance being noticed, but the main body of this Brigade was not to advance without orders from Divisional Headquarters (D.O.218.).

The situation on the Divisional front remained unchanged for the remainder of the day.

29th August.1918.

The situation remained unchanged during the night. No enemy Machine Gun or Artillery activity.

8 a.m. Divisional Cavalry Troop were ordered to send a patrol under a N.C.O. to report to B.G.C., 110th Infantry Brigade. The remainder of the troop was to be ready to move at short notice but not saddled up.(G.X.653.)

9.20 a.m. Owing to the 38th Division meeting no opposition in their attack this morning, 110th Infantry Brigade were ordered to push forward advanced guards followed by the remainder of the

/Brigade.....

Brigade if feasable, and make good the following successive lines:- LUISENHOF FARM ROAD - Road N.21 - N.9.a. Spur N.22.a.O.O. - Cross Roads N.9.d.7.2. along road to N.9.b.8.0. - Cross Roads N.24.a.5.1. - BEAULENCOURT and Road from N.11.d.5.0. to N.11.b.7.0. 62nd Infantry Brigade will be in Support to 110th Infantry Brigade and would move to LUISENHOF FARM Road when 110th Infantry Brigade had made good the road in N.21.a. N.9.a. moving on to the Spur in N.22.a. when 110th Infantry Brigade had reached BEAULENCOURT. Further orders would be issued for the move of 64th Infantry Brigade and Reserve Machine Gun Coy. (G.X.654).

10.40 a.m. 95th Brigade R.F.A. were placed under the orders of 110th Infantry Brigade and 94th Brigade R.F.A. under the orders of 64th Infantry Brigade. 94th Brigade R.F.A. were to assist however, in covering the advance of the 110th Infantry Brigade (G.X.659.)

11 a.m. Situation. Advanced Guards of the Right Battalion, 110th Infantry Brigade had reached the Ridge N.14.Central and reported it clear of the enemy. Divisional Cavalry Troop had gained touch with the 42nd Division and reported THILLOY to have been evacuated by the enemy.

12.10 p.m. Orders issued in continuation of G.X.654 for the 64th Infantry Brigade to become Support Brigade in place of the 62nd Infantry Brigade and to be prepared to move to YELLOW CUT on receipt of orders from Divisional Headquarters. 94th Brigade R.F.A. would now come under the orders of the 64th Infantry Brigade (G.X.661.).

12.15 p.m. Main Guards had occupied LUISENHOF FARM ROAD with vanguards advancing over high ground N.14 and 15. Some hostile Machine Gun fire encountered from N.3.c. otherwise no touch with the enemy yet obtained.

2 p.m. 64th Infantry Brigade ordered to move forthwith to YELLOW CUT (G.X.665).

Situation. Infantry Patrols had reached line in N.16.c. and were encountering Machine Gun fire from Sunken Road N.16 a and b. Infantry advanced guards were on Ridge N.15.a and c. and main body was crossing the LUISENHOF FARM ROAD.

4.30 p.m. 110th Infantry Brigade report timed 2 p.m. stated that advanced guards had reached the line of trenches in N.16, N.9. and were in touch with the 17th Division on the Right and 42nd Division on the left. Main body had reached line of the road N.21.a, N.9.a at 3.25 p.m.

6 p.m. Situation at 5.30 p.m. Main body had reached line of trenches N.16.d. to N.9.d. and were in touch on both flanks. Advanced guards were endeavouring to make progress towards BEAULENCOURT, but were encountering very heavy Machine Gun and rifle fire from the Western edge of the Village.

9.20 p.m. Message sent to Vth Corps asking for as much artillery fire as possible to be brought to bear on BEAULENCOURT during the night. All fire on the village to cease at 2 a.m. 30th inst, when patrols would enter the village (G.X.673.).

/10.20 p.m.....

<u>10.20 p.m.</u> Orders issued for the 110th Infantry Brigade to send forward fighting patrols to ascertain the situation as regards BEAULENCOURT and to occupy the village if found empty. 110th Infantry Brigade were also to endeavour to resume the advance to the fourth objective early tomorrow, August 30th. When this objective had been taken, one Coy and one Section of Machine Guns were to be sent to LUBDA COPSE to form defensive flank facing North. As soon as the PERONNE - BAPAUME Road had been crossed, the Division would come into Corps reserve about LE TRANSLOY. Until further orders the 64th and 62nd Infantry Brigades would remain in their present positions, the 64th Infantry Brigade being ready to occupy YELLOW CUT at short notice. The Cyclist Squadron and Divisional Cavalry Troop would remain under the orders of 110th Infantry Brigade (D.O.219).

<u>30th August 1918.</u>

The situation during the night remained unchanged with very little enemy activity.

<u>12 noon.</u> Divisional Hdqrs. closed at GUEUDECOURT and opened N.9.c.70.05.

<u>12.5 p.m.</u> Situation. Patrols report BEAULENCOURT still occupied. Machine Guns and snipers very active from the Western outskirts of the Village.

<u>7.15 p.m.</u> Situation throughout the day, remained unchanged. Enemy artillery fire was negligible. Our Artillery shelled BEAULENCOURT and engaged Machine Guns which had been located in the Western outskirts of the village. Large explosions occurred at N.11.d.5.8. and N.5.c.3.6. between 5.30 and 6.5 p.m.

<u>7.30 p.m.</u> Orders were issued to the Divisional Cavalry Troop to rejoin their Squadron near COURCELETTE by 8.30 a.m. 31st August (G.A.684).

<u>31st August 1918.</u>

<u>5.20 a.m.</u> The situation remained unchanged during the night. Patrols had endeavoured to enter BEAULENCOURT but were stopped by Machine Gun fire. Much enemy movement was heard in BEAULENCOURT during the night. At South end of the village wiring was believed to be in progress. There was considerable random shelling of our back areas during the night.

<u>8.50 a.m.</u> Under instructions received from Corps one Troop of Carabineers was placed under the orders of the Division as Divisional Cavalry. The Troop was ordered to bivouac near the BUTTE DE WARLENCOURT and was placed under the orders of 110th Infantry Brigade (G.A.688).

<u>10.25 a.m.</u> Instructions were received from Corps for intense harassing fire by Artillery not only on enemy known communications but also on all known positions held by him (Vth Corps R.A.30/44).

/9 p.m......

9 p.m. Orders were issued for 110th Infantry Brigade to capture and occupy BEAULENCOURT during the night, zero hour being 2.30 a.m. The infantry were to form up on the line N.10.Cent. N.11.b.2.9. and attack Southwards. When the village had been captured, 110th Infantry Brigade were to carry out a second operation at 5.40 a.m. (in conjunction with 17th Division who were to take LE TRANSLOY) with objective the SUGAR FACTORY N.24.Central. 64th Infantry Brigade were to take over the present positions of 110th Infantry Brigade when vacated by latter Brigade (D.O.220.). The situation throughout the night remained unaltered, all attempts by patrols to enter BEAULENCOURT being frustrated by Machine Gun fire.

1st September 1918.

7.45 a.m. 110th Infantry Brigade report that all objectives in the first attack had been gained and an enemy counter-attack easily beaten off. Our casualties were believed to be slight. About 100 prisoners were captured and two 77 mm guns. Touch had not yet been gained with 42nd Division but patrols were being sent out to do so.

9.50 a.m. Situation. 110th Infantry Brigade report timed 9.30 a.m. states that troops detailed to take the SUGAR FACTORY were unable to enter it owing to Machine Gun fire from LE TRANSLOY. They have occupied trench in N.24.a. just North of Factory. An Officer who had just returned from BEAULENCOURT reports many German dead in the Village. Touch had been gained with 42nd Division about N.11.d.3.9. 30 enemy Machine Guns had already been counted in the Village.

6.40 p.m. Situation remained unchanged throughout the day. Enemy shelled BEAULENCOURT and trenches in N.16. Shelling ceased about 6 p.m.

8.5 p.m. 62nd Infantry Brigade were ordered to take up the following dispositions by 5 a.m. 2nd September. One Battalion in YELLOW CUT, one Battalion WARLENCOURT, and one Battalion in bivouacs near LE SARS. (G.A.734).

8.15 p.m. Orders issued that in conjunction with the attack by IV Corps on September 2nd, the 110th Infantry Brigade were to capture the SUGAR FACTORY N.24.Central. After capture of SUGAR FACTORY, 110th Infantry Brigade were to push out a force not exceeding one Coy. to about 0.19.d.central with object of preventing withdrawal of garrison of LE TRANSLOY.

This attack to take place at 2 a.m.

In conjunction with main attack of IV and Vth Corps which was to take place later in the morning the 64th Infantry Brigade were to capture LABDA COPSE, at 5.15 a.m.at which hour the 42nd Division on the left would be attacking VILLERS AU FLOS. After capture of LABDA COPSE, 64th Infantry Brigade were to effect a junction with 42nd Division at Cross Roads 0.13,a.2.4. and were also to establish a line from LABDA COPSE to SUGAR FACTORY and get in touch with 110th Infantry Brigade. (D.O. 221).

2nd September 1918.

5.45 a.m. Report received from 110th Infantry Brigade that the SUGAR FACTORY had been captured but that the attacking Coys. of 7th Leicestershire Regt had been unable to gain touch with their

/supporting.....

Company. The runner who brought back the message states that enemy with Machine Guns were still in position between SUGAR FACTORY and BEAULENCOURT. The 1st Wiltshire Regt. were sending one Coy. forward to clear up the situation and to gain touch with troops of the 7th Leicester Regt. in the SUGAR FACTORY.

7.20 a.m. 64th Infantry Brigade reported LABDA COPSE to have been captured with about 30 prisoners and 6 - 77 mm guns. A pocket of Germans in N.18.b. was being dealt with by Stokes Mortars. Situation at SUGAR FACTORY now reported as being satisfactory.

10.40 a.m. Report received from 64th Infantry Brigade that owing to Machine Gun fire from the Southern outskirts of VILLERS AU FLOS and N.E. Corner of LE TRANSLOY, the 1st East Yorkshire Regt. had been withdrawn from LABDA COPSE. This Battalion was now holding trench from N.18.Central to about O.13.a.6.0. The road from LE TRANSLOY to BEAULENCOURT was being swept by Machine Gun fire from LE TRANSLOY. Touch with 110th Infantry Brigade in the SUGAR FACTORY had not been gained owing to fire from small enemy pockets about O.19.a.

11.15 a.m. 64th Infantry Brigade report~~-ed~~ that LABDA COPSE had been reoccupied. The line now ran O.13.b.3.1. where in touch with 42nd Division through O.13.d.3.0. to O.19.b.0.8. 110th Infantry Brigade report that counter-attack from LE TRANSLOY drove their troops out of all except N.W. portion of the SUGAR FACTORY. A fresh attack was being organized to retake the FACTORY.

12.30 p.m. 110th Infantry Brigade report-ed that 7th Leicester Regt. have retaken SUGAR FACTORY and are pushing up the Spur towards LABDA COPSE. Troops of the 17th Division had just passed through and could be seen on high ground in O.19.a.

6.15 p.m. Orders issued for 110th Infantry Brigade to relieve forward Battalion of 64th Infantry Brigade during night 2nd/3rd September. The 110th Infantry Brigade would then hold SUGAR FACTORY and LABDA COPSE, maintaining touch with 42nd Division at O.13.b.3.1. 110th Infantry Brigade were also to garrison the defences of BEAULENCOURT, maintaining at least one Battalion in Brigade reserve in Valley West of the main PERONNE - BAPAUME Road. The 64th Infantry Brigade, after relief of the 1st East Yorkshire Regt. by 110th Infantry Brigade, were to be prepared to hold general line N.22.Central - N.10.Central. 62nd Infantry Brigade were to move to area near LESBOEUFS forthwith (D.O.222.).

The situation during the day remained unchanged. Very little hostile fire of any kind.

3rd September 1918.

12.30 a.m. Instructions received from Corps to withdraw the 110th Infantry Brigade to Valley West of BEAULENCOURT as soon as possible to rest. Time of withdrawal to be arranged mutually between 21st and 17th Divisions (Vth Corps G.180.).

/5.45 a.m......

<u>5.45 a.m.</u> All moves ordered by Divisional Order No.222. were complete.

<u>3.30 p.m.</u> Orders issued to all Brigades to give instructions to Cyclists to concentrate at N.13.d.3.3. where they were to be ready to move at 1 hours notice. (G.X.780 and G.X.781).

<u>10.25 p.m.</u> Orders issued to the effect that 21st Division would remain in Corps Reserve on September 4th. The 62nd Infantry Brigade group would move to area about O.20 and O.21. on the 4th instant, so as to clear LE TRANSLOY by 10 a.m. Observation posts were to be established in the trench system East of ROCQUIGNY, as soon as this system was vacated by 17th Division. 110th Infantry Brigade and 64th Infantry Brigade Groups would probably not move but 64th Infantry Brigade group would be ready to move at one hour's notice. (D.O.223.).

During the above operations the following prisoners and guns were captured by the Division :-

	<u>Officers</u>.	<u>Other Ranks</u>.
Prisoners	45	1,242.
Guns.	12. (including two 8" hows.)	

Copy of Telegrams to accompany Summary of Operations
for period 20th Aug. to 3rd Sept.

G.X.449.

Send one N.C.O. and 12 men to report to 64th Inf. Bde. at Q.10.b.6.4 at once AAA Addsd Corps Cyclists reptd V Corps and 64th Inf. Bde.

G.X.452.

Our troops have entered ACHIET LE PETIT and are moving on IRLES AAA As soon as Brown Line captured 62nd Inf. Bde. will move two Reserve Companies preceded by patrols to line River ANCRE at R.4.c.6.7 Road junc. R.4.a.5.1 to R.4.a.0.5. AAA Picquets will be placed on all bridges over ANCRE between above line and Brown Line AAA 62 Inf. Bde. will push patrols from new line into S.W. outskirts of MIRAUMONT AAA 64th Inf. Bde. will place two Coys. at disposal of 62nd Inf. Bde. to act as Brigade Reserve AAA Ack

G.396 from Corps.

In event of IV Corps taking IRLES and the fire from THIEPVAL RIDGE not being heavy be prepared move your 3rd Bde. rapidly along BEAUCOURT - MIRAUMONT Road and cross ANCRE in R.3 and 4 moving thence on THIEPVAL holding BOOM RAVINE to cover movement AAA

G.X.455.

One Battalion 110 Inf. Bde. is placed at disposal of 64th Inf. Bde. AAA Battalion will reach BEAUMONT RESERVE Area about 2 p.m. AAA 64th Inf. Bde. will send orders to 110th Inf. Bde. H.Q. as to further move of Battalion AAA

G.X.460.

IRLES has not yet been captured by us AAA In consequence 42nd Div. have not yet entered MIRAUMONT AAA 64th Inf. Bde. will therefore take special precautions regarding his Eastern flank after crossing ANCRE AAA 62 Inf. Bde. will make every endeavour to throw bridges across the ANCRE between BEAUCOURT and GRANDCOURT so as to give 64th Inf. Bde. alternative line for withdrawal in case of necessity AAA 64th Inf. Bde. will send patrols towards GRANDCOURT after crossing ANCRE to connect with 62nd Inf. Bde. and to ensure connection between these bridge-heads AAA

G.X.461.

Reference G.X.455 AAA 110th Inf. Bde. will hold another Battalion in readiness to join 64th Inf. Bde, if ordered to do so from Div. H.Q. AAA Ack

G.421 from Corps.

21st Div. will consolidate final objective from River by BAILLESCOURT FARM Sunken Road to R.3.a.0.8 with one Bde. connecting with 42nd Div. on left AAA One Brigade in position to support front Bde. or to renew the offensive across the ANCRE at short notice AAA Rear Bde. S. and W. of BEAUMONT HAMEL in positions to be selected and reported AAA Ack

G.X.476.

Two rear Battalions 64th Inf. Bde. and 1 Battalion 110th Inf. Bde. attached 64th Inf. Bde. will NOT be ~~xxxxxx~~ moved forward without reference to Div. H.Q.

G.X.477.

Trend of hostile movement this evening has been towards MIRAUMONT and ACHIET LE GRAND AAA Hostile counter-attack is

therefore possible tonight or tomorrow morning AAA All Commanders will be warned accordingly AAA Action of two Rear Battalions of 64th Inf. Bde. and attached Battalion from 110 Inf. Bde. will be defensive until further orders AAA They will be prepared to support 62nd Inf. Bde. to meet a counter-attack from the East AAA At Dawn tomorrow Aug. 22nd 110 Inf. Bde. will endeavour to push patrols across the ANCRE to the Blue Line also a patrol in conjunction with 38th Div. AAA When Blue Line has been made good and consolidated 110th Inf. Bde. will push patrols to Red Line AAA 62 Inf. Bde. will push patrols to Blue Dotted Line AAA Leading Battalion of 64th Inf. Bde. will push patrols across ANCRE to try and get touch with enemy. AAA Ack

<u>22.9.18.</u> <u>G.X.486.</u>

62 Inf. Bde. will push patrols forward from Blue Line to portion of Red Line in their area as well as to GRANDCOURT AAA If Red Line occupied by our patrols 64th Inf. Bde. will be prepared to send two Coys. to garrison it AAA Ack

<u>G.466 from Corps.</u>

A Brigade 17th Division will relieve and take over a one Brigade front at present held by 110th Inf. Bde. 21st Division tonight (22nd/23rd) AAA Relief to be complete by 5 a.m. 23rd AAA Boundary between 21st and 17th Divs. will be line from R.21.d.0.0 - R.14.c.0.0 to Q.12.c.6.0 thence West along grid line between Q.11 and Q.17 AAA S. Boundary 17th Div. will be THIEPVAL Road (exclusive) to Q.24.a.6.0 thence West along grid line Q.23.Central - Q.22.Central AAA Ack

<u>R.A.1163 from Corps.</u>

Reference V Corps G.466 AAA 17th Divl. Arty. will come under orders of C.R.A. 17th Div. at 4 a.m. on 23rd AAA The two 60 - pdr. Batteries will remain under C.R.A. 21st Div. AAA Ack

<u>G.X.503.</u>

If Brown Line or any portion of it has been lost it must be restored by a counter-attack in conformity with attack of Div. on your left at 2.30 a.m. Aug. 23rd AAA Arrange Arty. support with affiliated Brigade R.F.A. AAA Gain touch with 42nd Div. after counter-attack AAA Ack

23rd ~~[illegible]~~ August, 1918.

<u>G.511 from Corps.</u>

A Company, Cyclists Battalion, is allotted to each Div. AAA Coy. has already been detailed to 21st and 38th Divs AAA Remaining Coy. now allotted to 17th Div. under arrangements to be made direct between Headquarters 17th Division and O.C. Cyclist Bn. AAA Lewis Gun Detachments now attached 21st Division will revert to their CompaniesAAA O.C. Cyclist Bn. and Adjutant will act as liaison Officers between Divisions ~~xxx~~ and will be attached 17th Division under arrangements to be made direct AAA Ack

<u>G.X.521.</u>

Order all Lewis Gunners N.I.H. except those belonging to "A" Squadron to rejoin their own Units AAA Ack

<u>G.X.535.</u>

Confirmation of telephone conversation AAA 62 Inf. Bde. will concentrate all troops less garrison of Brown Line at once AAA As soon as reliable information is received that MIRAUMONT has been captured the garrison of the Brown Line will concentrate with its own Units AAA You will then be prepared to cross the ANCRE either by the railway bridge or the bridge in GRANDCOURT AAA

25th August, 1918.

G.A.10.

Sit easy AAA Be prepared to move at 6 p.m.

G.A.11.

In confirmation of telephone message AAA 21st Division will probably remain in present position for today AAA However 62nd Inf. Bde. will be prepared to advance its left to keep touch with troops on its left should they go forward AAA Should 17th Div. advance and take EAUCOURT L'ABBAYE 110 Inf. Bde. will be prepared to carry on the general advance AAA

Order No.214.

17th Division are holding East of MARTINPUICH with their left in M.22.c. 63rd Division hold LE BARQUE and YELLOW CUT AAA 62 Inf. Bde. will hold present line in M.18 and 24. AAA 110th Inf. Bde. will protect the right of 62nd Inf. Bde. until 17th Div. left reaches M.24.c. when 110th Inf. Bde. will concentrate West of BLUE CUT and ready to hold that line AAA 64th Inf. Bde. will move to high ground M.15 and 20 and be prepared to hold this line AAA Reserve M.Gs will prepare to occupy positions on ridge R.12 and R.18 AAA 64th Inf. Bde. will advance at 5.30 a.m. Aug. 26th and move through 62nd Inf. Bde. with objective line of road N.21.b.6.0 - N.9.b.7.0. AAA When 64th Inf. Bde. has passed road N.19.b. N.7.b. 62nd Inf. Bde. will advance to it AAA When 64th Inf. Bde. ~~made~~ objective made good 62nd Inf. Bde. will advance to SAILLY SAILLISEL - BAPAUME Road AAA 110th Inf. Bde. if not already concentrated in M.17 will do so when 62nd Inf. Bde. advances and be in Divisional Reserve AAA One Coy. Cyclists works under 64th Inf. Bde. for first operation and 62nd Inf. Bde. for second AAA One Troop Div. Cav. under special instructions issued to O.C. will work in front of Infantry reporting situation to leading Brigade AAA 94th Bde. R.F.A. under orders 64th Inf. Bde. for first operation AAA 95th Bde. R.F.A. under 62nd Inf. Bde. for second AAA Mobile Newton Mortar works with leading Brigade reporting 62nd Inf. Bde. H.Q. early tomorrow AAA Infantry will not move extended across country unless under aimed small arm fire AAA Div. H.Q. remain GRANDCOURT AAA ACK

G.X.587.

Ref. Order No. 214 AAA 64th Inf. Bde. will first make good intermediate objective line of road N.19.b. N.17.b. reporting capture to Div. H.Q. AAA 64th Inf. Bde. will not advance to further objective without orders from Div. H.Q. AAA 62nd Inf. Bde. will not advance to their objective without reference to Div. H.Q. AAA As soon as 17th Division start advancing on right of 110 Inf. Bde., 110 Inf. Bde. will concentrate in M.17 AAA

G.X.589.

Reference instructions issued you today if Infantry have not relieved you by 7 p.m. you will withdraw to MIRAUMONT AAA If state of ground tomorrow does not permit of you moving faster than the Infantry you will return to MIRAUMONT and report to Div. H.Q. for further orders AAA

G.X.588.

If as is probable relief of your troops in our area not carried out tonight AAA Brigade which moves through our leading Bde. at 7.30 a.m. have particular orders to get their left on Northern Div. Boundary. AAA

29th August, 1918.

G.X.653.

Send a patrol under a N.C.O. to report to B.G.C. 110th Inf. Bde. as soon as possible AAA Remainder of Troop to be ready to move at short notice but not saddled up AAA

G.X.654.

38th Division report that they met no opposition this morning AAA There are other indications that enemy are retiring AAA 110th Inf. Bde. will push forward Advanced Guards followed if feasible by remainder of Brigade and make good following successive bounds AAA LUISENHOF FARM ROAD AAA Road N.21.a. N.9.a. AAA Spur N.22.a.00 to Cross Rds N.9.d.7.2 along road to N.9.b.8.0 AAA Cross Rds N.24.a.5.1 BEAULENCOURT and road from N.11.d.5.0 to N.11.b.7.0 AAA 62nd Inf. Bde. will support 110 Inf. Bde. moving to LUISENHOF FARM Rd. when 110 Inf. Bde. has made good road N.21.a. N.9.a. AAA N.2 Spur N.22.a.0.0 Cross Rds. N.9.d. when 110 Inf. Bde. has reached BEAULENCOURT AAA Moves of 64th Inf. Bde. and Reserve M.Gs will be ordered direct from Div. H.Q. AAA Successive Report Centres at BUTTE DE WARLENCOURT LUISENHOF FARM and Sunken Road N.15.d.4.7 AAA

G.X.659.

95th Bde. R.F.A. will act under orders of leading Brigade AAA 94th Bde. R.F.A.under orders of supporting Brigade but will assist in covering advance of leading Brigade AAA

G.X.661.

Ref. G.X.654 of today AAA 64 Inf. Bde. will become supporting Brigade instead of 62nd Inf. Bde. AAA 64 Inf. Bde. will be prepared to move to YELLOW CUT on receipt of orders from Divisional H.Q. AAA 94th Bde. R.F.A. now come under orders 64th Inf. Bde. AAA

G.X.665.

64 Inf. Bde. will move forthwith to YELLOW CUT AAA Completion of move to be reported to 21st Div. H.Q. AAA

G.X.673.

In confirmation of telephone conversation AAA As much Arty. fire as possible is required on BEAULENCOURT tonight AAA All fire on Village to cease at 2 a.m. 30th instant when patrols will enter the village AAA Could 4th Corps be asked to shell the village as well AAA

30th August, 1918.

G.X.684.

Under orders from Corps you are to rejoin your Squadron at Cross Roads COURCELETTE at 8.30 a.m. tomorrow August 31st AAA

31st August, 1918.

G.X.688.

You will bivouac near the BUTTE DE WARLENCOURT AAA Until further orders you will be under the 110 Inf. Bde. who will issue the necessary orders for your employment AAA Please report to these Brigade H.Q. at N.13.d.6.4 as soon as possible leaving the troop in bivouacs.

21st August, 1918.

R.A.30/44 from Corps.

It is essential that enemy should be prevented from improving his present positions by making secure M.G.posts improving his trenches and putting up wire AAA All Artillery will be active not only on communications but on the positions now held by enemy

1st September, 1918.

G.X.734.

62 Inf. Bde. will have one Battalion holding YELLOW CUT by 5 a.m. Sept. 2nd AAA Another Battalion of 62nd Inf. Bde. will be at WARLENCOURT and the third in bivouacs near LE SARS by same hour AAA 62nd Inf. Bde. will establish Brigade Headquarters at BUTTE DE WARLENCOURT xxx by 11 a.m. AAA

2nd September, 1918.

G.180 from Corps.

21st Division will withdraw Brigade now holding LABDA COPSE SUGAR FACTORY BEAULENCOURT as soon as possible to rest AAA Time of withdrawal to be arranged mutually between 21st and 17th Divs.

3rd September, 1918.

G.X.780.

110 Inf. Bde. will issue instructions to Cyclists to concentrate at the BUTTE forthwith AAA 62nd and 64th Inf. Bdes. will send all cyclists at present ~~to~~ with them to rejoin their Unit at the BUTTE AAA Cyclist Squadron will keep orderlies at the BUTTE Telephone Exchange AAA After concentration Cyclists will be ready to move at one hours' notice AAA

G.X.781.

Ref. G.X.780 AAA Cyclists will now concentrate at N.13.d.3.3 and NOT at the BUTTE AAA Cyclists will keep orderlies at 110th Inf. Bde. H.Q.

Appx 26

21 Div.
G. 989.

REPORT ON OPERATIONS FROM 4th SEPT. to 16th SEPT. 1918.

4th September, 1918.

Orders were issued for the Division to relieve the 38th Division in the line, the 62nd Inf. Bde. being the leading Brigade, with 64th Inf. Bde. in support and 110 Inf. Bde. in Reserve. (Order No.224 and G.X.806 and G.X.808).

Instructions received from Corps that operations on a large scale would not be undertaken for the present. The enemy rear-guards, however, were to be engaged and pressed by our advanced guards and every opportunity taken of gaining ground.(Corps G.247).

5th September, 1918.

12.40 p.m. Orders issued for the 64 Inf. Bde. to relieve the 113th and 115th Inf. Bdes., 38th Division, in the trench system U.5. U.11 U.17.a. and U.10. 110 Inf. Bde. were to move to the area West of SAILLY SAILLISEL. (Order No.224a).

3.30 p.m. Divisional Headquarters closed at M.9.c.70.05 and opened at LES BOEUFS. (T.3.d.4.4).

6.50 p.m. Orders issued for active patrolling to be carried out during the night and the following day. If enemy resistance showed signs of slackening, the 62 Inf. Bde. were to push forward advanced guards and be prepared to follow with remainder of the Brigade. The advance would be continued until the objective W.22.c.0.4 - REVELON - W.10.Central was reached, when orders for a fresh advance would be issued from Divisional Headquarters. The 62 Inf. Bde. were not to engage in a serious attack unless instructions were issued from Divisional Headquarters to that effect. The 64 Inf. Bde. were to be prepared to hold the line ST. MARTINS WOOD to LE MESNIL - en - ARROUAISE, but efforts were to be concentrated on keeping troops fresh. 110 Inf. Bde. were to remain in their present position. (Order No.225).

/6th Sept.......

6th September, 1918.

6.15 a.m. The relief of the 38th Division was complete and G.O.C. 21st Division assumed command of the sector. The line taken over ran V.9.a.7.2 - V.15.a.3.1 - V.14.c.2.5 - V.20.a.0.0. The enemy was inactive, but there was slight gas shelling of valley near MANANCOURT and ETRICOURT.

8.5 a.m. Left Battalion 62 Inf. Bde. reported that the enemy still held EQUANCOURT TRENCH. Touch had been obtained with troops on the left.

10.30 a.m. The line now ran V.3.d.3.2 - V.9.a.5.0 - V.15.a.3.1 - V.14.c.2.6 - V.20.a.0.0. Owing to troops of the 12th Division having withdrawn from FAUCON TRENCH this trench had been occupied by the Right Battalion, 62 Inf. Bde. and an unconfirmed report stated that touch had been gained with 12th Division about V.22.b.7.1.

1 p.m. Situation. 62 Inf. Bde. reported that their right Battn. was established in trenches V.22.b. & d. and were believed to be in trenches in V.16.d. Patrols of the Left Battalion were in EQUANCOURT WOOD.

1.15 p.m. Report received that EQUANCOURT Village and Wood were now occupied by our troops.

2 p.m. Two Mobile Newton Mortars were ordered to proceed to 62 Inf. Bde. under whose orders they would act. (G.X.856).

3.10 p.m. Situation. Right Battalion, 62 Inf. Bde., were holding trenches in V.23.b. & d. and V.17.d. Left Battalion was in trenches V.17.a.0.5 and along trench system V.11.a. & c. Touch had been gained with 12th Division on right. No definite opposition had been encountered.

3.45 p.m. Orders were issued to the 64 Inf. Bde. to move one Battalion to the high ground East of ETRICOURT. As soon as the 62 Inf. Bde. had cleared the trench system running through V.10. to V.22 the 64 Inf. Bde. were to move two Battalions up to this line, ready to occupy it in depth, one Battalion remaining West of the Canal. (G.X.864).

/4.35 p.m....

4.35 p.m. Situation. Right Battalion, 62 Inf. Bde. had reached the line of the road V.23.b.3.1 to V.18.c.1.9 with advanced guard pushing on to SOREL LE GRAND. The left Battalion had encountered opposition from the trenches V.11.b. and a. but this opposition was being dealt with.

5.15 p.m. Report received from the Corps Cavalry Troop, timed 4.5 p.m., that the 2nd Linc. Regt. had a patrol in SOREL LE GRAND, and that the 1st Linc. Regt. was pushing round the North of FINS.

8 p.m. Orders issued to the 62 Inf. Bde. to continue the advance on the following day, the main guard moving forward at 6 a.m.
Objectives :-
(1) Brown Line W.22.c. - W.16.Central - W.10.a.0.0 - W.9.a.8.9.
(2) Northern end of PEIZIERE - VAUCELLETTE FARM - CHAPEL CROSSING.
64 Inf. Bde. to move forward by stages until the EQUANCOURT TRENCH SYSTEM was occupied, when further orders would be issued. The 110 Inf. Bde. to remain in present position. (D.O.226).

10.15 p.m. Situation. Line ran, Spur in W.19.a. & c. SOREL LE GRAND inclusive. Touch had been gained with 17th Division in V.6.d. Situation in FINS was uncertain.

7th September, 1918.

12.45 a.m. FINS had been definitely captured and was being heavily gas shelled by the enemy.

5.15 a.m. With the exception of the gas shelling of FINS, the enemy were inactive during the night.

8.50 a.m. Report from 62 Inf. Bde. timed 8.30 a.m. stated that the left Battalion was advancing through W.8 and W.9, apparently without opposition. Right Battalion was echeloned in rear owing to troops on right not commencing the advance until 8 a.m. No news of progress of this Battalion had yet been received, but hostile M.G. fire had been heard.

9.45 a.m. Orders were issued to the effect that when the 62 Inf. Bde. had occupied the whole of the first objective, the 64 Inf. Bde. were to move one Battalion to occupy SOREL LE GRAND. When the reserve Battalion 62 Inf. Bde. had moved forward from first objective, the 64 Inf. Bde. were to send one Battalion to W.8.Central and another to about W.20.a. & c. keeping one Battalion in SOREL LE GRAND. When 62 Inf. Bde. had gained the whole of the /second....

second objective, the 64 Inf. Bde. were/to dispose their troops so as to be able to occupy the first objective in case of need, or to take up the advance on the following day. The 110 Inf. Bde. were warned that they would probably move to ground East of the Canal du Nord during the evening. (G.X.894).

10 a.m. Report received from the 62 Inf. Bde. timed 9.45 a.m. that the right Battalion held the ridge W.20.a. & c. but were held up by M.G. fire coming from about W.26.d. The left Battn. of the 12th Division held the ridge W.25. and were also held up by M.G. fire. The left Battalion 62 Inf. Bde. had reached W.9.Central and had been ordered to push on to REVELON RIDGE. Enemy had been seen retiring out of HEUDECOURT.

12 Noon. Divisional Headquarters closed at LES BOEUFS and opened at LE MESNIL EN ARROUAISE (U.5.c.3.2).

4 p.m. 110 Inf. Bde. were ordered to move to bivouacs in the area between Canal du Nord and a line running North and South through LE MESNIL en ARROUAISE before dark tonight. (G.X.899).

The reserve M.G. Coy. were ordered to reconnoitre positions in trench system V.22.b. - V.16.b. & d. - V.11.a. & c. These positions were to be occupied before dark. (G.X.900).

4.5 p.m. The 64 Inf. Bde. were ordered to move one Battalion to the neighbourhood of SOREL LE GRAND. (G.X.901).

4.25 p.m. 62 Inf. Bde. reported the situation at 1 p.m. as under :-

Right Battalion were in W.27.b. Left Battalion had been reported by the Corps Cavalry to be on the general line W.9.Cen. to railway North of HEUDECOURT. HEUDECOURT was reported to have been captured.

4.50 p.m. Situation. Right/Bn. 62 Inf. Bde. held trenches in W.23.a. & c. with advanced posts in W.22.d. Left Battalion held trenches in W.9.b. and W.10.c. and was advancing to the attack on REVELON RIDGE. The right Battalion was advancing to the spur W.23.Central in order to cover the left flank of the 12th Division.

8 p.m. Orders issued for the 62 Inf. Bde. to send forward advanced guards at 6 a.m. tomorrow to try and capture the second objective. If the enemy's resistance had slackened, advanced guards were to be supported, but no serious attack

/was......

was to be undertaken without reference to Div. H.Q. 94th and 95th Bdes. R.F.A. were placed under the orders of 62 Inf. Bde. Artillery and Machine Guns were to be freely used for harassing fire. 64 and 110 Inf. Bdes. would remain in their present positions but the 64 Inf. Bde. were to carry out the necessary reconnaissances with a view to relief of 62 Inf. Bde. on the night 8th/9th. (D.O.227).

8th September, 1918.

5.40 a.m. Situation unchanged during the night. There was spasmodic shelling throughout the night of roads, tracks and villages in the forward area. Hostile night bombing squadrons were very active.

8.45 a.m. Situation. Enemy held RAILTON - REVELON - W.10.Central. 1st Linc. Regt. had an encounter with an enemy patrol near RAILTON, in which four prisoners were captured. Enemy attempted to raid one of our posts at 5.30 a.m. but was repulsed before entering our lines.

9.45 a.m. Owing to the enemy putting down a very heavy barrage on the Division on our left, the 62 Inf. Bde. called on the leading Battalion of the 64 Inf. Bde. to form a defensive flank facing North in case of necessity. (G.X.919).

10.50 a.m. Situation. The right Battalion 62 Inf. Bde. attacked at 7.30 a.m. in conjunction with 58th Division on right and captured the KNOLL at W.23.Central with little opposition. The Battalion was moving on the second objective, the trench line W.24.c. - W.23.d. which objective was also later reported as captured. Troops were pushed down railway through W.24.c. & d. to connect with left of 58th Division who were believed to have captured PEIZIERE. This village, however, was not captured.

12.20 p.m. Trenches in W.23.Central and W.21.a & c. were being consolidated. RAILTON was being mopped up and a few prisoners had been taken.

1.10 p.m. Situation. REVELON FARM was reported captured and Battalions had been pushed forward to GENIN WELL COPSE. Heavy M.G. fire was being encountered from LOWLAND SUPPORT.

/2.30 p.m.

2.30 p.m. Report received from 62 Inf. Bde. that their troops had worked along the railway at W.24.d. but had been driven back by a counter-attack. They also reported that PEIZIERE was strongly held by the enemy.

10.10 p.m. Orders issued to the 64 Inf. Bde. to attack tomorrow at 4 a.m. in conjunction with the 17th Division on their left. The objectives were CHAPEL HILL and high ground in W.11.d. After capture of these objectives, the 62 Inf. Bde. were to push patrols to VAUCELLETTE FARM, which was to be occupied in absence of resistance. The 110 Inf. Bde. were to have two Battalions in the vicinity of, and ready to occupy, EQUANCOURT TRENCH SYSTEM by 6 a.m. tomorrow morning. The third battalion was to move to the neighbourhood of SOREL LE GRAND. The 62 Inf. Bde. would be withdrawn gradually under orders of Div. H.Q. to MANANCOURT and ETRICOURT and to ground just East of Canal. (D.O.228).

9th September, 1918.

5.30 a.m. Situation. Very little activity during the night. Enemy harassed RAILTON Cross roads with Artillery. No news had yet been received from the attacking Battalions.

7 a.m. 64 Inf. Bde. reported that the first objective in W.11.d. had been captured, but this report had not been confirmed. The enemy were heavily shelling RAILTON and REVELON.

8.10 a.m. Situation. Owing to GENIN WELL COPSE No.2 not having been held by our troops during the night it had to be taken by the attacking troops this morning, and consequently these troops lost the barrage. The line now reported ran W.18.c.9.9 along rly. to W.17.b.4.8. thence along LOWLAND SUPPORT to Northern Divl. Boundary.

Three Machine Guns and some prisoners were captured.

4.30 p.m. Situation remained unchanged. There was some hostile shelling of back areas.

5 p.m. 64 Inf. Bde. reported that they were continuing the attack at 5.30 p.m. in order to gain the final objectives.

/8 p.m.....

8 p.m. 64 Inf. Bde. were ordered that unless attack delivered at 5 p.m. was successful, the attack would be continued in conjunction with 17th Division at 4 a.m. the following day. The objectives would be CHAPEL HILL thence along CAVALRY TRENCH and LOWLAND TRENCH to junction with 17th Division at W.12.a.0.0. At 5.15 a.m. the 58th Division on the right were attacking EPEHY and PEIZIERE at which hour the 64 and 110 Inf. Bdes. were to advance and occupy the YELLOW LINE under a creeping barrage. In view of this the 110 Inf. Bde. would be relieving the 62 Inf. Bde. in the Brown Line and at KNOLL W.23.Central during the night. 110 Inf. Bde. were also to be prepared to occupy REVELON FARM and GENIN WELL COPSE No.1 if vacated by forward move of troops of 64 Inf. Bde. On relief, 62 Inf. Bde. was to move to the EQUANCOURT - ETRICOURT Area. (D.O.229).

10th September, 1918.

6.35 a.m. Situation. Heavy shelling of trench system W.24.a. & c. during the night. No news had yet been received of the attack. There was heavy rain and wind during the night.

10.40 a.m. Report received from 64 Inf. Bde. that the attack on CHAPEL HILL and high ground in W.11.d. was not successful. No details had yet been received.

11.30 a.m. Warning order issued that the 110 Inf. Bde. would relieve the 64 Inf. Bde. during the night. The 110 Inf. Bde. was also to be prepared to advance under a barrage and occupy the Yellow Line from CHAPEL HILL to Southern Divisional Boundary. On relief, the 64 Inf. Bde. would move to the EQUANCOURT TRENCH SYSTEM with one Battalion about SOREL LE GRAND. (G.X.693).

7.30 p.m. Orders issued for the 110 Inf. Bde. to advance under a barrage and make good the whole of the Yellow Line within the Divisional Sector. 110 Inf. Bde. would also relieve the 64 Inf. Bde. in the line. (D.O.230).

11.25 p.m. 64 Inf. Bde. reported that a patrol of the 15th Durham L.I. had reached point W.18.c.4.7 where they encountered heavy M.G. fire from both sides. Patrol reported the Yellow Line to be occupied in W.18.c. and W.24.a.

/11th Sept. ......

11th September, 1918.

5.20 a.m. Situation. The attack by the 110 Inf. Bde. started at 3 a.m. and the objectives were now reported as captured, but this report not yet confirmed. Enemy retaliation was slight in the forward area, but heavy on back area, where all valleys were being gassed. The relief of the 64 Inf. Bde. by the 110 Inf. Bde. was complete at 2.45 a.m.

12.30 p.m. Report received from the 110 Inf. Bde. giving situation as follows. One Coy. in trench system from W.23.d.85.30 to W.24.c.45.95. One Platoon in trench system W.24.a.6.2, one Coy. W.18.c.9.3 to W.18.c.9.6. Hostile counter-attack from direction of CHAPEL HILL had been repulsed. This trench system was being heavily shelled by the enemy and the dispositions of the remaining troops could not be ascertained.

2.15 p.m. 110 Inf. Bde. were informed that gas would be projected on CHAPEL CROSSING and VAUCELLETTE FARM between 1.30 a.m. and 2.30 a.m. Sept. 12th. (G.X.5).

2.15 p.m. Brigades were ordered to send all Cavalry and Cyclists attached to them to concentrate in EHRICOURT where they would be under the orders of the 62 Inf. Bde. (G.X.6.).

4.30 p.m. Situation. Line ran W.23.d.0.0 along line of trenches W.18.c.8.9 where a small gap still existed. Line was continued from W.18.a.8.4 along LOWLAND SUPPORT to Northern Divl. Boundary. Touch had been gained on both flanks. Endeavours were being made to clear up the situation in the gap. Enemy trench mortars were active from LOWLAND TRENCH, but were being engaged by Stokes mortars.

12th September, 1918.

12.30 a.m. Report received from the 110 Inf. Bde. that the 1st Bn. Wilts. Regt. had been unable to gain touch with the 7th Leic. Regt. in the Yellow Line. The patrol had been attacked with M.G. fire and bombed by the enemy who were holding a strong post about W.18.a.8.4.

6 a.m. Situation during the night unchanged. Gas was successfully projected at 1.30 a.m. Practically no hostile retaliation.

/11.30 a.m.

11.30 a.m. Situation. No activity on the right Battalion front. Left Battalion front was heavily shelled from W.17.b.9.9 to W.11.c.8.6 between 5 a.m. and 7 a.m. At 6 a.m. the enemy attempted to bomb down trench leading to our line at W.11.c.8.6. but were repulsed. Touch had not yet been obtained between 7th Leic. Regt. and 1st Wilts. Regt.

6 p.m. Situation unchanged during the day. At 2 p.m. the enemy attempted to raid the post at W.17.b.6.9 but was repulsed before entering our line.

13th September, 1918.

5.25 a.m. The situation remained quiet and unchanged during the night. Touch had now been gained between the 7th Leic. Regt. and the 1st Wilts. Regt., the enemy pocket which had existed between these two Battalions being cleared up.

9 a.m. 110 Inf. Bde. caught a deserter who stated that the enemy would make an attack on our present line on CHAPEL HILL at 10 a.m. The attack would be accompanied by flammenwerfer. This attack was carried out.

1.5 p.m. 110 Inf. Bde. were informed that gas would be projected on to the railway cutting W.35.b.95.70 between 1.30 a.m. and 2.30 a.m. 14th instant. (G.X.23).

2 p.m. Report received from 110 Inf. Bde. timed 12.30 p.m. that the enemy attacked with flammenwerfer at 10 a.m. and obtained a temporary footing in our line at the trench junction W.11.c.8.6. He was immediately counter-attacked and driven out, 12 men and 1 M.G. being captured. The enemy's losses were reported as being very heavy. Our line was intact and in touch on both flanks. None of our men were missing. The enemy attacks was accompanied by heavy Artillery and Trench Mortar bombardment.
The situation for the remainder of the day remained unchanged. There was no enemy activity.

14th September, 1918.

5.25 a.m. There was no change in the situation during the night which passed quietly. An enemy bombing aeroplane was brought down in our lines at 10.30 p.m., the Officer Pilot being captured.

/9.5 a.m......

9.5 a.m. Report received from the 110 Inf. Bde. that preceded by a Trench Mortar bombardment about 20 of the enemy attempted to enter our line at W.18.a.7.4 but were entirely repulsed by rifle and Lewis Gun fire.

4.30 p.m. Situation. Up to 1 p.m. the enemy artillery was fairly active on back areas, but after that hour there was practically no fire.

15th September, 1918.

5.15 a.m. Situation during the night remained unchanged. Enemy Artillery was comparatively quiet but increased slightly at 4 a.m. Some hostile trench mortar fire on the front line in the right sector.

4 p.m. Orders issued that the 110 Inf. Bde. would be relieved by the 19th Inf. Bde. in the line tonight 15th/16th instant. On relief, the 110 Inf. Bde. would move to ETRICOURT and MANANCOURT. The Coys. of the 21st Bn. M.G.C. in the line would not be relieved. (D.O.231).

5.35 p.m. Situation remained unchanged except for some shelling of HEUDECOURT. Our Artillery carried out the usual harassing fire.

16th September, 1918.

2.20 a.m. The relief of the 110 Inf. Bde. by the 19th Inf. Bde. was complete and command of the sector passed to the G.O.C. 33rd Division.

5.15 a.m. The enemy opened a bombardment of the area V.9.c. & d. V.15, V.16.c. & d. where the 62 and 64th Inf. Bdes. were bivouaced, with H.E. and gas. The bombardment ceased at 5.45 a.m. A few casualties were caused.

During the above operations, the following prisoners were captured by the Division.

Officers.	O.R.
5	246

Telegrams to accompany REPORT ON OPERATIONS from
4th to 16th September, 1918.

4th ~~xxxxxxx~~ September 1918.

G.X.806. Ref. 21st Div. Order 224 AAA Field Coys R.E. Pioneer Bn and M.G. Bn. less 3 Coys will move between 2 p.m. and 8 p.m. tomorrow Sept.5th to Bivouaacs on COMBLES - SAILLY SAILLISEL Rd. AAA Route via LES BOEUFS and MORVAL AAA Exact Location of bivouaacs from 'Q'

G.X. 808. Cyclist Squadron will come under orders of 62nd Inf. Bde. tomorrow and will report to 62nd Inf. Bde. H.Q.O.31.b.33 before 12 noon AAA 62nd Inf. Bde. will issue necessary orders for future employment.

G.247. Operations on a large scale will not be undertaken for the present and our resouces must be husbanded and communications improvised with a view to the resumption of a vigorous offensive in the near future AAA Divisions will be in depth on a one Brigade front AAA Corps Cav. will be withdrawn to BAZETIN LE GRAND keeping in touch with the situation by patrols AAA Adv. Guards will continue to press the enemy driving in his rearguards AAA On Adv. Guards gaining any hostile position they will be reinforced sufficiently from main bodies to resist any local counter-attack AAA Valleys should be avoided on account of gas shelling AAA Reserve Bdes. of forward Divisions and the Reserve Division will rest and train AAA

September 6th. 1918.

G.X.856. Two Mobile Newton Mortars being sent at once to 60 pounder Bridge MANANCOURT V.13.d.5.2. AAA Arrange guide to meet them.

G.X.864. 62nd Inf. Bde. has occupied Equancourt and is advancing on FINS and SOREL AAA 64th Inf. Bde. will move one Bn. to the high ground West of ETRICOURT AAA As soon as 64th Inf. Bde. has cleared the trench system running through V.10. to V.22. 64th Inf. Bde. will occupy with two Battns. disposed in depth the ground East of Canal AAA One Battn. will remain West of the Canal AAA 64th Inf. Bde. will be prepared to occupy the above trench system in case of necessity AAA

7th September 1918.

G.X.899. 110th Inf. Bde. will move to bivouaacs in area between CANAL DU NORD and a line due North and South through MESNIL before dark tonight AAA 110th Inf. Bde. will report hour of moving and hour of arrival AAA

G.X.900. Instruct Reserve M.G. ~~Battn.~~ Coy. to reconnoitre positions in Trench System V.22.b. - V.16.b and d - V.11 a and c. AAA These positions will be occupied before dark tonight AAA Coy. will report that positions have been taken up to Div. H.Q.

G.X.901. Confirming telephone conversation to 64th Inf. Bde AAA 64th Inf. Bde. will move one Battalion to neighbourhood of SOREL LE GRAND forthwith AAA 64th Inf. Bde. will report arrival and disposition of this Battalion.

8th September 1918.

G.X.919. Enemy are putting down a heavy barrage on Division on our left AAA 62nd Inf. Bde. have called on leading Battn. of 64th Inf. Bde.

to form defensive flank facing North in case of need AAA Battalion H.Q. 1st E.York Regt. at W.18.c.8.4 AAA

11th September, 1918.

G.X.5. Gas will be projected on CHAPEL CROSSING and VAUCELLETTE FARM between 1.30 and 2.30 a.m. September 12th AAA Further details will be sent to 110 Inf. Bde. AAA

G.X.6. Brigades will instruct all Cavalry and Cyclists attached to them to concentrate in ETRICOURT AAA Both Div. Cav. and Cyclists will come under orders of 62 Inf. Bde. until further orders AAA 62 Inf. Bde. will arrange billets and also baths AAA

13th September, 1918.

G.X.53. Gas will be projected on to railway cutting W.30.b.95.70 tonight AAA Position of projectors sunken road W.23.d. AAA Zero between 1.30 a.m. and 2.30 a.m. 14th instant AAA Further details to 110 Inf. Bde. later AAA

5th September 1918.

G.X.822./ Ref 21 Div Order No.224. AAA 64th Inf. Bde. group will relieve 113th and 115th Bdes. in Trench System U.5, U.11, U.17.a. and U.10. this afternoon AAA Both these Brigades are very weak AAA Exact positions occupied by 38 Div need not be taken up AAA Woods and valleys are full of gas and will be avoided AAA 64th Bde. H.Q. will be established at 113 Bde.H.Q. U.8.a.5.5. from 3 p.m. AAA Leading Troops 64th Bde. will cross main LE TRANSLOY - SAILLY SAILLISEL Road at 3.30 p.m. AAA Movement by Platoons AAA 64th Bde. will wire exact position of Battns. on completion of relief AAA Dispositions of 113 and 115 Bdes by wire for 64th Bde only. 110th Bde. will move to area W. of SAILLY SAILLISEL AAA Starting point LE TRANSLOY SUGAR FACTORY at 4.30 p.m. AAA 110th Bde. H.Q. will be established at 115th Bde.H.Q. U.14.a.0.4. from 5 p.m.

7th September 1918.

G.X.894. Ref. 21 Div. Order 226. When 62nd Inf. Bde. has occupied whole of 1st objective 64th Bde. will move one Battn. to occupy SOREL LE GRAND AAA When 62nd Bde. Reserve Bn. moves forward from 1st objective, 64th Bde. will move one Battn. to about W.8. Cent. and another to about W.20 a and c. maintaining one Battn. in SOREL AAA When 62nd Inf. Bde. reports whole of 2nd objective captured 64th Bde. will dispose Brigade so as to be able to occupy 1st objective in case of need or to take up advance tomorrow AAA 110th Bde. will probably move to ground E. of CANAL DU NORD this evening so all preparations should be made AAA Reserve M.G. Coy. will move via EQUANCOURT to about V.17.d. forthwith. AAA This Coy. will move in future when leading Bde.H.Q. moves and will maintain liaison Officer with latter AAA

10th September 1918.

G.X.963. Warning Order AAA Attack on CHAPEL HILL did not succeed this morning AAA 110th Inf. Bde. will relieve 64th Inf. Bde. tonight AAA 110th Inf. Bde. will also be prepared to advance under a barrage and occupy the YELLOW LINE from CHAPEL HILL to Southern Div. Boundary AAA On relief 64th Inf. Bde. will move to EQUANCOURT Trench System with one Battn. about SOREL LE GRAND AAA

App 32

21 Div.
G. 997.

REPORT ON OPERATIONS FROM 17th to 20th September 1918.

Map 57.c. S.E. 1/20,000.

Divisional Order No.233. issued for the attack on the enemy's positions on September 18th. The 62nd Inf. Bde. were ordered to capture VAUCELLETTE FARM and the line of ridge through X.19. and X.20.c. The 110th Inf. Bde. on the right and the 64th Inf. Bde. on left were to pass through the 62nd Inf. Bde. and attack and capture the line BEET Trench, MEUNIER Trench, MEATH Post and LIMERICK Post.

17th September 1918.

5.50 a.m. There was no change in the situation during the night. The enemy continually shelled the FINS - HEUDECOURT Road. Hostile bombing aeroplanes dropped bombs around MANANCOURT, EQUANCOURT and SOREL LE GRAND, which places were also occasionally shelled by H.V. guns.

6.10 a.m. The relief of the 19th Inf. Bde. 33rd, Division, by the 62nd Inf. Bde. was complete and G.O.C. 21st Division assumed command of the Sector.
Except for desultory enemy shelling in the forward area and occasional H.V. shelling of MANANCOURT and ETRICOURT, the day passed quietly. There was no change in the situation.

18th September 1918.

5.15 a.m. Situation during the night remained unchanged. The enemy fired a few gas shells into the HEUDECOURT Valley.

6.15 a.m. Situation at 6 a.m. Verbal report received by the 62nd Inf. Bde. stated that the left Battalion had gained the first objective , i.e., CAVALRY SUPPORT. Very little hostile retaliation to our barrage.

7.10 a.m. The 62nd Inf. Bde. reported verbally that the whole of the first objective had been gained on the Divisional front.

/8 a.m........

8 a.m. Situation 7.45 a.m. The whole of the second objective of the 62nd Inf. Bde. had been captured, except the extreme right at about X.26.a.5.9. where the situation was not yet known. The attack of the 64th Inf. Bde. on the final objective had started to time, but no news as to progress had yet been received.

8.45 a.m. The Cyclist Squadron attached to the Division was ordered to report to H.Q., 64th Inf. Bde. as soon as possible. (G.X.233 and 234).

9.10 a.m. 64th Inf. Bde. were ordered to communicate with Divisional Headquarters before using the Cyclists as the situation on the right of the 62nd Inf. Bde was not clear. Until the situation was satisfactory, the cyclists would be at the disposal of the 62nd Inf. Bde. to be used on their right flank. (G.X.236 and 239).

9.30 a.m. Situation 9 a.m. Situation as regards 62nd Inf. Bde. remained unchanged. Touch had been gained with the 58th Division on the right at X.19.c.2.0. but no news yet received as to touch in PLANE Trench. Touch had also been gained with the 17th Division on the left near VAUCELLETTE FARM. Both 110th and 64th Inf. Bdes. had passed through to the attack on the final objectives up to time.

10.25 a.m. Situation at 10.15 a.m. The 58th Division reported that their troops in POPLAR Trench stated that the 6th Leicestershire Regt. were well on ahead. No reports had yet been received from either the 64th or 110th Inf. Bdes, but F.O.O's reported the advance appeared to be going well and prisoners were coming in.

10.50 a.m. Pigeon message received from 15th Durham Light Infantry timed 8.30 a.m. stated that they had occupied RACKET Trench and Copse in X.13.b.

11.30 a.m. Left Battalion 64th Inf. Bde. report timed 10.40 a.m. stated that the Support Trench to MEUNIER Trench had been captured and prisoners and guns taken. One 10.5 c.m. battery had been captured with teams complete. No definite report had been received from the right Brigade, but our

/troops......

troops had been seen nearing MEATH Post and to be held up by heavy M.G. fire from LIMERICK Post.

11.30 a.m. The 62nd Inf. Bde. reported that touch had now been gained with the 58th Division at X.20.c.2.0.

11.45 a.m. The Cyclists were now placed at the disposal of the 64th Inf. Bde. for exploitation (G.X.245).

11.55 a.m. The Div. Cav. Troop was ordered to move at once to Headquarters 64th Inf. Bde. where they would come under the orders of that Brigade and be used for the exploitation of VILLERS GUISLAIN (G.X.246 and 247).

Situation 11.45 a.m. The right Brigade reported that steady progress was being made towards the final objective, but no touch could be gained with the 12th Division on the right and heavy M.G. fire was coming from LARK SPUR. The Left Battalion during the advance met a heavy counter-attack in LINNET VALLEY. Prisoners were taken and the advance resumed.

12.30 p.m. Report received from the left Battalion, 64th Inf. Bde. timed 10.25 a.m. that they had captured the whole of BENT Trench at 9 a.m. and held it with Platoon Posts from X.8.d.7.1. to X.8.a.5.4. They also held a portion of GUISLAIN Trench in X.8.d. Officer patrols had been pushed forward towards VILLERS GUISLAIN. Casualties were slight.

12.55 p.m. The 62nd Inf. Bde. were ordered to place one Coy. of their left Battalion at the disposal of the 64th Inf. Bde. who were to use this Coy. to relieve a Coy. of their Reserve Battalion. (G.X.252).

2.30 p.m. Situation. On right Brigade front MEATH LANE and MEATH POST believed to be occupied. The situation on the extreme right was obscure and further attacks on LIMERICK Post in conjunction with the 12th Division were being made.

3.30 p.m. 110th Inf. Bde reported that constant Machine Gun fire and sniping were coming from enemy pocket in X.25. Central.

Situation 3 p.m. 64th Inf. Bde. held the whole of the final objectives from left Boundary to LEITH WALK in X.15.d. 110th Inf. Bde. continued the line from MEATH POST (exclusive) then PARRS Trench to LIMERICK LANE. Situation on the extreme right was still obscure. Troops who had captured

/MEATH.....

MEATH Post earlier in the day had been heavily counter-attacked and forced to withdraw.

4.40 p.m. Report from 64th Inf. Bde. timed 3.40 p.m. stated that the enemy counter-attacked the left of the 9th K.O.Y.L.I. in BEET Trench about 2.30 p.m. Troops had been forced back slightly. The situation was quickly restored by an immediate counter-attack and the whole line regained.

5.35 p.m. 62nd Inf. Bde. were ordered to place the Coy. of the 1st Lincolnshire Regt. detailed to hold RACKET Trench at the disposal of the 64th Inf. Bde, to replace one Coy. 15th Durham Light Infantry. who had been used to reinforce the left flank (G.X.262).

7.30 p.m. Situation. 64th Inf. Bde. unchanged, with defensive flank from X.15.d.8.9. to X.15.c.Central, where the line was continued by the 110th Inf. Bde. to X.21.a.5.6. - MEATH LANE - Road in X.20.b. and d. The Division on right reported enemy to be still in POPLAR Trench, CHESTNUT AVENUE and CULLEN Post.

8 p.m. Orders issued for the 110th Inf. Bde. to relieve the 62nd Inf. Bde. in PLANE Trench during the night. The 62nd Inf. Bde. were to hold the VAUCELLETTE FARM Ridge from the Div. Southern boundary to SKITTLE ALLEY inclusive, taking over the N. portion of this line from the 17th Division. 64th Inf.Bde. were to hold the final objective and to use all their resources for this purpose. 62nd Inf. Bde. were to place one Battn. at the disposal of the 64th Inf. Bde. for the purpose of holding supporting position West of BEET FACTORY (X.14.a. The R.E. and Pioneers were to construct and wire a line of Posts on the general line PLANE Trench, Spur X.20.a. West of Factory, FIVES Trench. 110th Inf. Bde. were to be prepared to carry out an attack on LIMERICK Post the following morning. (Order No.234).

19th September 1918.

6 a.m. Situation. The enemy counter-attacked the 110th Inf. Bde. in Area X.21.a. at about 4.15 p.m. on the 18th inst,

/but.......

but was repulsed. During the night the enemy forced the 64th Inf. Bde. to withdraw from LEITH WALK in X.15.d. Northwards up MEUNIER TRENCH to about X.15.b.3.7. A counter-attack by the 64 Inf. Bde. to restore the situation was being made. Counter-preparation was fired at 4.45 a.m. and finished at 5.10 am. Considerable hostile M.G. fire throughout the night from LIMERICK POST.

3.30 p.m.
Orders issued for the relief of the Division by the 33rd Div. On relief 110 Inf. Bde. were to move to the area ETRICOURT and MANANCOURT. 62 Inf. Bde. to the area West and South West of LE MESNIL EN ARROUAISE. 64 Inf. Bde. to LES BOEUFS. (D.O.235).
The situation during the day remained unchanged with very little hostile activity.

5.45 p.m.
Under orders from Corps, the command of the Artillery covering the right sector would pass to the G.O.C. 33rd Division on completion of relief. (Corps G.668).

9.40 p.m.
64 Inf. Bde. were ordered to hand over the command of the Cyclist Squadron to the 98th Inf. Bde. on completion of the relief. (G.X.317).

20th September, 1918.

4.40 a.m.
The relief of the Division by the 33rd Division was complete and the command passed to G.O.C. 33rd Division.
Prisoners and guns captured during the above operations were :-

		Officers.	O.R.
Prisoners		27	667
Guns	...	15	

Telegrams to accompany REPORT ON OPERATIONS from 17th to 20th September 1918.

<u>18th September 1918.</u>

<u>G.X.233.</u> Cyclists being sent to you for use either as mobile reserve or exploitation purposes.

<u>G.X.234.</u> Report with your troop to General Edwards at 64th Inf. Bde. H.Q. in Sunken Road, W.22.c. as soon as possible AAA You should assemble troop some spot West of W.22.c. and proceed to Bde. H.Q. yourself for orders.

<u>G.X.236.</u> Reference G.X.233. AAA Situation on right of 62nd Inf. Bde. not yet clear AAA Communicate with Div. H.Q. before using Cyclists AAA If communication not possible, communicate with 62nd Bde. AAA Cyclists will be at disposal of 62nd Inf. Bde. for use on their right if required. AAA If 62nd Inf. Bde. satisfied as to situation on right Cyclists will be used by you in accordance with G.X.233.

<u>G.X.239.</u> Cyclists have been sent to report to 64th Inf. Bde. AAA They are placed under your orders until the situation on your right is clear AAA When situation is clear Cyclists revert to 64th Inf. Bde AAA

<u>G.X.245.</u> Cyclists will now be used by 64th Inf. Bde. for exploitation AAA

<u>G.X.246.</u> Cavalry Troop has been ordered to report your H.Q. forthwith AAA Troop to be used for exploitation of VILLERS GUISLAIN.

<u>G.X.247.</u> Move at once to H.Q. 64th Inf. Bde. in sunken road W.22.c. AAA On arrival you will come under orders of 64th Inf. Bde. and will be used for exploitation of VILLERS GUISLAIN.

<u>G.X.252.</u> 62nd Inf. Bde. will place one Coy. of their left Battn. at disposal of 64th Inf. Bde AAA If required, 64th Inf. Bde. will use this Coy. to relieve a Coy. of their Reserve Battn AAA 64th Inf. Bde. will inform 62nd Inf. Bde. if Coy. is used AAA

<u>G.X.262.</u> One Coy 1st Lincoln Regt. detailed to hold RACKET Trench, is placed at disposal of 64th Inf. Bde. to replace one Coy. 15th D.L.I. used to reinforce left Flank AAA

<u>19th September 1918.</u>

<u>G.668. from Corps.</u> Reference G.650 today AAA Command of artillery covering right Sector will pass on completion of infantry relief when command of Sector will pass from G.O.C. 21 Div. to G.O.C. 33 Div AAA C.R.A. 21 Div, will move to 33 Div H.Q. and remain for 24 hours with C.R.A. 33 Div AAA

<u>G.X. 317.</u> 64th Inf. Bde will hand over command of Cyclist Squadron to 98th Bde. to-night AAA On completion of relief Cyclist Sqdn. will come under orders of 33 Div AAA

SECRET.

21 Div.
G. 42.

App 28

SUMMARY OF OPERATIONS for period Sept. 26th to Oct. 10th.1918.

Ref; Sheet 57.C. S.E.) 1/20,000.
57.C. S.W.)

Orders were issued for the Division to relieve the 17th Division in the left Sector, V Corps front, on night 25th/26th instant. 110 Inf. Bde. relieving the 51st Inf. Bde. on the right and the 62 Inf. Bde. relieving the 50th Inf. Bde. on the left. The 64th Inf. Bde. relieving the 52nd Inf. Bde. in support.(D.O.236)

In conjunction with operations to the North, the 21st Division was ordered ;-

(a) To capture AFRICAN TRENCH from Q.31.a.6.5 to the Northern Divisional Boundary.

(b) To advance along the QUENTIN RIDGE and capture GONNELIEU at the same time as the 33rd Division on the right attacked VILLERS GUISLAIN. (D.O.237).

September 26th, 1918.

3.5 a.m. The relief of the 17th Division was complete and command of the Sector passed to G.O.C., 21st Division.

The situation throughout the night was quiet except for slight hostile shelling of back areas including a few gas shells.

4.50 p.m. Situation remained unchanged throughout the day. There was intermittent shelling of SOMME ALLEY, GAUCHE ALLEY, CHAPEL HILL and W.12.d., chiefly with 5.9".

September 27th, 1918.

At Zero hour, 7.52 a.m., in conjunction with the attack, 'K' Special Coy. R.E. successfully discharged 110 oil drums into the Western outskirts of GOUZEAUCOURT.

9.30 a.m. 62 Inf. Bde. reported that the right Coy. had reached their objective and were holding strong post in sunken road at Q.35.a.8.8. The situation on the left was not yet known.

/10.15 a.m.......

10.15 a.m. R.A.F. Observer reported our troops in strength at Q.29.c.90.50. Returning wounded also reported our troops on objective. Enemy were reported at Q.29.c.80.75. and Q.29.a.85.20. These were being dealt with by Stokes Mortars.

11.30 a.m. 62nd Infantry Brigade report timed 11.15 a.m. stated that three Coys. left Battalion attacked AFRICAN Trench at 7.52 a.m. The right and centre Coys. gained their objective but the left Coy. was held up by enfilade Machine Gun fire from the North. The Centre Coy. had worked Northwards up AFRICAN Trench and gained the remainder of the objective where a block had been established on the Divisional Boundary. No touch had been gained with the 5th Division on the left and it was understood that their right Battalion had been held up.

12 noon. Divisional Headquarters closed at U.5.c.3.2. and reopened at V.4.b.2.5.

5 p.m. Situation remained unchanged during the day. The enemy intermittently shelled the Divisional front.

Brigades were informed that the operation ordered in para 1(b) of Divisional Order No.237 would not take place tonight, but would probably take place on the night 28th/29th September (G.498).

28th September 1918.

5.10 a.m. During the night the enemy put down a heavy bombardment with Artillery and Trench Mortars on AFRICAN Trench and subsequent counter-attack forced our troops to withdraw. The 62nd Inf. Bde. now held their original line from Q.35.a.5.4. to Q.29.c.0.1. where they were in touch with the 5th Division.

10.40 a.m. The 62nd Infantry Brigade reported that the enemy had evacuated AFRICAN Trench as far North as the Divisional Boundary and that patrols were pushing forward towards GOUZEAUCOURT.

11.35 a.m. Orders issued to the effect that 110th Infantry Brigade were to occupy the line GREEN LANE, GREEN SWITCH, should they meet with no resistance and to get in touch with the 5th Division at R.26.a.9.1. When this line had been made

11 a.m. Report received from the 62nd Inf. Bde. that patrols of the 1st Linc. Regt. had reached trench running from Q.36.c.0. to road Q.36.a.0.2. and found it clear of the enemy. The patrol proceeded to the W. edge of GOUZEAUCOURT & met with no oppositio

good, patrols were to be sent to the BROWN Line (line of road X.3.a. - R.33.c. and a.) but no advance in force was to be made until touch had been established with the 5th Division on the left. Should patrols still report no resistance, 110th Infantry Brigade would occupy the BROWN Line and send patrols to the GREEN Line (ROSE TRENCH - RIBBLE TRENCH R.35). As soon as 110th Inf. Bde. had occupied GREEN LANE, GREEN SWITCH, and their patrols had reached the BROWN Line, 62nd Infantry Brigade were to assemble in GOUZEAUCOURT VALLEY (G.X.515).

1 p.m. 62nd Infantry Brigade reported a group of enemy snipers located in Quarry R.31.c.9.7. who were being dealt with.

3.10 p.m. 62nd Infantry Brigade reported that left Battn. had reached R.35.a.5.9. without opposition and had located party of enemy in FLAG RAVINE R.20.a.

4.35 p.m. Situation. Our troops occupied GREEN LANE and R.A.F. Observer reported that GREEN SWITCH as far North as R.26.a.6.0. was also occupied.

6.15 p.m. 21st Battalion Machine Gun Corps were ordered to send the two Companies 17th Battn. Machine Gun Corps attached to them for barrage work back to rejoin their own Unit. (G.X.526.).

7.30 p.m. Orders issued for the attack on the GREEN and BROWN Lines early the following morning. 110th Infantry Bde. were to attack on the right with 62nd Infantry Brigade on the left. Two Tanks were placed at the disposal of each Brigade. One Machine Gun Coy. was also detailed to accompany each Brigade (Div. Order No. 238).

9.10 p.m. Situation at 9 p.m. Line ran VILLERS TRENCH X.2.a.5.3. along GREEN LANE, GREEN SWITCH TO R.26.a.4.0. Enemy heavily shelled the Eastern edge of GAUCHE WOOD at 8.30 p.m.

10.20 p.m. Ref. Order No. 238, instructions were issued that when the GREEN Line had been captured patrols were to be sent forward to the Canal. If no opposition was met with the C.R.E was to begin making arrangements to bridge the Canal (G.X.536)

/11.25 p.m.....

11.25 p.m. The two supply tanks were placed under the orders of the 62nd Infantry Brigade (G.X.547).

September 29th,1918.

1.30 a.m. Report received from 110th Inf. Bde. timed 12.20 a.m. giving the situation as follows :- 6th Leicestershire Regt. held VILLERS Trench X.2.a.8.0. thence N.W. along VILLERS Trench GREEN LANE to cross roads R.31.d.9.1. where they were in touch with the 7th Leicestershire Regt. Line was continued N.W. along road thence North along GREEN LANE, GREEN SWITCH to cross Roads R.26.c.4.0.

5 a.m. Situation during the night remained unchanged. The attack started at 3.30 a.m. but no details had yet been received.

7.15 a.m. Situation. 110th Infantry Brigade position was obscure, but attack apparently held up by heavy Machine Gun fire from R.32.c. and also from the direction of the CEMETERY X.2.d. No reports yet received from the 62nd Infantry Brigade.

8 a.m. No change on the 110th Infantry Brigade front. The 62nd Infantry Brigade had been held up along the whole Brigade front West of GONNELIEU, which place was strongly held by the enemy with many Machine Guns. 62nd Infantry Brigade were now reorganizing in GREEN SWITCH. Considerable hostile Artillery and Machine Gun fire had been encountered.

9.20 a.m. 64th Infantry Brigade were ordered to hold two Battalions in readiness to move at quarter of an hours' notice to occupy LOWLAND TRENCH, HEATHER TRENCH and AFRICAN TRENCH within Divisional Boundaries. (G.X.556).

10 a.m. Report received from 110th Infantry Brigade timed 9 a.m. stated that the right Coy. 6th Leicestershire Regt held the CEMETERY X.2.d.9.9. - CROSS POST - Road junction X.2.b.65.20. thence N.E. for about 100 yards along the Sunken Road. This Coy. was in touch with the 33rd Division on the right. Remaining Coys. of this Battalion were along LANCASHIRE TRENCH, GREEN LANE to about R.31.d.5.2. A party was bombing down VILLERS TRENCH to gain touch with the forward Coy. near the Cemetery. 7th Leic. Regt. were established

/in.........

in GREEN LANE from R.31.d.5.2 to about R.31.d.Central whence line was continued along GREEN SWITCH. Attack had been held up by heavy Machine Gun fire from R.32.c. and VILLERS GUISLAIN.
Situation of 62 Inf. Bde. was unchanged. The enemy held RESERVE LINE and GIN AVENUE in strength.

10.50 a.m. 110 Inf. Bde. were ordered to place one Battalion at the disposal of the 62nd Inf. Bde. This Battalion was to move at once to the vicinity of Quarry R.25.d. Battalion would be used to advance along the BANTEUX SPUR. 62 Inf. Bde. were to send as much of the Brigade as could quickly be made available round the North of GONNELIEU towards R.28.Central and to get in touch with the right of the 5th Division at that place. 110 Inf. Bde. were to take over the defence of GREEN SWITCH as far North as R.26.c.3.0. (G.X.562).

11.10 a.m. 64 Inf. Bde. were ordered to move one Battalion forthwith to area Q.35.c - W.5.a. On arrival this Battalion was to be prepared either to hold AFRICAN TRENCH, HEATHER TRENCH within Divisional Boundaries or to concentrate quickly and move either North or South of GOUZEAUCOURT followed by remainder of Brigade to exploit success. (G.X.564).
The Cyclist Squadron was transferred from the 110 Inf. Bde. to the 62 Inf. Bde. and were ordered to move to 62 Inf. Bde. H.Q. as soon as possible. (G.X.565).

12.10 p.m. Situation at 12 noon. Two Battalions 62 Inf. Bde. moving through R.20 and R.21 with objective BANTEUX SPUR supported by one Battalion 110 Inf. Bde. The Third Battalion, 62 Inf. Bde., was working round the North of GONNELIEU.

2.50 p.m. 64 Inf. Bde. were ordered to move another Battalion to area Q.35.c. W.5.a. the third Battalion to remain in Q.32. (G.X.573).

4.35 p.m. Situation on Divisional Front unchanged. The Battalions of the 62 Inf. Bde. which were moving to the North of GONNELIEU were now in the following positions :- One Battalion in FERN TRENCH with right on road at R.21.c.7.0. Troops of the 5th Division were also in this trench. One Battalion in NEWPORT TRENCH and third Battalion in Sunken Road R.19.b. Enemy held JAM TRENCH and LA VACQUERIE Road in strength. Some enemy Machine Guns were still in LA VACQUERIE.

9.5 p.m. Instructions received from the Corps that the Division was to re-organise and rest during the 30th September. The Div. was to be prepared to follow up the enemy on any sign of a retirement. All enemy trenches and positions would be kept under intense harassing fire. (V Corps G.180).

/10.10 p.m...

10.10 p.m. Orders issued to the effect that active patrolling was to be carried out during the night. Should GONNELIEU and Brown Line be entered by patrols without resistance, they were to be at once occupied in force and patrols pushed on to the Green Line. Should this line be found empty, it was to be occupied and patrols pushed on to the Canal. All available Heavy Artillery and Field Howitzers were to bombard GONNELIEU from 4.5 a.m. to 5 a.m. 64 Inf. Bde. were ordered to remain in their present positions until further orders. (D.O.239).

September 30th, 1918.

5.20 a.m. Situation remained unchanged during the night, with very little hostile activity. The 62 Inf. Bde. reported that the Reserve Line was very strongly held by the enemy at 4.50 a.m.

10 a.m. Owing to 5th Division reporting that they had patrols in GONNELIEU and BANTEUX, 62 Inf. Bde. were ordered to send patrols through the 5th Division area so as to enter GONNELIEU from the North. These patrols were to be supported by stronger bodies. 110 Inf. Bde. were to send patrols to the Brown Line and to reinforce them as soon as VILLERS GUISLAIN was occupied by the 33rd Division. 62 Inf. Bde. were to send one Battalion round the North of GONNELIEU to work down GLASGOW and PRESTON TRENCHES with objective Green Line and Southern slopes of BANTEUX SPUR. (G.X.594).

10.50 a.m. 62 Inf. Bde. report timed 10.15 a.m. stated that one Battalion had gone through GONNELIEU and occupied Brown Line as far South as KITCHEN CRATER. Another Battalion was working round the North of GONNELIEU towards the Green Line, the third Battalion being in support. 110 Inf. Bde. reported that the Cemetery at X.2.d.9.9 was still strongly held.

11.50 a.m. 110 Inf. Bde. had occupied the Brown Line and were pushing on towards the Green Line, to which line the 62 Inf. Bde. were also advancing.

12.10 p.m. 110 and 62 Inf. Bdes. as soon as the Green Line had been made good were to send forward strong fighting patrols to the Canal to seize crossings and establish bridge-heads on the Eastern Bank. 64 Inf. Bde. were to move to area just West of QUENTIN RIDGE forthwith and to be prepared on receipt of orders to advance through the leading Brigades, to cross the Canal and occupy the HINDENBURG

/LINE.....

LINE between BANCOURT FARM and BANTOUZELLE (both exclusive). The Cyclist Squadron would be transferred from 62 Inf. Bde. to 64 Inf. Bde. when latter Brigade took up the advance. (D.O.240).

6 p.m. Patrols had now reached the West bank of the Canal but were prevented from crossing the Canal by Heavy Machine Gun fire from the Eastern bank. All bridges had been destroyed.

7.30 p.m. 110 and 62 Inf. Bdes. were ordered to continue to hold the Green Line and to push out patrols who were to try and cross the Canal by any available crossings. Should any bridges be found repairable, and if hostile fire permitted, the R.E. were to construct crossings. Such crossings were to be guarded by posts on the Western bank in order to prevent the enemy blowing them up. 64 Inf. Bde. were to remain in their present positions. (D.O.241).

10.20 p.m. Situation for the remainder of the day remained unchanged. The enemy were reported to be holding the trench line S.2.c. & a. to M.31.d. & b. The bridge at M.31.b.1.1 blew up just as our patrol was about to cross.

1st October, 1918.

5.25 a.m. The situation remained unchanged. Slight hostile shelling of the forward area at intervals during the night.

10 a.m. Patrols during the night reported that no enemy had been encountered on the West bank of the Canal. One German who had been left behind in HONNECOURT was captured. BANTOUZELLE was held by the enemy but in what strength could not be determined.

4.50 p.m. Situation remained unchanged throughout the day. Slight hostile Artillery and Machine Gun fire on area West of Canal.

2nd October, 1918.

During the night 62 Inf. Bde. succeeded in getting one bridge across the Canal South of BANTEUX but all attempts to pass troops over this bridge were stopped by heavy Rifle and Machine Gun fire from the Eastern bank.

Later in the day this bridge was destroyed by a direct hit from an enemy Trench Mortar.

Situation on the Divisional front remained unchanged.

(2nd Oct...

3rd October, 1918.

Situation remained unchanged. All attempts to cross the canal were stopped by heavy Machine Gun fire.

Orders issued for the 110 Inf. Bde. to extend their left during the night 3rd/4th October, and take over the front now held by 62 Inf. Bde. On relief, 62 Inf. Bde. to withdraw to the area Q.34, Q.35, W.4, W.5. (D.O.242).

12.30 p.m. The M.G.Coy. attached to 64 Inf. Bde. were ordered to reconnoitre defensive positions on the QUENTIN RIDGE. These positions were only to be occupied in case of hostile attack. (B.X.662).

6 p.m. In conjunction with the attack being made in a Northerly direction by the 50th Division from LE CATELET, the Divisional Artillery and Machine Gun Battalion were ordered to keep the HINDENBURG LINE under steady continuous fire whilst these operations were in progress. 110 Inf. Bde. were to keep touch with the enemy by means of patrols endeavouring to cross the canal by means of rafts. As soon as the 110 Inf. Bde. had gained bridge-head on East bank, 64 Inf. Bde. were to be prepared to cross the Canal and establish themselves in the HINDENBURG LINE within Divisional Boundaries. The Cyclist Squadron was placed under orders of 64 Inf. Bde. (D.O.243).

4th October, 1918.

During the day and night the situation remained unchanged. Patrols were unable to cross the canal owing to hostile fire. There was slight hostile shelling of BANTEUX SPUR throughout the day.

Under orders from Corps two extra Mobile Newton Mortars were placed at the disposal of the Division. (V Corps C.T.283).

5th October, 1918.

5.5 a.m. Situation remained unchanged during the night. Practically no enemy activity.

12.5 p.m. Owing to all indications pointing to the fact that the enemy had withdrawn opposite the Corps front, and R.A.F. Observers reporting the HINDENBURG LINE deserted, 110 Inf. Bde. were ordered to establish a bridge-head round the Eastern outskirts of BANTOUZELLE under cover of which the C.R.E. was to construct bridges to take Infantry in fours. As soon as this objective

/had.......

had been gained, 110 Inf. Bde. were to seize a more extended bridge-head as follows :- ARNOULD QUARRY - C.T. through M.33.a. and M.27.d. - HINDENBURG SUPPORT LINE from M.27.d.3.5 to M.27.b.0.3, thence via RED FARM to Canal. Fighting patrols were then to be sent to HINDENBURG SUPPORT LINE between RANCOURT FARM exclusive and M.27.d. As soon as patrols had reached this line, 110 Inf. Bde. were to occupy it. 64 Inf. Bde. were to move the heads of leading Battalions to BANTEUX forthwith and to start crossing canal as soon as 110 Inf. Bde. had gained the larger bridge-head. 64 Inf. Bde. would then pass through the 110 Inf. Bde. with the following objectives :- HINDENBURG SUPPORT LINE if not already captured by the 110 Inf. Bde. Line of road MONTECOUVEZ FARM - BONNE ENFANCE FARM within Divisional Boundaries. When latter objective had been made good, patrols were to be sent to the MASNIERES - BEAUREVOIR TRENCH SYSTEM to ascertain if it was occupied by the enemy or not. 62 Inf. Bde. were ordered to move to area R.28.c. & d. R.29.c. & d. R.24. as soon as vacated by 110 and 64 Inf. Bdes. (D.O.244).

__2.40 p.m.__ 110 Inf. Bde. reported that the larger bridge-head had been gained and their patrols had been seen in M.33.d. and M.34.c. Troops of the Division on the right had been seen in and about RANCOURT FARM.

__3 p.m.__ Divisional Headquarters closed at V.4.b.3.5 and opened at W.11.c.5.8.

__4.30 p.m.__ The HINDENBURG SUPPORT LINE had been captured within the Divisional Boundaries. Patrols had been pushed on to the line MONTECOUVEZ FARM - BONNE ENFANCE FARM, from both of which hostile Machine Gun fire was coming and also from Copse M.36.c. Touch had been gained with troops on the right. Troops on the left were reported to be on the line M.23.c. - M.17.d.

64 Inf. Bde. reported that 15th Battalion, Durham Light Infantry were crossing the Canal and Cyclists had reached M.34.Cen. at 3 p.m. and reported enemy Machine Gun in GRATTE PANCHE FARM. At 3.15 p.m. this farm was seen to be on fire.

__5 p.m.__ 64 Inf. Bde. reported that Cyclists had reached M.35.b.2.9 but were encountering M.G. fire from both flanks. Dismounted patrol was being sent out.

__5.30 p.m.__ 64 Inf. Bde. were now passing through 110 Inf. Bde. on their way to the line MONTECOUVEZ FARM - BONNE ENFANCE FARM.

/7.15 p.m.....

7.15 p.m. Report from Cyclists timed 4 p.m. stated BONNE ENFANCE FARM clear of enemy. Machine Gun fire was still coming from the direction of MONTECOUVEZ FARM.

Two bridges at R.36.c.9.9 and R.36.c.9.8 had now been completed for Infantry in fours and pack animals.

8.45 p.m. Orders issued for the advance to be continued on the 6th October, 64 Inf. Bde. acting as Advance Guard Brigade. Objectives as follows :-

(a) Line of road M.33.d. & b. - HAUT FARM - HURTEBISE FARM.

(b) WALINCOURT Village and high ground N.18.a. patrols being pushed forward into SORVAL CHATEAU and SELVIGNY.

Touch was to be gained if possible on both flanks at the conclusion of each bound, but the advance was not to be delayed for this purpose. 78th Bde. R.F.A. would come under the direct orders of 64 Inf. Bde. 110 Inf. Bde. would act as Supporting Brigade and would move to the line MONTECOUVEZ FARM - BONNE ENFANCE FARM as soon as the 64 Inf. Bde. had completely passed over the MASNIERES - BEAUREVOIR TRENCH SYSTEM. 62 Inf. Bde. would be reserve Brigade and was to move to the HINDENBURG SUPPORT LINE as soon as the 110 Inf. Bde. was clear of this line. The policy for the 64 Inf. Bde. was to manoeuvre the enemy out of any positions he might be holding without engaging the Brigade in a frontal attack on a strong position. (D.O.245).

10.50 p.m. Cyclists reported the enemy still holding MONTECOUVEZ FARM. No further reports had been received as to the situation of the 64 Inf. Bde.

Two bridges at the lock M.25.d.8.6 had been completed to carry Infantry in fours. One of these bridges was capable of taking field guns. Six other bridges had been completed for Infantry only.

6th October, 1918.

5.20 a.m. 64 Inf. Bde. held the line BONABUS FARM exclusive to BONNE ENFANCE FARM inclusive. Enemy still held MONTECOUVEZ FARM. Very little hostile activity during the night.

/8 a.m......

8 a.m. 64 Inf. Bde. reported that MONTECOUVEZ FARM had been captured. Our troops were also reported to be entering BEAUREVOIR LINE in T.2.a. but this report was not yet confirmed.

11.30 a.m. 64 Inf. Bde. reported the situation at 10 a.m. as follows :- The Right Battalion had two Coys. in sunken road T.1.b. - N.31.c. One Coy. MONTECOUVEZ FARM. One Coy. in support M.36.c. Left Battalion one Coy. along road N.25.a., one Coy. BONNE ENFANCE FARM. Two Coys. in trench line M.29.b. & d. Right Battalion was endeavouring to work down sunken road T.2.c. but was meeting with heavy opposition.

11.55 a.m. In conjunction with the attacks to be made by Divisions on the right, 64th Inf. Bde. were ordered to attack and occupy ANGLES CHATEAU at Dusk, the 110 Inf. Bde. being ordered to place one Battalion at the disposal of 64 Inf. Bde. to protect the right flank. These orders were afterwards cancelled.

5.15 p.m. Situation. Right Battalion 64 Inf. Bde. remained unchanged. Troops of the 64 Inf. Bde. who were occupying BONNE ENFANCE FARM were withdrawn from the buildings owing to hostile shell fire and now held sunken road M.30.b. & d.

9 p.m. Under instructions received from V Corps 2 Coys. 17th Bn. M.G.C. were placed at the disposal of the Division for barrage work. (V Corps G.389).

10.30 p.m. Right Battalion 64 Inf. Bde. now held trench line T.1.c.5.6 to T.1.b.8.5. Otherwise there was no change in the situation.

7th October, 1918.

5.30 a.m. Situation remained unaltered during the night with very little enemy activity. Touch had been gained with the 38th Division on the right.

9.30 a.m. Situation unchanged. Patrols reported that the BEAUREVOIR LINE was strongly held and the wire to be in good condition. Attempts to extend Northwards along the trench from T.1.b.8.5 were strongly resisted and no progress made.

7.30 p.m. Orders issued for the attack on the enemy's positions to be continued on Oct. 8th, the objectives of the Division being as follows :-

(a) ANGLES CHATEAU to trench N.33.a.1.6.

(b) Trench N.33.a.1.6 - HAUT FARM - HURTEBISE FARM.

(c) WALINCOURT and high ground N.18.a.

The attack on the first objective was to be carried out by the 64th Inf. Bde. on the right and the 110 Inf. Bde. on the left, Zero hour would be 1 a.m. The attack on the second objective would be carried out by the 110 Inf. Bde., Zero hour being 5.15 a.m. The attack on the third objective would be carried out by the 62nd Inf. Bde., Zero hour being 8 a.m. After the capture of the third objective, the 62nd Inf. Bde. was to send out patrols to the Eastern edge of GARD WOOD - SORVAL CHATEAU - SELVIGNY Village. The Cyclist Squadron was placed at the disposal of the 62nd Inf. Bde. for this purpose. Should SELVIGNY be found unoccupied, reconnoitring patrols were to be pushed out towards CAULLERY. (D.O.246).

[illegible] : Situation remained unchanged throughout the remainder of the day. Enemy shelled MONTECOUVEZ and BONNE ENFANCE FARMS.

<u>October 8th, 1918.</u>

<u>5 a.m.</u> 64 Inf. Bde. reported that the BEAUREVOIR LINE had been occupied but no news yet received of further progress. Wounded Coy. Comdr. from the 110th Inf. Bde. stated that he had been wounded about 200 yards from the objective. Touch had been gained on both flanks. Hostile shelling during the assembly of the troops was negligible.

<u>8 a.m.</u> Divisional Headquarters closed at REVELON FARM and opened at M.32.b.7.1.

<u>9 a.m.</u> Both 64th and 110th Inf. Bdes. reported the first objective had been captured. 64 Inf. Bde. were in touch with the 38th Division at ANGLES CHATEAU. 110 Inf. Bde. reported the assembly and forming up of troops for the second attack was carried out successfully and troops had moved off well under the barrage. ARDISSART FARM had been captured. Many prisoners were reported coming in.

<u>9.15 a.m.</u> 110 Inf. Bde. reported second objective had been captured and the 62nd Inf. Bde. were passing through on their way to the third objective. There was considerable hostile shelling of the BEAUREVOIR LINE.

/9.40 a.m.

9.40 a.m. 64 Inf. Bde. and 110 Inf. Bde. were ordered to collect all available troops less one Battalion each to be ready on receipt of orders, to advance in support of 62nd Inf. Bde. Each Brigade was to keep one Battalion and 8 Machine Guns as garrison of the first and second objectives. (G.A.102).

10.45 a.m. No report had yet been received as to the progress of the 62nd Inf. Bde. The situation in ANGLES CHATEAU was not yet clear, as some enemy still appeared to be in the building. These were being 'mopped up'. Troops in HAUT FARM reported that the enemy could be seen retiring Eastwards and that hostile Artillery was also being withdrawn.

12.20 p.m. The 62nd Inf. Bde. line ran ANGLE WOOD inclusive - trench line through N.28.b. & d. to about N.22.c.8.4. Gap existed from this point to about N.21.b. whence line was believed to run through HURTEBISE COPSE - but this was not yet confirmed. Hostile field guns were firing from N.23.d.3.2 and were being engaged by our forward sections. The situation at ANGLES CHATEAU had been cleared up and our troops were in touch with 113th Inf. Bde. in the Quarry T.3.b.

1.30 p.m. Situation on right was unchanged. Further advance out of ANGLE WOOD was stopped owing to intense M.G. fire from MALINCOURT. The left Battalion of the 62nd Inf. Bde. had reached N.16.c. where touch had been gained with 37th Division. Patrols were being pushed across the stream and towards high ground N.18.a. but were meeting with considerable opposition, especially from GUILLEMIN FARM. 110 Inf. Bde. were ordered to be prepared to attack GUILLEMIN FARM and the high ground N.18.a. during the afternoon, probable Zero Hour being about 5 p.m. As a preparatory measure, two Battalions were to be moved forthwith to area West of BRISEUX WOOD (G.X.808).

3.5 p.m. 62 Inf. Bde. reported that the whole of the NAUROY - AUDIGNY LINE within Divisional Boundaries had been captured. Touch had been gained on both flanks. Enemy were seen to be limbering up guns in N.35.c. These were engaged by L.G. fire and casualties inflicted.

3.35 p.m. 64 Inf. Bde. were ordered to move one Battalion forthwith to ANGLES WOOD where it came under the orders of 62nd Inf. Bde. It would be used to assist 62nd Inf. Bde. in their advance on MALINCOURT. (G.X.813).

/5.20 p.m.....

5.20 p.m. The West edge of WALINCOURT and sunken road N.17.b. & d. were strongly held by enemy Machine Guns and further progress without a barrage was impossible. Attack would be re-newed with a barrage at 6 p.m.

11 p.m. Orders issued to the effect that when the 17th Division had passed through the 62nd Inf. Bde. on the 9th October, Brigades were, on orders being received from Division, to concentrate and re-organise in the following areas :-

62 Inf. Bde.	...	In Squares	N.17, 23 and 29.
64 : :	...	: :	N.28, 27 and 32.
110 : :	...	: :	N.22, 21 and 20.

The 17th and 21st Divisional Artilleries would come under orders of G.O.C., 17th Division as soon as that Division had passed through the 62nd Inf. Bde. (G.X.827).

The Cyclist Squadron was transferred to 17th Division (G.X.830).

9th October, 1918.

1.10 a.m. 62 Inf. Bde. reported the situation at 11 p.m. 8th Oct. to be as follows :- Line ran N.29.d.9.5 along sunken road N.9.b.5.7 - N.23.Central - thence to stream N.22.b.5.4 - thence along stream to N.16.Central. Posts had been established along the N.W. edge of MILL WOOD and also on the W. outskirts of WALINCOURT. The enemy was shelling all sunken roads in N.29. . and N.23. and also WALINCOURT with gas shell. GUILLEMIN FARM was strongly held by the enemy.

During the day the 62nd Inf. Bde. concentrated in WALINCOURT and the 64th and 110th Inf. Bdes. re-organised their Battalions in the present positions.

10th October, 1918.

9.5 a.m. 64 Inf. Bde. were ordered to move to billets in WALINCOURT. (G.X.864).

12.40 p.m. 110 Inf. Bde. were ordered to move during the afternoon to billets in CAULLERY. (G.X.869).

3.5 p.m. Divisional Headquarters closed M.32.b.7.1 and opened in WALINCOURT.

The following prisoners and guns were captured during these operations :-

	Officers.	O.R.	Guns.
Sept. 26th - Oct. 10th. ...	14	802.	5

Copy of Telegrams to accompany 21st Division Summary of Operations for period 26.9.18 to 10.10.18.

28th September, 1918.

G.X.526. 2 Coys. 17th M.G.Bn. attached to you will rejoin their own Battalion forthwith.

G.X.536. Ref: Order No.238. When Green Line objective has been captured patrols will be sent forward to the Canal. Reports will be rendered as to whether opposition is met. If no opposition C.R.E. will begin arrangements to bridge canal.

G.X.547. Supply tank will be under orders of 62nd Inf. Bde.

29th September, 1918.

G.X.556. Hold two Bns. in readiness to move at ¼ of an hours' notice to occupy LOWLAND TRENCH, HEATHER AND AFRICAN TRENCHES within Divl. Boundaries.

G.X.562. 110 Inf. Bde. will place one Bn. at disposal of 62 Bde. Bn. to move at once to vicinity of Quarry R.25.d. pushing reconnaissance ahead through R.20 - R.21. Object of reconnaissance to find covered approach for Bn. to GOUZEAUCOURT - CAMBRAI Road, from which advance can be made on BANTEUX SPUR. Bn. detailed by 110 Inf. Bde. will send Officer to report 62 Bde. H.Q. Q.35.a.5.6. 62 Inf. Bde. will establish report centre at Station R.31.a.9.9 to which reconnaissance sent out by Bn. of 110 Bde. will send reports. 62 Bde. will send as much of his own Bde. as can quickly be made available round N. of GONNELIEU towards R.28.Central and to get touch with right of 5th Division there. 110 Bde. will take over GREEN SWITCH as far N. as R.26.c.3.0.

G.X.564. 64 Bde. will move one Bn. forthwith to area Q.35.c. W.5.a. On arrival Bn. will be prepared either to hold AFRICAN TRENCH HEATHER TRENCH within Divl. Boundaries or to concentrate quickly and move either N. or S. of GOUZEAUCOURT followed by remainder of Bde. to exploit success.

G.X.565. Cyclist Squadron will be transferred forthwith from 110 Bde. to 62 Bde. O.C. Squadron to report 62 Bde. at once and Squadron to move to 62 Bde. H.Q. as soon as possible.

G.X.573. In confirmation of G.X.564 64 Bde. will move another Bn. to area about Q.35.c. W.5.a. ~~in~~ and will maintain remaining Bn. in Q.32. 64 Bde. will report on completion of move.

G.180 from V Corps.

G.172 is cancelled. 33rd and 21st Divs. will re-organise and rest their troops tomorrow rectifying their present front line where necessary. They will be prepared to immediately follow up the enemy and take prisoners on any signs of a retirement. The enemy's trenches on the Corps front will be kept under a constant bombardment. The G.O.C. 21st Div. will inform Corps H.Q. as soon as the situation is such as to allow of his pushing into GONNELIEU so that until this time the Village may be kept under bombardment.

/30th Sept...

<u>30th September, 1918.</u>

<u>G.X.594</u>. 5th Div. report they have patrols in GONNELIEU and BANTEUX. 62 Bde. will push patrols round through 5th Division area so as to enter GONNELIEU from North. These patrols to be supported by stronger bodies. If GONNELIEU occupied by us patrols to work down Reserve Line and KITCHEN STREET to join hands with 110 Inf. Bde. 110 Inf. Bde. will send patrols to BROWN LINE and reinforce them when VILLERS GUISLAIN is occupied by 33rd Div. 62 Bde. will send one Bn. round N. of GONNELIEU to work down GLASGOW and PRESTON TRENCHES with objective GREEN LINE and Southern slopes of BANTEUX SPUR getting touch with 5th Div. on left.

<u>3rd October, 1918.</u>

<u>G.X.662</u>. The M.G.Coy. attached 64th Bde. will reconnoitre defensive positions on QUENTIN RIDGE. These positions will not be occupied except in case of hostile attack.

<u>4th October, 1918.</u>

<u>G.T.283. from T.M.O. V Corps.</u> Two more Mobile Newton Mortars being sent your Division 6th instant.

<u>6th October, 1918.</u>

<u>G.389 from V Corps</u>. Ref: G.375 of today. Two Coys. 17th and ~~21st~~ 33rd M.G.Bns are alotted 21st and 38th Divs. respectively for barrage purposes. Details as regards their temporary attachment to be arranged direct between Divns.

<u>8th October, 1918.</u>

<u>G.A.102.</u> 64 and 110 Bdes. will each collect all available troops less one Bn. each ready on receipt of orders to advance in support of 62 Bde. 64 and 110 Bdes. will leave one Bn. and 8 M.Gs each to garrison RED LINE. Dividing line between Brigades HAUT FARM incl. to 64 Bde. thence via road running Westwards to N.26.d.1.5. 64 and 110 Bdes. will each report as soon as one Bn. is ready to move forward.

<u>G.X.808.</u> 110 Bde. will be prepared to attack GUILLEMIN and high ground N.18.a. this afternoon. Probable Zero about 17.00 hrs. As preparatory measure two Bns. will be moved forthwith to area W. of BRISEUX WOOD. Completion of move to be reported.

<u>G.X.813</u>. 64 Bde. will move one Bn. forthwith to ANGLE WOOD where it will come under the orders of 62 Bde. It will be used to assist 62nd Bde. in their advance on WALINCOURT. C.O. to report 62 Bde. H.Q.

<u>G.X.807</u>. The ~~62 Bde.~~ 17th Div. will pass through the 62 Bde. early tomorrow morning and resume the advance. When the 17th Div. have passed through orders will be issued to Bdes. to concentrate and re-organise in the following areas :- 62 Bde. in squares N.17,23 & 29. 64 Bde. in Squares N.28, 27 and 32. 110 Inf. Bde. Squares N.22, 21 and 20. M.G.Coys. re-organise with affiliated Bdes. Cyclists will re-organise with 62 Bde. and will not be transferred without further orders. 17th and 21st D.As come under orders G.O.C. 17th Div. on completion of relief.

/G.X.830.....

S E C R E T.

21 Div.
G, 498.

All recipients of Div. Order No.237.

Reference para. 1 (b) of 21st Division Order No.237 dated 26th September, 1918.

This operation will NOT take place to-night, but will probably take place on night 28th/29th instant.

A.H. Macdougall. Major.
for Lt. Col.
General Staff,
21st Division.

27th September, 1918.

TELEGRAM.

URGENT
OPERATIONS
PRIORITY TO

Bdes
HG

Words

Sent.
At...............
To...............
By...............

DADE	LODE	33rd Div.
BASU	ZEJU	5th Corps.
VUFE	5th Div.	15th Sqn. R.A.F.

G.X.515 / 28 / AAA

IVth Corps report that enemy have withdrawn from their front AAA DADE has occupied AFRICAN TRENCH and is pushing patrols towards GOUZEAUCOURT AAA If patrols sent out by VUFE meet no resistance VUFE will occupy line GREEN LANE GREEN SWITCH getting touch with 5th Division at R.26.a.9.1 AAA When this line made good by VUFE patrols will be sent to BROWN LINE but no advance in force until touch established with 5th Division on left AAA When 5th Division have occupied FUSILIER RIDGE and if patrols still report no resistance VUFE will make good BROWN LINE and send patrols to GREEN LINE AAA In addition to above VUFE will send one special reconnoitring patrol at once to KITCHEN CRATER and another to GONNELIEU to report if enemy occupy these places or not AAA When VUFE has occupied GREEN LANE GREEN SWITCH and when patrols have reached BROWN LINE DADE will assemble Brigade in GOUZEAUCOURT VALLEY assuming that GOUZEAUCOURT is found empty AAA DADE will be prepared on receipt of orders to move through VUFE and occupy GREEN LINE AAA BASU will be at half hours' notice to move AAA ACK AAA Added all concerned

---

H. V. Franklyn

ZOWU
11.35 a.m.

Lieut.Colonel,
General Staff,

TELEGRAM.

Words

Sent.

DRLS.
S.&R. 5th Div
33rd "

At....................
To....................
By....................

DADE	JESO	33rd Div.	15th Sqn. R.A.F.
BASU	ZOHO		Cyclist Troop.
VUFE	DUFA	V Corps.	
LODE	A/Q.	V Corps R.A.	
ZOKI	5th Div.	V Corps H.A.	
ZEJU		'B' Coy. Tanks.	

- / 28th / AAA

ZOWU Order No.238 AAA Enemy have withdrawn opposite Vth and IVth Corps fronts but to what extent is not yet known AAA ZOWU has been ordered to capture BROWN and GREEN LINES early tomorrow morning AAA VUFE will attack on right and DADE on left AAA Dividing line between Brigades R.31, R.33, R.36.Central AAA 33rd Division will be attacking VILLERS GUISLAIN and GREEN LINE in conjunction with us AAA 5th Division will be attacking FUSILIER and CEMETERY RIDGES and subsequently BANTEUX AAA Two Tanks will work with VUFE and two Tanks with DADE AAA The former rendezvous X.8.a.1.9 and latter R.25.d.2.0 about 11 p.m. AAA Right pair Tanks will work via Cemetery X.2.d. KITCHEN CRATER TURNER CRATER and clear GREEN LINE AAA Left pair Tanks work round each side GONNELIEU and down GLASGOW TRENCH and prepared to deal with BANTEUX SUPPORT if Infantry in difficulties AAA All Tanks rally KITCHEN CRATER after operations where available for immediate counter-attack AAA Artillery starting line for barrage X.2.d.3.5 to R.26.d.3.8 AAA Barrage moves 100 yards in six minutes to BROWN LINE and 100 yards in four minutes from BROWN to GREEN LINE AAA Barrage will be amended and added to according to most Easterly line reached by Infantry this evening AAA Barrage Tables issued to Brigades show other details AAA One M.G.Coy. will accompany each Brigade AAA Unless otherwise detailed Barrage for attack on BROWN LINE will come down at 3.30 a.m. and for attack from BROWN to GREEN LINE at 5.50 a.m. AAA Ack AAA addsd all concerned

---

H.L. Franklyn
Lieut.Colonel,
General Staff.

ZOWU
7.30 p.m.

TELEGRAM.

URGENT OPERATIONS
PRIORITY to 3 Bdes.

Words

Sent.
At....................
To....................
By....................

DADE	JESO	V Corps.
BASU	ZOHO	V Corps R.A.
VUFE	DUFA	V Corps H.A.
LODE	A/Q.	15 Sqn. R.A.F.
ZOKI	5th Div.	Divl. Cyclists Troop.
ZEJU	33rd Div.	

\- / 29th / AAA

ZOWU Order No.239 AAA Owing to success of both flanks today it appears probable that the enemy will withdraw shortly from our immediate front AAA Active patrolling will be carried out by VUFE and DADE tonight AAA If GONNELIEU and BROWN LINE are entered by patrols without resistance either tonight or tomorrow they will at once be occupied in force and patrols pushed on to GREEN LINE AAA If GREEN LINE is occupied by patrols this line will also be occupied in strength and patrols pushed down towards CANAL AAA Boundary between Brigades Sunken Road at R.26.c.3.0 - R.32.Central - R.34.Central - R.36.Central AAA Patrolling must be carried out by strong fighting patrols and minor resistance must be overcome AAA Patrols must be sent out at least once every hour and be particularly active just before Dawn AAA All available heavy Artillery and Field Howitzers will bombard GONNELIEU from 4.5 a.m. to 5 a.m. and then Cease AAA DADE will inform Div. H.Q. by 3 a.m. if bombardment is not to take place owing to their being in occupation of village AAA Any barrage required by Brigades for patrols to work under will be arranged with affiliated Artillery AAA DADE will have call on 122 Brigade as well as 79th Brigade for this purpose AAA BASU will remain in present positions till further orders AAA Ack AAA Adsd all concerned

H. W. Laudlyn

Lieut.Colonel,
General Staff.

ZOWU
10.10 p.m.

TELEGRAM.

Words

Urgent
Operations
Priority to
3 Bdes. HWT

Sent.
At...............
To...............
By...............

DADE	JESO	V Corps.
BASU	ZOHO	V Corps R.A.
VUFE	DUFA	V Corps H.A.
LODE	A/Q.	15 Sqn. R.A.F.
ZOKI	5 Div.	Divl. Cyclist Troop.
ZEJU	33 Div.	

- / 30th / AAA

ZOWU Order No.240 AAA Prisoners state that enemy will withdraw to distance of 4 kilo-metres East of Canal AAA When GREEN LINE has been made good on Divl. Front DADE and VUFE will send forward to Canal sieze crossings and establish bridgeheads on East bank AAA BASU will move to just West of QUENTIN RIDGE forthwith and will be prepared on receipt of orders to advance through VUFE and DADE cross Canal and occupy HINDENBURG LINE between RANCOURT FARM and BANTOUZEELE both exclusive AAA Report Centres will be established by Div. Signals at KITCHEN CRATER TURNER QUARRY successively ARNOLD QUARRY AAA DADE will transfer Cyclists in R.33c to BASU when latter takes up advance AAA Addsd all concerned AAA Ack

---

H. W. Faulkner

ZOWU
12.10 p.m.

Lieut.Colonel,
General Staff.

TELEGRAM.

URGENT OPERATIONS
PRIORITY to
3 Bdes.

Words

Sent
At....................
To....................
By....................

DADE	JESO	V Corps.
BASU	ZOHO	V Corps R.A.
VUFE	DUFA	V Corps H.A.
LODE	A/Q.	15th Sqn.R.A.F.
ZOKI	5th Div.	Div. Cyclist Troop.
ZEJU	33rd Div.	

– / 30th / AAA

ZOWU Order No.241 AAA VUFE on right and DADE on left will continue to hold GREEN LINE AAA Front line to be held thinly and Brigades disposed in depth AAA BASU will remain in present positions AAA Patrols will be sent to Canal bank tonight accompanied by R.E. AAA If any bridges are found to be repairable and hostile fire permits R.E. will carry out repairs protected by Infantry patrol on East bank AAA Risk of heavy casualties will NOT be run AAA If any bridges are found intact or are repaired by R.E. post will be established on West bank to cover bridge with fire and so prevent demolition by enemy AAA If patrols can cross canal they will work towards HINDENBURG LINE to report if enemy hold this line or not AAA All troops East of GREEN LINE except those detailed to guard Bridges or to occupy tactical points selected by Brigadiers will be withdrawn before daylight AAA Troops to be rested as much as possible tonight and tomorrow unless situation changes AAA Ack AAA Adsd all concerned

ZOWU
7.30 p.m.

H L Knatchbull [signature]

Lieut.Colonel,
General Staff.

TELEGRAM.

	Words
Urgent Operations Priority to 3 Bdes.	Sent At.................... To.................... By....................

DADE	JESO	38th Div.
BASU	ZOHO	V Corps.
VUFE	DUFA	V Corps R.A.
LODE	A/Q.	V Corps H.A.
ZOKI	33rd Div.	15 Sqn. R.A.F.
ZEJU	37th Div.	Div. Cyclists.

~ / 3rd / AAA

ZOWU Order No.243 AAA The 50th Div. have reached Northern outskirts of CATELET and GOUY and are to attack high ground S.28. S.29 this evening AAA 38th Div. will then relieve them and will tomorrow attack LA TERRIERE and clear crossings for 33rd Div. at OSSUS AAA 33rd Div. will then cross Canal and form offensive flank facing North between LA TERRIERE and HONNECOURT AAA C.R.A. and M.G.Bn. will keep HINDENBURG LINE and ground between it and Canal under steady continuous fire during these operations AAA VUFE will keep touch with the enemy tonight with patrols endeavouring to pass patrols across Canal on rafts AAA Patrols to withdraw before daylight. AAA VUFE will be prepared from tomorrow inclusive as pressure from South increases to push patrols across Canal and to support them AAA C.R.E. will arrange for bridges to be thrown whenever and wherever VUFE obtains lodgement on East bank AAA BASU will be prepared to cross by these bridges or via HONNECOURT and establish themselves in HINDENBURG LINE within Div. Boundaries AAA Cyclist Sqn. comes under orders of BASU from tomorrow inclusive AAA O.C. will report BASU H.Q. during morning AAA Ack AAA Adsd all concerned.

300 4/as E of

H L Knaubbyn

ZOWU
1800 hrs.

Lieut.Colonel,
General Staff.

TELEGRAM.

URGENT OPERATIONS
PRIORITY to 3 Bdes.

Words

Sent.
At..................
To..................
By..................

DADE	JESO	38th Div.
BASU	ZOHO	V Corps.
VUFE	DUFA	V Corps R.A.
LODE	A/Q.	V Corps H.A.
ZOKI	33rd Div.	15 Sqn. R.A.F.
ZEJU	37th Div.	Div. Cyclist Troop.

\- / 5th / AAA

ZOWU Order No.244 AAA All indications show enemy have withdrawn opposite Corps front AAA Aeroplanes report HINDENBURG LINE appears deserted AAA 33rd Div. reported to have patrol in or near LA TERRIERE AAA VUFE will establish bridge-head round outskirts of BANTOUZELLE forthwith under cover of which C.R.E. will throw bridges to take Infantry in fours AAA When this objective made good VUFE will occupy more extended bridge-head as follows AAA ARNOULD QUARRY - C.T. through M.33.a. and M.27.d. - HINDENBURG SUPPORT Line from M.27.d.3.5 to M.27.b.O.3 thence via RED FARM to Canal AAA Fighting patrols will then be sent to HINDENBURG SUPPORT Line between RANCOURT FARM excl. and M.27.d. AAA This line will be occupied by VUFE as soon as made good by patrols but VUFE will continue to hold bridge-head strongly until further notice AAA BASU will move heads of leading Battns. to BANTEUX forthwith and will start crossing Canal as soon as VUFE has made good larger bridge-head AAA Objectives for BASU as follows AAA HINDENBURG SUPPORT Line from RANCOURT FARM exclusive to M.27.d. if not already made good by VUFE AAA Line of road MONTECOUVEZ FARM - BONNE ENFANCE FARM within Divl. Boundaries AAA When latter objective made good patrols will be sent to MASNIERES BEAUREVOIR Trench System to ascertain if occupied by enemy or not AAA Minor resistance must be overcome by VUFE and BASU AAA Touch must be obtained and kept with 33rd Div. AAA Care must be taken to protect left flank throughout operations until 37th Div. are up in line AAA DADE will move to area R.28.c. & d. R.29.c. & d. R.34. as soon as vacated by VUFE and BASU AAA One M.G.Coy. with each Bde. AAA Successive Report Centres will be established by Divl. Signals at ARNOULD QUARRY GRATTE PANCHE FARM and ARDISSART FARM AAA Ack AAA Adsd all concerned

ZOWU
1205 hrs.

Lieut.Colonel.
General Staff.

TELEGRAM.

URGENT OPERATIONS
PRIORITY to 3 Bdes.

Words

Sent.

At....................
To....................
By....................

DADE	JESO	38th Div.
BASU	ZOHO	5 Corps.
VUFE	DUFA	5 Corps R.A.
LODE	A/Q.	5 Corps H.A.
ZOKI	33rd Div.	15 Sqn. R.A.F.
ZEJU	37th Div.	

\- / 5th / AAA

ZOWU Order No.245 AAA Line reached today not yet certain but we hold BONNE ENFANCE FARM-M.24.c. - M.17.d. AAA Aeroplane reports enemy seen retiring from BEAUREVOIR Line this evening AAA Advance will be resumed tomorrow Oct. 6th AAA BASU will act as advanced guard Brigade AAA First objective line of road N.33.d. & b. - HAUT FARM - HURTEBEISE FARM AAA Second objective WALINCOURT Village and high ground N.18.a. with patrols into SERVAL CHATEAU and SELVIGNY AAA Touch will be gained if possible on flanks at conclusion of each bound but advance must not be delayed for this purpose AAA 78th Bde. R.F.A. come under direct orders of BASU for tomorrow AAA VUFE will act as supporting Brigade and will move to line MONTECOUVEZ FARM - BONNE ENFANCE FARM as soon as BASU has completely cleared BEAUREVOIR front line AAA DADE will be Reserve Brigade and will move to HINDENBURG SUPPORT LINE as soon as VUFE has completely cleared this line AAA Policy for BASU will be to manoeuvre enemy out of positions he may be holding and to act vigorously without engaging Brigade in frontal attack on strong position AAA 38th Div. on our right are being directed on high ground in O.27.Central AAA Objective for 37th Div. not yet known AAA Ack AAA Added all concerned

ZOWU
20.45 hrs.

Lieut.Colonel,
General Staff.

Escarmain
Ghissignies
Vertain
Romeries
Vertigneul
Salesches
Neuvilly
ENEMY ORGANISATION 12-10-18
Solesmes
Grand Champ
Beaurain
Vendegies-sur-Bois
Poix-du-Nord
Wagnonville
Red House
Vendegies Wood
Ovillers
Slaughter House
Present Line
Amerval
Richemont
Croix
Bousies
Lannoy
Forest
Malgarni
Montay
Pommereuil
LE CATEAU
Scale 1 : 20,000
Corrections to detail made 27-10-17
Ordnance Survey, November 1917.

G.S.G.S. 2743. Field Survey Bn. [10650]. 1-10-18

Scale 1 : 20,000

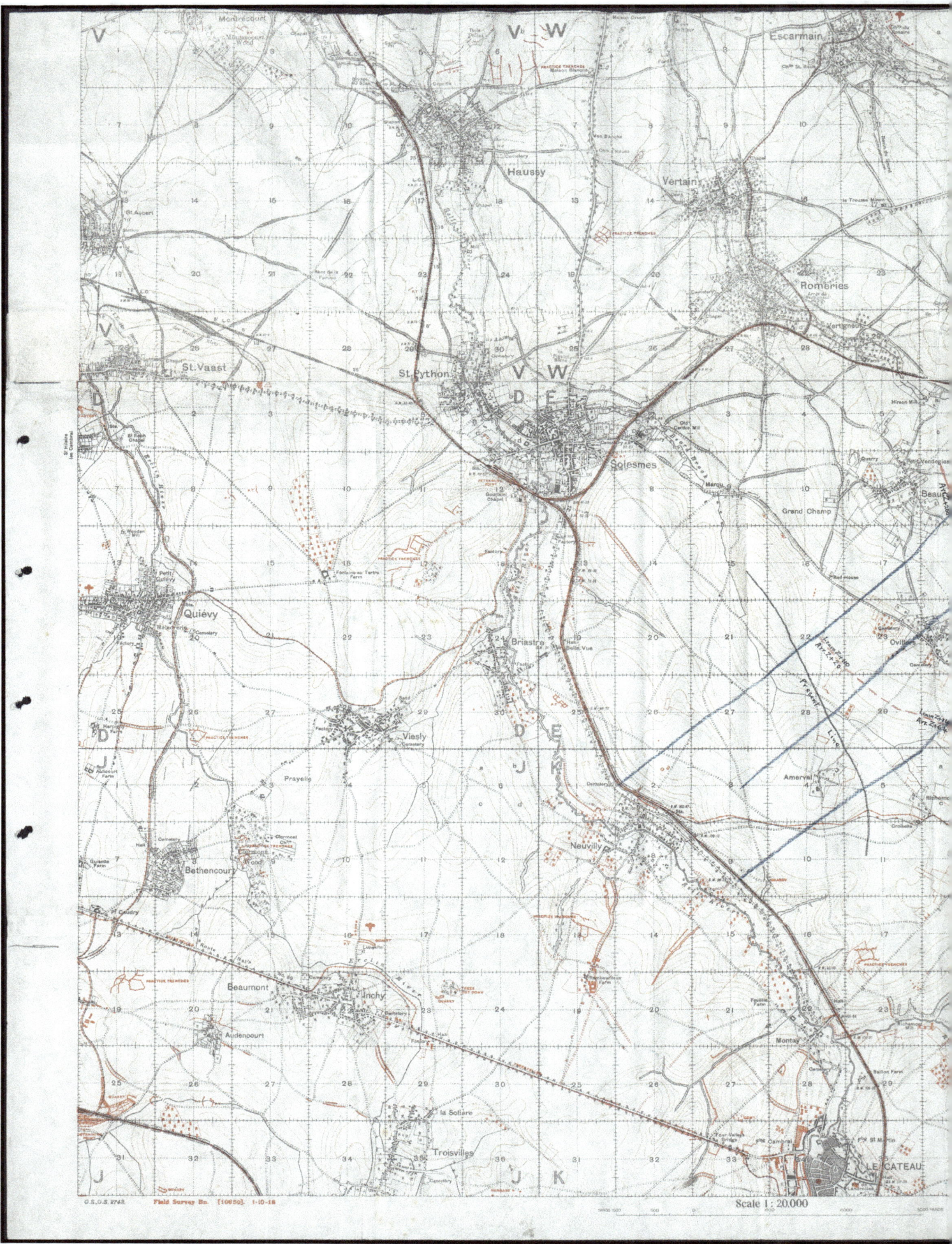

21st Div
map

21st Div
map

Appx XII

S E C R E T.

21 Div.
G. 643.

ACCOUNT OF OPERATIONS FROM 22nd OCTOBER to 26th OCTOBER, 1918.

Ref: Maps.
57.B.)
51.A.) 1/40,000.
51.)

22nd October, 1918.

The Division relieved the 17th Division in the Left Sector of the V Corps front, relief being complete at 10.45 p.m., at which hour G.O.C. 21st Division assumed command of the Sector.

The 64th Inf. Bde. were on the right, 110th Inf. Bde. on the left, and 62nd Inf. Bde. in support at INCHY.

Divisional Headquarters closed at WALINCOURT and opened at INCHY at 3 p.m.

Objectives for the attack on 23rd October were as follows :-

1. RED DOTTED LINE - high ground E.30.a. - E.29.b and a - E.22.d.
2. RED Line - F.19.c. and a. - E.18.Central.
3. GREEN DOTTED LINE - Road F.13.d.7.0. - F.13.d.6.9. - F.7.d.4.1. - F.7.a.2.4.
4. GREEN LINE - high ground F.9.Central - F.2.d. - Cross Roads F.2.c.
5. BROWN LINE - high ground X.89.a. - X.22.Central - SALESCHES Station.

23rd October.

12.15 a.m. Enemy opened a very heavy counter preparation on the area occupied by the 7th Leicester Regt. 110th Infantry Brigade. This bombardment was continued Northwards into the 5th Division area and lasted for about one hour. As the result, severe casualties were suffered and the Battalion became somewhat disorganized.

Up to 2 a.m. the right Brigade Sector was fairly quiet except for some scattered Gas shelling over the Brigade area.

2 a.m. Troops of both Brigades advanced to the attack well up to the barrage.

/6 a.m.......

6 a.m. Both Brigades reported the first objective - RED DOTTED LINE - had been gained and that troops were advancing towards the second objective. Hostile shelling of the forward area was very heavy.

7.50 a.m. 64th Inf. Bde. report timed 6 a.m. stated that the enemy still appeared to be holding OVILLERS. Elements of the 1stWilts Regt. could be seen dug in on the S.W. edge of the Village.

A verbal report received by the 110th Inf. Bde. stated that at 7 a.m., 7th Leicester Regt. were East of the Sunken Road in E.17.d. but were rather disorganized. The 6th Leicester Regt. were going through them. Considerable M.G. fire was being encountered from BEAURAIN.

8.40 a.m. R.A.F. observers reported that at 8 a.m. our troops were advancing through OVILLERS and that tanks could be seen advancing in E.30.a.

9.40 a.m. The second objective - The RED LINE - captured. The 64th and 110th Inf. Bdes. reported that their troops were advancing towards the 3rd objective, followed by troops of 62nd Inf. Bde. Hostile M.G. fire was heavy up to 8.15 a.m. when it died down. Hostile shelling was still heavy but scattered.

10 a.m. Divisional Headquarters closed INCHY and opened NEUVILLY.

10.10 a.m. Report received from 64th Inf. Bde. that at 9 a.m. the O.C. 9th K.O.Y.L.I. reported from personal reconnaissance that his troops were on the third objective. The right Battalion of the 62nd Inf. Bde.were passing through, no touch had been gained on his right. Considerable M.G. fire had been encountered from DUKES WOOD and casualties were fairly heavy.

No report had yet been received as to situation of 110th Inf. Bde.

11.25 a.m. 62nd Inf. Bde. reported the situation at 11 a.m. as follows :- Right Battalion had crossed the third objective. Left Battalion reported its advanced troops in VENDEGIES but this was not yet confirmed. The reserve Battalion was pushing on to the W. edge of DUKES WOOD.

For page 3. see beyond pages 6 & 7 /11.50 a.m....

11.50 a.m. Orders issued to 64th Inf. Bde. to keep touch with the progress made by 62nd Inf. Bde. As soon as the progress of 62nd Inf. Bde. allowed, 64th Inf. Bde. were to move one Battalion to about F.14.a. As soon as the right of the 62nd Inf. Bde. had crossed the road running S.E. through F.8.Central, 64th Inf. Bde. were to move another Battalion to about F.8.d. These Battalions were to be prepared either to support the 62nd Inf. Bde. or to form a defensive flank facing S.E. between the third and fourth objectives.(G.X.151).

12.55 p.m. 62nd Inf. Bde. situation at 12 noon. Right Battalion in F.14.a. and b. and F.8.c. Left Battalion in F.7.b. VENDEGIES had been completely 'mopped up'. No touch with 33rd Division on right, but touch had been gained with 37th Division at F.1.d.0.0. The advance was being continued and a fair amount of opposition was being encountered. Our casualties fairly heavy.

1.15 p.m. 110th Inf. Bde. were warned that they would probably move across the HARPIES RIVER during the afternoon and that Coys. should therefore, be kept concentrated.(G.X.157).

2.45 p.m. Situation at 1 p.m. - Line ran F.9.c.0.7. - F.8.b.0.8. - F.8.a.5.9. - F.8.a.1.6. - F.1.d.Central, where in touch with 37th Division. No touch had yet been gained with 33rd Division. Many enemy dead were reported in VENDEGIES which was now being heavily shelled by the enemy. M.G. and Artillery fire was coming from the N.W. edge of VENDEGIES WOOD.

3.45 p.m. 62nd Inf. Bde. reported that the fourth objective - the GREEN LINE - had been captured. Two Coys. on the right were advancing towards POIX DU NORD. Troops of 33rd Division could be seen on high ground about F.9.d.9.1.

4 p.m. 21st Bn.M.G.Corps. were ordered to move two Sections from the Reserve M.G.Coy. to the fourth objective forthwith. These sections were to reconnoitre positions, but were only to occupy them in case of necessity. The remainder of this Coy. would remain on the second objective (G.X.161).

/5 p.m.....

5 p.m. Warning Order issued that the advance would be continued on October 24th with objective, Line of Road X.24.a.9.0. - GRAND GAY FARM - HALTE (X.11.a.5.6.). The 64th Inf. Bde. would attack on the right, the 62nd Inf. Bde. on the left (G.X.162).

5.15 p.m. Situation 5 p.m. Heavy enemy opposition had been encountered by right Battalion on the fourth objective and the advance had been momentarily held up.

6 p.m. 62nd Inf. Bde. report timed 5 p.m. stated that on the right the advance from the fourth objective had been held up owing to heavy shelling and M.G. fire. Touch had been gained with troops of the 33rd Division who were about 800 yards away on the right. The left Battalion was in touch with the 37th Division in F.2.b.

8.20 p.m. Situation at 8 p.m. At 5.45 p.m. enemy put down a very heavy artillery barrage followed by counter-attack. Situation on right was rather obscure, but as far as was known the line ran along the road F.8.b. and F.9.c. No change on left.

8.30 p.m. Orders issued for the advance to be continued on October 24th in accordance with warning order already issued. The first objective would be the line of Road X.29.c.7.7. to X.21.b.7.1. Advance to this line would be carried out under a barrage. Advance to the second objective would be carried out without a barrage. When the second objective had been captured it was to be consolidated in depth, advanced guards being sent forward to make good . an outpost zone. The 110th Inf. Bde. would pass through the 64th and 62nd Inf. Bdes. after the capture of the second objective and advance to the main JOLIMETZ- LE QUESNOY ROAD (Div.Order No. 248).

11.55 p.m. Situation remained unchanged. The right Battalion 62nd Inf. Bde. held the line of the road through F.8.d. with outposts on the road running through F.8.b. and F.9.c.

/24th Octr.....

24th October 1918.

6.30 a.m. 62nd Inf. Bde. reported that the night had passed quietly up to 4 a.m. at which hour our barrage came down and troops advanced to the attack. Enemy put down a very heavy barrage almost immediately ours started. Not much enemy M.G. fire was heard at first, but it was now increasing.

7.5 a.m. 62nd Inf. Bde. reported that the attack was progressing steadily but hostile artillery fire was extremely heavy. 64th Inf. Bde. reported that at 5 a.m. left Battn. was held up in F.9.a. by heavy M.G. fire which was now reported to be dying down. Right Battalion was advancing steadily.

7.25 a.m. 62nd Inf. Bde. reported that from reports received it appeared that the first objective had been captured. Touch had not been gained with the 64th Inf. Bde. on the right but troops of this Brigade were seen passing through POIX at 6.30 a.m. and were advancing steadily.

8.35 a.m. Situation 8.15 a.m. First objective on the whole Divisional front had been definitely captured. No touch had been gained with the 33rd Division on the right. Considerable opposition had been met in POIX where a large number of the enemy had been killed. Enemy's barrage in reply to ours was extremely heavy and had come down on the Eastern outskirts of VENDEGIES and also upon the forming up area.

8.59 a.m. 62nd Inf. Bde. reported two Coys. of 12/13th Northumberland Fusiliers had passed through 1st Lincoln. Regt. on the first objective at 7 a.m.

10.50 a.m. Situation unchanged. Further advance along the whole line had been held up for the present owing to very strong opposition from the high ground X.22.Central. Enemy artillery fire was very heavy.

/1 p.m.....

1 p.m. Situation remained unchanged. Troops had twice been on the high ground in X.23.a. but each time were forced to withdraw owing to intense M.G. fire from X.23.a. and d. One Coy. 62nd Inf. Bde. were working along the Railway in X.16. in order to gain touch with the 37th Division and also to attack the Farms in X.17. from the N.W.

110th Inf. Bd . were ordered to have all their troops between VENDEGIES incl. and the River running through POIX (G.X.190).

2.40 p.m. Orders issued that 64th Inf. Bde. on the right and 62nd Inf. Bde. on left were to attack the second objective during the afternoon, Zero hour being 4 p.m. Attack would be carried out under a barrage. (Div.Order 249).

4.20 p.m. 62nd and 64th Inf. Bdes. were ordered after the capture of the second objective, to send forward patrols to the line of the ENGLEFONTAINE - LOUVIGNIES ROAD and to S.W. edges of the orchards in X.12.a. in order to ascertain whether the enemy were holding this line or not. (G.X.196).

6.15 p.m. No news had yet been received as to progress of the attack. Enemy artillery was inactive during our barrage but was now shelling POIX.

9.50 p.m. Situation - Whole of objective had been captured but touch had not yet been gained with the 37th Division on the left. 64th Inf. Bde. had established a post at X.24.a.9.0. where they were now in touch with the 33rd Division. Enemy were holding the line of the objective and the Farms in X.17 in considerable strength and heavy M.G. fire was encountered during the advance, but on approach of our troops enemy withdrew. Enemy were still holding the main road in X.30.a. and X.24.c.

9.50 p.m. The Cyclist Squadron attached to the Division was ordered to send one troop to be attached to each Brigade, troops were to leave their present billets at 7 a.m. 25th Oct. (G.X.204.)

10.15 p.m. Orders issued that as it was considered possible

/ that....

that the enemy might withdraw from opposite the Divisional front during the night, the 62nd and 64th Inf. Bdes. were to send out patrols at dawn to search the ground between our present front line and the Orchards about 1000 yards N.E. of it. If no enemy were encountered these patrols were to be supported and were then to be sent on to the line of the Road through CROIX ROUGE and into LOUVIGNIES. If the enemy were not yet encountered the 110th Inf. Bde. would pass through the 62nd and 64th Inf. Bdes. and take up the advance until the line of the JOLIMETZ - LE QUESNOY ROAD had been reached. If 62nd and 64th Inf. Bdes. encountered the enemy, it was not the Divisional Commander's intention to make ground by fighting. (Div. Order 250).

Situation remained unchanged with very little enemy activity.

25th October 1918.

6 a.m. Situation remained unchanged during the night. Patrols sent out during the night encountered heavy M.G. fire from the ridge in X.12.c. Enemy heavily shelled POIX during the night.

[?].20 a.m. Patrols sent out at dawn were unable to make progress owing to heavy M.G. fire from the orchards in X.12.a.

9.10. a.m. Orders issued that if 110th Inf. Bde. did not pass through the 62nd and 64th Inf. Bdes. during the day, they would relieve these Brigades in line during the night 25/26th October, On relief the 62nd Inf. Bde. would withdraw to the area round POIX and would be prepared to hold the BROWN LINE running through X.29.a. and X.22.a. and d. or to form defensive flank facing S.E. 64th Inf. Bde. would withdraw to the area round VENDEGIES and would be prepared to hold GREEN LINE running through F.9.a., F.2.c. and d. 62nd Inf. Bde. were to hold two Battalions in readiness to move at quarter hours notice and 64th Inf. Bde. to hold one Battalion ready to move at half hours notice. The reserve M.G.Coy. was to be disposed for the defence of the GREEN LINE. (Div.Order 251.)

/ 10 a.m.

10 a.m. Divisional Headquarters closed NEUVILLY and opened OVILLERS.

2.5 p.m. Warning order received from Corps that the Division would be relieved by the 17th Division on October 26th and during the night October 26/27th. (Vth Corps G. 393.).

2.45 p.m. Situation unchanged. Some hostile Gas shelling of the Eastern outskirts of POIX and also scattered shelling in the forward area.

3.50 p.m. Orders issued that in conjunction with an operation to be carried out by the 33rd Division to capture the village of ENGLEFONTAINE, the 110th Inf. Bde. were to establish an outpost zone on the line S.13.d.0.4. - X.11.d.8.8. - X.11.b.1.9. Platoons to establish this line of posts would advance under a barrage which would come down at 1 a.m. 26th October. At dawn reconnoitring patrols were to be sent forward to ascertain if the orchards in X.12. a. were held. If no enemy were encountered the action detailed in order No. 250 of 24th October would be carried out. The whole of the Cyclist Squadron would come under the orders of 110th Inf. Bde. on completion of the Brigade relief. (Div. order 252).

21st Bn. M.G.C. were ordered to place 8 guns from the reserve Coy. at the disposal of 110th Inf. Bde for the defence of their right flank. (G.A. 219).

5.30 p.m. Situation remained unchanged. Enemy Artillery was much less active.

6.45 p.m. 64th Inf. Bde. were ordered to place one Battalion on and about the GREEN LINE, the remaining Battalions being in VENDEGIES. (G.A. 229).

7.30 p.m. Warning order issued that the Division less Artillery, would be relieved by the 17th Division, less Artillery on Oct. 26th and during the night 26/27th October. On relief 64th Inf. Bde. would be billeted in INCHY, 62nd Inf. Bde. in NEUVILLY and 110th Inf. Bde. in OVILLERS and AMERVAL. (G.A. 228).

/ 26th October ....

26th October 1918.

1 a.m. Relief of 62nd and 64th Inf. Bdes by 110th Inf. Bde. was complete.

5.35. a.m. Situation during the night unchanged. Heavy enemy Artillery fire on forward area.

110th Inf. Bde. reported at 8.45 a.m. that the left Battalion had established a post at X.12.c.0.5. Heavy M.G. fire had been encountered from X.11.b.2.2. and X.11.d.

8.30 a.m. 110th Inf. Bde. reported that posts had now been established at S.13.d.0.4., X.17.d.9.9., X.12.c.0.5., X.11.b.2.2. Considerable M.G. fire was encountered on any movement taking place in the forward area.

1.30 p.m. Orders issued for the relief of the Division by the 17th Division. (Div. Order 253).

4.30 p.m. Divisional Headquarters closed at OVILLERS and opened at NEUVILLY.

6.30 p.m. 110th Inf. Bde. reported that 1st Wilts. Regt. had sent out a daylight patrol which reached point X.11.d.6.6., where they came under heavy M.G. fire from X.12.c.5.9.

10.15 p.m. The relief of the Division by 17th Division was complete and command of the Sector passed to G.O.C. 17th Division.

During the above operations the following prisoners were captured by the Division.

	Officers.	O.R.
Prisoners. -	17	648
Guns.		1.

-----------oOo---------------

App XIII

S E C R E T.

- 3 -

21 Div.
G. 321.

Proceedings of Conference held at Divisional Headquarters, 28th Oct. 1918.

Present :-

B.G.C. 62 Inf. Bde.
B.G.C. 64 : : A.A.Q.M.G.
B.G.C. 110 : : D.M.G.C.
C.R.A. O.C.Signals.

1. Relief of 17th Division.

The G.O.C. said that he had decided to take over the front line with two Brigades, the 110th Infantry Brigade being on the right and the 62nd Infantry Brigade on the left.

2. Barrages.

B.G.C. 64th Infantry Brigade considered that in the present form of warfare it was better to have a barrage only for about the first 1,000 yards of an advance and then barrage should gradually die away, the troops continuing the advance without it. By this means he considered that objectives could be more distant, and that the advance would be carried out more rapidly. The B.G.C. 62nd Infantry Brigade considered that no definite rule could be laid down, and that when he had to pass through another Brigade he would prefer that Brigade to have a barrage the whole way to their objective as he considered troops were more likely to get their objective with a barrage. The Divisional Commander said that this question was worth considering. The C.R.A. also agreed, especially as he thought the enemy would have more strength in front owing to the enclosed nature of the country that we were now passing through.

The point was raised that troops were liable at night to get into our own barrage owing to them thinking the superimposed H.E. barrage, being more visible than the shrapnel barrage, was the one to follow. It was agreed that the H.E. barrage should be continued as it was of great value.

3. Rate of Advance.

B.G.C. 64th Infantry Brigade considered that in the recent attacks the whole rate of advance was too slow, caused chiefly by the very long halts on objectives. The Divisional Commander agreed but said that these halts had to take place in order to comply with the rate of advance of Corps on either flank.

4. Pace of Barrage.

The Divisional Commander asked Brigadiers if they had any points which they wished to raise with reference to the recent memorandum issued on this subject. There were no points raised.

5. Smoke.

Brigadiers agreed that smoke in the barrage was useful, both by day and night, but considered that the amount to be used should depend on the direction of the wind. The C.R.A. said that this point would be borne in mind in future.

6. Gas.

Now that our guns fired a certain amount of shell filled with a very volatile gas, the Divisional Commander asked

/Brigadiers....

Brigadiers whether they thought troops should be told or not. B.Gs.C. 64th and 110th Infantry Brigades were of opinion that troops should not be told. B.G.C. 62 Infantry Brigade thought that troops should be warned that they would probably encounter gas after the attack had started but that gas was innocuous and was only fired to induce the enemy to wear gas masks. The Divisional Commander said that he was inclined to tell the troops but only if there was sufficient time to explain the situation fully to them.

7. The Divisional Commander asked the C.R.A. what was the probable minimum time that would be taken for the Artillery to fire a new barrage if the guns had advanced 2,000 yards. The C.R.A. said that, provided the going was good, and guns could get across country, he considered there would be a delay of about 2 hours. This delay was due to the insufficient training of present personnel.

The Divisional Commander considered that when Brigades and Batteries had to move forward, they should move to forward positions of readiness during the time the Brigade or Battery Commander was reconnoitring for new positions, so that there would be practically no delay in the Battery moving to the new position as soon as it had been decided on. The C.R.A. said that this matter would be gone into.

8. Reconnaissance of the Infantry Situation.

Brigadiers considered that Artillery Officers relied too much on getting news from Brigade Headquarters instead of finding out the situation for themselves, the consequence being that Infantry Brigade Headquarters became flooded out with Artillery Officers. The Divisional Commander agreed and thought that Artillery Officers should make more use of Mounted Orderlies to ascertain the situation. The C.R.A. agreed.

9. Tools.

B.G.C. 62 Infantry Brigade said that in the recent attacks each Battalion took two pack animals carrying 80 shovels with them. These were found to be invaluable. B.Gs.C. 64th and 110th Infantry Brigades agreed that this was the best method.

10. Communications.

It was agreed that the Brigade going through the Brigades attacking the first objectives should be responsible for laying the Divisional cable to the report centre immediately in rear of these objectives.

The question of Brigades laying light cable would be considered and instructions issued on the subject.

11. Machine Guns.

The Divisional Commander considered that whenever it was possible Machine Guns should fire indirect barrages. After the first attack the firing of these barrages was purely a question of the supply of ammunition.

Brigadiers all agreed that the Machine Gun Companies attached to Brigades did very good work during the recent/attacks.

12. Administrative.

(a) First Line Transport has now been divided into 'A' and 'B' Echelons.

/B.G.C.....

B.G.C. 110th Infantry Brigade said that he had sub-divided 'A' Echelon placing a proportion of it directly under the Battalion Commander, the remainder being under Brigade control. He found that this method worked extremely well during the recent attacks.

The Divisional Commander considered that Battalion Commanders should have the fighting limbers under their own control but that by day limbers could not, as a rule, go further forward than Brigade Headquarters. Beyond Brigade Headquarters pack animals would have to be used. This was agreed to.

B.G.C. 64th Infantry Brigade considered that the transport lines for Echelon 'B' were too far behind. The A.A. & Q.M.G. said that this was a question of supply of water, but that as water in the area we were now passing through was more plentiful, transport lines would be placed as far forward as the situation permits.

(B) Burials.

B.G.C. 64th Infantry Brigade considered that troops in rear e.g. Artillery, Kite Balloon Sections etc. should bury all corpses lying in their immediate area. He thought that recent orders issued on this subject prevented this from being carried out.

The Divisional Commander said that this question would be taken up with the Corps.

(C) Traffic Control.

B.G.C. 64 Infantry Brigade suggested that in view of the recent orders issued by the Corps reference troops moving across country, cross country tracks should be marked out. The Divisional Commander agreed.

The Divisional Commander considered that Traffic Control Posts should be got forward quicker and should go as far forward as limbers normally went. The A.A. & Q.M.G. said that this matter would be taken up with the A.P.M.

13. Transport with Troops.

The Divisional Commander said that if Brigadiers considered that it was a tactical move, Companies could march with their own Lewis Gun Limbers, but that all other transport should move together in rear of the Battalion.

14. R.E.

Brigadiers agreed that the Section of R.E. attached to each Brigade during the recent operations had done good work and were invaluable.

Strong Points. The Divisional Commander said that the orders were for the R.E. to construct the strong points and then hand them over to the Infantry. Some doubt existed as to whether the strong points made during the recent operations had been so handed over and the Divisional Commander wished Brigadiers and the C.R.E. to go into this matter and to report to Div. H.Q.

15. Horses and Transport.

The Divisional Commander again emphasised the necessity for Battalion Commanders to use their horses in the present operations. However, he wished to impress on everyone the necessity of taking as much care as possible of horses owing to their scarcity and tf the difficulty of getting remounts.

/The Divisional...

The Divisional Commander said that he was not satisfied with the turnout of the transport taking into consideration the fact that the Division had recently been 12 days out of the line.

16. Consolidation.

The Divisional Commander said that the tendency at present was to crowd too many troops into the front line instead of defence in depth. The policy he laid down was that the front line should be held by posts, with strong bodies of men in suitable positions in rear ready to counter-attack to retake the front line, should it be captured by the enemy. He considered that a buffer of about 500 yards in depth was sufficient.

A. H. Macdougall. Major for Lt Col.
General Staff,
21st Division.

29.10.18.

Distribution.

62 Inf. Bde.
64 " "
110 " "
C.R.A.
C.R.E.
"Q"
D.M.G.C.
Signals

Copy of Telegrams to accompany 21st Division Summary of Operations for period 26.9.18 to 10.10.18.

28th September, 1918.

G.X.526. 2 Coys. 17th M.G.Bn. attached to you will rejoin their own Battalion forthwith.

G.X.536. Ref: Order No.238. When Green Line objective has been captured patrols will be sent forward to the Canal. Reports will be rendered as to whether opposition is met. If no opposition C.R.E. will begin arrangements to bridge canal.

G.X.547. Supply tank will be under orders of 62nd Inf. Bde.

29th September, 1918.

G.X.556. Hold two Bns. in readiness to move at ¼ of an hours' notice to occupy LOWLAND TRENCH, HEATHER AND AFRICAN TRENCHES within Divl. Boundaries.

G.X.562. 110 Inf. Bde. will place one Bn. at disposal of 62 Bde. Bn. to move at once to vicinity of Quarry R.25.d. pushing reconnaissance ahead through R.20 - R.21. Object of reconnaissance to find covered approach for Bn. to GOUZEAUCOURT - CAMBRAI Road, from which advance can be made on BANTEUX SPUR. Bn. detailed by 110 Inf. Bde. will send Officer to report 62 Bde. H.Q. Q.35.a.5.6. 62 Inf. Bde. will establish report centre at Station R.31.a.9.9 to which reconnaissance sent out by Bn. of 110 Bde. will send reports. 62 Bde. will send as much of his own Bde. as can quickly be made available round N. of GONNELIEU towards R.28.Central and to get touch with right of 5th Division there. 110 Bde. will take over GREEN SWITCH as far N. as R.26.c.3.0.

G.X.564. 64 Bde. will move one Bn. forthwith to area Q.35.c. W.5.a. On arrival Bn. will be prepared either to hold AFRICAN TRENCH HEATHER TRENCH within Divl. Boundaries or to concentrate quickly and move either N. or S. of GOUZEAUCOURT followed by remainder of Bde. to exploit success.

G.X.565. Cyclist Squadron will be transferred forthwith from 110 Bde. to 62 Bde. O.C. Squadron to report 62 Bde. at once and Squadron to move to 62 Bde. H.Q. as soon as possible.

G.X.573. In confirmation of G.X.564 64 Bde. will move another Bn. to area about Q.35.c. W.5.a. ~~xx~~ and will maintain remaining Bn. in Q.32. 64 Bde. will report on completion of move.

G.180 from V Corps.

G.172 is cancelled. 33rd and 21st Divs. will re-organise and rest their troops tomorrow rectifying their present front line where necessary. They will be prepared to immediately follow up the enemy and take prisoners on any signs of a retirement. The enemy's trenches on the Corps front will be kept under a constant bombardment. The G.O.C. 21st Div. will inform Corps H.Q. as soon as the situation is such as to allow of his pushing into GONNELIEU so that until this time the Village may be kept under bombardment.

/30th Sept...

30th September, 1918.

G.X.594. 5th Div. report they have patrols in GONNELIEU and BANTEUX. 62 Bde. will push patrols round through 5th Division area so as to enter GONNELIEU from North. These patrols to be supported by stronger bodies. If GONNELIEU occupied by us patrols to work down Reserve Line and KITCHEN STREET to join hands with 110 Inf. Bde. 110 Inf. Bde. will send patrols to BROWN LINE and reinforce them when VILLERS GUISLAIN is occupied by 33rd Div. 62 Bde. will send one Bn. round N. of GONNELIEU to work down GLASGOW and PRESTON TRENCHES with objective GREEN LINE and Southern slopes of BANTEUX SPUR getting touch with 5th Div. on left.

3rd October, 1918.

G.X.662. The M.G.Coy. attached 64th Bde. will reconnoitre defensive positions on QUENTIN RIDGE. These positions will not be occupied except in case of hostile attack.

4th October, 1918.

G.T.283. from T.M.O. V Corps. Two more Mobile Newton Mortars being sent your Division 6th instant.

6th October, 1918.

G.389 from V Corps. Ref: G.376 of today. Two Coys. 17th and ~~21st~~ 33rd M.G.Bns are alotted 21st and 38th Divs. respectively for barrage purposes. Details as regards their temporary attachment to be arranged direct between Divns.

8th October, 1918.

G.A.102. 64 and 110 Bdes. will each collect all available troops less one Bn. each ready on receipt of orders to advance in support of 62 Bde. 64 and 110 Bdes. will leave one Bn. and 8 M.Gs each to garrison RED LINE. Dividing line between Brigades HAUT FARM incl. to 64 Bde. thence via road running Westwards to N.26.d.1.5. 64 and 110 Bdes. will each report as soon as one Bn. is ready to move forward.

G.X.808. 110 Bde. will be prepared to attack GUILLEMIN and high ground N.18.a. this afternoon. Probable Zero about 17.00 hrs. As preparatory measure two Bns. will be moved forthwith to area W. of BRISEUX WOOD. Completion of move to be reported.

G.X.813. 64 Bde. will move one Bn. forthwith to ANGLE WOOD where it will come under the orders of 62 Bde. It will be used to assist 62nd Bde. in their advance on WALINCOURT. C.O. to report 62 Bde. H.Q.

G.X.807. The ~~62 Bde.~~ 17th Div. will pass through the 62 Bde. early tomorrow morning and resume the advance. When the 17th Div. have passed through orders will be issued to Bdes. to concentrate and re-organise in the following areas :- 62 Bde. in squares N.17, 23 & 29. 64 Bde. in Squares N.28, 27 and 32. 110 Inf. Bde. Squares N.22, 21 and 20. M.G.Coys. re-organise with affiliated Bdes. Cyclists will re-organise with 62 Bde. and will not be transferred without further orders. 17th and 21st D.As come under orders G.O.C. 17th Div. on completion of relief.

/G.X.830....

G.X.830. Under orders from Corps the Squadron N.I.H. will be transferred to 17th Divisiom from 05.20 hours tomorrow.

10th october, 1918.

G.X.864. Your Bde. will move this morning to Billets in WALINCOURT

G.X.869. 110 Bde. will move this afternoon to Billets in CAULLERY.

- - - - - - - - - - - - - - - - -

App 25

21 Div.
G. 787.

SUMMARY OF OPERATIONS FROM AUGUST 1st TO 31st, 1918.

August 1st to August 8th.

On August 1st the Third Army was opposed by eight German Divisions in the line and seven in Reserve. In accordance with the German policy before an offensive, the majority of the Divisions in the line were of doubtful quality. From aeroplane photographs and other sources of information it was evident that the enemy were making general preparations for an offensive in sectors suitable for offensive action between YPRES and MONTDIDIER.

Documents captured in recent operations confirm this. The enemy contemplated a British counter-offensive, but it was thought that this would be easily dealt with. A statement made by LUDENDORF early in August welcomed such an event as an easy means of destroying the Allied Reserves, and so paving the way for a decisive victory before the winter. There were practically no signs of organization for defence in the territory gained by the enemy during his earlier offensives, and his intention seems to have been to at least gain a footing in undestroyed land, commanding the forward Railway systems, if a decisive Military victory could not be obtained before the winter.

August 8th to 14th.

The operations South of ALBERT on August 8th took the enemy by surprise. The Germans admit the fact that the Allies had no numerical superiority, and attribute their defeat to the use of Tanks.

From August 8th to 14th the Reserves opposite the Third Army were gradually drawn into the battle South of the SOMME, although the Divisions in the line remained the same, namely 8.

During this period the enemy withdrew to the E. bank of the ANCRE opposite the S. Divisional Sector of the Corps front.

August 14th to 21st.

On August 14th the enemy withdrew from his forward zone opposite the remainder of the Corps front. Probable intention of the enemy was to shorten his line, and, by so doing, withdraw sufficient Divisions to stem the attack South of the SOMME without drawing further Divisions from his strategic Reserve. It is evident from the lack of preparations for demolition, and the amount of guns and material captured, that a forced retirement was not contemplated. Prisoners taken on August 14th stated that it was thought improbable that we should discover the enemy withdrawal for at least a week, and that we should only follow it up timidly.

From August 14th onwards the enemy became distinctly nervous as to our intentions. Many fruitless local counter-attacks were made to regain portions of land from which the enemy had withdrawn.

About August 19th the enemy withdrew many of his heavy guns to rear positions. Prisoners state that this was done on account of signs of an impending British offensive.

It is therefore certain that the enemy was not taken entirely by surprise on Aug. 21st, and that he had had time to make preparations to meet an attack.

/ Aug. 21st.

August 21st to 31st.

On August 21st there were still eight Divisions in the line opposite the Third Army. Two Divisions were known to be in reserve, and Divisions which had fought South of the SOMME on August 8th were on their way to rest in the BAPAUME - CAMBRAI area. In addition train activity from LILLE to CAMBRAI indicated the arrival of fresh Divisions from the North.

The success of operations on August 21st and 23rd threw the enemy into a state of great confusion. Fresh and tired Divisions have been liberally thrown into the fight to stem the advance and have failed to do so. Prisoners all testify to the confusion which exists behind the enemy lines, and attribute our success to the fact that we gave them no time to rest and re-organise their troops. This is borne out by the fact that twenty German Divisions have already been identified by this Corps alone, of which eight have been identified by this Division (namely, 3rd Naval Division, 16th Reserve Division, 52nd Division, 49th Reserve Division, 44th Reserve Division, 14th Reserve Division, 183rd Division, and 87th Division).

Thirty two German Divisions have been engaged against the Third Army since August 21st. Between the SCARPE and the AISNE 95 Divisions have been engaged since August 8th. The total German Army on the Western Front consists of 196 Infantry Divisions and four Cavalry Divisions. Many of the Divisions engaged since August 21st have suffered sufficient casualties, in prisoners alone, to render them unfit for action for some considerable period (the 2nd Guard Reserve Division lost 80 Officers and 2,313 O.R. in prisoners alone).

Prisoners state that the enemy is withdrawing to the HINDENBURG LINE, and that the enemy intention is to hold up our advance by rearguards for a sufficient length of time to rest and re-organize his troops in rear.

In the North the First Army has turned the HINDENBURG LINE by breaking through the DROCOURT - QUEANT Switch, and it is there that the enemy is making his biggest effort to drive us back.

These operations have forced the enemy to withdraw from KEMMEL and the BAILLEUL Salient in order to shorten his line.

In conjunction with the operations by the First, Third and Fourth British Armies, the 1st, 3rd and 10th French Armies are also attacking. The Battle front now extends from ARRAS to SOISSONS.

SUMMARY.

There is evidence to prove that at least 6 German Divisions have been disbanded and that the personnel drafted away to fill up gaps in other Divisions.

The man power situation in Germany is critical at the present moment. At the end of this month it will be greatly relieved by the appearance in the field of the 1920 Class.

The enemy realises that it is a neck and neck race as to whether we are to drive him over the HINDENBURG LINE and reach the undestroyed land before the winter sets in. He also realises and will attempt to make full use of the fact that only six weeks of fighting weather remain.

/SUMMARY OF PRISONERS.....

SUMMARY OF PRISONERS ETC.

Taken by British Army from August 1st to 29th :-

57,318 prisoners (including 1,283 Officers).

657 Guns (including 153 heavy guns).

5,750 Machine Guns.

Over 1,000 Trench Mortars.

Taken by Third Army from August 21st to September 2nd :-

596 Officers, 20015 Other Ranks.

138 Guns.

Taken by Vth Corps from August 21st to September 2nd :-

111 Officers, 4,709 Other Ranks.

Taken by 21st Division from August 21st to September 2nd :-

45 Officers, 1,242 Other Ranks.

12 Guns.

The average depth of the advance is 12 miles.

23rd October 1918.

G.X.151.
64th Inf. Bde. will keep touch with progress of 62nd Inf. Bde. As soon as progress of 62nd Inf. Bde. allows 64th Inf. Bde. will move one battalion to about F.14.a. As soon as right of 62nd Inf. Bde. crosses road running S.E. from F.8.central 64th Inf. Bde. will move another battalion to about F.8.d. These battalions of 64th Inf. Bde. will be prepared either to support 62nd Inf. Bde. or to form defensive flank facing S.E. between GREEN and GREEN DOTTED LINES. When 62nd Inf. Bde. vacates GREEN LINE 64th Inf. Bde. will occupy as previously ordered remaining battalion moving to N.E. of VENDEGIES.

G.X. 157.
It is probable that your Bde (110th Inf. Bde.) will have to move across RIVER HARPIES some time during afternoon. Coys. should therefore be kept as concentrated as possible.

G.X. 161.
21st Bn. M.G.C. will move two sections from Reserve Coy. to GREEN LINE forthwith. These sections will reconnoitre positions but will not occupy them unless necessary. Two sections reserve Coy. will remain on RED LINE. Whole Coy. will probably be required to fire a barrage to assist advance to-morrow.

24th October 1918.

G.X.190. Under present conditions G.O.C. does not consider it necessary for your H.Q. being in POIX and suggests you returning to VENDEGIES. No troops of your Bde. to be East of the stream running through POIX or West of VENDEGIES. No objection to one Bn. being in VENDEGIES. 110th Inf. Bde. will be prepared to hold GREEN LINE if necessary.

Div. Order No.249.
64th Inf. Bde. on right and 62nd Inf. Bde. on left will attack and capture second objective this afternoon. Artillery comes down at 16.00 hours on line 300 yards in front of LES TUILERIES - SALESCHES Rd on right Bde. front and about 400 yards in front of this road on left Bde. front. Exact Artillery starting line has been given to those concerned. Barrage lifts at 16.12. hours and advances at rate of 100 yards in 3 minutes until 300 yards beyond objective and then ceases. Heavy Artillery will bombard objective and orchards West of objective from Zero till safety compels lift. Heavy Artillery then lifts on to high ground 500 yards beyond objective for 20 minutes and then ceases.

G.X. 196.
After capture of objective this afternoon 64th Inf. Bde. will send forward patrols to line of ENGLEFONTAINE - LOUVIGNIES Road and 62nd Inf. Bde. to S.W. edges of Orchards between objective and LOUVIGNIES. It is very important that information should be received if enemy are encountered or not.

G.X. 204.
You will move from present billets at 07.00 hours to-morrow October 25th sending one troop to each Bde. 62nd Inf. Bde. and 64th Inf. Bde. H.Q. POIX. 110th Inf. Bde. H.Q. VENDEGIES CHATEAU. When 110th Inf. Bde. passes through 62nd Inf. Bde. and 64th Inf. Bde. all troops will come under orders of 110th Inf. Bde.

/ Vth Corps G.39

25th October 1918.

Vth Corps G.393.

Warning order. 17th Division will relieve 21st Division left Division Sector on 26th and night 26/27th. Command of Artillery covering left Sector will pass to G.O.C., R.A. 17th Division on completion of relief. 21st Division on relief will be disposed Div. H.Q. INCHY. One Bde. Group OVILLERS - AMERVAL area. One Bde. Group NEUVILLY. One Bde. Group INCHY. G.O.C., 17th Division on relief will establish his H.Q. at present H.Q. 21st Division. O.C. 5th Cyclist Regt. will allot one Squadron Cyclists to 17th Division and will keep one Squadron in Corps reserve.

G.X. 219.

21st Bn. M.G.C. will place eight guns from reserve Coy. at disposal of 110th Inf. Bde for defence of right flank. Details of attachment will be arranged between D.M.G.O. and 110th Inf. Bde.

G.X. 229.

Reference 21st Div. order No. 251. One Bn. will be located on and about the GREEN LINE. Remaining Bns. may be in VENDEGIES.

------------ooo------------

TELEGRAM

Urgent operations priority to Brigades.

Words

Sent.

To......................

At......................

By......................

DADE	LODE	LEJU	ZODU	17 Div.	5th Corps.
BASU	ZOKI	A/Q	5th Div.	37 Div.	
VUFE	DUFA	ZOHO	33 Div.	15th Sqn.	

G.X. 162 c / 23 / AAA

Zowu Warning Order AAA. Advance will be resumed tomorrow by ZOWU AAA Objective Line of road X.24.a.9.0. GRAND GAY FARM to Halt X.11.a.5.5. AAA Right Div. Boundary from X.29.Cent. to Cross Roads S.3.c.8.7. AAA Left Div. Boundary from X.6.a.0.2. M.31.b.3.0. M.26.b.5.0. M.21.c.3.0. AAA Inter-brigade boundary POIX SPINNING MILL to road junction X.23.d.1.4. just inclusive to right Brigade thence straight line to X.22.d.6.5. South of Road to X.17.b.3.1. thence straight line to M.33.c.0.8. AAA BASU will attack on right and DADE ON LEFT AAA Jumping off line depends on progress of DADE today AAA After capture of objective advance guards will be sent forward to make as much ground as possible towards JOLIMETZ - LE QUESNOY Road AAA Cancelling previous instructions BASU will now take over GREEN line on right Brigade front and VUFE on left Brigade front as soon as vacated by DADE AAA BASU will push forward troops to protect right rear of DADE during latters advance today and will take over right Brigade front from DADE ON final line reached tonight AAA VUFE will be disposed tonight between GREEN Line inclusive and RED line exclusive and will be in Div. Reserve tomorrow AAA Further orders later. ACknowledge. X.28.c.1.4

ZOWU
1200

General Staff.
21st Division.

TELEGRAM.

Words

URGENT OPERATIONS
PRIORITY 3 Bdes.
D.M.G.C. H G Lt Col

To....................
At....................
By....................

DADE	ZOKI	ZEJU	ZODU	17 Div.	V Corps.
BASU	LODE	A/Q.	5 Div.	37 Div.	
VUFE	DUFA	ZOHO	33 Div.	15 Sqn. R.A.F.	

\- / 23 / AAA

ZOWU Order No.248 AAA Ref. Warning Order G.X.162 of today AAA Advance is being continued tomorrow AAA 33rd Div. attack LANDRECIES - LE QUESNOY Road AAA 37 Div. attack high ground North of GHISSIGNIES AAA BASU on right and DADE on left will attack with first objective line of road from X.29.c.7.7 to X.21.b.7.1 AAA Second objective line of road from rd. junc. X.24.a.9.0 GRAND GAY FARM to Halt X.11.a.5.5 AAA Advance to first objective under barrage AAA NO barrage for advance beyond first objective AAA Artillery starting line 300 yards in advance of road F.9.c.6.6 F.2.a.3.5 AAA Barrage dwells on starting line for 8 minutes and then advances at rate of 100 yards in 4 minutes AAA Protector beyond first objective for 8 minutes and then ceases AAA No barrage for right Brigade through Village of POIX DU NORD AAA BASU will pick up barrage on far side of village AAA Advance through village will be calculated at rate of 100 yards in 4 minutes AAA Reserve Coy. Machine Guns will barrage 400 yards ahead of Artillery AAA One M.G.Coy. remains with each Brigade AAA 95th Bde. R.F.A. will support advance from first to second objectives and keep liaison with BASU and DADE H.Q. AAA Second objective will be consolidated in depth when captured AAA Liaison post with 33rd Div. at rd. junc. X.24.a.9.0 and with 37th Div. on rly. at X.5.c.9.5. AAA After capture of objectives all three Divs. will send advanced guards forward to make good outpost zone. AAA 33 Div. to FUTOY and JOLIMETZ AAA 37th Div. to East of LE QUESNOY AAA Objective for ZOWU adv. Guards main JOLIMETZ - LE QUESNOY Road AAA VUFE will act as Adv. Guard leading troops crossing Green Line at 07.00 hours and advancing through BASU and DADE after capture of second objective AAA 95th Bde. R.F.A. will support advance of VUFE AAA Most important for VUFE to protect right of 37th Div. during advance AAA Ack AAA Addsd all concerned

H C Franklyn
Lieut Col

ZOWU

General Staff.

Words

URGENT
OPERATIONS
PRIORITY 3 Bdes.

Sent
At....................
To....................
By....................

DADE	LODE	ZEJU	ZODU	17 Div.	V Corps.
BASU	ZOKI	A/Q.	5 Div.	37 Div.	
VUFE	DUFA	ZOHO	33 Div.	15 Sqn. R.A.F.	

G.X. / 24 / AAA

ZOWU Order No.250 AAA It is considered possible that the enemy may withdraw from opposite our front tonight AAA BASU and DADE will send out patrols at Dawn to search ground between our present front line and line of orchards about 1,000 yards N.E. of it AAA If no enemy encountered these patrols will be supported and patrols sent on again to line of road through CROIX ROUGE and into LOUVIGNIES AAA If still no enemy encountered DADE and BASU will NOT be required to send patrols further AAA VUFE will have two Coys. between Brown Line and POIX inclusive by 07.00 hrs. tomorrow Oct. 25th AAA Remainder of Bde. will be disposed in depth and obtain as much rest as possible until leading Coys. are ordered to move AAA VUFE will keep close touch with situation through BASU and DADE H.Q. AAA If patrols report no enemy on this side of line of orchards VUFE will order leading Coys. to advance and take over work of patrolling from DADE and BASU AAA These two Coys. will patrol by bounds and will support patrols on conclusion of each bound AAA VUFE will support leading Coys. by remainder of Bde. making good as first objective line of JOLIMETZ - LE QUESNOY Rd. AAA When this road made good patrols will be sent forward to Railway but no further advance except by patrols until ordered from Div. H.Q. AAA If BASU and DADE encounter enemy it is not the Divl. Comdr's intention to make ground by fighting AAA Divs. on flanks will be taking similar action AAA One Bde. R.F.A. will be held in readiness and come under orders of VUFE if latter moves forward AAA One Troop Cyclists will be sent to report to each Bde. about 08.00 tomorrow and will be used to get touch with the enemy if Inf. patrols fail to do so AAA Div. H.Q. closes NEUVILLY 10.00 and re-opens OVILLERS same hour AAA Ack

H. C. Chaubleyn[?]

ZOWU.
22.15 hrs.

Lieut.Col.

TELEGRAM

Urgent operations priority to Bdes.

Words.

Sent.
At..................
To..................
By..................

DADE	LODE	ZEJU	ZODU	17 Div.	15th Sqn.R.A.F.
BASU	ZOKI	A/Q	5th Corps.	33rd Div.	
VUFE	DUFA	ZOHO	5th Div.	37th Div.	

- / 25 / AAA

ZOWU order No.251 AAA If VUFE does not pass through DADE and BASU today VUFE will relieve DADE and BASU tonight 25/26 inst AAA Details will be arranged between Brigadiers AAA On relief DADE will withdraw to the area between the BROWN and GREEN lines both exclusive AAA BASU will withdraw to the area between the GREEN line and VENDEGIES both inclusive AAA DADE will be prepared to hold the BROWN line or to form a defensive flank facing S.E. AAA BASU will be prepared to hold the GREEN line AAA DADE will hold two Battns. in readiness to move at quarter hours notice and BASU will hold one Batten. ready to move at half hours notice AAA Reserve M.G. Coy. will be disposed for the defence of the GREEN line AAA Completion of relief will be reported to ZOWU AAA Ack.

ZOWU
0910.

Major
for Lt. Col.

21ST DIV

G. S.,

NOVEMBER, 1918

...s Majest... Service.

R

R 38 FIELD POST OFFICE 10 NO 17 D.29

FIELD POST OFFICE 10 NO 17 D.29

13 NOV 1917

D.A.G.

G.H.Q.

3rd Echelon

AFC 2118

CONFIDENTIAL.

WAR DIARY

"G" Branch, Headquarters, 21st Division.

November 1st - 30th 1918.

Instructions regarding War Diaries and Intelligence Summaries are contained in F. S. Regs., Part II. and the Staff Manual respectively. Title pages will be prepared in manuscript.

GENERAL STAFF. H.Q. 21ST DIVISION

WAR DIARY
or
INTELLIGENCE SUMMARY.
(Erase heading not required.)

Army Form C. 2118.
ORIGINAL.

Place	Date	Hour	Summary of Events and Information	Remarks and references to Appendices
OVILLERS.	Nov.	1st.	21st Division order No. 256 issued detailing the relief of the 21st Division by the 17th Division on the night 2/3rd November. Readjustment of Boundaries complete 10.15 p.m. Intermittent shelling of POIX-DU-NORD.	App. I
NEUVILLY.	:	2nd.	Conference held at Divisional Headquarters at 10 a.m. to discuss & future operations. Situation unchanged. 21st Div.O/257 issued detailing orders for attack by 21st Div. on Nov. 5th.	App. II
	:	3rd.	Relief of 21st Division by 17th Division complete 1.30 a.m. Division preparing for action.	
POIX.DU NORD.	:	4th.	17th Division reported attack going according to programme. During the day Brigades moved to assembly areas in accordance with 21st Division O./No.257. Appdx "A".	
			11.10 p.m. 21st Division Order No. 258 issued giving situation on Corps front. Owing to 17th Division failing to reach GREEN Line, 62nd Inf. Bde. were to attack GREEN Line, 110th Inf. Bde. the BLACK Line and 64th Inf. Bde. the YELLOW LINE. Zero 5.30 a.m. for 62nd Inf.Bde.	App. III
	:	5th.	6.30 a.m. 62nd Inf. Bde. report advance going well, very little opposition. 2 Machine Guns and 12 O.R. captured in T.13 Central.	
FORESTERS INSTITUTE, near LOCQUIGNOL.			9 a.m. Div. H.Q. opened FUTOY, subsequently moving to the FORESTERS INSTITUTE, near LOCQUIGNOL.	
			10.15 a.m. Our troops in BERLAIMONT, mopping up Village. 110th Inf. Bde. moved to TETE NOIR, 64th Inf. Bde. ordered not to advance E. of a line running N. and S. through U.19.Cent. Heavy M.G. fire encountered from E. bank of SAMBRE and all bridges blown.	
			2.45 p.m. 21st Div. G.X.494 issued stating that if crossing of SAMBRE could not be effected today, bridges must be thrown over during the night by 62nd Inf. Bde. and 110th Inf. Bde. be prepared to pass through at dawn.	App. IV
			3.45 p.m. Line runs as follows :- U.27.c.0.9. - U.27.a.1.9. - U.21.c.3.4. - U.21.c.2.9. -	

D. D. & L., London, E.C.
(A7883) Wt W809/M1672 350,000 4/17 Sch. 52a Forms/C/2118/14

Instructions regarding War Diaries and Intelligence Summaries are contained in F. S. Regs., Part II, and the Staff Manual respectively. Title pages will be prepared in manuscript.

WAR DIARY
or
INTELLIGENCE SUMMARY.
(Erase heading not required.)

Army Form C. 2118.

Place	Date	Hour	Summary of Events and Information	Remarks and references to Appendices
			U.20.b.5.3. - U.20.b.0.7. - U.14.c.5.2. - U.14.a.0.7. - U.13.b.9.1. - U.13.b.5.6. - U.13.b.7.9. Enemy still in U.21.a.Central - U.14.a, b & d. and U.8.c.	
			10 p.m. 21st Div. Order No. 259. issued giving general situation and orders for advance on 6th inst by 110th Inf. Bde.	App. V
	Nov.6th.		5.25 a.m. 62nd Inf. Bde. got two Coys. across SAMBRE in U.21.c. and 27.a. Heavy M.G. fire encountered whilst crossing. Hostile artillery shelling Western outskirts of BERLAIMONT.	
			9.40 a.m. 110th Inf. Bde. passed two Battalions across SAMBRE but advance held up by heavy M.G. fire from E.of SAMBRE.	
			1 p.m. Two Coys. left Battalion 110th Inf. Bde. entered AULNOYE at U.22.a.0.3. and U.21.d.6.4; in touch with right Battalion.	
			3.30 p.m. 110th Inf. Bde. hold line of road U.23.c.0.5. U.22.b.7.7. and are advancing to high ground U.23.Central. AULNOYE and LE BOUVIER clear of the enemy.	
			10.10 p.m. 21st Division Order No. 260 issued giving general line and orders for advance by 64th and 110th Inf. Bdes. on 7th inst.	App. VI.
			10.45 p.m. Line now reported on road U.17.d. - U.23.b. except on right flank, where M.G. fire is still coming from LE QUATRE BRAS.	
	Nov. 7th.	7 a.m.	110th Inf. Bde. reported advancing without opposition.	
			8.35 a.m. 21st Division G.3. 100 issued detailing 62nd Inf. Bde. to move to AYMERIES at once.	
			8.35 a.m. 21st Division G.3.101 issued detailing 110th Inf. Bde. to be prepared to move one Battalion to high ground V.22.	
			10.10 a.m. 62nd Inf. Bde. passed through 110th Inf. Bde. who had gained the RED Line without opposition.	

D. D. & L., London, E.C.
(A7883) Wt. W809/M1672 350,000 4/17 Sch. 52a Forms/C/2118/14

Instructions regarding War Diaries and Intelligence Summaries are contained in F. S. Regs., Part II. and the Staff Manual respectively. Title pages will be prepared in manuscript.

WAR DIARY
or
INTELLIGENCE SUMMARY.
(Erase heading not required.)

Army Form C. 2118.

Place	Date	Hour	Summary of Events and Information	Remarks and references to Appendices
BERLAIMONT.	Nov.	7th.	11 a.m. Divisional Headquarters moved to BERLAIMONT.	
			12.20 p.m. 64th Inf. Bde. held up on line V.16. and 22 Cent. by heavy M.G. fire from LIMONT FONTAINE.	
			4 p.m. 21st Division Order No. 261. and G.X.547 issued detailing relief of 21st Division by 17th Division and consequent moved of Brigades.	App. VII
			7.45 p.m. 64th Inf. Bde. in an attack at 5.45 p.m. captured LIMONT FONTAINE and ECLAIBES together with 100 prisoners.	
	Nov.	8th.	Division resting and re-organizing :- Div.H.Q. BERLAIMONT. 62nd Inf. Bde. AYMERIES. 64th : : BERLAIMONT. 110th : : BERLAIMONT.	
	Nov.	9th &10th.	Division resting and re-organizing.	
	Nov.	11th.	Armistice signed and hostilities ceased at 11 a.m. Day passed quietly.	App. X
	Nov.	12th.	Division moved to BACHANT - BEAUFORT Area and was disposed as follows :-	
AULNOYE.			Div. H.Q. .... AULNOYE. 62nd Inf. Bde. BACHANT. 64th : : FONTAINE & ECLAIBES. 110th : : BEAUFORT.	App. VIII App. IX
	Nov 13th to 30th.		Division training and carrying out sports.	
			The Field Companies, 21st Divisional R.E. moved to the CAVILLON Area for the purpose of erecting Huts, etc.,	App. XI

D. D. & L., London, E.C.
(A7883) Wt. W809/M1672 350,000 4/17 Sch. 52a Forms/C/2118/14

Instructions regarding War Diaries and Intelligence Summaries are contained in F. S. Regs., Part II, and the Staff Manual respectively. Title pages will be prepared in manuscript.

Army Form C. 2118.

WAR DIARY
or
INTELLIGENCE SUMMARY.
(Erase heading not required.)

Place	Date	Hour	Summary of Events and Information	Remarks and references to Appendices
			Account of the Operations of the 21st Division from 22nd to 26th October, 1918.	App. XII
			Proceedings of Conference held at Divisional Headquarters 28th October, 1918.	App XIII
			do do do do 11th November, 1918.	App XIV
			[signature] Lieut Col GS for Major General Commanding 21st Division.	

D. D. & L., London, E.C.
(A7883) Wt W809/M1672 350,000 4/17 Sch. 52a Forms/C/2118/14

SECRET.

Words

To.....................
At.....................
By.....................

DADE	LODE	ZEJU	ZODU
BASU	ZOKI	A/Q	JESO
VUFE	DUFA	ZOHO	

GX. 228. / 25 / AAA

Warning Order AAA ZOWU less LODE will be relieved by 17th Division less Arty tomorrow and night 26/27 inst AAA DADE and BASU will be relieved by 50 and 51 Inf. Bdes. respectively AAA Reliefs to be complete by 1530 hrs AAA VUFE will be relieved by 52 Inf. Bde. AAA On relief BASU to INCHY DADE to NEUVILLY VUFE to OVILLERS and AMERVAL AAA 3 Coys ZEJU will be relieved with affiliated Bdes AAA ZEJU H.Q. and Res. Coy. to NEUVILLY AAA ZOKI will arrange reliefs of Field Coys.R.E. and DUFA AAA Added DADE, BASU, VUFE, ZEJU, ZOKI repeated LODE, DUFA, A/Q, JESO, ZOHO, ZODU.

ZOWU.
1930.

A.T. Macdougall Major for
Lt. Col
General Staff.

War Diary.

App III

TELEGRAM.

Words

Sent

URGENT OPERATIONS
PRIORITY 3 Bdes.

At.....................
To.....................
By.....................

DADE	ZOKI	ZOHO	V Corps.	17th Div.
BASU	DUFA	D.A.P.M.	V Corps H.A.	33rd Div.
VUFE	"Q"	ZEJU	V Corps R.A.	15 Sqn. R.A.F.
LODE	JESO	ZODU	5th Div.	Div. Cyclists.

\- / 4 / AAA

ZOWU Order No.258 AAA Ref Order No.257 AAA Front line 17th Div. not definitely ascertained but believed to run S.30.b.Central - T.19.c.5.0 - T.19.c.2.9 - T.13.c.5.9 - T.13.a.0.5 - T.13.a.0.9 AAA Left of 38th Div. believed in S.30.a. AAA 37th Div. believed in BIG WOOD T.1.2.7 and 8 AAA DADE will capture GREEN LINE tomorrow morning working S.E. with right on ROUTE DE LA FLAQUETTE and clearing LOCQNIGNOL from North and East AAA DADE will cross line of road running N.E. through S.18.c. a. & b. at 05.00 hours AAA VUFE is detailed to capture BLACK LINE timing advance so as to cross GREEN LINE at 0800. hours AAA BASU is detailed to capture YELLOW LINE timing advance to cross BLACK LINE at 11.00 hours AAA DADE will reform after capture of GREEN LINE and will be prepared to advance across River SAMBRE moving on orders from Div. H.Q. AAA Above times only to be taken as a guide if real opposition is met AAA It is of supreme importance that crossings over River SAMBRE should be seized at earliest possible moment therefore if little or no opposition leading Brigade will push on as rapidly as possible to BLACK and YELLOW LINES until opposition is met when next Brigade will pass through AAA Rear Bdes. must keep touch during advance with Brigade next in front but must avoid getting crowded on top of it AAA Barrage will be arranged in accordance with Appendix 'F' order No.257 AAA Artillery starting line T.19.d.3.8 - T.14.b.6.5 . At 05.30 hours AAA Barrage will move S.E. AAA Otherwise arrangements detailed in Order No.257 hold good AAA Ack

for DADE

ZOWU
23.10 hrs. 5.11.18

Lt.Col. G.S.

"A" Form

Army Form C. 2121 (In pads of 100.)

MESSAGES AND SIGNALS.

No. of Message............ App IV

Prefix.........Code.........m. Office of Origin and Service Instructions	Words / Charge. Sent At.......m. To........ By........	This message is on a/c of: War Diary Service. (Signature of "Franking Officer")	Recd. at......m. Date.......... From.......... By..........
Pty			

TO	DADE	LUDE	JESO	
	BASU	ZOKI	ZEJU	
	VUFE	Q		

Sender's Number.	Day of Month.	In reply to Number.	AAA
GX 496	5		

Warning Order aaa Intact crossings over SAMBRE gained today bridges must be thrown over tonight aaa DADE will form necessary bridge heads aaa VUFE will be prepared to pass through DADE at Dawn tomorrow and capture BROWN DOTTED LINE aaa BASU will be in Div Reserve aaa ack

From ZOWU

Place

Time 1445 hrs

The above may be forwarded as now corrected. (Z) Major

Censor. Signature of Addressor or person authorised to telegraph in his name

* This line should be erased if not required.

Order No. 1625. Wt. W3253/ P 511. 27/2. H. & K., Ltd. (E. 2624)

TELEGRAM.

War Diary

Words.

App I

S D R
to Bdes
[initials]

Sent.
At....................
To....................
By....................

DADE	ZOKI	ZOHO	V Corps	17 Div.
BASU	DUFA	D.A.P.M.	V Corps R.A.	33rd Div.
VUFE	"Q"	ZEJU	V Corps H.A.	15th Sqn R.A.F.
LODE	JESO	ZODU	5th Div.	Div Cyclists.

ZOWU Order No. 259. AAA The advance is progressing on whole Army front and on fronts of flank Armies AAA Orders have been received that no respite is to be allowed the enemy AAA DADE will capture remainder of YELLOW LINE as soon as possible and will push patrols down to river in U.16.a. AAA DADE will also establish bridgehead tonight on line U.21.d.0.7. - U.21.d.9.2. - U.27.d.5.8. and thence back to river AAA Under cover of bridge-head C.R.E. will throw bridges over SAMBRE exact positions selected will be notified later AAA VUFE will advance tomorrow so as to pass advanced troops of DADE holding bridgehead at 05.30 hrs AAA Vufe will capture successively BROWN DOTTED LINE AAA Ridge running through V.21. and V.15.Central to be known as RED LINE AAA Main AVESNES - MAUBEUGE Road to be known as BLUE LINE AAA BASU will support VUFE and will start crossing river when leading troops of VUFE reach BROWN DOTTED LINE probably about 07.30 hrs AAA BASU will occupy BROWN DOTTED LINE when vacated by VUFE AAA DADE will be in Div. Reserve AAA One Brigade R.F.A. under VUFE finding advanced sections with Battalions AAA DADE will transfer Cyclists and Mobile Mortars to VUFE AAA Div. Signals will establish Report Centre B.L. VUFE will establish E.T. and new Report Centre at V.16.c.3.2. to be known as R.E. AAA One M.G. Coy. affiliated to each Brigade AAA One Section R.E. and One Coy. Pioneers under VUFE AAA Acknowledge AAA Added all concerned.

ZOWU
20,00 hrs.
5.11.18

[signature]
Lt. Col.
General Staff.

War Diary

App VI

TELEGRAM.

Words

S D R Bdes
33rd Div
5th Div

SENT
To...............
At...............
By...............

DADE	DUFA	ZEJU	5th Corps H.A.	15 Sqn R.A.F.
BASU	"Q"	ZODU	5th Divn.	Div Cyclists.
VUFE	JESS	5th Corps.	17th Divn.	
LODE	ZOHO	5th Corps R.A.	33rd Divn.	
ZOKI	D.A.P.M.			

- / 6 / AAA

ZOWU Order No. 260 AAA 33rd Div. believed to be on BROWN DOTTED LINE AAA 5th Divn hold BROWN DOTTED LINE from U.11.a.Cent. Northwestwards AAA Enemy were still in S. portion of PONT SUR SAMBRE AAA Advance will be continued tomorrow AAA VUFE will begin advance under barrage AAA Barrage will come down on artillery starting line 300 yds. in advance of and parallel to main road in U.17.d. U.23.b. U.24.c. at 0545 hrs AAA Barrage rests on above line for 8 mins. and then advances at rate of 100 yds in 4 mins. for 1000 yards and will then cease AAA Barrage will skip village of BACHANT AAA VUFE will continue advance to RED LINE AAA BASU will move so as to begin crossing River SAMBRE at 05.30 hrs and will take up advance from RED LINE or earlier if VUFE held up AAA BASU will make good successively the BLUE LINE and village of BEAUFORT and will establish outposts on line W.16.Cent. W.22.Cent. AAA If VUFE held up BASU will make progress by working round the S. flank AAA Owing to probable delay in crossing River SAMBRE by 5th Div. Brigades must take precautions to guard their left flank AAA One Brigade R.F.A. under BASU AAA VUFE will transfer cyclists and Mobile Mortars to BASU when latter takes up advance AAA VUFE will lay Div. Signal line to BT and BASU from E.T. to R.E. and to new report centre X Roads W.13.d.1.1. to be known as H.F. AAA Acknowledge AAA Addsd all concerned.

ZOWU
2010 hrs.

Lt. Col.

"A" Form

MESSAGES AND SIGNALS.

Army Form C. 2121
(in pads of 100.)

No. of Message ....

Prefix .... Code .... m. | Words. | Charge.

Office of Origin and Service Instructions.

Urgent operations .... m.
PRIORITY to BASU
and VUFE.

Sent ... By ...

This message is on a/c of. .... *Service.*

War Diary

(Signature of "Franking Officer.")

Recd. at .... m. Date .... From .... By ....

TO			
DADE Signals.	BASU	VUFE	17th Div.

Sender's Number.	Day of Month.	In reply to Number.	AAA
* G.X. 547	7th		

In continuation of ZOWU order No. 261 VUFE will be billeted to-night as under AAA Two Bns. AULNOYE AAA Bde. less two Bns. BERLAIMONT AAA On Nov. 8th following moves will take place AAA Two Bns. VUFE to LA TETE NOIRE head to pass Road junction U.21. d.6.4. at 0815 hrs. AAA BASU to BERLAIMONT head NOT to pass AULNOYE CHURCH U.21.d.7.8. before 0900 hrs. AAA 52 Bde will be moving to AULNOYE and will be clear of River crossings by 0800 hrs. AAA ACK. AAA Addsd BASU Vufe reptd. 17 Div and Sigs.

From 21st Division.

Place

Time 1830 hrs.

The above may be forwarded as now corrected. (Z) Signed AIM Major G.S.

Censor. Signature of Addressor or person authorised to telegraph in his name.

* This line should be erased if not required.

(1539). Wt. W3253/P511. 200,000 Pads. 2/18. H. C. & L., Ltd.

21 Div.
G. 617.

App XIV

62nd Inf. Bde.
64th " "
110th " "
"Q"

Herewith Proceedings of Conference held at Divisional Headquarters today, 11th November.

H. J. Macdougall Major
General Staff.
21st Division.

11th November 1918.

PROCEEDINGS OF CONFERENCE HELD AT DIVISIONAL HEADQUARTERS
November 11th, 1918.

Present :- B.G.C. 62nd Inf. Bde.
B.G.C. 64th : :
B.G.C. 110th : :
A.A.Q.M.G.

1. The Divisional Commander told Brigadiers that the Commander in Chief had been to see him yesterday and had given great praise to the Division for its work throughout the year. The Divisional Commander wished Brigadiers to inform all troops of this fact.

2. The Divisional Commander said that the Division would probably be 25 days in the new area. It was important not to allow Officers or men to diminish their efforts as far as training, etc., went and that it was important to keep the Division up to its present very high standard. The Divisional Commander wishes, during this period, special attention to be paid to the turn out, guards, arms drill and the march past.

The Commander in Chief told the Divisional Commander that if it was possible he would inspect the whole Division.

3. March Discipline.

The Divisional Commander said that it was probable the Division would have to do a lot of marching in the future, and that, therefore, he wished special attention paid to march discipline during the period the Division would be in rest.

4. Tactical Work.

The Divisional Commander said that it was important to get Battalion and Company Commanders to handle their Commands and to work together. He considered that in tactical schemes it was a mistake to employ a skeleton enemy before the men had grasped the principles of the movements to be carried out.

The Divisional Commander impressed on Brigadiers the necessity of holding tactical exercises for Officers, with a special view of teaching Platoon Commanders to rely on themselves and not to wait in all cases for orders from their Company Commanders.

5. Transport. The Divisional Commander said that the transport was in bad condition at present and he wished special attention to be paid to improving it. It was essential that all vehicles should be packed in the correct manner and that Company Commanders should know what each wagon belonging to their Company contained.

The special points the Divisional Commander wished Brigadiers and Battalion Commanders to see to were :- care and fitting of harness, cleaning of collar chains, cleanliness of wagons, greasing of wheels, all parts of wagon that is not painted to be burnished or polished, condition of horses.

/The....

The Divisional Commander said he would inspect all transport on his return from leave, not more than about 12 hours warning being given for the inspection.

The A.A.Q.M.G. said that he would try to hasten the provision of paint for wagons.

6. Sports.

Each Brigade was being given money for Sports etc., in addition, Divisional Sports would be held towards the end of the period in rest, at which the Corps Boxing Cup which had been won by the Division, would be fought for and would become the property of the Battalion winning the Divisional Boxing Competition.

Committees for the Sports were being formed; instructions on this subject were being issued.

37TH DIV
17TH DIV
38TH DIV
5TH DIV
21ST DIV
33RD DIV
4TH ARMY
V
FORET DE MORMAL
Louvignies
ENGLEFONTAINE
Locquignol
BERLAIMONT
Aulnoye
Aymeries
Bachant
Pont sur Sambre
Tête Noire
SASSEGNIES
CARNAGNOLE
PETIT PARIS
PETIT MAUBEUGE
Brewery
LEVAL
Petit Landrecies
ST WAAST
MONCEAU ST WAAST
Rombise
Le Corbeau
Water Supply
Furnaces
Carrefour de la Tourraille
Les Grandes Patures
Carrefour de l'Ermitage
Carrefour du Chene à Meronnis
Carrefour du Chene la Guerre
HECQ
PLANTY
Pont Sabion
Route de Landrecies
Route Tortenelle
Laie du Magonlau
le Croisil Inn
Route de Sassegnies
Le Champ de Sassogne
TREES FELLED

21 DIVISION

GEN STAFF

1918 DEC — 1919 MAR

21st DIV.

G. S.,

DECEMBER, 1918

J. LYONS & Co. LTD.
UNIVERSAL CATERERS
J. LYONS & Co. LTD.
HEAD OFFICES & STEAM BAKERIES
Cadby Hall, Kensington, W.

19

VIII 40

C O N F I D E N T I A L.

WAR DIARY

OF

"G" Branch, Headquarters, 21st Division.

FROM:- 1st December 1918. TO:- 31st December 1918.

Instructions regarding War Diaries and Intelligence Summaries are contained in F. S. Regs., Part II. and the Staff Manual respectively. Title pages will be prepared in manuscript.

WAR DIARY
or
INTELLIGENCE SUMMARY.
(Erase heading not required.)

Army Form C. 2118.

Place	Date	Hour	Summary of Events and Information	Remarks and references to Appendices
	1918.			
AULNOYE.	Dec. 1st-3rd.		Division Training and carrying out Sports in the BEAUFORT - AULNOYE Area.	
	4th		Warning Order issued re move of Division to CAVILLON Area. Appendix	I
	: 5th.		14th Northumberland Fusiliers (Pioneers) moved to CAVILLON Area, Battalion proceeding by train and Transport by Road. Appendix	II
	: 6th-11th.		Division Training in BEAUFORT - AULNOYE area. 21st Division Order No. 266 issued on 8th December, detailing the move of the 21st Division to the CAVILLON Area. Appendix	III.
	: 12th		D.M.G.C. moved to VENDEGIES and 64th Inf. Bde. Group to BERLAIMONT.	
	: 13th-19th		Moves continued in accordance with 21st Division Order No. 266.	
	: 20th.		Divisions disposed as follows in the new area :- Divisional H.Q. MOLLIENS VIDAME. 62nd Inf. Bde.H.Q. PICQUIGNY. 64th : : PISSY. 110th Inf. Bde. BOVELLES.	
	: 21st-31st.		Division Resting and carrying out Sports, Education Schemes & Demobilization. ------------	
			Proceedings of Conference held at Divisional H.Q. on 21st December 1918. Appendix	IV
			: : : : : 30th : 1918. Appendix	V

A H Macdougall Major
G.S. for
Major General
Commanding 21st Division.

D. D. & L., London, E.C.
(A7883) Wt. W809/M1672 350,000 4/17 Sch. 52a Forms/C/2118/14

TABLE TO ACCOMPANY WARNING ORDER G.840.

Serial No.	Unit.	Date.	From.	To.	Route.
1.	64th Bde.Group.	Dec. 12th.	LIMONT-FONTAINE area.	BERLAIMONT.	No restrictions.
2.	- do -	13th	BERLAIMONT.	VENDEGIES	LOCQUIGNOL.
3.	- do -	14th	VENDEGIES.	INCHY	NEUVILLY.
4	110th Bde Group	14th	BEAUFORT	BERLAIMONT	No restrictions.
5.	- do -	15th	BERLAIMONT	VENDEGIES	LOCQUIGNOL.
6.	64th Bde.Group.	15th	INCHY	PISSY area	Move by bus.
7.	110th Bde.Group.	16th	VENDEGIES	INCHY	NEUVILLY.
8.	- do -	17th	INCHY.	BOVELLES area	Move by bus.
9	62nd Bde.Group.	17th	BACHANT-AYMERIES area	ENGLEFONTAINE	LOCQUIGNOL.
10.	- do -	18th	ENGLEFONTAINE.	INCHY	FOREST.
11.	- do -	19th	INCHY	OISSY area	Move by bus.

App I

WAR DIARY.

SECRET.

21 Div.
G. 840.

21st DIVISION WARNING ORDER.

Ref. Maps Sheets
VALENCIENNES and
AMIENS 1/100,000.

4th December 1918.

1. The Division will probably move to the CAVILLON area (West of AMIENS), in accordance with the attached Table.

2. The Machine Gun Battalion will be split up for the purposes of the move amongst Brigade Groups. Details as to this will be notified later.

3.(a). Transport will march from INCHY to the CAVILLON area.

(b). Transport will leave INCHY on the day on which the Brigade Group to which it belongs embusses.

(c). Successive staging areas for transport will be as follows :-
WALINCOURT - VILLERS OUTREAUX area.
TINCOURT area.
PROYART area.
BLANGY, GLISY, LONGEAU area.

4. The Divisional Artillery will probably march from NEUVILLY on December 13th, and will stage on successive nights in areas given in para.3.

5. Distances laid down in G.R.O.5586 of Novr. 16th, 1918, will be observed in all marches connected with this move.

6. ACKNOWLEDGE.

H.H. Hawkslyn

Lieut.-Colonel.
General Staff.
21st Division.

Distribution.

62nd Inf. Bde.	D.M.G.C. D.A.P.M.	V Corps.	
64th : :	Pioneers.D.G.O.	17th Div.	File.
110th : :	Signals. Train.	33rd Div.	"Q".
C.R.A.	A.D.M.S. M.T.Coy.	38th Div.	Div. Reception Camp.
C.R.E.	Camp.Comdt.	War Diary.	

App II

C O P Y.

21 Div.
G. 829.

14th North'd Fus. Pioneers.
"Q"

---

1. The 14th Northumberland Fusiliers Pioneers, less Transport, will move to ENGLEFONTAINE on the 5th instant, entraining at SALESCHES at 09.30 hours on December 6th. The detraining Station will be AMIENS, whence Battalion will march to MONTIERES.

2. The Transport will move to FOREST on the 5th instant, subsequently moving as follows :-

Dec. 6th	to VILLERS-OUTREAUX.	)	No restrictions as to route or time of starting.
: 7th	: TINCOURT.	)	
: 8th	: PROYART.	)	
: 9th	: BLAGNY-GLISY Area.	)	
: 10th	: MONTIERES.	)	

3. Details as to rations, lorries, etc. will be issued by 21st Division 'Q'.

(Signed) G.Tooth, Captain,

General Staff,
21st Division.

3/12/18.

App III

S E C R E T.

Copy No. 34

21st DIVISION ORDER No.266.

Ref. VALENCIENNES, ST.QUENTIN
and AMIENS 1/100,000.

8th December 1918.

1. The Division will move to the CAVILLON Area by bus and march route in accordance with the attached Table.

2. Administrative Instructions will be issued by 21st Div."Q".

3. Distances laid down in G.R.O.5586 of Nov.16th, 1918, will be observed in all marches connected with this move.
Attention is directed to the Memorandum "March Discipline" forwarded under this Office G.847 dated 6th December 1918.

4. Completion of moves of personnel and transport to new area will be reported to Divisional Headquarters.

5.(a). Divisional Headquarters will close at AULNOYE and open at INCHY at 10.00 hrs. December 14th, 1918.

(b). Divisional Headquarters will close at INCHY and open at MOLLIENS VIDAME at 10.00 hrs, December 19th.1918.

(c). The D.A.A.G. will be at MOLLIENS VIDAME from 14th December inclusive.

6. ACKNOWLEDGE.

A F Macdougall. Major
for

Lieut.-Colonel.
General Staff.
21st Division.

Issued through Signals at 13.30 p.m. to

	Copy No.		Copy No.		Copy No.
62nd Inf. Bde.	1	Train.	13	Area Comdt. BERLAIMONT	26
64th : :	2	M.T.Coy.	14	: : ENGLEFONTAINE	27
110th : :	3	V Corps.	15/16	: : VENDEGIES	28
C.R.A.	4	V Corps H.A.	17	: : INCHY	29
C.R.E.	5	V Corps R.A.	18	: : CAVILLON	30
D.M.G.C.	6	17th Div.	19	: : PICQUIGNY	31
Pioneers.	7	33rd Div.	20	: : FLUY	32
"Q"	8	38th Div.	21	: : BOVELLES.	33
Signals.	9	15th Sqn.R.A.F.	22	War Diary	34
A.D.M.S.	10	Div. Rec.Camp.	23	File.	35
D.A.P.M.	11	Camp Comdt.	24		
D.G.O.	12	D.O.	25		

TABLE TO ACCOMPANY 21st DIVISION ORDER No. 266.

Serial No.	Date.	Unit.	From	To	Route	Staging areas	Remarks
1	Dec. 12th	21st Bn.M.G.Corps.	BERLAIMONT.	VENDEGIES	LOCQUIGNOL	-	To be clear of BERLAIMONT by 10.00 hours.
2	12th	64th Bde. Group.	LIMONT-FONTAINE area	BERLAIMONT.	No restrictions.	-	-
3	13th	21st Bn.M.G.Corps.	VENDEGIES.	INCHY.	NEUVILLY	-	Not to enter NEUVILLY before 11.00 hrs. Will come under orders of G.O.C. 110th Bde.Group on Dec. 16th.
4	13th	64th Bde. Group.	BERLAIMONT.	VENDEGIES.	LOCQUIGNOL.	-	To be clear of BERLAIMONT by 10.00 hrs.
5	13th	Transport & mounted personnel, Div.H.Q.	AULNOYE.	VENDEGIES.	LOCQUIGNOL.	-	Not to enter BERLAIMONT before 10.00 hrs. On arrival at VENDEGIES will come under orders of G.O.C. 64th Bde.Group, who will issue orders for further marches.
6	14th	64th Bde. Group.	VENDEGIES	INCHY.	NEUVILLY	-	-

/7.......

Serial No.	Date	Unit	From	To	Route	Staging Areas	Remarks.
7	Dec. 15th.	64th Bde. Group.	INCHY.	CAVILLON area (FLOXICOURT-FLUY -PISSY sub-area)	BY BUS.	Transport by road staging as under:- 15/16 VILLERS-OUTREAUX. 16/17 TINCOURT. 17/18 PROYART. 18/19 GLISY-LONGEAU	-
8	13th	21st Div. Arty. less dismounted portion.	NEUVILLY	CAVILLON area (LA CHAUSEE - ST. SAUVEUR - ARGOEVRES sub-area)	-	Staging as under :- 13/14 WALINCOURT-VILLERS OUTREAUX 14/15 TINCOURT. 15/16 PROYART. 16/17 BLANGY-GLISY-LONGEAU.	To be clear of NEUVILLY by 11.00 hrs. Dec.13th. Dismounted portion will embus on Dec.19th (vide Serial Nos. 9 and 16
9	17th	Dismounted portion 21st Div. Arty.	NEUVILLY.	INCHY	-	-	Will come under orders of G.O.C. 62nd Bde.Group on Dec.18th. Not to enter INCHY before 12.00 hrs 17th Decr.
10	14th	110th Bde.Group.	BEAUFORT.	BERLAIMONT.	No restrictions	-	-
11	15th	- do -	BERLAIMONT.	VENDEGIES	LOCQUIGNOL	-	-
12	16th	- do -	VENDEGIES	INCHY.	NEUVILLY	-	-

Serial No.	Date.	Unit	From	To	Route	Staging area	Remarks
13	Dec. 17th.	110th Bde.Group.	INCHY.	CAVILLON area (AILLY-FERRIERES-BOVELLES sub-area).	By Bus.	Transport by road staging as in Serial No.7.	21st Bn.M.G.C. to BREILLY.
14	17th	62nd Bde.Group.	BACHANT-AYMERIES area	ENGLEFONTAINE	LOCQUIGNOL	-	-
15	18th	- do -	ENGLEFONTAINE	INCHY	FOREST	-	-
16	19th	- do -	INCHY	CAVILLON area (CAVILLON-FOURDRINOY-SAISSEVAL sub-area)	By bus.	Transport by road staging as in serial No.7.	-

War Diary

21 Div.
G. 935.

Recipients of Div. Order No. 266.

Reference Divisional Order No. 266, para.5.(b) is cancelled and the following substituted :-

Divisional Headquarters will close at INCHY and open at MOLLIENS VIDAME at 12.oo hrs. 18th December, 1918.

Rear Divisional Headquarters will remain at INCHY until 09.00 hrs, 19th December, 1918.

A H Macdougall Major.
General Staff.
21st Division.

15th December 1918.

Appx IV

PROCEEDINGS OF CONFERENCE HELD AT DIVISIONAL HEADQUARTERS ON 21st DECEMBER, 1918.

21 Div.
G. 49.

Present :- Divisional Commander.
G.O.C. 62nd Inf. Bde.
O.C., 64th : :
G.O.C. 110th : :
C.R.E.
D.A.Q.M.G.
Education Officer.

1. The Divisional Commander stated that the chief thing to bear in mind during the succeeding months was to keep the men happy, contented and usefully employed. He wished every effort to be made to make the men comfortable in billets. In connection with this all Officers must look after their men and should go round to see that the men are doing everything possible to make themselves comfortable.

The Divisional Commander stated that every Battalion was to have an Orderly Officer whose duties should be laid down by the Battalion Commander and who should render a report to the Orderly Room at the end of his tour of duty.

He also stated that Brigades should appoint a Field Officer every week, but this he left entirely to the discretion of Brigade Commanders.

2. POLICY. The Divisional Commander decided that three days a week should be spent in Military Training and three days in Educational Training. He had no objection to one of the days allotted for Military Training being used for Sports.

Stress was laid on the importance of not allowing troops to become bored.

It was not necessary for all Educational Training to take place on the same three days of the week, as it would probably be more convenient to hold Educational Classes on every day of the week.

Military Training was to include route marching, physical training, ceremonial drill and musketry.

/Educational.....

Educational Training was to be purely voluntary.

3. <u>TRAINING OF YOUNG REGULAR OFFICERS AND N.C.Os. AND THOSE INTENDING TO JOIN THE REGULAR ARMY.</u>

The Divisional Commander suggested that Brigade Classes should be held for such Officers and N.C.Os. on days set apart for Educational Training. Subjects to be taught should include Drill, musketry, tactical exercises, field engineering, map reading, military law, interior economy and [illegible] riding

Brigade Commanders agreed to this.

4. <u>RECREATIONAL TRAINING GROUND.</u> It was stated that Battalions can hire ground 200 sq.yards in extent for this purpose. If any difficulty was experienced or if more ground was required, the Division should be informed and the Corps Rents Officer would take the matter up. It was decided that Football ground should be extra.

5. <u>HUTTING.</u> The C.R.E. stated that the supply of Huts was sufficient but that the whole difficulty was a question of transport. The D.A.Q.M.G. stated that transport was improving every day.

It was decided that Huts should be erected in the following order :-

1. For accommodation.
2. For Recreation.
3. For Education.

The C.R.E. stated that all Huts allowed for in the present estimates would be erected in 4 or 5 weeks and that it would be 6 weeks before the extra huts which had recently been asked for would be finished.

G.O.C., 62nd Inf. Bde. suggested that Hospital Beds should be provided for the use of Officers. This matter would be referred to Corps.

The C.R.E. stated that he was getting a supply of timber for the erection of cook-houses, washing benches etc. Units would be responsible for making these.

/6......

- 4 -

6. Recreation Huts. It is essential that these Huts should be made really comfortable and the Divisional Commander stated that Divisional Funds would be used for this purpose. He also suggested that Committees of men should be formed to send in suggestions as to what furniture etc., should be bought. Brigades were asked to send in these suggestions to Div.H.Q. as soon as possible.

Corps would be asked if they could provide indoor games.

7. TENTED HANGARS. Corps had said that one tented hangar would be available for the Division.

8. BATHS AND FUEL. It was decided that three Bath houses should be erected in each Brigade area. The priority of erection should be decided by the Brigadier.

The D.A.Q.M.G. stated that fuel dumps in each area were now being made.

9. LAMPS. The D.A.Q.M.G. stated that a sufficient number of lamps had been demanded from Corps and were expected immediately. It was believed that the oil supply would be sufficient.

10. DIVISIONAL REST CAMP. A Rest Camp in each Brigade area had been suggested to the Corps who stated that, owing to the probability of only one Field Ambulance per Div. being kept up to strength, this would not be feasable. The A.D.M.S. was to decide on a suitable location for a Div. Rest Camp.

The Divisional Commander wished a suitable building set aside in each Battalion area for the inspection of sick and for the retention of sick until they could be removed to Field Ambulance.

11. REDUCTION OF OFFICE HOURS. A suggestion had been made to Corps that all Offices should be closed at 19.00 hours. Corps were going to issue orders on this subject.

/12......

12. RECREATIONAL KIT. A sufficient quantity been demanded from Corps.

13. MUSICIANS. The Divisional Commander stated that it would probably be possible to get extra musicians from Units which had been partially disbanded. Brigadiers were to inform Division of their requirements.

14. EDUCATION. The Education Officer stated that it would be about three weeks before the Educational Scheme was in full running order.

It was decided that Battalions should report when they were ready to start education, but in no case should it start before accommodation was ready.

Books and stationery were at present very scarce, but it was hoped that the position with regard to these would improve by the end of January.

A Divisional Library of Fiction was being formed. The G.O.C. 62nd Inf. Bde. suggested that all books should be kept in boxes containing a suitable number and that these boxes should be distributed to Units according to their requirements. This suggestion was approved.

The Divisional Commander stated that 2,000 Francs would be allotted to each Brigade Group for the provision of Educational Books. It was left to Brigade Group Commanders to decide what type of book should be bought.

A second course for Instructors would commence at the Corps Schools on 1st January and would last three weeks.

The Divisional Commander thought it would be advantageous to send Instructors to these courses owing to the fact that it would probably be three weeks before they were required by Units. Vacancies for these Courses have already been allotted.

The Divisional Commander stated that it would be possible to obtain lecturers from home, if they were specially asked for. The G.O.C. 62nd Inf. Bde. was asked to forward the names of any suitable lecturers who would undertake to come out to France to lecture to the troops.

/it.....

It was decided that all Education Officers should be excuded all parades and Regimental duties so that they could spend their whole time on educational work.

Brigade Commanders were asked to report to Division whether any troops would like to work on the land under French farmers. If troops wished to do this the matter would be taken up with the French Authorities.

It was thought that if we provided free labour for the farmers a great amount of the present ill feeling towards the troops would be removed.

15. PAYMENT FOR BILLETS. A number of cases had come to notice where civilians had not been paid the amount of billoting money due to them. The Divisional Commander wished for house owners to be given either a copy of the Billeting Certificate or a chit showing the amount of money due to him. It is of the utmost importance that we should get on good terms with the inhabitants. Every care should be taken to avoid damage to crops, trees and property.

16. COMPETITIONS. The Divisional Commander wished as many competitions as possible to be arranged, but he laid great stress on all competitions, sports and games being carried out in a sporting spirit. There should be no booing or hissing or questioning the decision of the referee at any game.

He wished Battalion and Unit Commanders to talk to their men on this subject and to point out to them the un-British spirit of such behaviour.

He suggested that a senior Officer should be present at every match or game to check anything of this nature.

17. CHRISTMAS DAY. The Divisional Commander wished every Unit to make out a full programme for Christmas Day and he also wished all Officers to be with their men as much as possible.

/18.......

18. FIRE ORDERS. Fire orders were being printed and would be issued in large numbers to all Units. The Divisional Commander wished steps to be taken to ensure that every man knew these orders and also that the orders should be read out on parade at least once per month. Several cases had already occurred where Officers have had to pay large amounts for damage by fire owing to it being proved that their men had never been given any orders for the prevention of fire.

19. HOLIDAYS. Until Hutting was sufficiently advanced to allow men being reasonably comfortable, work on the erection of huts should take place on Sundays, otherwise Sundays were to be observed as a holiday.

20. A further Conference would be held in a week's time to discuss points brought up at this Conference and any further points suggested by Brigadiers.

Distribution :-

62nd Inf. Bde.
64th " "
110th " "
C.R.A.
C.R.E.
Pioneers.
D.M.G.C.
A.D.M.S.
"Q"
Education Officer.

App V

21 Div.
G. 128.

PROCEEDINGS OF CONFERENCE HELD AT DIVISIONAL HEADQUARTERS, 30th DECEMBER, 1918.

Present :- Divisional Commander.
G.O.C., 62nd Inf. Bde.
O.C., 64th " "
G.O.C., 110th " "
C.R.A.
C.R.E.
D.M.G.C.
O.C., Pioneers.
D.A.A.G.
E.O.

1. DEMOBILIZATION.

The Divisional Commander asked Units to send in a list of all difficulties that had cropped up with reference to demobilization. When all lists were in they would be forwarded to G.H.Q. for answer. Units were also to report what men they considered were essential to carry on the work of a unit. Authority would then be asked for these men to be returned to their units when they went on leave. It was agreed that transport could not be demobilized unless horses and wagons were also sent away. G.O.C., 62nd Inf. Bde. suggested that transport personnel should be diluted with men in low categories so as to allow of transport men being demobilized in their turn. This was agreed to.

It was suggested that as Battalions became weaker a certain amount of transport should be demobilized. Brigadiers were not in favour of this.

The Divisional Commander said that it was essential that good Officers and N.C.Os. should be retained in order to keep up the moral and discipline of the troops. He also said that he wished the reason why a man was being ordered to return from leave to be explained to him by an officer.

/2......

2. POLICY.

Owing to the provision of the recent G.R.O. ordering the demobilization of students and teachers, it was considered that three days a week for educational work was too much. The Education Officer was to report what amount of time he considered necessary for education. The Divisional Commander considered that three days a week for military training was also excessive under present circumstances and he wished some of this time taken up with sports. It was essential that men should be kept occupied and it was agreed that this was a matter to be decided by Battalion Commanders.

3. EDUCATION.

The grant of 2,000 Francs per Brigade Group decided on at the last Conference, is now cancelled. Under the circumstances, the G.O.C., 62nd Inf. Bde. suggested that cheap exercise books should be bought to tide over the delay in the issue of Government ones. This was agreed to and the G.O.C., 62nd Inf. Bde. was asked to buy and send out to the Division 5,000 exercise books.

The provision of Text Books out of Divisional Funds would be considered later when the situation was clearer.

4. TRAINING OF YOUNG OFFICERS ETC..

G.O.C. 110th Inf. Bde. said that this was being arranged by Battalions. The G.O.C., 62nd Inf. Bde. said that there was no difficulty about officers, but owing to the non-arrival of the necessary forms there was considerable difficulty about enrolling men for these Courses.

The Divisional Commander wished all arrangements for these courses to be ready, so that, as soon as the forms arrived, courses could be started for the N.C.Os and men enrolling in the post war army. He also wished Brigades to report any difficulties they experienced in this scheme.

5. HUTTING.

The C.R.E. stated that satisfactory progress was being made and that he saw no reason to suppose that Huts would take longer to erect than was originally estimated. He expected a train load

/of.....

of duckboards to arrive on December 30th, which would contain sufficient for all requirements. The work on baths was also proceeding and the C.R.E. asked Brigadiers to state definitely the sites on which they wanted the new baths to be set up. The Divisional Commander stated that baths were of great importance in connection with the demobilization scheme. O.C., 64th Inf. Bde. asked if Sawyer Stoves could be procured as their use would do away to a great extent with the present difficulty in regard to baths. The D.A.A.G. said that 50 had been demanded for the Division.

At present there appeared to be no great complaint with regard to fuel. It was agreed that if fuel was getting short lorries would be taken off hutting and used for the transport of fuel. An extra ration would be necessary when all huts had been erected. Units were to report when this extra ration was required.

6. CIVILIANS.

Civilians appeared to be becoming more friendly, but G.O.C. 110th Inf. Bde. stated that the civilians in his area were not helpful.

7. The Divisional Commander said he wished to address all Battalions, and that he would commence with the 110th Inf. Bde, on January 4th.

8. BOOTS.

The C.R.A. and C.R.E. said that owing to the present state of the ground, the present issue of boots was not sufficient. D.A.A.G. was instructed to go into this matter.

9. PROSPECTS OF REGULAR N.C.Os. WHO TAKE PERMANENT COMMISSIONS.

The G.O.C., 110th Inf. Bde. asked if there was any information available as to the prospects of these Officers as regards pension etc., if they decided to serve on. This matter will be referred to higher authority.

10. TEMPORARY OFFICERS WISHING TO TAKE PERMANENT COMMISSIONS.

G.O.C., 110th Inf. Bde. asked if the conditions of service etc., had been laid down. The Divisional Commander thought that owing to the large surplus of permanent officers already in the

/army.....

Army, it was not probable that Temporary Officers would be allowed to join, but the matter would be referred to higher authority.

11. WORK ON LAND.
The G.O.C., 110th Inf. Bde. stated that the 1st Wilts. Regt. had 42 men who wished to work on the land for instruction. It was decided that arrangements for this should be made direct between the Brigade and French Farmers.

12. PAYMENT FOR BILLETS.
The 110th Inf. Bde. thought that it was against the French Regulations to give a copy of the Billeting Certificate to the house owner. This matter will be referred to Corps.

13. WATER POINTS.
The C.R.A. stated that the roads to existing water points were in a very bad state of repair and were rapidly becoming worse. The C.R.E. said that their repair was entirely a question of transport for the material, but that it would be taken in hand as soon as possible.

14. LIGHTING.
The D.A.A.G. stated that lamps are now beginning to arrive. Acetylene lamps had also been received and the question of their distribution would be decided by Div H.Q. The C.R.E. stated that he had asked the Corps to re-allot to this Division all lamps at present allotted to the 33rd. Division.

15. RECREATION HUTS.
All Brigades were of opinion that deck chairs should not be bought, but that ordinary rush bottomed chairs were the best. This was agreed to. It was also agreed that table lamps and tables should be bought. The G.O.C., 110th Inf. Bde. stated that some form of floor covering should be provided. The C.R.E. thought that camouflage would answer for this purpose and it was agreed that supplies should be demanded.

/16.....

16. BOYS FROM GRADUATED BATTALIONS.
No further orders had been received with regard to these boys being sent to units in France. It was thought that they would be very useful in units during the period of demobilization. This matter would be referred to Corps.

17. CONCENTRATION OF BRIGADE.
The O.C., 64th Inf. Bde. wished to move the Battalion at present at BOUGAINVILLE to huts at FLUY in order to have the whole Brigade in a more concentrated area. At present, the difficulty owing to the distance between units of organizing sports etc., was very great. The Divisional Commander said that this move was again a question of the provision of transport and that at present it could not be done. It was decided to hold the matter over until other hutting had been finished.

18. CROCKERY FOR STANDING CAMPS.
It was suggested that the present Battalion Camps might be regarded as Standing Camps and crockery demanded in accordance with G.R.O. The matter will be referred to Corps.

Distribution :-

62nd Inf. Bde.
64th : :
110th : :
C.R.A.
C.R.E.
Pioneers.
D.M.G.C.
A.D.M.S.
"Q"
Education Officer.

Vol 41

C O N F I D E N T I A L.

WAR DIARY

of

"G" Branch., Headquarters, 21st Division.

FROM:- 1st January 1919. TO:- 31st January 1919.

Instructions regarding War Diaries and Intelligence Summaries are contained in F. S. Regs., Part II, and the Staff Manual respectively. Title pages will be prepared in manuscript.

Army Form C. 2118.

WAR DIARY
or
INTELLIGENCE SUMMARY.
(Erase heading not required.)

Place	Date	Hour	Summary of Events and Information	Remarks and references to Appendices
January 1st to 31st, 1919.			Division Disposed as follows :-	
			Divisional Headquarters. MOLLIENS VIDAME.	
			62nd Inf. Bde. CAVILLON.	
			64th : : PISSY.	
			110th : : BOVELLES.	
			The month was spent carrying out training, sports and demobilization.	
			[signature] Brig.-General Commanding 21st Division.	

GENERAL STAFF, H.Q., 21ST DIVISION.
No.
Date.

D. D. & L., London, E.C.
(A7883) Wt W809/M1672 350,000 4/17 Sch. 52a Forms/C/2118/14

14

V.8.42

C O N F I D E N T I A L.

WAR DIARY

OF

"G" Branch, Headquarters, 21st Division.

FROM:- 1st February 1919. TO:- 28th February.1919.

Instructions regarding War Diaries and Intelligence Summaries are contained in F. S. Regs., Part II. and the Staff Manual respectively. Title pages will be prepared in manuscript.

WAR DIARY
or
INTELLIGENCE SUMMARY.
(Erase heading not required.)

Army Form C. 2118.

Place	Date	Hour	Summary of Events and Information	Remarks and references to Appendices
February 1st to 28th.1919.			Division Disposed as follows :-	
			Divisional H.Q. — MOLLIENS VIDAME.	
			62nd Inf. Bde. — CAVILLON.	
			64th : : — PISSY.	
			110th : : — BOVELLES.	
			Major General Sir. D.G.M. CAMPBELL, K.C.B., left the Division on 9th February 1919 to take over command of 33rd Division.	
			Brig.-General H.R.CUMMING, D.S.O., [redacted], took over command of Division on the same day.	
			The month was spent carrying out training, sports and demobilization.	

for [illegible] Capt

Brig.-General
Commanding 21st Division.

GENERAL STAFF.
H.Q.
21ST DIVISION.
No.............
Date...........

D. D. & L., London, E.C.
(A7883) Wt W809/M1672 350,000 4/17 Sch. 52a Forms/C/2118/14

Instructions regarding War Diaries and Intelligence Summaries are contained in F. S. Regs., Part II, and the Staff Manual respectively. Title pages will be prepared in manuscript.

WAR DIARY
or
INTELLIGENCE SUMMARY.
(*Erase heading not required.*)

Army Form C. 2118.

Vol 43

Place	Date	Hour	Summary of Events and Information	Remarks and references to Appendices
Molliens Vidame.	March 1st to 31st. 1919.		Division disposed as follows :-	
			Divisional Headquarters. - MOLLIENS VIDAME.	
			62nd Infantry Brigade. - CAVILLON.	
			64th : : - PISSY.	
			110th : : - BOVELLES.	
			The month was spent in carrying out training, sports and demobilisation.	

Brigadier General,

Commanding 21st Division.

D. D. & L., London, E.C.
(A7883) Wt. W809/M1672 350,000 4/17 Sch. 52a Forms/C/2118/14

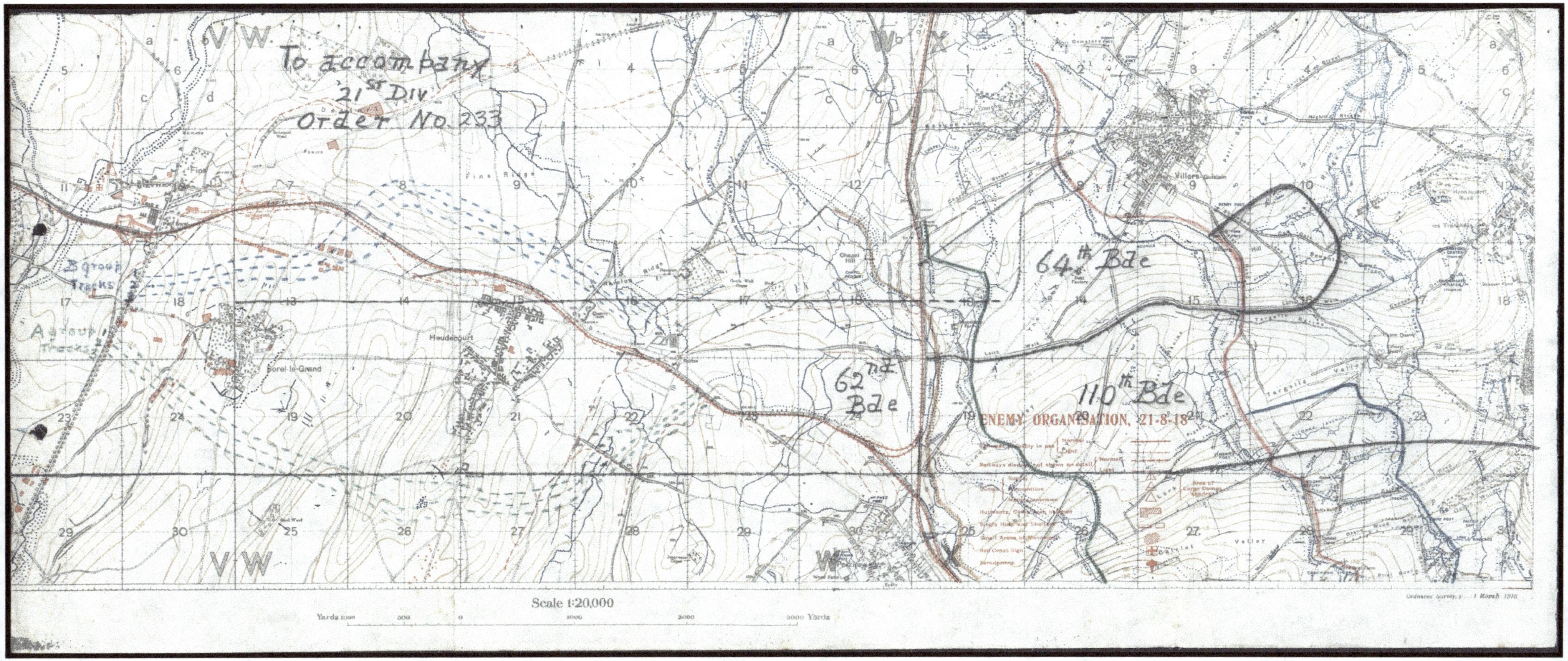
To accompany
21st Div
Order No. 233
64th Bde
62nd Bde
110th Bde
ENEMY ORGANISATION, 21-8-18
Villers-Guislain
Heudecourt
Sorel-le-Grand
Fins Ridge
Chapel Hill
B group Tracks
A group Tracks
Scale 1:20,000
Yards 1000 500 0 1000 2000 3000 Yards

GENERAL STAFF.
V CORPS.
G. 496/7
25.9.18

S E C R E T.

21 Div.
G. 419.

V Corps.

1. Herewith Map showing proposed objectives for an attack along QUENTIN RIDGE and on GONNELIEU. The objectives are :-

(a) Green dotted line

(b) Red line.

(c) Blue line.

2. The attack will be carried out by two Infantry Brigades. The objectives allotted to each are shown on the attached Map.

Inter-Divisional Boundaries are shown Black and Inter-Brigade Boundaries Brown.

3. It is essential that :-

(a) The attack should be carried out by night.

(b) The IV Corps should simultaneously attack FUSILIER and CEMETRY RIDGES.

4. GOUZEAUCOURT will be kept under a bombardment by Artillery and 6" Newton Mortars throughout the operation and will be mopped up at a later hour from the East.

5. The four Tanks allotted to the Division will move as shown by Yellow Lines on the Map.

H.C. Franklyn Lieut.Col.
GS

for Major-General,

24.9.18. Commanding 21st Division.

Copy to :-

5th Division.

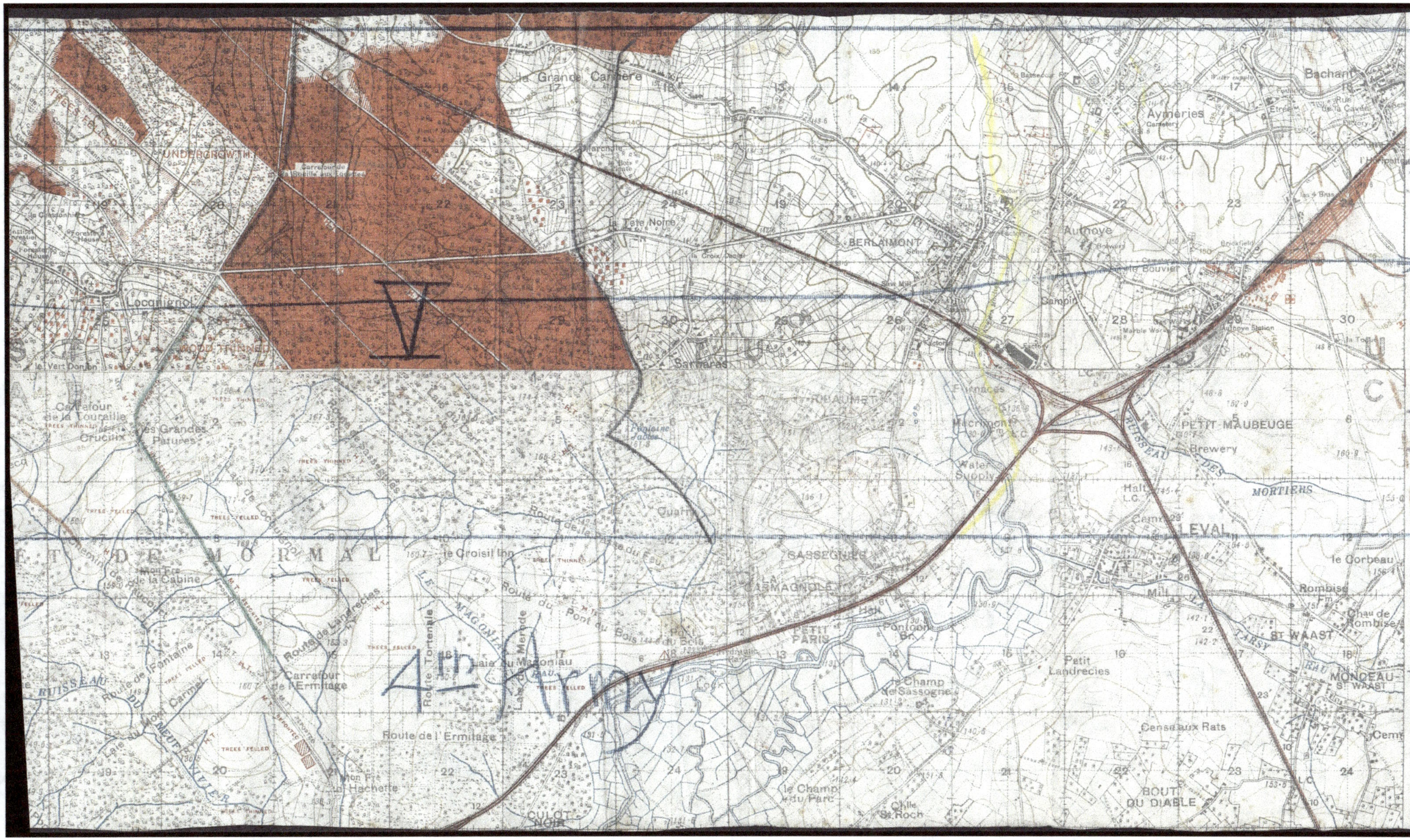

21 Div
33 Div
4th Army
V
BERLAIMONT
Aymeries
Bachant
Aulnoye
PETIT MAUBEUGE
LEVAL
SASSEGNIES
PETIT PARIS
ST WAAST
MONCEAU ST WAAST
BOUT DU DIABLE
Petit Landrecies
Censeaux Rats
le Corbeau
Rombise
la Grande Carrière
la Tête Noire
Sambres
Locquignol
UNDERGROWTH
ROUTE DE LANDRECIES
Route de l'Ermitage
Carrefour de l'Ermitage
Carrefour de la Tourelle
Crucifix
Les Grandes Patures
Route Tortenale
RUISSEAU DES MORTIERS
Brewery
To Maubeuge
To Avesnes
TREES FELLED
TREES THINNED
CULOT NOIR
le Champ du Parc
Chlle St Roch
Champ de Sassogne
Pontoon Br.

17th Div
38th Div
ENEMY ORGANISATION 22-10-18
Salesches
Salesches Station
Neuville
Poix-du-Nord
Englefontaine
Vendegies-au-Bois
Vendegies Wood
Wagnonville
Beaurain
Duke's Wood
Spinning Mill
La Fourquette
Paul Jacques Farm
Bousies Wood Farm
Renuart Farm
Hecq
Petit Planty
Preux-aux-Bois
Ruisseau
Trees Felled
Locquignol
Carrefour de la Touraille
Carrefour du Chene la Guerre
Carrefour du Chene à Maronne
Route du Chene Cuplet
Route d'Hecq
Fontaine St Saulve
Chlle du Carmel
Chlle St Roch
Rutoy
Forêt de Mormal

File

Map to Accompany 21st Div. Order No2
FRANCE
EDITION 2. a (Local)
Trenches revised from information received to 14-10-18
SHEET 51 S.W.
FORET
DE MORMAL
VI
IV
V
4TH ARMY
Gommegnies
Amfroipret
Petit Gommegnies
Bavisiaux
Mecquignies
le Trechon
Obies
le Cheval Blanc
la Haute Rue
la Porquerie
Pont-sur-Sambre
Aymeries
Bachant
Hargnies
Vieux Mesnil
Pantigny
Quartes
la Grande Carriere
Berlaimont
Aulnoye
Sassegnies
Leval
Petit Maubeuge
Rombies
St Waast
Monceau St Waast
Petit Landrecies
Bout du Diable
Lambresart
Champ de Sassegnies
Hachette
Noyelles
Locquignol
UNDERGROWTH
TREES FELLED

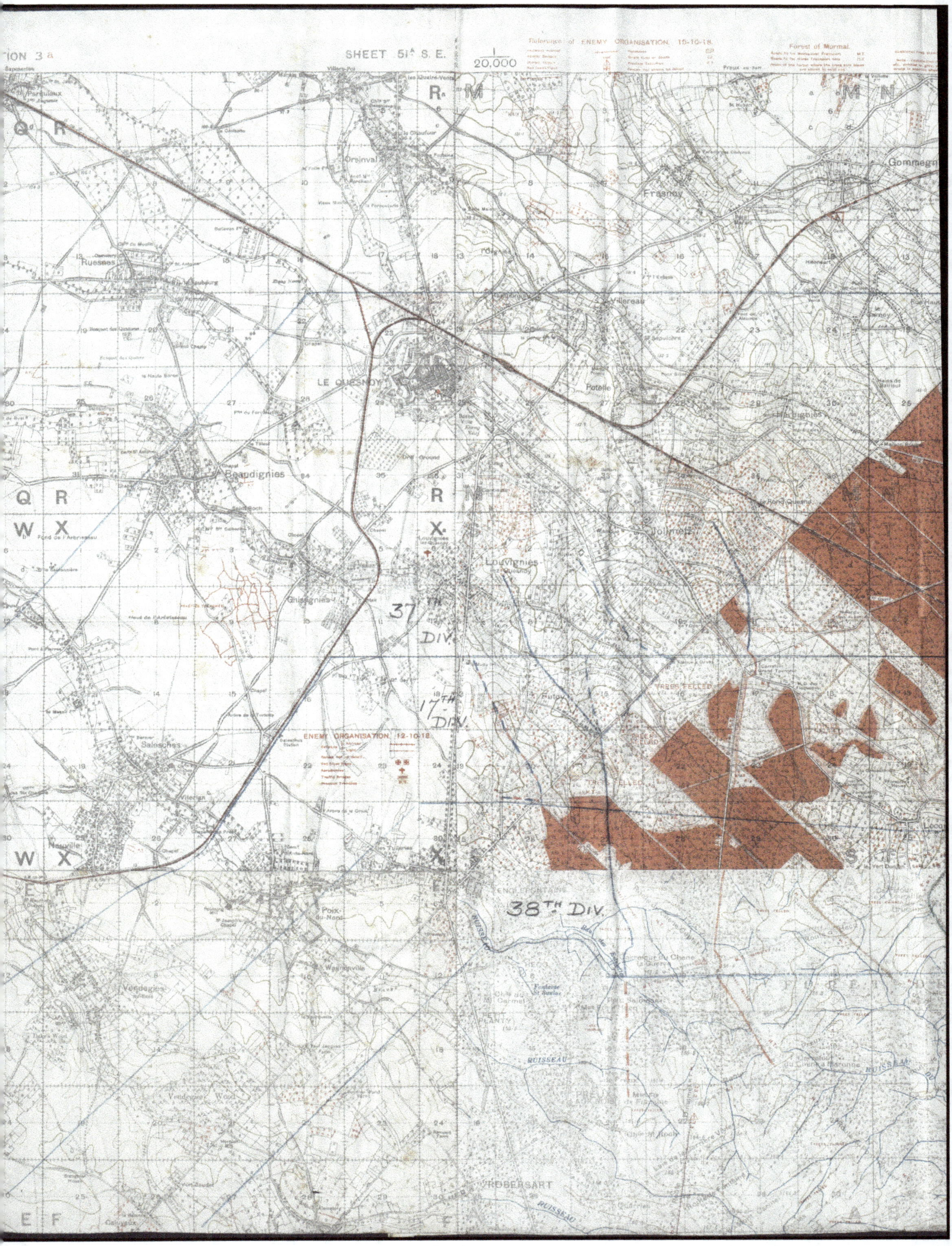
SHEET 51A S.E.
1/20,000
Reference of ENEMY ORGANISATION 15-10-18.
Forest of Mormal
Orsinval
Frasnoy
Gommegnies
Ruesnes
Villereau
LE QUESNOY
Potelle
Herbignies
Beaudignies
Jolimetz
Louvignies
Ghissignies
37TH DIV.
17TH DIV.
TREES FELLED
ENEMY ORGANISATION 12-10-18
Salesches
Englefontaine
38TH DIV.
Poix-du-Nord
Wagnonville
Vendegies
RUISSEAU
ROBERSART

D O No 257

H O

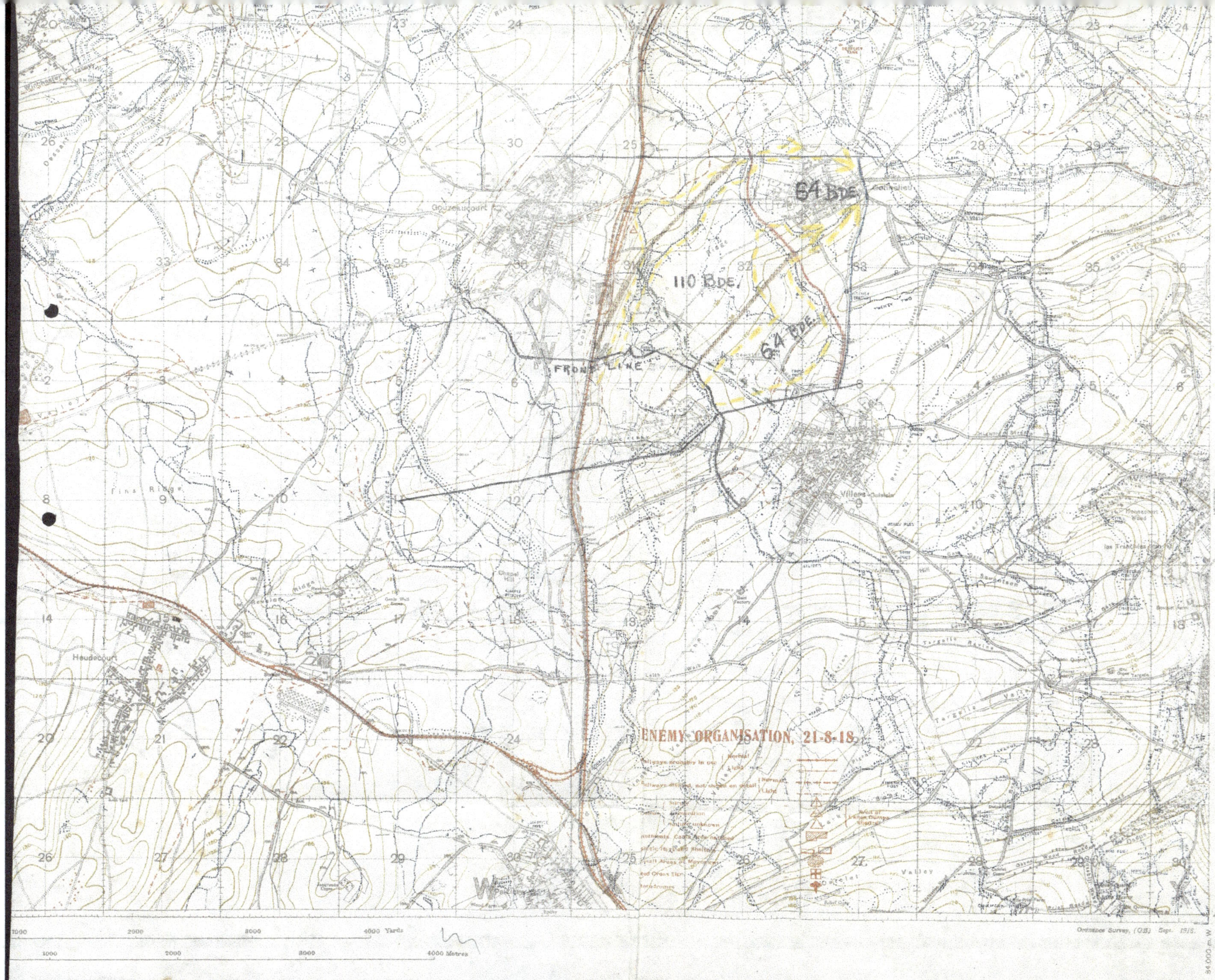

ENEMY ORGANISATION, 21-8-18.
64 BDE.
110 BDE.
64 BDE.
FRONT LINE
Gouzeaucourt
Villers-Guislain
Heudecourt
Fins Ridge
Chapel Hill
Valley
Ordnance Survey, (O.B.) Sept. 1918.
4000 Yards
4000 Metres

War Diary

APPENDIX D.

REFERENCE 21st DIVISION OPERATION ORDER No.257.

1. TRANSPORT.

(a) 'B' Echelon First Line Transport will move with Brigades on Z day until they start to advance to Assembly positions.

When Brigades advance to Assembly positions First Line Transport will concentrate as follows :-

62nd Inf. Bde.	X.27.c.
64th " "	X.28.d.
110th " "	F.3.b.
21st M.G.Bn.	F.3.a.
R.E.	F.3.d.
14th N.F. (P.)	F.3.d.

If circumstances permit 'B' Echelon will move to the neighbourhood of FUTOY on Z day.

(b) Div. Train will move to F.7.a. on Z day, not to pass railway bridge on NEUVILLY - AMERVAL road before midday.

2. AMMUNITION AND GRENADES.

(a) A.R.P. will be at ~~S.7.a.~~ S.9.d.
(b) Div. Grenade Dump is at X.27.d.9.9. and F.8.a.4.1. The advanced Grenade Dump will be formed by 17th Division at S.21.a.5.9.
(c) A Dump will be formed at LOCQUIGNOL as soon as possible, but Brigades must be prepared to come on to the normal system of supply as outlined in this Office letter No. Q.1199.

3. S.A.A. Section D.A.C.

n S.A.A. Section D.A.C. will move to F.3.d.8.2. on Z day not to pass cross roads F.8.a. before 17.30 hours.

4. SUPPLIES.

(a) Supply Wagons with Supplies for Z plus 1 day will join First Line Transport before 10.00 hours on Z day and will move with First Line Transport until Brigades start to move to concentration areas. After they have delivered their supplies they will rejoin Train Coys. at F.7.a.

Men will go into action carrying rations for Z plus 1 day.

(b) Refilling point on Z day will be at NEUVILLY Station, on Z plus 1 day, at POIX, or, if circumstances do not permit, at F.7.a.

5. ROADS.

Transport not actually moving with troops will move East of POIX DU NORD by the road ARBRE DE LA CROIX -F.6.a.7.9. - X.24.a.9.0. - S.26.a.3.1. The ENGLEFONTAINE - BAVAY road south west of S.26.a.3.1. has to be kept clear for the right Division.

Transport will whenever possible move off the roads.

6. PACK TRANSPORT.

After entering the FORET DE MORMAL Brigades will be prepared to send up all ammunition and supplies by Pack Transport.

P.T.O.

7. WATER.

Reports on Streams or other Water Supply will be forwarded to Div. H.Q. as early as possible.

8. PACKS AND BLANKETS.

Packs and Blankets will be stored under Brigade arrangements as near a lorry route as possible. The exact locations of stores will be reported to Div. H.Q.

9. TRAFFIC CONTROL.

D.A.P.M. will be responsible for Traffic Control East of the line captured by 17th Division.

6 Officers and 60 extra men are being lent to D.A.P.M. for Traffic Control.

In the first instance, this party will be used to ensure that the Infantry are not blocked when moving forward from their concentration areas.

10. STRAGGLERS POSTS.

D.A.P.M. will arrange for Stragglers Posts to be placed on the following roads as circumstances permit.

(1) ENGLEFONTAINE - LOUVIGNIES road.
(2) RED LINE.
(3) GREEN LINE.
(4) BLACK LINE.
(5) Road West of YELLOW LINE.

11. PRISONERS OF WAR CAGE.

Prisoners of War Cage will be established at S.17.a.8.8.

One Troop of Cavalry will be taken over from 17th Division by D.A.P.M.

They will patrol the forward ...... roads and take over prisoners of war from infantry escorts.

12. CASUALTIES.

Attention is again called to the importance of reporting estimated casualties as early as possible.

A rough estimate only is required.